Wahhabism and the World

T0355136

RELIGION AND GLOBAL POLITICS

Series Editor
John L. Esposito
University Professor and Director
Prince Alwaleed Bin Talal Center for Muslim-Christian Understanding
Georgetown University

ISLAMIC LEVIATHAN
Islam and the Making of State Power
Seyyed Vali Reza Nasr

RACHID GHANNOUCHI
A Democrat Within Islamism
Azzam S. Tamimi

BALKAN IDOLS
Religion and Nationalism in Yugoslav States
Vjekoslav Perica

ISLAMIC POLITICAL IDENTITY
IN TURKEY
M. Hakan Yavuz

RELIGION AND POLITICS IN POST-
COMMUNIST ROMANIA
Lavinia Stan and Lucian Turcescu

PIETY AND POLITICS
Islamism in Contemporary Malaysia
Joseph Chinyong Liow

TERROR IN THE LAND OF THE
HOLY SPIRIT
*Guatemala under General Efrain Rios Montt,
1982-1983*
Virginia Garrard-Burnett

IN THE HOUSE OF WAR
Dutch Islam Observed
Sam Cherribi

BEING YOUNG AND MUSLIM
*New Cultural Politics in the Global South
and North*
Asef Bayat and Linda Herrera

CHURCH, STATE, AND DEMOCRACY IN
EXPANDING EUROPE
Lavinia Stan and Lucian Turcescu

THE HEADSCARF CONTROVERSY
Secularism and Freedom of Religion
Hilal Elver

THE HOUSE OF SERVICE
The Gülen Movement and Islam's Third Way
David Tittensor

ANSWERING THE CALL
Popular Islamic Activism in Sadat's Egypt
Abdullah Al-Arian

MAPPING THE LEGAL BOUNDARIES OF
BELONGING
*Religion and Multiculturalism from Israel
to Canada*
Edited by René Provost

RELIGIOUS SECULARITY
A Theological Challenge to the Islamic State
Naser Ghobadzadeh

THE MIDDLE PATH OF MODERATION
IN ISLAM
The Qur'ānic Principle of Wasaṭiyyah
Mohammad Hashim Kamali

ONE ISLAM, MANU MUSLIM WORLDS
*Spirituality, Identity, and Resistance Across
Islamic Lands*
Raymond William Baker

CONTAINING BALKAN NATIONALISM
*Imperial Russia and Ottoman Christians
(1856-1914)*
Denis Vovchenko

INSIDE THE MUSLIM BROTHERHOOD
Religion, Identity, and Politics
Khalil al-Anani

POLITICIZING ISLAM
The Islamic Revival in France and India
Z. Fareen Parvez

SOVIET AND MUSLIM
The Institutionalization of Islam in Central Asia
Eren Tasar

ISLAM IN MALAYISA
An Entwined History
Khairudin Aljunied

SALAFISM GOES GLOBAL
From the Gulf to the French Banlieues
Mohamed-Ali Adraoui

JIHADISM IN EUROPE
European Youth and the New Caliphate
Farhad Khosrokhavar

ISLAM AND NATIONALISM IN MODERN
GREECE, 1821-1940
Stefanos Katsikas

Wahhabism and the World

Understanding Saudi Arabia's Global Influence on Islam

Edited by

PETER MANDAVILLE

OXFORD
UNIVERSITY PRESS

OXFORD
UNIVERSITY PRESS

Oxford University Press is a department of the University of Oxford. It furthers
the University's objective of excellence in research, scholarship, and education
by publishing worldwide. Oxford is a registered trade mark of Oxford University
Press in the UK and certain other countries.

Published in the United States of America by Oxford University Press
198 Madison Avenue, New York, NY 10016, United States of America.

© Oxford University Press 2022

Library of Congress Control Number: 2021924413

ISBN 978–0–19–753257–7 (pbk.)
ISBN 978–0–19–753256–0 (hbk.)

DOI: 10.1093/oso/9780197532560.001.0001

Contents

Preface   vii
List of Contributors   xi
Note on Transliteration   xv

PART I. ORIGINS AND EVOLUTION

1. Wahhabism and the World: The Historical Evolution, Structure,
   and Future of Saudi Religious Transnationalism   3
   Peter Mandaville

2. Wahhabism and Salafism in Global Perspective   35
   Natana J. DeLong-Bas

3. From Dir'iyya to Riyadh: The History and Global Impact of
   Saudi Religious Propagation and Education   53
   Christopher Anzalone and Yasir Qadhi

4. Salafi Publishing and Contestation over Orthodoxy and
   Leadership in Sunni Islam   76
   Andrew Hammond

5. Transnational Wahhabism: The Muslim World League and the
   World Assembly of Muslim Youth   93
   Reinhard Schulze

6. Humanitarian and Relief Organizations in Global Saudi Da'wa?   114
   Nora Derbal

PART II. COUNTRY CASE STUDIES

7. Salafism, Education, and Youth: Saudi Arabia's Campaign for
   Wahhabism in Indonesia   135
   Noorhaidi Hasan

8. Saudi Influence in Kyrgyzstan: Beyond Mosques, Schools,
   and Foundations   158
   Emil Nasritdinov and Mametbek Myrzabaev

9. Saudi Arabia: A South Asian Wrecking Ball 186
   James M. Dorsey

10. "Working for a Living in the Land of Allah": Labor Migration
    from Bangladesh to Saudi Arabia and Remittances of Wahhabism 208
    Nazli Kibria and Sultan Mohammed Zakaria

11. Ethiopia and Saudi Arabia: Between Proximity and Distance 221
    Terje Østebø

12. Wahhabi Compromises and "Soft Salafization" in the Sahel 238
    Alexander Thurston

13. Unpacking the Saudi-Salafi Connection in Egypt 255
    Stéphane Lacroix

14. Arab Brothers, Arms, and Food Rations: How Salafism
    Made Its Way to Bosnia and Herzegovina 272
    Harun Karčić

15. The Shifting Contours of Saudi Influence in Britain 290
    Hira Amin

Index 315

Preface

The idea that, for more than half a century, Saudi Arabia's petrodollar-fueled export of the austere and rigid breed of Islam known as Wahhabism has had profound and far-reaching effects around the globe is by now something of an article of faith among observers of the contemporary Muslim world. For some, the kingdom's vast portfolio of global religious-propagation activities serves first and foremost to disseminate ultra-conservative interpretations of Islam in ways that generate cultural intolerance and also affect social attitudes toward (as well as the status and precarity of) women and nonconforming religious groups in receiving countries. Others, however, go much further, drawing direct links between Saudi support for religious causes and various forms of violent conflict, militancy, extremism, and terrorism. Some even see in Saudi Wahhabism the wellspring of the Salafi-jihadi worldview associated with groups such as Al-Qaeda and Islamic State (ISIS). And while bold, often categorical declarations regarding Wahhabism's impact in various countries are commonplace, systematic research on Saudi religious transnationalism and its effects remains scarce.

The purpose of this volume is to provide an analytical portrait of the Saudi global *daʿwa* (religious propagation or "call") apparatus, explaining its history, structure, evolution, and role within the kingdom's broader portfolio of external relations. Additionally, the various case studies offered in the following pages seek to contextualize and assess the effects of Saudi religious transnationalism in various and varying national contexts. Drawing on extensive fieldwork undertaken by an international team of scholars across multiple world regions, this study explores the complex—sometimes counterintuitive and contradictory— interplay between religious influences emanating from Saudi Arabia and local religious actors and religious cultures in receiving countries. It offers assessments of how transnational Wahhabism has affected various settings around the world and provides analytic insights which help to explain how and why these effects differ from context to context. In addition to presenting cross-cutting research findings with respect to the broad field of Saudi religious transnationalism, this study also engages with the debate on the kingdom's export of Wahhabism as an object of analysis in its own right and looks at some of the methodological and epistemological challenges associated with gathering data, navigating indeterminate terminology, and identifying clear mechanisms of causality linking Saudi religious influences to specific social, political, and security outcomes.

The timing of this study is also significant. It comes in the context of a politically ascendant crown prince, Muhammad bin Salman ("MbS," the kingdom's most powerful figure by any measure other than his formal title), who has issued a range of intriguing pronouncements and has undertaken actions that suggest he may be preparing to throw the standard Saudi playbook on religion—or, at least, aspects of it—out the window. However, in many dimensions of his ambitious and aggressive agenda, MbS is forced to confront inevitable tensions between his unorthodox instincts and the vast equities that have been built up around previous Saudi ways of doing business. This is no different with respect to religion and the religious dimensions of the kingdom's external relations. It is therefore my hope that detailing and explaining the nature and evolution of Saudi religious transnationalism over the past half century will also aid in assessing the extent to which prevailing structures and norms may shape what MbS can (and cannot) do in the realm of religion, both domestically and around the world.

While not usually one to self-consciously insert authorial position into my writing, I do feel in this case an obligation to explain certain aspects of my perspective on the issues treated in this volume. As someone born in Saudi Arabia, the third generation of my family to live and work in the kingdom as an American expatriate, I grew up regularly hearing accounts of how Saudi Arabia nefariously funded the "Wahhabization" of the Muslim world. My tendency was to regard such narratives with skepticism, not least of all because they seemed so at odds with my personal experience of most Saudis who—while certainly socially conservative and religiously observant—invariably came across as warm, kind, and generous. So while I did not doubt that certain Saudi and Saudi-funded religious activities outside the kingdom's borders might have negative effects (after all, I had had enough of my own run-ins with the kingdom's notorious *mutawa*, or religious police, to know that rigid and aggressive religiosity was a reality in Saudi Arabia), the idea that Saudi religious transnationalism was having a systemic impact on global Islam struck me as rather far-fetched, or an idea most likely to be promoted by political opponents of the kingdom. However, over the years, and as my research on comparative Muslim politics took me to more and more settings across the Muslim majority (and minority) world, I could not ignore the fact that, almost everywhere I went, I encountered in local informants and interview subjects some version of a narrative that talked about how things "used to be" before the arrival of religious influence from Saudi Arabia, and how things had changed as a result of those influences. And as pervasive as this discourse on global Wahhabization seemed to be, one was always hard pressed to find much in the way of detailed and systematic analysis of the phenomenon. I therefore felt the desire and need for a more thorough, objective, nuanced, and research-driven analysis of Saudi religious export activity, and this is what led me to embark on the process of producing this volume.

This volume would not have been possible without the support of a great number of people and institutions, several of which I would like to acknowledge by name. The Carnegie Corporation of New York made the project possible in the first place, and I owe a great debt of gratitude in particular to Hillary Wiesner for her encouragement and early championing of the core idea. She and her Carnegie colleague Nehal Amer have been unwaveringly supportive throughout. The Henry Luce Foundation and especially Toby Volkman also provided important support that helped the project to get off the ground. I was fortunate to spend a year at Georgetown University's Berkley Center for Religion, Peace, and World Affairs while the project was in its most active phase. The Center's leadership and staff—particularly Shaun Casey, Tom Banchoff, Michael Kessler, Claudia Winkler, Randolph Pelzer, and Ruth Gopin—provided an incredibly warm and supportive environment in which to work. My thanks also to Ray Kim and Grant Marthinsen for their research assistance. Henry Brill shepherded the manuscript through the copyediting process with amazing skill and efficiency. In addition to benefiting from early brainstorming with Will McCants, several colleagues offered valuable feedback at an author workshop in December 2019, namely Nathan Brown, Duke Burbridge, Yasmine Farouk, Sarah Feuer, Shadi Hamid, and Annelle Sheline. I owe special gratitude to Christopher Anzalone who, in addition to coauthoring one of the volume's chapters, provided invaluable support in preparing the final manuscript. Finally, I would like to thank Cynthia Read, Drew Anderla, Brent Matheny, and the entire team at Oxford University Press.

Peter Mandaville
Washington, DC, September 2021

Contributors

Hira Amin holds a PhD in History from the University of Cambridge. She is currently a Visiting Associate Professor in the Islam and Global Affairs division of the College of Islamic Studies at Hamad Bin Khalifa University. Her research interests include Muslims in the West and global Muslim trends and thought in modernity. She is working on a monograph about Salafism and Islamism in Britain, as well as a new project on disability in Muslim communities. She is the cofounder of the Maker-Majlis, an annual experiential conference that explores the Sustainable Development Goals in the Muslim world.

Christopher Anzalone is a Visiting Assistant Professor of Islamic Studies, History, and Government at George Mason University and a Visiting Scholar at the Ali Vural Ak Center for Global Islamic Studies. He has a PhD in Islamic Studies from McGill University and an MA in Near Eastern Languages and Cultures from Indiana University, Bloomington. His research focuses on political Islam, radical and militant movements and organizations, Shi'i Islam, Islamic visual cultures, and religious narratives of martyrdom and self-sacrifice. He has published articles and book chapters, including with Oxford University Press and Princeton University Press. He blogs about his research at https://ibnsiqilli.com/ and on Twitter at @IbnSiqilli.

Natana J. DeLong-Bas is the author of *Shariah: What Everyone Needs to Know* (Oxford University Press, 2018, with John L. Esposito), *Islam: A Living Faith* (Anselm Academic, 2018), and *Wahhabi Islam: From Revival and Reform to Global Jihad* (rev. ed., Oxford University Press, 2008, translated into Arabic, Russian, and French), among other books, and is Editor-in-Chief of *Oxford Bibliographies Online—Islamic Studies*. Past President of the American Council for the Study of Islamic Societies (ACSIS), she is an expert on Islam and Christianity, women and gender, Islamic law, the environment, and the Arabian Gulf countries. She is Associate Professor of the Practice of Theology and Islamic Civilizations and Societies at Boston College.

Nora Derbal is a Postdoctoral Fellow at the Martin Buber Society of Fellows (MBSF) in the Humanities and Social Sciences at the Hebrew University in Jerusalem. She holds a PhD in Islamic Studies from Freie Universität Berlin. Before joining the Hebrew University in 2019, she spent two years as a Postdoctoral Teaching Fellow at the American University in Cairo (AUC). She has conducted extensive fieldwork in Saudi Arabia since 2009, with long-term fellowships at the King Abd al-Aziz University and Effat University in Jeddah, as well as the King Faisal Center for Research and Islamic Studies in Riyadh.

James M. Dorsey is a Senior Fellow at the S. Rajaratnam School of International Studies and Middle East Institute in Singapore, co-director of the Institute for Fan Culture of the

University of Wuerzburg in Germany, and the author of the globally syndicated column and blog, "The Turbulent World of Middle East Soccer."

Andrew Hammond is a historian of modern Islamic thought, with a focus on Turkey, Egypt, and Saudi Arabia. Currently teaching Turkish history at the University of Oxford, he is the author of *The Islamic Utopia: The Illusion of Reform in Saudi Arabia* (Pluto Press, 2013), *Popular Culture in North Africa and the Middle East* (ABC-CLIO, 2017), and numerous journal articles on Salafism, Arabic media, and Middle East politics. He previously worked as a journalist with BBC Arabic, in Egypt and Saudi Arabia with Reuters, and as a Middle East policy analyst with the European Council on Foreign Relations.

Noorhaidi Hasan is a Professor of Islam and Politics at Sunan Kalijaga State Islamic University of Yogyakarta, Indonesia. Currently he also serves as the Dean of the Graduate School at the same university. His research interests are broadly interdisciplinary, covering topics such as Salafism, identity politics, religious diversity, popular culture, and youth. He received his PhD from Utrecht University, the Netherlands (2005). Apart from his active participation in various academic forums at home and abroad, he has published books, papers and articles with academic presses and refereed international journals. Recently he was appointed as a member of the Indonesian Academy of Sciences (AIPI), a state institution formed by the Indonesian president for the advancement of the sciences and humanities.

Harun Karčić is a journalist and political analyst based in Bosnia and Herzegovina, covering the Balkans, Turkey, and the Near East. He has written extensively on Islam in the Balkans, religious revival after communism, Islamic norms in a secular state, and has compared Saudi, Turkish, and Iranian Islamic influence in the region. He is also a Fellow at the Center for Advanced Studies (CNS) in Sarajevo and the author of *A Short Introduction to Shariʻa* (2017) and *Shariʻa and Legal Pluralism in Europe* (2018), both published in Bosnian.

Nazli Kibria is Professor of Sociology at Boston University. A scholar of migration, identities, and families, her books include *Muslims in Motion: Islam and National Identity in the Bangladeshi Diaspora* and *Race and Immigration* (with Cara Bowman and Megan O'Leary).

Stéphane Lacroix is an Associate Professor of Political Science at Sciences Po and a researcher at Sciences Po's Centre de Recherches Internationales (CERI). His work deals with religion and politics, with a focus on the Gulf and Egypt. He is the author or editor of *Awakening Islam: The Politics of Religious Dissent in Contemporary Saudi Arabia* (Harvard University Press, 2011); *Saudi Arabia in Transition: Insights on Social, Political, Economic and Religious Change* (Cambridge University Press, 2015, with Bernard Haykel and Thomas Hegghammer); *Egypt's Revolutions: Politics, Religion, Social Movements* (Palgrave Macmillan, 2016, with Bernard Rougier); and *Revisiting the Arab Uprisings: The Politics of a Revolutionary Moment* (Oxford University Press, 2018, with Jean-Pierre Filiu).

Peter Mandaville is a Professor of International Affairs at the Schar School of Policy and Government and Director of the Ali Vural Ak Center for Global Islamic Studies, both at George Mason University. He is also a Senior Research Fellow at Georgetown University's Berkley Center for Religion, Peace, and World Affairs. He is the author of the books *Islam and Politics* (4th edition, 2020) and *Transnational Muslim Politics: Reimagining the Umma* (2001), and has also edited several volumes of essays in the fields of Islamic studies and international relations.

Sultan Mohammed Zakaria is a Visiting Research Fellow at the Centre for Peace and Justice, BRAC University, and a Researcher at Amnesty International. His research interests include democratic transitions, political developments, and human rights issues in South Asia.

Mametbek Myrzabaev is Director of the Research Institute for Islamic Studies, Bishkek, Kyrgyzstan. Since completion of his PhD in the Sociology of Religion from Ankara University, Turkey, he has been engaged in a large number of research projects on religion and the religious situation in Kyrgyzstan. He also taught at the Theology faculties of Arabaev Kyrgyz State University and Osh State University.

Emil Nasritdinov is an Associate Professor and Coordinator of the Anthropology, Urbanism and International Development Master's program at the American University of Central Asia (AUCA). He is also the director of AUCA's Social Innovations Lab Kyrgyzstan (SILK). His main areas of research and teaching expertise are migration, religion, and urbanism. He teaches undergraduate and graduate subjects and publishes in all three fields.

Terje Østebø is currently the Chair of the Department of Religion and Associate Professor at the Center for African Studies and the Department of Religion, University of Florida—and the founding director of the UF Center for Global Islamic Studies. His research interests are Islam in contemporary Ethiopia, Islamic reformism, ethnicity and religion, and Salafism in Africa. His publications include *Islam, Ethnicity, and Conflict in Ethiopia: The Bale Insurgency (1963–1970)* (Cambridge University Press, 2020); *Muslim Ethiopia: The Christian Legacy, Identity Politics, and Islamic Reformism* (Palgrave-Macmillan, 2013, co-edited with Patrick Desplat); *Localising Salafism: Religious Change among Oromo Muslims in Bale, Ethiopia* (Brill, 2012).

Yasir Qadhi is the Dean of The Islamic Seminary of America based in Dallas, Texas, and the Resident Scholar of the East Plano Islamic Center. He has a BSc in Chemical Engineering from the University of Houston; a BA (Ḥadīth) and an MA (Theology) from the Islamic University of Medina (Saudi Arabia); and a PhD from Yale in Islamic Studies. His research focuses on early Islamic theology, Salafism, Ibn Taymiyya, and Qur'anic studies. He is extremely active on social media, where he has large followings, and has also established himself as a voice for modern American Muslims, straddling both clerical and academic roles.

Reinhard Schulze, after studying at the University of Bonn, has held professorships in Islamic Studies and Middle East Studies at the Universities of Bochum and Bamberg and has occupied the Chair of Islamic and Middle Eastern Studies at the University of Bern since 1995. Since 2018, he has directed the Forum Islam and the Middle East at the University of Bern. His research mainly deals with Islamic history from early modernity to the present, as well as early Islamic history.

Alexander Thurston is Assistant Professor of Political Science at the University of Cincinnati. His research focuses on Islamic scholars and movements in northwest Africa, including both nonviolent and violent actors. He is the author of three books, including *Jihadists of North Africa and the Sahel: Local Politics and Rebel Groups* (Cambridge University Press, 2020). He has conducted fieldwork in Mali and elsewhere in the Sahel region and West Africa. He writes regularly at Sahel Blog, where he has been analyzing Sahelian politics since 2009.

Note on Transliteration

This book uses a modified form of transliteration from Arabic to English, based on the system used by the *International Journal of Middle East Studies*. In order to simplify the text for general and nonspecialist readers, diacritical marks (macrons and microns) are not used, with the exception of ʿ for the *ayn* (for example: *ʿulama*) and ʾ in some instances for *hamza* (for example: Qurʾan). Names and words from languages other than Arabic are transliterated according to the preferences of the individual chapter authors. Words originating in foreign languages which have entered into common usage in English are not italicized (for example: "Qurʾan" and "jihad"). Names of organizations are not italicized. All other words in the book originating in foreign languages are italicized.

PART I
ORIGINS AND EVOLUTION

1

Wahhabism and the World

The Historical Evolution, Structure, and Future of Saudi Religious Transnationalism

Peter Mandaville

Introduction

Religious proselytization activities funded by and emanating from Saudi Arabia have played a significant role in shaping the religious, social, and cultural landscapes of numerous Muslim majority and minority countries for the past half century. Since the 1960s, the Saudi religious establishment as well as its Ministry of Islamic Affairs have spent billions of dollars to undertake a wide range of religious propagation (*da'wa*) activities, including mosque building; funding religious schools; distributing religious literature; proving preachers and religious educators scholarships for religious study in Saudi Arabia; and media campaigns focused on religion and religious identity. In addition to *da'wa* carried out by the Saudi government, numerous other Saudi and Saudi-linked entities have been major contributors to this effort, including parastatal organizations such as the Muslim World League and the World Assembly of Muslim Youth; humanitarian relief groups such as the International Islamic Relief Organization; and various private charities such as Waqf al-Islami.

The motivations for this proselytization have varied and evolved over time. At some level, it has always been driven by a sense on the part of the Saudi religious establishment that, as the historical cradle of Islam and the home of its holiest sites, the country has an obligation to promote the distinctly Saudi variant of Salafi Islam (commonly called "Wahhabism") globally. But there have been additional driving factors. In the 1960s, when Arab nationalism was at its height, Saudi *da'wa* sought to provide an alternative to the secular ideology of Nasserism. From the 1980s, religious propagation was seen as a tool for countering growing Iranian influence in the Muslim world in the wake of the Islamic Revolution. During the 1990s, particularly in sub-Saharan Africa, Islamic *da'wa*—much of it funded from the Arab Gulf region—reached new heights in response to the rising influence of Pentecostal and Evangelical Christian groups. More recently, a perception of rising Iranian dominance regionally and beyond

Peter Mandaville, *Wahhabism and the World* In: *Wahhabism and the World*. Edited by: Peter Mandaville, Oxford University Press. © Oxford University Press 2022. DOI: 10.1093/oso/9780197532560.003.0001 has once again become a defining factor in Saudi global proselytization. In sum, the outward projection of Saudi religious influence often reflects multiple and competing agendas within the kingdom itself as various entities—public, private, and somewhere in between—vie for influence around the world.

The purpose of this chapter is to provide the reader with a broad overview and introduction to the historical evolution, structure, and potential futures of transnational religious activity emanating from Saudi Arabia. The discussion proceeds as follows. The first section begins by framing the debate on Saudi Arabia's export of Wahhabism, clarifying the scope of the research inquiry, and exploring some of the methodological considerations that bear on the challenge of reaching clear and sound conclusions. This section also includes a brief discussion of Wahhabism and its relationship to the broader doctrinal current known as Salafism. The second section of the chapter provides an overview of the ecosystem of Saudi religious transnationalism. It explores the origins and historical evolution of Saudi religious export activity, with particular attention to the relationship between religious propagation activity and the kingdom's geopolitical interests during various periods. This section also offers an analysis and "inventory" of the global Saudi *da'wa* apparatus, identifying the diverse range of organizations, agencies, and actors involved in religious propagation and providing an overview of the kinds of activities and programs associated with their efforts. It also discusses some of the effects most commonly associated with Saudi religious transnationalism around the world. The chapter then concludes with a brief discussion of what the future may hold with respect to Saudi religious transnationalism in the era of Crown Prince Muhammad bin Salman.

Debating and Defining Saudi Religious Transnationalism

One reason Saudi Arabia's export of Wahhabism poses such a quandary for analysts arises from the fact that there is an underlying politics to the question itself. While discussions of Islam's role in Saudi foreign policy date back to at least the early 1980s, the last 20 years in particular have seen an upsurge in the number of books, articles, and reports exploring connections between Saudi religion and Islamist militancy.[1] More specifically, in the aftermath of the September 11, 2001, terrorist attacks on the United States—where 15 of the 19 perpetrators turned out to be Saudi citizens—new questions started to be asked about Saudi Arabia's possible support for terrorist groups. To some degree, this debate is entangled with the larger question of America's complex and, to some, contentious relationship with the kingdom. Put simply, political groups opposed to Washington's alliance with Riyadh are often at the forefront of efforts to promote the idea of clear linkages between Saudi religious propagation and terrorism, whereas allies of the kingdom tend to play down or ignore such ties. These already murky waters turn rather muddy once we bring into the picture the frequency with which observers elide or outright conflate direct Saudi support for specific militant and terrorist groups (a fairly undisputed phenomenon) and the question of whether Saudi support for Islamic causes around the world might be linked to intolerance, conflict, and violence.[2] Some of the confusion here is understandable: it is well documented that the activities of certain Saudi Islamic charities, humanitarian aid organizations, and conduits of religious education have been tied to militant and terrorist activity. Nonetheless, much of the existing commentary and analysis posits a rather direct—albeit often vague in terms of precise causal mechanisms—connection between the global propagation of something called Wahhabism and support for jihadi violence. The following depiction is relatively typical:

> Through lectures, booklets, videos, CDs, *fatawah*, Facebook, blogs, YouTube and television stations such as Iqra, Saudi scholars disseminate their call for *jihad*. Published and produced in KSA, Wahhabi propaganda of this sort, much of it little more than hate literature, finds its way into mosques and *madrassas* throughout the international community. Moreover, many Muslim students go to KSA to study at Saudi universities, returning to their home countries with their minds trained in Wahhabist-*jihadist* ideology. Countless other Muslims visit KSA as pilgrims and, coming across Wahhabi teaching and practice, return home as missionaries of Wahhabism. (Valentine 2015, 243)

It is precisely this kind of narrative that the research underpinning this volume aims to explore and assess. Given the nature of the ongoing debate about Saudi Arabia's export of Wahhabism and the various forms of analytical conflation and slippage which surround it, there are two important points to make up front about the scope of the present inquiry. First, this study is focused primarily on the question of how we should understand the transnational currency and impact of activities undertaken and/or funded by Saudi Arabia that are clearly religious in nature. It therefore excludes direct financial and political support the kingdom provides to various militant groups, including some Islamists, in pursuit of its own policy interests and objectives. The one exception is to note cases where Saudi Arabia has specifically used religious activities or support for religious causes as vehicles for providing such assistance. Second, the question of whether Saudi Arabia's global propagation of Wahhabism causes violent extremism is not a major focus of this research. Rather, this work seeks to understand the full range of diverse effects and outcomes associated with Saudi religious propagation around the world, and to begin identifying the various factors and societal patterns that govern these outcomes. Much of this relates

primarily to questions of intercommunal tolerance, sectarianism, diversity, pluralism, gender, minorities, and human rights. That said, where it is possible to
provide an account of how Saudi religious influence intersects with dynamics
surrounding conflict, violence, extremism, and militancy in a given setting, such
connections are certainly noted.

Even though this chapter and the broader volume in which it is situated focus
almost exclusively on Saudi Arabia, it is also important to recognize that the
kingdom is not the only country in the Arab Gulf region involved in transnational religious propagation.[3] Although their smaller petrodollar economies lead
them to operate at a more modest scale compared to their large neighbor, Qatar,
Kuwait, and the United Arab Emirates have to varying degrees also provided
significant support for many of the same Islamic causes, engaged in mosque
building, and funded religious education in ways that are similar to Saudi Arabia.
Qatar's religious establishment, for example, has long been influenced by scholarship and religious trends from Saudi Arabia, and its national mosque is named
in honor of Muhammad ibn Abd al-Wahhab (Dorsey 2017c, Roberts 2014).
While some aspects of wider Gulf Cooperation Council (GCC) religious propagation have been carried out in alignment with Saudi Arabia's efforts, there have
also been examples of rivalry and competition—a particularly relevant issue to
track in this time of heightened factionalization within the GCC bloc.

Having delimited the scope of this research, it is probably worth saying something about the object of inquiry itself and some of the specific terminology
I use to describe and define it. While this chapter employs a variety of shorthand
phrases to refer to the phenomenon under study (e.g., "Saudi religious propagation," "Saudi da'wa," "Wahhabi exports"), the title of this chapter follows Madawi
al-Rasheed in more properly defining its object of analysis in terms of *Saudi religious transnationalism*. For Al-Rasheed, "Saudi religious transnationalism
involves the establishment of connections with Muslims using institutions under
state sponsorship and agents who are not necessarily Saudi nationals. It entails
the transfer of funds and religious knowledge from Saudi Arabia to Muslims in
other countries" (Al-Rasheed 2005, 150). To focus on the transnationalism of
these religious influences is to recognize that while the relevant flows of finances,
media, personnel, and ideas certainly move across the borders of nation-states,
the actors involved on both the sending and receiving sides include a range
of entities from state agencies to subnational institutions to networks of individuals. This point also highlights the one qualification I would add to Al-
Rasheed's definition. While the (Saudi) "state sponsorship" she emphasizes is
certainly pervasive across most of the religious transnationalism addressed by
this study, there are also dimensions of Saudi religious propagation that involve
exclusively private and civil society actors—some of which occurs without the
knowledge or backing of the kingdom's authorities. Focusing on Saudi religious

transnationalism also allows us to avoid reducing the issue to, or framing it exclusively in terms of, Wahhabism. As will become clear in the following, this term—while absolutely central to our analysis—carries its own complexities and baggage.

The Challenges of Studying Saudi Religious Transnationalism

There are a number of specific challenges that face scholars and analysts trying to understand the nature and impact of what we are calling Saudi religious transnationalism. Three in particular are worth highlighting in the present context since they relate very directly to common framings and questions surrounding Saudi Arabia's religious propagation in foreign policy and national security contexts. These concern issues around the availability and reliability of data, particularly with respect to levels of Saudi funding for religious causes around the world (or, put another way, "how much Saudi religious transnationalism exists or has existed in the world?"); the presence of considerable conceptual and terminological fluidity in existing accounts of Saudi religious propagation which renders comparisons across cases difficult (or, "are we all talking about same thing when we describe and make claims about Saudi religious influence in different countries?"); and challenges regarding the levels of confidence with which we can advance causal claims in connection with Saudi transnational religious influence (or, "how certain can we be that a given effect or outcome occurred because of influence from Saudi Arabia?"). Let us briefly address each of these in order.

Availability and Reliability of Data on Saudi Religious Transnationalism

One of the persistent challenges associated with studying Saudi-sponsored religious propagation efforts pertains to the stark unevenness of available data and information about the extent and scale of such activities. This is in part a function of the fact that—as we will see in the next section of this chapter—there are a wide range of entities involved in *da'wa* emanating from the kingdom, and they vary significantly in terms of the extent and specificity with which they disclose their activities. For example, there are some high-profile projects, often associated with senior members of the Saudi royal family, which are the focus of press releases and public affairs campaigns. For example, the King Fahd Complex for the Printing of the Holy Qur'an publishes copious statistics on the number of

Qur'ans it prints in various global languages each year.[4] Move over to another dimension of Saudi *da'wa*, however, that of private support for the construction of mosques around the world, and it becomes almost impossible to quantify anything. This is because prior to the 9/11 attacks, Saudi Arabia did not track or require declaration of private charitable donations. Much of the money flowing out of the kingdom to support the construction of mosques around the world during the 1970s and 1980s took the form of donations from private individuals. As explained to me by an informant in London who was frequently present when such donations were made, "the head of the family would simply pull out a checkbook, write a check for millions of riyals, and hand it to the petitioner from the Muslim community in Australia or wherever. No record, no follow-up, no accountability whatsoever." Even where copious amounts of data are reported, it is often difficult to know how to interpret their significance or reliability. For example, the Saudi Ministry of Islamic Affairs, Da'wa, and Guidance publishes annual "Statistical Books" that quantify in great detail various aspects of Saudi domestic and international religious outreach.[5] However, given the level of abstraction involved in its reporting, one has little idea how to understand the significance of, for example, the 350,000 religious lectures it reported supporting around the world in 2016–2017.

Such widely varying levels in the availability and quality of data on Saudi funding for religion, not to mention lack of consensus with respect to how such funding levels should be measured, means that it is very difficult to put an aggregate number on how much Saudi Arabia has spent over the years on supporting religious causes and activities around the world. There is no shortage of impressive sounding figures cited in the existing literature, but little is ever said about how analysts and authors arrive at these numbers. Nonspecific hearsay ("some estimate . . .", "it is believed . . .") seems to be the standard mode for reporting these figures. Sometimes sources are even internally inconsistent on this question. For example, Valentine's *Force and Fanaticism: Wahhabism in Saudi Arabia and Beyond*, cites a *U.S. News & World Report* article to claim that Saudi Arabia has spent $87 billion propagating Wahhabism abroad, only to claim 20 pages later that the kingdom has spent $100 billion on Wahhabi causes in the West alone (Valentine 2015, 235, 255). A 2003 *Washington Post* article on a congressional hearing dealing with Saudi support for terrorism cites $70 billion having been spent on "Saudi aid projects" without clarifying whether and how these projects relate to the article's primary focus on spreading Wahhabism (Mintz 2003). Given the aforementioned tendency for many observers to conflate any form of Saudi external funding, the kingdom's support for militant groups, and export of Wahhabism, it becomes all but impossible to separate out different funding streams and arrive at a reliable figure for religion alone.

For all of these reasons, this research has refrained from trying to posit even an order of magnitude estimate for the overall level of Saudi funding for religion around the world. The one thing we feel relatively confident about saying is that there has been an overall downward trend in levels of funding for Saudi transnational religious propagation activities over the past 20 years. This trend—which we address in more detail in the concluding section—has been reported in numerous recent analyses and also shows up in the kingdom's own data, with the Ministry of Islamic Affairs Statistical Books for 2012–2017 showing year-on-year declines in the levels of international *da'wa* activities (Varagur 2020, 187).[6] This general trend is also confirmed by several of the country case studies that appear later in this volume.

The Indeterminacy of Wahhabism and Salafism

A second major challenge facing anyone who tries to map, inventory, and assess Saudi religious transnationalism arises from the imprecision and slipperiness associated with some of the relevant key terms such as "Wahhabism" and "Salafism." While it is possible for academics in the field of Islamic Studies to advance relatively clear and distinctive definitions of such concepts, the ways in which these terms tend to be used by nonspecialist observers and in everyday conversation can lead to considerable confusion. "Wahhabism" is often invoked—by local populations, governments, and media alike—as a broad and derogatory term referring to any religious idea or practice deemed highly conservative or reflective of nonlocal norms (regardless of its actual origins). For example, as societies in Central Asia and the Caucasus opened up to the world after the Cold War, it was not uncommon for local governments, suspicious of foreign religious influences, to use the label "Wahhabism" to refer to any religious group or movement whose origins lie outside the region—including patently non-Wahhabi groups such as the Hizmet movement associated with the Turkish preacher Fethullah Gülen (Bashirov 2018). Similarly confusing are references to things like "Wahhabist-*jihadist* ideology," as seen in the passage from Valentine quoted earlier (and not uncommon in journalistic and other non-academic writing), as a description of the main religious thrust emanating from the kingdom's global *da'wa* apparatus. This is because the bedrock Wahhabism of the Saudi religious establishment, which represents the discourse found in most of the kingdom's religious export products, is predominantly quietist and preaches loyalism to established authority rather than activism and revolution. While it might be accurate to describe as Wahhabi-Jihadi the ideology and political orientation of figures such as the Syrian Muslim Brotherhood leader Muhammad Surur (1938–2016) and various dissident figures from the Egyptian Muslim

Brotherhood who sought refuge in Saudi Arabia in the 1960s and whose cross-fertilization of Saudi Salafism and Brotherhood activism formed the basis of the kingdom's Sahwa movement, this distinctly minoritarian trend is frowned upon by the Saudi authorities and therefore excluded from officially sponsored trans-national religious outreach efforts.[7]

In addition to widely varying usage of the term "Wahhabism," those seeking to evaluate Saudi religious transnationalism today must also contend with the challenge of distinguishing Wahhabism from the widely prevalent and, in many respects, doctrinally similar trend known as Salafism.[8] The confusion is very understandable since the similarities in question arise from the fact that Wahhabism represents, essentially, a Saudi-specific variant of the broader Salafi current. Chapter 2 in this volume, by Natana Delong-Bas, explores the question of Wahhabism's relationship with global Salafism in considerable detail.

Wahhabism takes its name from the eighteenth-century Arabian religious revivalist Muhammad Ibn Abdul Wahhab (1703–1792). Deeply influenced by the ideas of the medieval jurist Ibn Taymiyya (1263–1328), Ibn Abdul Wahhab's main concerns related to the centrality of monotheism (tawhid) and the dangers posed to Islam by what he saw as corrupting innovations (bid'a), such as Sufism. His political alliance with the Al-Saud family, and the fact that the Saudi religious establishment is founded on his teachings, have led Wahhabism to be strongly identified with the Saudi practice (and projection) of Islam. While sharing, as we have noted, much of the same doctrinal orientation as Salafis, the public and social implications of Salafism have been interpreted in very particular ways by Wahhabis. The social structure and political environment of eighteenth-century Arabia, for example, led followers of Wahhabism to place a strong emphasis on differentiating true believers from infidels in the name of justifying political ex-pansion and the use of violence against other Muslims. This has led to an em-phasis among Wahhabis on the practice of takfir—that is, the act of declaring someone to be an infidel or an apostate from Islam. The fact that takfir is also a central concept in modern jihadi ideology is one of the reasons that Wahhabism is often seen as an inspiration for Islamist militancy. The Salafi/Wahhabi dis-tinction is further confused by the fact that many of the most prominent Salafi scholars known and followed around the world are Saudis or scholars who spent part or most of their career within the Wahhabi religious establishment of Saudi Arabia. These include 'ulama such as Muhammad Nasiruddin al-Albani (d. 1999), Muhammad ibn al-Uthaymeen (d. 2001), and Rabee' al-Madkhali (b. 1931).

Another complicating factor here comes from the fact that, as many scholars have noted, interest in Salafism has been on the rise across the Muslim world over the past 20 years.[9] It is common to assume—not incorrectly, we hasten to add—that Saudi financial support for religious propagation is a key factor in this upsurge. It is inarguable that the subsidized mass dissemination by Saudi Arabia of texts central to Salafism has facilitated access to Salafi ideas in many settings around the world. The error comes when analysts and observers start to view *all* manifestations of Salafism as evidence of Saudi Arabia's influence. There are at least two explanations for the presence and currency of Salafism in some settings that are largely unrelated to the kingdom's global *da'wa* efforts. First, it is important to recognize that some countries possess their own indigenous traditions of Salafism, such as the Ahl-e Hadith movement in Pakistan, whose existence predates the development of religious connections with Saudi Arabia. Salafi and Salafi-like movements also have a historical basis in West Africa and Southeast Asia. The Salafi sector that began to emerge in Egypt in the 1920s, while certainly in active conversation with like-minded peers in the Arabian Peninsula, has roots in intellectual trends closer to home. This picture is rendered even more complex when we recognize that the natural affinities between emerging Saudi religious connections and existing local Salafi groups in various countries made it easy for the latter to quickly develop close collaborative ties with new Saudi partners. It therefore becomes relevant to talk about the cross-fertilization of indigenous traditions of Salafism with new Saudi approaches, leading—as we explain in the following—to the multidirectional flow of religious ideas. Like the aforementioned conflation of Wahhabism with "conservative Islam," it is not uncommon for conservative-leaning religious movements in some countries to be described (once again, exonymically and usually by their critics) as "Salafi" even if their theological and legal positions do not correspond to widely accepted definitions of Salafism. Such is the case, for example, with the Hanafi-based Deoband movement in South Asia, a more conservative and literalist trend in South Asian Islam which, while possessing characteristics that have enabled a degree of interoperability and partnership with Salafis (including Saudi Salafis), is firmly grounded in a school of Islamic jurisprudence, Hanafism, viewed as illegitimate by most purist Salafis.

Finally, it is important to recognize that there are wider sociological reasons that may explain why Salafism appears attractive to many young Muslims today. First, in many Muslim-minority settings in Europe and North America, the current generation of young Muslims have sought to move away from what they perceive as their parents' "culturally tainted" understanding of religion—a type of religiosity viewed as reflective of localized religious culture in the countries from which the older generation emigrated, rather than something embodying "authentic" Islam. Salafism, with its moorings in the earliest period of Islamic history prior to the religion's expansion to other world regions, is better able to represent itself as a purer expression of the religion's original essence. Furthermore, in the highly mediated information environments that all young people, including Muslims, inhabit today, anyone searching online or on social media for reliable religious guidance is likely to encounter such a wide and varying range of information, opinions, claims, and fatwas that it becomes very difficult to know whom to trust or which sources should be viewed as religiously authentic. Here again, Salafism, with its more circumscribed set of sources and rigid methodology for deriving legal opinions, sometimes seems the safer option. To make this point is not to say that religious ideas emanating from Saudi Arabia are not part of this picture—certainly young Muslims do often end up being exposed to the views of Saudi-based scholars and theologians during their online explorations—but only to make the point that there exist today reasons for embracing Salafi doctrine that arise from something other than Saudi religious transnationalism.

The Origins and Evolution of Saudi Religious Transnationalism

The motivations for Saudi Arabia's involvement in religious export activity have evolved over time, with shifts in the regional environment, as well as in Saudi domestic politics, shaping its promotion of religious soft power. While consolidating stewardship of the annual *hajj* pilgrimage was a priority for the kingdom's founder, 'Abdul-Aziz, neither he nor his son and successor, Saud bin 'Abdul-Aziz, emphasized Islam as a major dimension of Saudi Arabia's external relations. Rather, most historians and observers agree that the kingdom's third monarch, Faysal (r. 1964–1975), was the chief architect of modern Saudi religious transnationalism. Faysal's embrace of Islam within Saudi foreign policy had both international and domestic dimensions. Internationally, Saudi Arabia's projection of conservative religion in the 1960s was a key pillar of Faysal's response to the secular nationalist Pan-Arabism emanating from Gamal 'Abd al-Nasser's Egypt, then the kingdom's chief regional rival.[10] King Faysal presided over the founding of the Muslim World League in 1962 (see later discussion), an initiative that emerged out of a major Saudi-sponsored conference on combating secularism and socialism around the world (Commins 2009, 152).

But even in the infancy of Saudi religious soft power, there were motivations other than pure *realpolitik* at work. Domestic considerations also played a role. For example, many within the kingdom's religious establishment viewed the global propagation of Islam as a religious obligation deeply intertwined with Saudi Arabia's role as home to Islam's two holiest sites. And after the Senior Council of 'Ulama played a key role in supporting Faysal's efforts in 1963–1964 to remove his brother Saud from the throne, the new Saudi monarch was even more inclined to support their agenda of international Islamization. Faysal continued to place Islam at the forefront of the kingdom's geopolitical identity, playing a key role in the establishment in 1970 of the Organization of the Islamic Conference (OIC, known today as the Organization of Islamic Cooperation), an Islamic rival to the secular-nationalist dominated Arab League, and, in 1971, the Islamic News Agency, Islamic Broadcasting Agency, and Islamic Development Bank—all based in Saudi Arabia (Rundell 2020, 191). As David Commins puts it, by the time of Faysal's assassination in 1975, "he had put Saudi Arabia at the centre of a robust set of pan-Islamic institutions [and] contributed to a new consciousness of international Muslim political issues, ranging from Jerusalem to Pakistan's troubles with India over Kashmir to the suffering of South Africa's Muslims under the apartheid regime" (Commins 2009, 153).

The year 1979 was pivotal with respect to the role of Islam in Saudi Arabia's international relations. Domestic considerations rose to the fore once again with the royal family seeking to burnish its religious credentials after the seizure of the Grand Mosque in Mecca by a group of rebels led by Juhayman al-ʿUtaybi. This prompted a new infusion of funding into a wide range of Islamic causes, including a noteworthy increase in the scale and range of religious activities funded outside the kingdom. Two major international events that same year served to catalyze Saudi global *daʿwa*: the revolution in Iran and the Soviet Union's invasion of Afghanistan.

The establishment of the Islamic Republic of Iran and Khomeini's efforts to export its revolution marked a new phase of "geo-religious" competition between Saudi Arabia and Iran—each of them vying to assert supremacy among Muslim countries. Saudi Arabia also worried about Iranian influence with respect to its own significant Shiʿa minority population, a community subject to high levels of discrimination and de facto second-class citizenship. In the eyes of some of Saudi Arabia's hardline religious scholars, the Shiʿa were little more than heretics.

During the 1970s, certain dimensions of Saudi religious outreach had already come to reflect the kingdom's Cold War alignment with the United States, which saw in Islam an ideological counterbalance to Soviet influence. This was thrown into high gear with the Soviet invasion of Afghanistan, and in the 1980s South Asia became a major destination for Saudi funding. Saudi Arabia was a key broker in the various networks of US support flowing to Mujahidin resistance fighters in Afghanistan. Much of this flowed through Pakistan, where Riyadh also formed a close relationship with military ruler Zia ul-Haq, whose "Islamization" drive—including a significant expansion in funding for madrasas and religious higher education—were enacted with partnership and financial assistance from a wide range of benefactors in the kingdom.

The 1990s saw a diversification in the geographic scope of Saudi outreach, with a surge of funding for mosques and religious education in sub-Saharan Africa, in part as a response to the growth of Pentecostal Christianity. Over the years, other regions have also attracted the attention of religious benefactors in the Persian

Gulf, including Southeast Asia (especially Indonesia and the Philippines), Muslim communities in Europe and North America, and the various Central Asian republics after the fall of the Soviet Union. Concerns about Iranian influence have been the primary driver of Saudi Arabia's religious outreach efforts since 2003, when Tehran began asserting itself more forcefully in the Arab world as a response to its perceived encirclement by US forces in Afghanistan, the Gulf, and Iraq.

The Ecosystem of Global Saudi *Da'wa*

What exactly is implied by the idea of "Saudi Arabia" exporting Wahhabi influence? To think of such activity as a calculated and coordinated aspect of the Saudi government's foreign policy conduct is to miss a much more complex reality. While some of the entities involved are indeed governmental ministries and agencies, others are private or quasi-governmental. Some are funded by the Saudi royal family—but independent of the government bureaucracy. Still others are firmly linked to the kingdom's religious establishment, which at times has enjoyed considerable independence from both the government and the House of Saud. In some cases, Saudi benefactors have relied on non-Saudi groups and networks—such as the Muslim Brotherhood in the 1970s and 1980s—to manage and implement aspects of its global religious outreach. In practice, this means that whatever original intentions Saudi actors may have had, they become diluted by other agendas. In short, to fully understand the global Saudi *da'wa* apparatus, it is imperative to get past a "black box" image of the kingdom so as to fully appreciate the diverse array of Saudi entities—both public and private—involved in transnational religious propagation.[11] Several of these institutions and organizations—such as the Muslim World League, the World Assembly of Muslim Youth, and the Islamic University of Medina—are covered in greater detail by subsequent chapters in this volume.

The many and varied actors involved in global Saudi *da'wa* efforts comprise an "ecosystem" of sorts, including the following key components:

- *Ministry of Islamic Affairs, Da'wa, and Guidance:* The governmental body primarily responsible for the management of religious affairs and a major provider of resources (money, books, personnel) for international proselytization activities, including mosque building, the development of religious schools, and the organization of lecture tours by religious scholars and *du'at* (preachers). Ministry officials sometimes serve as "religious attachés" at Saudi diplomatic posts around the world, acting as liaisons with local Muslim communities and religious leaders.

- *Muslim World League (MWL):* A parastatal organization established in 1962 through royal patronage to promote Muslim solidarity and encourage the propagation of Islam globally. While formally independent of the Saudi government, the MWL is traditionally headed by a Saudi, headquartered in Mecca, and largely dependent on the kingdom for its finances. Although representatives from various regions and diverse Islamic trends have been part of the League's governing council over the years (including the Muslim Brotherhood and its South Asian cognate, the Jamaat-e-Islami, both of which were highly influential during the League's early phase), the growing centrality of Saudi figures in its executive functions has led most observers to regard the MWL as a vehicle for securing and promoting Saudi religious hegemony (Schulze 1990).

- *World Assembly of Muslim Youth (WAMY):* An organization established in 1972, originally for the primary purpose of preparing young Saudis and other Muslims planning to study in non-Muslim settings—mainly Europe and North America—to protect and preserve their religious beliefs.[12] Over time, its activities began to cross-fertilize with Muslim Brotherhood–linked networks, particularly in Europe and, given WAMY's close ties to the Saudi religious establishment (in contrast to the MWL's alignment with the al-Saud family), it became more directly involved in activities focused on the propagation of Wahhabi doctrine ("Muslim Network and Movements in Western Europe" 2010).

- *Islamic University of Medina (IUM):* An institution of higher education established in 1961 and closely tied to the kingdom's religious establishment, with a primary mission of providing training in the classical Islamic sciences to Muslims from around the world. IUM's provision of generous scholarships for international students has made it an attractive destination for higher religious study. While a number of other Saudi higher education institutions, such as Umm Al-Qura University (Mecca) and Imam Muhammad bin Saud University (Riyadh), are considered important centers of Wahhabi scholarship, IUM represents a particularly important component within the kingdom's global *da'wa* portfolio because of its primary focus on international students. Frequently viewed as a direct conduit for exporting Wahhabism via the training of religious scholars and preachers (*du'at*) (Sardar 2004, 145), recent scholarship has painted a more complex picture regarding the transnational circulation of religious ideas within and through this institution. Michael Farquhar's study of IUM, for example, demonstrates that aspects of its teaching have come to reflect the diverse range of cultural settings and theological orientations represented within its very global corpus of students (Farquhar 2017).

In their heyday, these institutions collectively formed what Krithika Varagur terms "the backbone of a cosmopolitan postcolonial Muslim world, which had an international circuit somewhat like the Davos-to-Aspen thought leadership junket of today" (Varagur 2020, 31).

In addition to the dedicated global *da'wa* organizations and institutions outlined here, there are four other sectors whose activities are relevant to understanding Saudi religious transnationalism: charities and humanitarian organizations; media; labor migration; and pilgrimage.

Saudi *Da'wa* and Humanitarian Aid

A wide variety of Saudi and Saudi-funded charitable organizations incorporate elements of proselytization into their provision of aid, relief, and social services around the world. Some of the main players here are the International Organization for Relief, Welfare and Development (formerly known as the International Islamic Relief Organization, an affiliate of the MWL), the al-Haramain Foundation, and al-Waqf al-Islami. While the vast majority of their activities fall into the realm of legitimate and valuable charitable services, some have been accused—alongside cognate Christian relief organizations—of proselytizing to particularly vulnerable populations (Racimora 2013, Byman 2017).[13] All three organizations have also had to deal with accusations (and, in some cases, actual convictions) of specific personnel and country programs being linked to funding for militant groups such as Hamas and Lashkar-e-Taiba. After 9/11, the Saudi authorities began to regulate charities much more tightly, but this reach does not necessarily extend to smaller private or family-based charities, some of which enjoy cover from various members of the royal family (US Department of the Treasury 2006, US Department of the Treasury 2008, Gall 2016).

Saudi Publishing, Media, and Global Religious Propagation

Various Saudi publishing and media activities constitute a key component of the kingdom's global *da'wa* apparatus. The worldwide ubiquity of religious texts produced or funded by Saudi entities probably says more about the massive scale at which the kingdom's publishing operations are able to operate than it does about the actual appeal of Wahhabi ideas. Massive Saudi governmental subsidies to support the production and dissemination of religious texts means that at almost any Islamic bookstore around the world, customers are likely to find a wide selection of texts whose contents reflect the religious worldview of the Saudi clerical establishment. There is little doubt that the King Fahd Complex for the

Printing of the Holy Qur'an, producing by its latest reporting some 18 million copies of Islam's holy book each year (in dozens of languages), has fundamentally transformed global Qur'an "supply chains" since its founding in the mid-1980s. While the text of Arabic language Qur'ans printed in Saudi Arabia is identical to any other Arabic edition, it is the kingdom's outsize role in the printing and distribution of the Qur'an as rendered in other languages that becomes relevant in the present context. For example, the English translation of the Qur'an officially supported by Saudi Arabia, by Muhammad Muhsin Khan and Muhammad Taqi ud-Din al-Hilali, contains in its rendering of the main text parenthetical additions that modify the meaning of certain Qur'anic passages. As Khaleel Mohammed (2005) points out:

> From the beginning, the Hilali and Muhsin Khan translation reads more like a supremacist Muslim, anti-Semitic, anti-Christian polemic than a rendition of the Islamic scripture. In the first *sura*, for example, verses which are universally accepted as, "Guide us to the straight path, the path of those whom You have favored, not of those who have incurred Your wrath, nor of those who have gone astray" become, "Guide us to the Straight Way, the way of those on whom You have bestowed Your Grace, not (the way) of those who have earned Your anger (such as the Jews), nor of those who went astray (such as the Christians)."

In other words, elements of Qur'anic exegesis associated with the Salafi worldview are added directly to the holy book's main text, rather than set apart in footnotes or separate ancillary passages, as would usually be the case with such commentary. Similar problems with the depiction of Jews, Christians, and a general climate of intolerance have also been associated with religious textbooks used in Saudi schools and frequently exported around the world by some of the organizations and agencies described earlier.[14] While these textbooks have been a major focus of recent efforts—including efforts by the US government—to address the deleterious effects of Saudi religious transnationalism, they are but one aspect of the vast Saudi religious publishing and dissemination machinery.

Saudi Arabia has also been an active producer and sponsor of religious content in the realm of electronic media, both with respect to broadcasting and, more recently, digital and online formats. The kingdom has been active in the religious media space since 1962 with the founding of the first pan-Islamic radio station, "Nida al-Islam" ("Call of Islam"), but the most significant efforts with respect to our current focus date to the late 1990s when Saudi businessmen began to develop a range of satellite television channels dedicated to religious content. Many of the most-watched Islamic channels, such as Iqraa', Al-Resala, Al-Nas, and Al-Khalijiya, are owned by Saudis, even if the geography of their editorial and production activities encompasses other countries in the Middle East and other regions. While these channels certainly provide ready global platforms for the voices of highly conservative Saudi clerics (and thereby serve as force multipliers with respect to the presence and prevalence of Salafi discourse), in recent years their programming has been linked more specifically to heightened levels of sectarianism and growing anti-Shiʿa sentiment across the Middle East. Mohammad Yaghi's research on Saudi Arabia's dominance in the Islamic media space, for example, suggests that some shows on these channels have the effect of reinforcing the message frames and strategic communications of groups such as Islamic State (ISIS) even without specifically endorsing that group (Yaghi 2017). Beyond satellite channels owned and operated by Saudi Arabia or Saudi entities, it is also relevant to note that controversial figures such as the Indian preacher Zakir Naik, founder of Peace TV (whose programs have been accused of promoting extremism), have been linked to various countries in the Arab Gulf region in terms of funding sources—including reports that Naik was granted Saudi citizenship in 2017 ("Indian Preacher Granted Saudi Citizenship" 2017).

Saudi religious scholars are also very active on platforms such as Twitter and Facebook and are among the most highly followed figures on social media in the Middle East. Most prominent are Salafi scholars who have had a vexed relationship with the Saudi government, such as Muhammad al-ʿArifi and Salman al-Awdah. Also popular are feeds and sites connected with major figures from the kingdom's religious establishment, such as ʿAbd al-Aziz Al-Fawzan, ʿAbd al-Rahman Al-Sudais, and current Grand Mufti ʿAbd al-Aziz Al-Shaykh. A number of late Saudi Salafi "superstars," such as Muhammad Ibn Al-Uthaymeen (d. 2001) and the luminary former Grand Mufti ʿAbd Al-Aziz Ibn Baz (d. 1999), also have large followings for their social media feeds operated in their names by family members, followers, and foundations. As with satellite television, analysts have viewed Saudi religious voices on social media as contributing to heightened levels of sectarian tensions, as well as normalizing domestic violence against women and anti-Semitism (Schanzer and Miller 2012).

Labor Migration and "Religious Remittances"

Another aspect of Saudi Arabia's transnational religious influence worth mentioning relates to labor migration and the concomitant diffusion of culture and religion. Since the 1970s, large numbers of workers from South and Southeast Asia, Africa, and the Arab world began flocking to Saudi Arabia due to the significantly higher wages they could earn during the kingdom's oil-fueled construction boom. Many of them came from Muslim-majority countries such as Pakistan and Bangladesh, or from countries with significant Muslim minorities such as

India, Sri Lanka, and the Philippines. A smaller but still significant number of skilled workers—engineers, doctors, and government advisors—came from Egypt, Jordan, and other Arab countries. They returned to their home countries exposed to stricter, more conservative forms of Islamic practice. This helped to create a new, influential, and Islamically minded bourgeoisie that would give added strength to religious revivals that were already underway.[15] In Jordan, for example, there was one mosque for every 13,181 residents in 1973, while, by 1984, there was one for every 6,908 residents (Rogan 1986, 36). In Jordan and the Palestinian territories, remittances from labor migration were coupled with economic aid, particularly from Saudi Arabia until a falling out during the Gulf War. Financial assistance from Gulf donors, along with remittances from Jordanian expatriates, accounted for as much as nearly half of Jordan's GNP (Satloff 1986, 7). This kind of transnational religion does not necessarily represent evidence of a desire on Saudi Arabia's part to generate specific outcomes in Jordan or South Asia as part of its overall foreign policy. Still, it is worth looking at "religious remittances" as one dimension of the point we made earlier about the projection of religious influence outside a state's borders not necessarily reflecting a coherent or deliberate policy impulse.

The Religious Geopolitics of Pilgrimage

A final dimension of Saudi Arabia's international role in Islamic affairs worth considering pertains to pilgrimage and, more specifically, the annual *hajj* season. Each year, 2–3 million pilgrims participate in *hajj*, in addition to 6–7 million Muslims who visit the kingdom annually for *umrah* (the minor pilgrimage). Their stays are relatively short, typically ranging anywhere from one week to a month, and so pilgrimage is not generally associated with extensive exposure to alternative religious ideas of a sort likely to significantly affect participants' religious norms or practices. However, the *hajj* nonetheless provides the kingdom with an opportunity to showcase its unique role and stature in the Muslim world and, through the quota system by which the Saudi authorities allocate varying numbers of *hajj* visas to each country, an opportunity to communicate favor or disfavor through the use of religious soft power (Bianchi 2004). For example, the number of pilgrimage visas granted to Iranians is a persistent point of tension in Riyadh's contentious relationship with Tehran. It is also worth noting that the aforementioned King Fahd Complex for the Printing of the Holy Qur'an provides each pilgrim with a copy of the Qur'an as a gift, and many *hajj* and *umrah* participants return home with additional religious literature and media acquired in the kingdom. In addition to the large volume of Muslims around the world who gain some level of exposure to Saudi Islam through the *hajj*, it is also clear that pilgrimage serves as a mechanism for creating and sustaining networks of religious elites (e.g., scholars, 'awqaf directors, preachers) that, over time, consolidate into mechanisms for supporting Salafi da'wa outside the kingdom (Lauzière 2016, 192–193).

Assessing the Impact of Saudi Religious Transnationalism

There has been no end to the debate about the impact of Saudi funding on Islam around the world. Skeptics point to evidence that the arrival of Wahhabism created a fertile environment for extremist groups to grow and recruit, citing in certain cases—such as Pakistan—direct ties between Saudi-funded mosques or schools and recruitment into militant organizations (Gall 2016). In his book-length treatment of soft power, Joseph Nye seems to subscribe to this account of Saudi Wahhabism directly inspiring radical Islamism. "The soft power of Wahhabism has not proved to be a resource that the Saudi government could control," he writes. "Instead it has been like a sorcerer's apprentice that has come back to bedevil its original creator" (Nye 2004, 96).

Others have focused on Wahhabism's impact on society more broadly, including a shift toward more conservative norms and practices—including an apparent correlation between the arrival of Saudi funding and the adoption of previously unfamiliar practices such as women wearing full face veils (niqab). For others, the effects are apparent in shifting attitudes toward religious minorities, nonconforming Muslim groups that Wahhabism views as illegitimate (such as Shi'a), and forms of religious practice it regards as deviant (such as Sufism). Taken collectively, these various effects are commonly said to generate over time a distortion of local culture through the transplantation of "foreign" or "Arabized" religious practices—a narrative in which, for example, funds for mosque building also entail the acceptance of Saudi-approved imams and specific texts in religious schools (Shane 2016, Varagur 2017, Al-Buluwi 2014, Sito-Sucic 2007). One expert likened the effect to that of climate change, viewing Saudi Arabia's vast religious influence around the world as a force that generates gradual and incremental shifts in the nature of Islamic religious culture in various settings. Over time, these initially modest changes snowball into cascade effects of increasing magnitude and significance.[16] The perspectives of an observer from Sri Lanka's Muslim community are typical and worth quoting at length to understand the perceived "life cycle" of Saudi Arabia's religious influence:

Over the past 30-odd years, an insidious change occurred in our community. It's hard to pinpoint when. It might have been when Sri Lanka began sending droves of housemaids to the Middle East in the early 1980s, among them many Muslim women. Many of these women had adopted the abaya and hijab in their countries of employment and, on their return, continued wearing them in Sri Lanka. Initially, they were the most vociferous that Sri Lankan Muslims were practicing a diluted version of Islam, that their prayers were not said in the correct Arabic accent, that they should stop praising the Prophet Muhammad and saints, and that they were not dressed properly according to Islamic guidelines—especially the women.

This strict interpretation of Islam began to take hold. I noticed it the first time a Muslim man refused to shake my hand, and when Muslims began to sprinkle their conversations with religious Arabic phrases. Young Muslim men I knew from the city began going to rural areas to preach on how to practice their faith better. Muslim weddings began to be held in male-only mosques, without the presence of the bride, instead of at home or in hotels. The most visible change was that Muslim women stopped wearing their traditional sari or shalwar kameez in favor of the hijab, abaya or niqab. Muslim men soon followed suit. Robes replaced sarongs or trousers, and more of them sported beards.

Today, Sufism has gone underground, while radical Wahhabis and Salafis have taken over many of Sri Lanka's mosques. Saudi-funded religious schools with puritanical preachers have persuaded many in our community that Sufism is a threat to the practice of a "pure," original Islam. While some families still cling to their Sufi roots, others have found it easier to accept the Wahhabi-enforced norms, which have affected Muslims regardless of class, city or sect. (Hussein 2019)

Across the various countries included in this study, one of the most commonly reported narratives about the impact of Saudi proselytization involves something we might describe in terms of a reconfiguration of local "religious grammar." This encompasses shifts in the nature of religious discussions and debates, as well as aspects of religious practice. While some things that fall in the latter category— such as the question of how to place one's hands during prayer—may seem relatively mundane, they often become the focus of debates about authenticity and purity, feeding into or catalyzing more existential debates about who counts as a "true" Muslim. With respect to the nature and focus of religious discourse and discussion, the Salafi focus on purity becomes more pronounced through Saudi religious transnationalism, with an increased emphasis on determining what is permissible (*halal*) and what is forbidden (*haram*). Local informants and interview subjects engaged through our research tend to report this phenomenon in terms of Islam turning into "a list of dos and don'ts" rather than a source of spiritual strength and inspiration.

However, the notion of wholesale bulldozing of pristine local culture by foreign ideologies is far too simplistic. Saudi support for religion is actually welcome in some communities where, for instance, the local authorities have viewed an emphasis on religion and religious education as contradictory to national development and modernization agendas. If there is a demand for religious education—and there often is—there will be incentives and pressures for someone, or some country, to provide it. In other cases, local rulers seek Saudi support to burnish their own religious credentials (Dorsey 2017a). In such situations, resources from the Middle East are often vital for creating religious infrastructure. It is also *not* the case that Saudi religious norms simply "replace" local Islam. Rather, a far more complex process of adaptation—on both the sending and receiving sides—takes place. Indeed, some countries on the receiving end of Wahhabi proselytization seem capable of absorbing these influences without seeing much in the way of local disruption or social change. We discuss this in more detail in the following.

Among the more contentious—and complex—questions surrounding the impact of Saudi religious transnationalism around the world concerns the relationship between Wahhabism, conflict, violence, and terrorism. What seems incontrovertible and frequently reported out of a wide range of settings—including the country-specific research associated with this project—is a clear relationship between religious influence emanating from Saudi Arabia and increased levels of sectarian and intercommunal tension. In some cases, such as Pakistan, Saudi religious influence seems to be positively correlated with rising sectarianism—specifically targeting Shiʿa and members of the Ahmadiyya community (Dorsey 2017b). Elsewhere in South Asia, as well as in West Africa and the Sahel, Saudi religious transnationalism has been associated with increased tensions between Sufi communities and purveyors of a self-described "pure" Islam that rejects such traditionalist practices. Where preexisting social cleavages in a given country fall out across sectarian lines, Saudi Arabia's religious influence can serve to sharpen identities and religious debates in ways that exacerbate tensions and catalyze conflict—including violent conflict (Basedau and Schaefer-Kehnert 2019).

Far less clear-cut is the question of the relationship between Saudi religious transnationalism and violent extremism or terrorism. It is worth reiterating that we are not asking here about Saudi support for established militant groups in the context of ongoing conflicts, but rather the question of whether funding for religious propagation emanating from the kingdom functions as a driver of radicalization. The clearest and best-known cases of Saudi support for religious causes overlapping with militant activities—the madrasas of Pakistan in the 1980s and Islamic charities in the Balkans and Southeast Asia in the 1990s—represent examples in which religious causes were used as conduits for transferring resources to known insurgent networks, or where religious institutions funded by Saudi Arabia were effectively taken over by violent insurrectionary groups (Chosky and Chosky 2015). In such examples, while it is clear that the kingdom's religious influence intensified, exacerbated, or extended levels of violence, it is more difficult to make the case that Saudi religious transnationalism generated radicalization since the militancy in question predates the presence of—and is driven by a logic separate from—Saudi religious doctrine. It is worth reiterating here that Saudi Salafism is by its nature politically quietist and emphasizes fidelity to incumbent authority and is therefore in and of itself unlikely to advocate violent activism.

This is not to say that there is no connection to be drawn between Saudi religious transnationalism and violent extremism or terrorism, only that direct and linear causality is usually difficult to establish. Rather, the historical record and our project research suggest that we need to focus on two somewhat more diffuse mechanisms through which the kingdom's propagation of religion functions as a contributing factor in radicalization. The first of these is something we might call the *denationalization and recontextualization of Wahhabism*, a process through which the transmission of Saudi religious ideas into new contexts de-emphasizes or removes altogether the emphasis on political quietism that generally accompanies the teaching of religion within the kingdom. Stripped of its loyalist underpinnings, the exclusionary religious doctrine of Saudi Salafism becomes recontextualized in new settings where different political environments, social structures, and local conflict dynamics allow Wahhabi ideas to take on new meanings. Saudi Salafism becomes, in effect, an ideological resource capable of being harnessed by local conflict actors to enhance mobilization and to justify their designation of particular groups or religious communities as legitimate targets. The second mechanism, which we might term the *promotion of exclusionary religious identities and depluralization of religious culture*, relates to the ways in which Muslims whose socialization into Islam or whose formative religious education occurs in settings defined by high levels of Saudi influence become over time more susceptible or receptive to the messages of groups—such as ISIS—whose worldview is premised on drawing hard and fast distinctions between authentic and deviant Muslims.

Given that the overall thrust of this analysis suggests we need to pay just as much attention to the "destination" (i.e., receiving country) side of the equation as the "sending" (i.e., Saudi) side, how should we think about the question of whether and how particular features of local political, social, and religious environments shape the nature and extent to which Saudi religious transnationalism affects various settings? One of the major factors bearing on this question is likely the strength of local religious institutions and the state's regulatory capacity vis-à-vis religion. In countries where local religious institutions are strong and, moreover, strongly connected to the state, such as in Turkey, transnational influences may have less dramatic effects. Another variable to consider is the presence and strength of mass-based Islamist movements, such as the Muslim Brotherhood, that can make it more difficult for Salafi organizations to gain traction (since they are often appealing to the same conservative constituencies). Finally, a factor likely to serve as a constraining effect on foreign religious influence is the strength of specific local religious structures and practices—either in the form of an identification between national identity and specific expressions of Islam (as in the case of Morocco, where the king is understood to play at least a ceremonial religious function), or in the dominance and pervasiveness of Sufi brotherhoods, which have forced transnational Salafi influences in regions such as West Africa to modulate their conventional hostility to (or become more accommodating of) Sufism in order to make inroads with local populations.

Key Systemic and Cross-Cutting Research Findings

Saudi religious transnationalism has touched dozens of countries around the world and, given the importance of local context and other dimensions of the receiving environment, many of the resulting effects are highly idiosyncratic in nature. The case studies found in this volume explore in detail the experience of numerous and diverse countries with respect to the impact of Saudi religious propagation. Looking across them, it is possible to identify certain patterns and similarities that cut across multiple cases. Four in particular are worth highlighting.

A clear geopolitical steer, but no consistent, centrally planned, and coordinated strategy for exporting Wahhabism. The extent to which the various Saudi actors and activities discussed earlier can be said to collectively constitute an official religious soft power strategy on the part of the Saudi state remains unclear. At certain historical junctures—most notably in the early 1960s and early 1980s—the kingdom's political and religious leadership rallied around a common global cause (combating socialism or secular Arab nationalism), and these moments generated the highest levels of coordinated transnational religious propagation. While some of the entities most directly involved in Wahhabi propagation are organs of the Saudi government, it would be wrong to assume that all of them view the kingdom's international challenges and opportunities in exactly the same way. Indeed, some manifestations of Saudi Arabia's external religious outreach over the years are best understood as a function of domestic politics and horse trading between and within, for example, the royal family and the religious establishment.[17] Similarly, the religious attachés stationed at Saudi embassies in many countries (a practice that commenced under King Fahd)—many on secondment from the Ministry of Islamic Affairs—were viewed with suspicion by the kingdom's foreign ministry, which worried that their less than subtle activities would create tensions with the local government and population. In many cases, such religious activity is just that: proselytization carried out under the auspices of the Ministry of Islamic Affairs (rather than the foreign ministry) or by WAMY, bearing little relationship to Saudi geopolitical designs. However, in other respects—particularly with regard to blunting Iranian influence—there does seem to be a broad convergence among the various Saudi stakeholders. If Shiʻa Islam in the eyes of most Saudis equals Iran, and Wahhabism is doctrinally opposed to Shiʻa, then almost by definition Wahhabism becomes a useful tool for countering Iranian influence across the Muslim world. In summary, Saudi Arabia's global machinery for religious propagation is too vast and multifaceted—reflecting a wide and diverse range of entities and equities inside and beyond the kingdom—to tolerate a single command and control point. Nonetheless, it is clear that over the years the Saudi authorities, and particularly individual monarchs, have been able to control the magnitude and overall direction of flow in line with their domestic and geopolitical priorities.

Saudi religious transnationalism is far from monolithic and can only be fully understood by appreciating the diverse (and sometimes competing) interests of the many actors involved. Despite a tendency in the existing literature to characterize the export of Wahhabism in broad brushstrokes, important nuances emerge when we move past the monolithic connotations of formulas like "Saudi funding for Islam" to better understand the wide range of actors within the kingdom involved in these activities, alongside a vast array of global partners. This is not to suggest that the Saudi authorities are not ultimately responsible for what comes out of their country and its impact on the world. Rather, this insight makes it possible to understand why constituent elements of the Saudi daʻwa apparatus have focused on specific countries during particular periods of time and how complex bureaucratic interests and differing conceptions of the kingdom's global role interact and compete with one another in the context of transnational religious propagation.

Various third-party mediators and processes of local adaptation mean that the specific nature, impact, and even directionality of Saudi religious transnationalism are often different than originally intended. While Saudi and Saudi-funded organizations and financial mechanisms often serve as the main conduits for transmitting religious influence from the kingdom, a wide range of additional actors exert influence on the agenda and messages reflected in such efforts. More specifically, as Saudi entities became more reliant on third parties to manage and implement daʻwa work, their direct control over this work decreased. In some cases, such as WAMY during the 1970s–1990s, premier organizations associated with Saudi religious transnationalism became heavily influenced by other ideological trends such as the Muslim Brotherhood movement. This means that it sometimes becomes difficult to discern whether the ultimate import of a given religious propagation activity reflects the original intent of its Saudi benefactor or the preferences of various middlemen and intermediary organizations involved in its implementation. Literature on activities of the "global Islamic movement" during this period portray a situation in which transnational activists of widely varying ideological and political orientations sought funding and positions within Saudi religious organizations in the hope of leveraging the available resources in support of their own agendas.[18]

Furthermore, our research suggests that countries on the receiving end of Saudi religious transnationalism are far from being passive actors in the transaction. It seems that a wide range of entities on the downstream side of the equation—including national and local governments, religious institutions, and civil society figures—are involved in complex processes of local adaptation that often inflect the nature and content of religious ideas as they interact with local "users" and "consumers." For example, in countries where the practice of Sufism is a bedrock aspect of local religiosity, those dimensions of Saudi religion that frown on traditionalist Islam may be downplayed even as the overall conservative thrust of Salafism is preserved. The capacity of local actors in this regard—or, put another way, the resilience of local Islam—is a function of numerous factors. In a majority-Muslim society with pervasive and deeply entrenched local religious norms (such as Morocco or Senegal), external influences seem less likely to have a systemic effect on local religious culture. In Muslim-minority contexts such as Sri Lanka (cited earlier) where a neglected Muslim community lacks well-developed religious infrastructure and where some community members may view Salafism—which easily turns into a discourse about Islam's supremacy vis-à-vis other religious groups—as an attractive prospect, Saudi religious influence may more readily find a receptive audience.

Finally, it is wrong to assume that the directionality of religious influence—or the worldwide Wahhabism supply-and-demand dynamics—universally reflect a one-way, hegemonic effort by Saudi Arabia to reshape global Islam in its image. In some cases, notably in a number of African settings, the demand for Saudi religious engagement originated locally and was driven by local social, political, and religious factors. Such flows also go both ways, and once the transnational connection is established it becomes possible for the kingdom itself to import Islamic influences from outside.[19] Moreover, non-Saudi scholars have been a fixture within the kingdom's religious establishment for more than a century, meaning that Wahhabism as an intellectual project has always been more international than is commonly recognized (Lauzière 2016, DeLong-Bas 2004). From the international reception and debate about Muhammad Ibn Abdul-Wahhab's ideas in the nineteenth century to the role of non-Saudi faculty at the International Islamic University of Medina to efforts by the Saudi Ministry of Islamic Affairs and Da'wa to develop tailored curriculum for teaching Islam in various world regions, Wahhabism has long been in contact, and has been forced to contend, with a broader range of global influences and contexts.

Saudi support for religious propagation is declining globally, but its "legacy effects" endure. Recent media reporting, academic analysis, and, indeed, the research undertaken for this project all suggest that over the past 20 years there has been a distinct downward trend in levels of Saudi support for religious causes worldwide. The drivers of this trend are varied. To some extent it reflects increased pressures on the kingdom's economy as global energy markets undergo significant changes and as other international projects—such as Crown Prince Muhammad bin Salman's vast Vision 2030 strategy—take priority. Increased regulation of Saudi religious charities and their overseas activities have also served to constrain global flows of resources that support religious (and other) causes. In other cases, decline in Saudi religious influence is more closely linked to changes within countries that were previously beneficiaries of its religious largesse. In Western Europe, for example, early immigrant Muslim communities in the 1960s relied enormously on foreign support in order to have even a basic infrastructure for religious life. By the 1990s, however, it became possible to identify an emerging Muslim middle class in places like the United Kingdom, France, and Germany. As the community's capacity to provide for its own religious needs increased, so naturally did its reliance on foreign religious sponsors wane.

However, the fact that aggregate levels of Saudi religious transnationalism have been declining should not detract attention from the fact that in some settings the kingdom's religious influence has been profound, pervasive, and enduring. With respect to a country such as Somalia, for example, active religious linkages to Saudi Arabia were at their high point in the 1970s and 1980s and have declined sharply since. Nonetheless, the extent to which a previously unfamiliar strain of purist Salafism (mediated through Muslim Brotherhood networks) gained a foothold in Somalia's Islamic sector during the 1980s, paving the way to some extent for the rise of Al-Shabab and its precursor groups, is difficult to overstate (Menkhaus 2002).[20] Once again, the aforementioned climate change metaphor has relevance here. It suggests that once certain inevitably vague and highly context-specific threshold points have been reached, the local impact of transnational religious influence is likely to be far-reaching and to last over time, even if active lines of religious engagement are subsequently halted. In such cases the effect of Saudi religious transnationalism cannot be addressed simply by interceding with the kingdom's political leadership and asking them to "stop." Rather, other mechanisms for dealing with the specific societal effects arising from Saudi *da'wa* activities will need to be explored.

MbS and the Future of Saudi Religious Transnationalism

How should we think about the future role of Islam in Saudi Arabia's external relations under Crown Prince Muhammad bin Salman (MbS)? The rise to prominence of MbS has been associated with a variety of statements and actions that, on their face, appear to signal that the kingdom's likely next monarch is ready and willing to significantly rock the boat when it comes to matters of religion. MbS has gone out of his way to signal Saudi Arabia's commitment to countering the extremist ideology of ISIS, establishing various centers and initiatives focused on counter-messaging and the dissemination of moderate Islam.[21] Within the kingdom itself, MbS has sharply curtailed the mandate and resources of the *mutawa* (religious police), virtually removing them from the streets of major Saudi cities. In the fall of 2017, speaking at an investment conference in Riyadh, MbS made the intriguing statement that Saudi Arabia would "return to moderate Islam"—prompting a raft of speculation about what exactly he meant by this. Figures associated with the Saudi lobbying and public affairs machinery in places like Washington, DC, were quick to spin a narrative about MbS's commitment to religious reform and pluralism, and the possibility of "a cultural awakening that is set to revolutionize the Islamic world" (Al-Ansari 2018). More sober analysts viewed the MbS statement as indicative of his desire to counteract and eradicate any and all politicized interpretations of Islam—from the Muslim Brotherhood movement to Al-Qaeda and ISIS—in order to blunt any possible threat to his authority. They likewise viewed his recent moves against the religious police as part of a broader effort to consolidate political authority, rather than as evidence that he prefers a kinder, gentler approach to Islam.[22]

There have also been interesting developments with respect to the explicitly external dimensions of Saudi religion under MbS. At the center of almost all of this is Shaykh Muhammad al-ʿIssa, a former minister of justice handpicked by the crown prince in 2016 to become the new secretary general of the MWL.[23] From his MWL perch, Al-ʿIssa has steered the League into previously unnavigated waters, turning heads in the process. For example, he has appeared and spoken at international conferences on the dangers of anti-Semitism (something the MWL has previously been accused of promoting) and, in early 2020, took part in a visit to Auschwitz to pay homage to victims of the Holocaust— a first for a senior Saudi figure. Al-ʿIssa used this same occasion to announce that Saudi Arabia would soon stop funding mosques outside the kingdom and would oversee a process to ensure that these facilities were transferred to appropriate local management structures ("Saudi Arabia to Stop Funding Mosques in Foreign Countries" 2020). In 2018, the government of Belgium assumed control of the Brussels Grand Mosque—whose facilities had been leased for years by Saudi Arabia—out of concern that its preaching was contributing to extremism

(Birnbaum and Ariès 2018). The 2020 announcement about ending foreign funding for mosques likely represents an effort by the kingdom to get out ahead of similar headlines in the future. However, as with other aspects of the apparent MbS religious reforms, the grand statements have been short on detail and so far have little to show by way of subsequent action. For example, while the MWL committed in 2019 to promote education about the dangers of anti-Semitism, there does not yet seem to be evidence that any of its country offices around the world have started implementing such programs. And while some analysts have seen in recent MWL pronouncements evidence of an important "course correction," it seems premature at this time to affirm any significant new directions in the organization's work (Feuer 2019). Much of the reform talk, while certainly welcome, appears to be rhetoric aimed at pleasing the kingdom's Western security partners.

In summary and in conclusion, the signals seemed mixed with respect to the future of Saudi religious transnationalism. Three points are worth bearing in mind when thinking about likely directions for Saudi global *da'wa* efforts under MbS. First, the crown prince is, above all, a pragmatist. There is very little evidence to suggest he has an ideological motivation to invest in the export of Wahhabism. Rather, where he sees religious propagation as potentially threatening things he cares about—such as concern on the part of allies in Europe that Saudi mosque funding promotes extremism within their borders—he will scale back those activities. On the other hand, it also seems likely that if he senses utility in religion as a political tool, he will not hesitate to deploy it. The idea of promoting anti-Shi'a discourse via media as a means of counterbalancing Iranian influence in the kingdom's near abroad is a case in point. Second, when looking to predict future changes in the geographic locus of Saudi religious transnationalism, it is worth bearing in mind that MbS—like so many global investors—is betting on Asia. The success of Vision 2030 is heavily dependent on emerging markets in East, South, and Central Asia, and on integration with aspects of China's expansive and equally ambitious Belt & Road Initiative. It is reasonable to expect Saudi Arabia to deploy religion as a form of soft power in support of this strategy, and we already perhaps see some evidence of such an approach in the fact that over the past few years the increasingly rare announcements about increased Saudi funding for religion center on Asia (Scott 2016, "Bangladesh to Build Hundreds of Mosques with Saudi Cash" 2017). One final consideration with respect to the future of Saudi religious transnationalism concerns the question of whether MbS will be able to overcome—and where necessary to defy—the long-standing equities that a wide range of influential Saudi entities have built up over time around certain ways of doing business with respect to the kingdom's worldwide propagation of Islam. To date, MbS has shown little hesitation to directly confront other elites within Saudi Arabia's political and economic establishment, but this strategy may begin to yield diminishing returns—particularly if and as he encounters obstacles to realizing his ambitious goals. For example, should he find himself requiring support from or needing to placate the kingdom's religious establishment, providing them with new opportunities to extend their international influence may be a more attractive prospect than giving them more space on the domestic front. While we may be well past the halcyon days of the 1970s through 1990s when seemingly unlimited petrodollars supported Wahhabi export activity, Saudi Arabia's unique stature in the Muslim world ensures that religion will continue to represent a viable and usable resource in its external relations, even if such efforts become smaller in scale and scope.

Notes

1. For an important early effort, see Piscatori (1983). For an example of more recent framings of the issue, see Gold (2003).
2. See, for example, Ward (2018).
3. Some authors of country case studies in this volume compare Saudi-funded da'wa with the religious propagation efforts of other GCC countries in their respective settings.
4. See https://qurancomplex.gov.sa/kfgqpc/statist/.
5. See https://www.moia.gov.sa/Statistics/Pages/default.aspx.
6. For the Ministry of Islamic Affairs Statistical Books, see https://www.moia.gov.sa/Statistics/Pages/default.aspx.
7. I might qualify my conclusion here somewhat by pointing to one of the cross-cutting research findings explained in the final section of the chapter to the effect that Islamic movements and groups whose ideology differs from the quietist orientation of the Saudi religious establishment have sometimes managed to co-opt the kingdom's da'wa mechanisms and use them to pursue agendas beyond generic religious education and propagation.
8. The following characterization of the relationship between Wahhabism and Salafism is adapted from Mandaville (2020).
9. See, for example, the various essays in Meijer (2009). For a general overview of the origins and evolution of modern Salafi thought, see Lauzière (2016).
10. Gamal 'Abd al-Nasser's influence within the House of Saud appeared even more pernicious after several senior members of the royal family, including King 'Abdul-Aziz's son Talal, endorsed Pan-Arabism and created a short-lived dissident schism based in Cairo known as the Free Princes Movement.
11. The following overview of the Saudi global da'wa apparatus is adapted from Mandaville and Hamid (2018).
12. See Mandaville (2010, 207) and Schulze (2009).
13. On the co-mingling of proselytization and humanitarian relief, see Rohde (2005).

14. See, for example, Doumato (2007).
15. See, for example, Gardner (2001) and Ahmad (2017).
16. Quoted in Shane (2016).
17. While Saudi Crown Prince Mohammed bin Salman has moved to constrain the power of some elements of the religious establishment—such as the *mutawwa*, or religious police—it is not yet clear whether or to what extent his actions will affect Saudi Arabia's global religious propagation activities.
18. See, for example, Sardar (2004); numerous author interviews with key figures in transnational Islamic activist networks from the 1980s and 1990s also confirm this general account.
19. For an example of how this has occurred with respect to religious ties between Saudi Arabia and Mauritania, see Farquhar and Thurston (2018).
20. Somalia, and the broader Horn of Africa subregion, are once again in the crosshairs of Arab Gulf countries, this time in relation to intra-GCC rivalries and concerns about containing Iranian influence. See Plaut (2017).
21. Chief among these are the Saudi Ministry of Defense's Intellectual Warfare Center (www.fekerksa.org) and Etidal, the Global Center for Combating Extremist Ideology (www.etidal.org).
22. On both points, see Lacroix (2019).
23. Al-'Issa is dual-hatted as director of the Ministry of Defense Intellectual Warfare Center, suggesting that MbS sees continuities between the two roles.

References

Ahmad, Attiya. 2017. *Everyday Conversions: Islam, Domestic Work, and South Asian Migrant Women in Kuwait*. Durham, NC: Duke University Press.

Al-Ansari, Salman. 2018. "The Crown Prince, Mohammed bin Salman Could Succeed in Restoring Islam." *The Hill*. February 7, 2018. https://thehill.com/opinion/internatio nal/372702-the-crown-prince-mohammed-bin-salman-could-succeed-in-restoring-islam (accessed September 20, 2021).

"Bangladesh to Build Hundreds of Mosques with Saudi Cash." 2017. *The Straits Times*. April 26, 2017. https://www.straitstimes.com/asia/south-asia/bangladesh-to-build-hundreds-of-mosques-with-saudi-cash (accessed September 20, 2021).

Basedau, Matthias, and Johanna Schaefer-Kehnert. 2019. "Religious Discrimination and Religious Armed Conflict in sub-Saharan Africa: An Obvious Relationship?" *Religion, State and Society* 47(1): 30–47.

Bashirov, Galib. 2018 "Islamic Discourses in Azerbaijan: The Securitization of 'Non-traditional Religious Movements.'" *Central Asian Survey* 37(1): 31–49.

Bianchi, Robert. 2004. *Guests of God: Pilgrimage and Politics in the Islamic World*. New York: Oxford University Press.

Birnbaum, Michael, and Quentin Ariès. 2018. "Belgium Ends Saudi Mosque Lease, Citing 'Foreign Influence' and Extremism." *Washington Post*. March 19, 2018. https://www. washingtonpost.com/world/europe/belgium-ends-saudi-mosque-lease-citing-fore ign-interference-and-extremism/2018/03/19/eebd3912-2b7a-11e8-8dc9-3b51e02 8b845_story.html (accessed September 20, 2021).

Al-Buluwi, Abdulmajeed. 2014. "The Saudi-Turkey Cold War for Sunni Hegemony." *Center for Geopolitical Analyses*. April 1, 2014. http://icmu.nyc.gr/The-Saudi-Turkey-cold-war-for-Sunni-hegemony?page=1 (accessed September 20, 2021).

Byman, Daniel L. 2017. "Getting Real With Riyadh." *Brookings Institution*. April 17, 2017. https://www.brookings.edu/research/getting-real-with-riyadh/ (accessed September 20, 2021).

Chosky, Carol E. B., and Jamsheed Chosky. 2015. "The Saudi Connection: Wahhabism and Global Jihad." *World Affairs* 178(1): 23–34.

Commins, David. 2009. *The Wahhabi Mission and Saudi Arabia*. London: I. B. Tauris.

DeLong-Bas, Natana. 2004. *Wahhabi Islam: From Revival and Reform to Global Jihad*. New York: Oxford University Press.

Dorsey, James M. 2017a. "Spreading the Gospel: Asian Leaders Wary of Saudi Religious Diplomacy." *The Huffington Post*. March 23, 2017. https://www.huffingtonpost.com/entry/spreading-the-gospel-asian-leaders-wary-of-saudi-religious_us_58ce7059e4b07112b6472eb4 (accessed September 20, 2021).

Dorsey, James M. 2017b. "Pakistan's Lurch Towards Ultra-Conservativism Abetted by Saudi-Inspired Pyramid Scheme." Unpublished paper. April 18, 2017. http://dx.doi.org/10.2139/ssrn.2954341.

Dorsey, James M. 2017c. "Qatari Wahhabism vs. Saudi Wahhabism and the Perils of Top-Down Change." *The Huffington Post*. December 4, 2017. https://www.huffingtonpost.com/entry/qatari-wahhabism-vs-saudi-wahhabism-and-the-perils_us_5a257240e4b05072e8b56b29 (accessed September 20, 2021).

Doumato, Eleanor Abdella. 2007. "Saudi Arabia: From 'Wahhabi' Roots to Contemporary Revisionism." In *Teaching Islam: Textbooks and Religion in the Middle East*, edited by Eleanor Abdella Doumato and Gregory Starrett, 153–176. Boulder, CO: Lynne Rienner.

Farquhar, Michael. 2017. *Circuits of Faith: Migration, Education, and the Wahhabi Mission*. Stanford, CA: Stanford University Press.

Farquhar, Michael, and Alexander Thurston. 2018. "How Mauritania Exports Religion to Saudi Arabia—and Not Just the Other Way Around." Washington, DC: Brookings Institution. December 13, 2018. https://www.brookings.edu/blog/order-from-chaos/2018/12/13/how-mauritania-exports-religion-to-saudi-arabia-and-not-just-the-other-way-around/.

Feuer, Sarah. 2019. *Course Correction: The Muslim World League, Saudi Arabia's Export of Islam, and Opportunities for Washington*. Washington, DC: Washington Institute for Near East Policy. https://www.washingtoninstitute.org/policy-analysis/view/course-correction.

Gall, Carlotta. 2016. "How Kosovo Was Turned into Fertile Ground for ISIS." *New York Times*. May 21, 2016. https://www.nytimes.com/2016/05/22/world/europe/how-the-saudis-turned-kosovo-into-fertile-ground-for-isis.html (accessed September 20, 2021).

Gardner, Katy. 2001. *Global Migrants, Local Lives: Travel and Transformation in Rural Bangladesh*. Oxford: Oxford University Press.

Gold, Dore. 2003. *Hatred's Kingdom: How Saudi Arabia Supports the New Global Terrorism*. Washington, DC: Regnery.

Hussein, Ameena. 2019. "Fighting for the Soul of Islam in Sri Lanka." *New York Times*. May 2, 2019. https://www.nytimes.com/2019/05/02/opinion/sri-lanka-bombing.html (accessed September 20, 2021).

"Indian Preacher Granted Saudi Citizenship." 2017. *Middle East Monitor*. May 19, 2017. https://www.middleeastmonitor.com/20170519-indian-terror-suspect-granted-saudi-citizenship/ (accessed September 20, 2021).

Lacroix, Stéphane. 2019. "Saudi Arabia and the Limits to Religious Reform." *The Review of Faith & International Affairs* 17(2): 97–101.

Lauzière, Henri. 2016. *The Making of Salafism: Islamic Reform in the Twentieth Century*. New York: Columbia University Press.

Mandaville, Peter. 2010. "The New Transnationalism: Globalising Islamic Movements." In *Muslims and Modernity: Culture and Society since 1800*, edited by Robert W. Hefner, 198–217. Vol. 6 of *The New Cambridge History of Islam*. Cambridge: Cambridge University Press.

Mandvaille, Peter. 2020. *Islam and Politics*. 3rd ed. New York: Routledge.

Mandaville, Peter, and Shadi Hamid. 2018. *Islam as Statecraft: How Governments Use Religion in Foreign Policy*. Washington, DC: Brookings Institution. https://www.brookings.edu/research/islam-as-statecraft-how-governments-use-religion-in-foreign-policy/.

Meijer, Roel, ed. 2009. *Global Salafism: Islam's New Religious Movement*. New York: Oxford University Press.

Menkhaus, Ken. 2002. "Political Islam in Somalia." *Middle East Policy* 9(1): 109–123.

Mintz, John. 2003. "Wahhabi Strain of Islam Faulted." *Washington Post*. June 27, 2003. https://www.washingtonpost.com/archive/politics/2003/06/27/wahhabi-strain-of-islam-faulted/f2eb68be-daae-4bbd-a824-d0ca31ace6c4/ (accessed September 20, 2021).

Mohammed, Khaleel. 2005. "Assessing English Translations of the Qu'ran." *Middle East Quarterly* (Spring): 58–71.

"Muslim Network and Movements in Western Europe." 2010. Washington, DC: Pew Research Center. http://www.pewforum.org/2010/09/15/muslim-networks-and-movements-in-western-europe/ (accessed September 20, 2021).

Nye, Joseph S. 2004. *Soft Power: The Means to Success in World Politics*. New York: Public Affairs.

Piscatori, James P. 1983. "Islamic Values and National Interest: The Foreign Policy of Saudi Arabia." In *Islam in Foreign Policy*, edited by Adeed Dawisha, 33–53. Cambridge: Cambridge University Press.

Plaut, Martin. 2017. "Faith and Money from the Middle East Fuelling Tensions in the Horn of Africa." *The Conversation*. February 9, 2017. https://theconversation.com/faith-and-money-from-the-middle-east-fuelling-tensions-in-the-horn-of-africa-72636 (accessed September 20, 2021).

Racimora, William. 2013. *Salafist/Wahhabite Financial Support to Educational, Social and Religious Institutions*. Brussels: European Parliament's Committee on Foreign Affairs.

Al-Rasheed, Madawi. 2005. "Saudi Religious Transnationalism in London," In *Transnational Connections and the Arab Gulf*, edited by Madawi Al-Rasheed, 149–167. London: Routledge.

Rohde, David. 2005. "Mix of Quake Aid and Preaching Stirs Concern." *New York Times*. January 22, 2005. https://www.nytimes.com/2005/01/22/world/worldspecial4/mix-of-quake-aid-and-preaching-stirs-concern.html (accessed September 20, 2021).

Rogan, Eugene L. "Physical Islamization in Amman." *The Muslim World* 76 (January): 24–42.

Roberts, David. 2014. "Qatar and the Muslim Brotherhood: Pragmatism or Preference?" *Middle East Policy* 21(3): 84–94.

Rundell, David. 2020. *Vision or Mirage: Saudi Arabia at a Crossroads*. London: I. B. Tauris.

Sardar, Ziauddin. 2004. *Desperately Seeking Paradise: Journeys of a Sceptical Muslim*. London: Granta.

Satloff, Robert. 1986. *Troubles on the East Bank: Challenges to the Domestic Stability of Jordan*. Washington, DC: Center for Strategic and International Studies.

"Saudi Arabia to Stop Funding Mosques in Foreign Countries." 2020. *Middle East Monitor*. January 25, 2020. https://www.middleeastmonitor.com/20200125-saudi-ara bia-to-stop-funding-mosques-in-foreign-countries (accessed September 20, 2021).

Schanzer, Jonathan, and Steven Miller. 2012. *Facebook Fatwa: Saudi Clerics, Wahhabi Islam and Social Media*. Washington, DC: Foundation for Defense of Democracies. https://www.fdd.org/analysis/2012/05/07/facebook-fatwa-saudi-clerics-wahhabi-islam-and-social-media-2/ (accessed September 20, 2021).

Schulze, Reinhard. 1990. *Islamischer Internationalismus im 20. Jahrhundert: Untersuchungen zur Geschichte der Islamischen Weltliga*. Berlin: Verlag.

Schulze, Reinhard. 2009. "*Da'wah* from Saudi Arabia: Transnationalism in the Context of the Muslim World League." Unpublished paper.

Scott, Margaret. 2016. "Indonesia: The Saudis Are Coming." *Financial Review*. October 21, 2016. https://www.afr.com/world/asia/indonesia-the-saudis-are-coming-20161 017-gs3u7j (accessed September 20, 2021).

Shane, Scott. 2016. "Saudis and Extremism: 'Both the Arsonists and the Firefighters.'" *New York Times*. August 25, 2016. https://www.nytimes.com/2016/08/26/world/mid dleeast/saudi-arabia-islam.html (accessed September 20, 2021).

Sito-Sucic, Daria. 2007. "Bosnia's Muslims Divided over Inroads of Wahhabism." *Reuters*. January 21, 2007. https://www.reuters.com/article/us-bosnia-wahhabi/bosnias-muslims-divided-over-inroads-of-wahhabism-idUSL2972174820061229 (accessed September 20, 2021).

US Department of the Treasury. 2006. "Treasury Designates Director, Branches of Charity Bankrolling Al Qaida Network." Press release. August 3, 2006. https://www.treasury. gov/press-center/press-releases/Pages/hp45.aspx (accessed September 20, 2021).

US Department of the Treasury. 2008. "Treasury Designates Al Haramain Islamic Foundation." Press release. June 19, 2008. https://www.treasury.gov/press-center/ press-releases/Pages/hp1043.aspx (accessed September 20, 2021).

Valentine, Simon Ross. 2015. *Force and Fanaticism: Wahhabism in Saudi Arabia and Beyond*. London: Hurst.

Varagur, Krithika. 2017. "Indonesia's Moderate Islam Is Slowly Crumbling." *Foreign Policy*. February 14, 2017. http://foreignpolicy.com/2017/02/14/indonesias-moderate-islam-is-slowly-crumbling/ (accessed September 20, 2021).

Varagur, Krithika. 2020. *The Call: Inside the Global Saudi Religious Project*. New York: Columbia Global Reports.

Ward, Terence. 2018. *The Wahhabi Code: How the Saudis Spread Extremism Globally*. New York: Arcade.

Yaghi, Mohammad. 2017. "Media Sectarianism in the Middle East: Saudi Hegemony over Pan-Arab Media." *International Journal of Media & Cultural Politics* 13(1–2): 39–56.

2

Wahhabism and Salafism in Global Perspective

Natana J. DeLong-Bas

In the aftermath of 9/11, intelligence, security, and policy circles have identified the global phenomena of Wahhabism and Salafism as central concerns due to their presumed association with violent and extremist manifestations of Islam in the public sphere, typically associated with or connected to Saudi Arabia as their purported epicenter. Most of the studies written since 9/11[1] analyze Wahhabism and Salafism through the lens of security studies, privileging information relevant to intelligence and military needs and often marginalizing other dimensions, even where they are statistically more important. Identification of and connections between individuals, organizations, and movements are often assumed based on the presence of broad, yet often vague, ideas for which all members either claiming or assigned a particular label are presumed to have identical views. While these connections and networks may exist in some instances, it should not be assumed that every person within a particular network has identical views on any single issue (Voll 2009). In reality, "Wahhabism" and "Salafism" cover a range of views, from theological and creedal to political or legal orientations, not all of which are associated with violence, and within which exist a range of opinions, however singular their method of interpretation claims to be. In addition, because the labels "Wahhabi" and "Salafi" are used as both endonyms and exonyms, they often mean different things to different interpreters. "Wahhabi," for example, carries such a pejorative, parochial connotation today that those following the teachings and methodology associated with the Wahhabi tradition tend to self-identify alternatively as simply Muslims, *Muwahhidun* (adherents of *tawhid*), or, in some cases, Salafis, connecting themselves to the first three generations of Muslims (*al-salaf al-salih*), all of which have more positive and global connotations.

Beyond issues of labels, determining the global impact of Wahhabism and Salafism requires careful attention to analytical focus, such as an individual's or group's adoption of a particular group of texts, hermeneutic, jurisprudential methodology, mode of performativity, or produced outcomes. Interactions between Wahhabism and Salafism and other influences and variables, whether in

Natana J. DeLong-Bas, *Wahhabism and Salafism in Global Perspective* In: *Wahhabism and the World*. Edited by: Peter Mandaville, Oxford University Press. © Oxford University Press 2022. DOI: 10.1093/oso/9780197532560.003.0002 thought or praxis, must also be considered, as influence flows in many directions, with populations adopting, discarding, protesting, and/or reinterpreting ideas, concepts, and orientations in locally meaningful ways (Al-Rasheed 2006). Ultimately, while it may be possible to identify broadly universal "Wahhabi" or "Salafi" trends or markers, their particularities in specific contexts are malleable and encompass a range of adherents from political-activist to pietist-quietist to jihadi extremist (Wiktorowicz 2006), to the point where some scholars question the utility of using "Wahhabism" and "Salafism" as frameworks for determining sources of violence or tracing genealogies of doctrines and practices (Hegghammer 2009). This chapter argues that it may be more useful to understand Wahhabism and Salafism as orientations, rather than fixed identities, in light of the reality that there is more than one way to be a Wahhabi or Salafi, and that the boundaries between them are fluid, whether for influences or critiques.

Wahhabism

Frequently described as a rigid, localized, conservative Saudi doctrine focused on the recreation of and strict adherence to the past, Wahhabism's appeal would seem to be relatively limited and unlikely to have survived without the support of the Al Sa'ud political dynasty (Meijer 2009, 8). Yet, it not only has survived, including, at times, beyond the Saudi state itself, but also has been declared a Saudi export and global threat in the twenty-first century. Although Wahhabism is often presumed to be monolithic, it appears in many forms and relationships, both within and outside of Saudi Arabia, infiltrating and adapting to new environments ranging from Africa to Eastern Europe and Southeast Asia.[2]

The Saudi state claims a monopoly on religious interpretation, yet Saudis are not religiously monolithic—Saudi Shi'ites and some Sunnis, particularly those living in the Hijaz, do not consider themselves "Wahhabis." In addition, Saudi Arabia does not hold an exclusive claim to Wahhabi identity, as Qatar also claims to be Wahhabi, albeit of a different variety. Furthermore, whatever their religious affiliation, all Saudi citizen-subjects retain the theoretical religious right, if not obligation, to offer private advice (nasiha) to the monarchy in cases where a person believes that the monarchy has strayed, creating some fluidity of exchange in religious interpretations, even if such advice is not always offered or received graciously. There is also not a singular mode of interaction between the state and religious scholars. While some religious scholars ('ulama) serve in official capacities on the state's payroll—such as the grand mufti, the Council of Senior 'Ulama, judges, and government-appointed imams—and are expected to approve and command compliance with state-issued directives, others function as independent state critics or even opponents, whether through statements or armed resistance (Lacroix 2011; Hegghammer and Lacroix 2007). The relationship between the Saudi state, religious scholars, and citizen-subjects has thus been variously described as subservient, co-dependent, or a matter of social capital that fluctuates between strength and weakness depending on the degree to which the state does or does not follow religious advice or the degree to which religion is used to critique the state (Wagemakers 2012).

A case in point was the 1927 conflict between King ʿAbd al-Aziz and his Ikhwan military unit following the king's refusal to allow the Ikhwan to declare excommunication (*takfir*) on the Shiʿite populations in al-Hasa and al-Qatif with the goal of either converting or exterminating them. While the Ikhwan prioritized ideological commitment and critiqued the king for failing to follow his own religious commitment to the fullest extent, the king focused on pragmatic state-building as a priority. In the end, the king fought religion with religion, seeking a religious juridical opinion (*fatwa*) from prominent Najdi religious scholars to reclaim *takfir* as the state's prerogative (Steinberg 2009, 114–115). Thus, while "Wahhabism" is typically portrayed as upholding and inherent to the legitimacy of the Saudi state, it also serves to critique and correct the state, such that there is no one singular mode of being Wahhabi in relationship to the state.

In terms of relationships to others, Wahhabism is presumed to be inherently violent due to the doctrine of *al-walaʾ wa-l-baraʾ* (loyalty and disavowal), which asserts that the true believer must demonstrate belief through open enmity (disavowal) of and breaking ties with non-adherents to Wahhabism, even to the point of declaring jihad against them, and befriending and being loyal only to fellow adherents. This approach asserts an absolute division of the world into a binary of believers and unbelievers. Although this concept became centrally important to the Wahhabi movement in the nineteenth century (Wagemakers 2012; Commins 2016; Firro 2018), the phrase does not appear in the foundational eighteenth-century Wahhabi theological literature, which focused instead on missionizing and education about the practical meanings of *tawhid* (absolute monotheism) and *shirk* (associationism). While *shirk* was clearly denounced from the movement's outset, some room was left for the possibility that associated behaviors might be accidental because a person was unaware that a given behavior was problematic. Thus, an unintentional *mushrik* (practitioner of *shirk*) would not necessarily be considered an unbeliever (*kafir*) outside of the fold of believers (DeLong-Bas 2008, 67–68). In order to prevent this kind of situation from occurring, religious education became a central corrective, assuring that people thought through and understood the consequences of their actions. Once properly instructed, they were expected to correct wrong behaviors. Refusal to change was considered an intentional act of disbelief (*kufr*) with serious consequences.

The threat of violence seems inherent to such a worldview. Yet the relationship between Wahhabism and violence is more complex, as the use of violence is neither the exclusive prerogative of Wahhabism nor unidirectional. In reality, the Saudi state claims exclusive legitimate use of violence, rendering any violence not enacted through the state illegitimate by nature. So, while there are some Wahhabis who have engaged in violence, including at the state's directive against the state's declared enemies—whether political or sectarian, internal or external, such as the Ikhwan, the Shi'ites, or Al-Qaeda in the Arabian Peninsula (AQAP)— or to maintain social order and public morality, as in the case of the notorious Commission for the Promotion of Virtue and the Prevention of Vice (CPVPV), or *mutawwa'*, there are also Wahhabis who have engaged in violence against the state and even civilians, such as the armed militants who took over the Grand Mosque in 1979 (Hegghammer 2010). Finally, there are some Wahhabis who do not engage in violence at all—and these constitute the majority of the population. Ultimately, focusing exclusively on the use of violence, even if deemed useful for security studies and risk assessments, reduces Wahhabism to a singular manifestation of public behavior, ignoring other motivating factors, actors, and surrounding context that may ultimately be more representative.

Another frequently assumed characteristic of Wahhabism is the rejection of modernity, as evidenced in the plethora of Saudi religious decrees from the twentieth century that reject "the West," seen in everything from technology to modern ideas, such as democracy and human and women's rights (Al-Rasheed 2006). Yet, because Najd was never colonized or even invaded by Western powers, there was no "confrontation with modernity" as such in the foundational period of the Saudi state, only concerns about intellectual and doctrinal innovations (*bid'a*) that had been introduced into Islam historically—fears rooted in the past, rather than the present or future. In addition, just because a religious decree is issued does not mean that everyone follows it. Many Saudis actually reject such rejectionism, choosing to travel to the West for education and finding value in Western holidays such as American Thanksgiving and Mother's Day, despite numerous *fatwas* condemning them as innovations. Although there have been historical moments of rejection of technology, such as radio and television when they were first introduced, technology is omnipresent in the kingdom today. Saudis constitute the highest percentage of Twitter users in the world (Hubbard 2019) and cell phones are ubiquitous, including among conservative *shaykhs*, many of whom also recognize the internet's potential for expanding efforts in *da'wa* (missionizing). While there remain some Saudis who prefer to avoid the trappings of what has come to be associated with Western culture, including what they perceive to be the corrupting influence of the monarchy's modernization efforts, even to the point of removing themselves from society, they remain a minority (Kechichian 1986).

Security circles frequently express grave concerns about the connection of Wahhabism to strong financial resources and the capacity this provides for projecting Wahhabism around the global arena. There has been tremendous pressure on Saudi Arabia post–9/11 to establish greater surveillance and control over charitable donations to assure that they are channeled to legitimate organizations and purposes, such as the Red Crescent Society and the International Islamic Relief Organization, and funding for charitable social services, such as *hajj* sponsorship for economically disadvantaged persons, supporting orphans, or hosting mass weddings,[3] and not used as covers for financing terrorism, support for rebel groups, or illicit arms purchases, as occurred most notoriously in Afghanistan throughout the 1990s (Rashid 2000, 2002) and through the Al-Haramayn Islamic Foundation. Some scholars have argued that Saudi government funding of various institutes and scholars has allowed them to forge loyalty and allegiance where it would not otherwise exist (Bonnefoy 2009), pointing to state-connected financial outreach such as scholarship programs offered through Saudi embassies abroad, charity organizations, and the personal fortunes of Saudi establishment ʿulama, which have been used to recruit foreign students from around the world, expanding Wahhabi influence far beyond the borders of Saudi Arabia (Farquhar 2016, esp. 98–108).[4]

Since the 1960s, the Saudi state has injected billions of petrodollars into religious propagation (*daʿwa*). The King Fahd Complex for the Printing of the Holy Qurʾan annually prints and globally exports 10 million copies of the Qurʾan in 39 languages, translations that have come under heavy criticism for including Wahhabi commentaries, often inserted directly into the text (*Translation of the Meanings of the Noble Qurʾan* 1999). Saudi petrodollars have also funded mosque and madrasa construction and reconstruction, most controversially in Bosnia following the 1992–1995 genocide. Briefly, instead of replacing damaged or destroyed historical mosques, including UNESCO heritage sites, Saudi funds were used to build new, Saudi-style mosques. Following Bosnian and international outcry, the Saudis were ordered to restore the mosques to their original state.[5] Saudi financing has also been used to train preachers and religious educators in other countries, as well as establish parastatal and international organizations, such as the Muslim World League, the World Assembly of Muslim Youth, and the Organization of Islamic Cooperation (formerly the Organization of the Islamic Conference).[6] Still, even though financial soft power is used to spread influence, whether Saudi, Wahhabi, or otherwise, it cannot always be equated with direct support for terrorism or extremism and does not necessarily explain Wahhabism's global reach and appeal on its own, particularly in instances where those on the receiving end are antagonistic to the Saudi government and policies to the point of declaring them illegitimate and heretical (Haykel 2009, 37).

Despite the importance of the purported manifestations of Wahhabism discussed so far, they focus more on means and outcomes (state power, violence, rejectionism, and monetary power) than methods and tell us little about Wahhabism's essence and origins. Wahhabism began as a theological movement, suggesting that understanding its associated methodologies, orientations, worldviews, and models of leadership and community-building would help to create a more accurate picture of what it is and where its appeal lies, not just why it is to be feared in certain manifestations.

As a theological orientation, Wahhabism was, from its outset, a revivalist and reformist movement, led by a renewer (mujaddid) whose role involved teaching and missionizing (da'wa), either opposing or supporting a state by offering religious advice and spiritual guidance to its leadership, but without necessarily being a part of it—a pattern that was neither distinctive nor unique to Wahhabism (Voll 2009, 154–156). It did not seek to re-establish the caliphate. It was not messianic in the sense of projecting the End Times through the political leadership of a Mahdi, a salvational and apocalyptic figure in Islamic eschatology.[7] Neither was it revolutionary in the sense of overthrowing existing systems, whether political or religious. Instead, it called for a "return" to a purer form of religion, solidly rooted in the Qur'an and Sunna (the Prophet Muhammad's traditions), leading to the socio-moral reconstruction of society through invitation (da'wa) engaged via missionary activities (preaching and teaching). Rather than representing something "new" or "innovative" (bid'a), it called for recovery of the basic fundamentals of an older time. Although resistance was, at times, met with coercion and even violence, and there were instances of religious declarations of takfir and active destruction of monuments, shrines, and tombs deemed to represent idolatry, not all violence was religiously motivated or intended as a coercive missionizing tactic. At times, the violence was related to state expansionism as a political activity—and there was often tension between the religious and political leadership in the foundational era over its use (DeLong-Bas 2008, esp. 193–225).

Methodologically, Wahhabism is rooted in a return to scripture for direct interpretation (ijtihad), rather than "blind imitation" of the historical tradition of interpretation (taqlid), at least in theory. The foundational writings of Wahhabism demonstrate familiarity with a multiplicity of historical and legal opinions (ikhtilaf), placing it within the broader Islamic tradition, rather than necessarily breaking from it altogether (DeLong-Bas 2008, 94–95). Since that time, in practice, on legal matters, Wahhabi scholars have tended to follow the Hanbali madhhab (legal school)—one of Salafism's main critiques of Wahhabism. The main exception today is among certain female Saudi preachers (da'iyat), some of whom are reviving the practice of ikhtilaf to demonstrate to followers that a variety of opinions existed historically on certain topics in a pushback against the tendency of male Wahhabi *'ulama* to be univocal, following only Hanbali interpretations (Al Saud 2012, esp. chapter 6).

The direct return to scripture proposed by Muhammad Ibn 'Abd al-Wahhab assigned different levels of authority to different sources. The hierarchy was simple: the Qur'an, as the revealed Word of God, at the top, followed by the Sunna (Muhammad's example, largely recorded in the *hadith* and biographical literature), and then consensus of the Companions (*ijma'*) where known. Although Wahhabism is often presumed to be literal in its approach to scripture, Ibn 'Abd al-Wahhab was more concerned about understanding and practical application than he was about simple memorization. He believed in the importance of being able to cite scripture, but did not encourage literal interpretations, favoring instead discovery of the underlying values and themes (DeLong-Bas 2008, 42–43). In addition to a more thematic and value-oriented approach to the Qur'an, Ibn 'Abd al-Wahhab also proposed a reformed approach to the *hadith*, authenticating them according to their coherence, or lack thereof, with the Qur'an, and giving attention to their content (*matn*), rather than the traditional method of authenticating the chains of transmission (*isnad*) and verifying the reputations of the various parties listed (DeLong-Bas 2008, 46–51).

Doctrinally, Wahhabism has given its greatest attention to creed (*'aqida*), rather than jurisprudence (*fiqh*), due to the central focus on *tawhid* and how it is to be lived out as both belief and behavior. Concerns about upholding *tawhid* and violations through *shirk* permeate much of Wahhabi literature, beginning with Ibn 'Abd al-Wahhab's famous catechism *Kitab al-Tawhid* (The Book of Monotheism) and continuing through treatises dedicated to assuring that believers know what behaviors—and people—to avoid, not befriend, denounce, or, in some extreme cases, fight—although fighting and killing were deemed the prerogative of the state to enact, not vigilantes. Such strong attention to correctness of belief and behavior, particularly active engagement of *tawhid*, expressed not only by acceptance of belief but also by rejection of anything or anyone opposed to it, served as the impetus for the reform of society to the point of exclusion of those not sharing the same beliefs or practices—expressions of *shirk*—as subject to excommunication (*takfir*), provided that the parties involved had received proper instruction and then chose to act against it. This necessitated constant and ongoing engagement of *da'wa*, both internal to the Muslim community by calling Muslims, both men and women, to righteous living, and external by calling people outside of Islam to the faith. During the foundational era, *da'wa* was generally directed outward as the movement expanded. That changed during the nineteenth century with a shift in state needs away from expansionism, largely due to external threats from the Ottoman and British empires, and toward homogenization of religious belief and practice within and discouraging migration outward to the point of declaring living in non-believer lands as grounds for *takfir*. In the twentieth and twenty-first centuries, a combination of internal and external projects have been used to maintain national cohesion (Commins 2016, 14; Al-Rasheed 2009; Firro 2018).

Some analysts have argued that the obligation of *da'wa* necessitates a constant and inherent threat to the integrity of the community, rendering it a tool for state-securitization and consolidation, as well as a source of identity construction and performance (Rich 2017, 8). The constant shift in priorities as to which threat is the most important to address at any given moment provides the state with some maneuverability in the face of dynamic circumstances, as can be seen in various "security concerns" about Shi'ites, Sufis, domestic terrorists, drug traffickers and other criminals, the Sahwa, sexual deviants, subversive women, journalists, or vague perceptions of *fitna* (chaos) or *bid'a* (innovation) within, or Iran, the Shi'ite triangle, the Cold War, neo-colonialism, or "the West" externally. Yet *da'wa* is arguably not the only factor at play in Saudi security, identity, or stability. Other realities, such as fluctuating oil prices and broad social and economic changes in light of Vision 2030, may ultimately present as great a security threat, if not more so, than religious deviancy (Rundell 2020).

One other critique of this security-focused model is that it insists upon state use of violence and threats to maintain the religious message of Wahhabism. If this were true, the collapse of the state should lead to populations freed from control, throwing off the mantle of Wahhabism. While this has happened in some cases where the Wahhabi message had been resisted all along, the fact that the revivalist project survived in certain places where the state had come to an end, such as nineteenth-century Najd, indicates the robust nature of the message itself, independent of political apparatus. At the same time, the state does not hold a monopoly on *da'wa*, given the divide between religious and political powers, such that other parties can use *da'wa* either to support or push back against the state. Finally, *da'wa* need not always be negatively generated. While it can be preached as movement away from negative behaviors, such as sin and idolatry, it is also possible to proclaim *da'wa* as movement toward positive behaviors, such as charitable giving, increased religious observance, and care for the less fortunate.

Salafism

As with Wahhabism, Salafism manifests in different ways, ranging from politically quietest and discrete while offering advice to political leaders, to covertly denouncing political participation while nevertheless acting politically, to openly activist in calling for political reform (Meijer 2009, 17). Like Wahhabis, Salafis have sometimes been linked to acts of coercion and violence, even as nonviolence and "quietist pietism" are more common. In extreme cases where Salafism has become connected to jihadism, violence often occurs against Shi'ites, although other Muslims deemed insufficiently observant or non-Muslims may also be targets (Steinberg 2009).

In some respects, Salafis resemble Wahhabis in their focus on 'aqida, particularly through the concept of tawhid. Wahhabis and Salafis share a tripartite understanding of tawhid as belief in Oneness of Lordship (tawhid al-rububiyya), Oneness of Godship (tawhid al-uluhiyya), and Oneness of Names and Attributes (tawhid al-asma' wa-l-sifat) (DeLong-Bas 2008, 57; Haykel 2009, 38–39). They differ in that Wahhabis historically tended to be more concerned about the first two, seeing the Oneness of Names and Attributes growing out of and defined by the Oneness of Lordship and Godship (DeLong-Bas 2008, 57), while Salafis place distinctive emphasis on literal understanding of the divine names and attributes, criticizing other scholars, both past and present, who have allowed interpretation of them (Nahouza 2018, 9–10).

Salafis and Wahhabis also share concerns about avoidance and condemnation of shirk, bid'a, and kufr; exclusive reliance upon the Qur'an, Sunna, and consensus of the Companions as sources of authority; and attention to da'wa. But whereas Wahhabis tend to focus more on externalities, many Salafis see da'wa as a comprehensive way of life that must be both internalized and embodied through lifestyle choices. At times, such choices may be extreme, such as insisting upon living separately from non-Salafis and calling out scholars for failure to support this practice, as occurred in a confrontation between Saudi Wahhabi establishment scholar Shaykh Salih ibn Fawzan al-Fawzan and Al-Qaeda ideologue Sultan al-'Utaybi. Although al-Fawzan has long been known for his conservatism and anti-Westernism—exemplified in his call for Muslims living in non-Muslim countries to emigrate to the Islamic world in order to avoid loyalty to unbelievers—al-'Utaybi accused him of not going far enough in avoiding unbelievers. He proposed instead opposition to and/or overthrow of nominally Muslim governments that he deemed insufficiently pure, specifically Saudi Arabia, a critique often repeated by jihadi ideologues (Lia 2009).

On a smaller scale, some Salafis call for violent vigilantism at the community level as an expression of individual responsibility for enforcing correct behaviors and principles where the state is perceived to have abandoned its religious obligations (Hegghammer 2010, 6–7) or has focused on facilitating and financing modernization at the expense of da'wa (Alsaif 2013, 382). Examples of such vigilantism include campaigns in the 1960s that targeted stores with "inappropriate" displays, photography studios perceived to be violating tawhid through the reproduction of images of living beings, and coffee houses, and against video rental sites in the 1980s (Al-Rasheed 2006, 26). Although some Wahhabis historically have also opposed modern technology, such as Ikhwan opposition to the automobile, telephone, and telegraph as "inventions of the devil" when first introduced (Habib 1978, 122), King ʿAbd al-ʿAziz simply overrode their concerns in the name of nation-building and they did not engage in vigilantism (Rundell 2020, 100).

In the majority of cases, embodiment is engaged nonviolently through personal behaviors and individual choices, such as manner of dress and self-presentation, a reflection of a "purist" approach to Salafism focused on strict adherence to creed and embodying ever-increasing levels of religious purity. For men, this means having the right length of beard, hair, and thobe, and not wearing the black circlet (ʿiqal) used to fasten a headcloth (Rock-Singer 2019; Lacroix 2009, 72). Women are expected to wear the full face covering (niqab) and gloves. Although Wahhabis are also known for modest dress, particularly for women, the niqab became a point of strong and public disagreement between Wahhabis opposed to it (represented by Grand Mufti ʿAbd al-ʿAziz bin Baz) and Salafis in support (represented by Shaykh Nasir al-Din al-Albani) (Lacroix 2009, 61–66).

These violent extremist and "purist" approaches are not, however, the only expressions of Salafism. Another trend, identified as "modernist moderate," also existed up through the 1970s, mainly in Morocco. Briefly, modernist moderate Salafism sought reforms to religious, social, political, and educational institutions in keeping with the needs of nation-state development in the twentieth century, often borrowing from the discourse of Western modernity even as it claimed anchoring in authentic Islamic tradition. Despite its arguably more progressive objectives, the modernist moderate trend of Salafism appears to have died out with independence from colonial regimes, leaving the field to the purists and violent extremists (Lauzière 2016, 4–6).

Parallel to the challenges presented by the terminology of "Wahhabism," the term "Salafism" has therefore been critiqued for being too broad and ill-defined, particularly where focused on political aspects to the detriment of attention to ʿaqida, despite the clear importance of theological and legal doctrines, which some scholars consider to be Salafism's distinguishing characteristics (Haykel 2009, 33–35; Farquhar 2016, 1). Despite its claim to roots in the example of the first three generations of Muslims, there are no mentions of a specific group known as "Salafis" prior to the twentieth century (Nahouza 2018, 9). Even then, "Salafiyya" seems to have been the mistaken creation of a French Orientalist scholar, although the term was later appropriated by Muslims for their own purposes (Lauzière 2016, 4–6). Some scholars have been tempted to dismiss "Salafism" as an ossified yet constantly reproduced set of beliefs and practices with a "seemingly endless ability to cite scripture" and interpret it literally (Haykel 2009, 36), rendering it a set body of material, transmitted from one generation to the next. Other scholars argue that Salafism is better understood as an orientation or overarching framework of inquiry brought to bear upon a particular body of texts, practices, and styles of reasoning in diverse ways as new circumstances and problems present themselves in different social and historical contexts—a "tradition within a tradition" (Farquhar 2016, 5). As with Wahhabism, this suggests the need to give careful attention not just to outcomes, but, more importantly, to modes of discourse, particularly how arguments and justifications are formulated and structured and on what basis. In this way, Salafism is not the outcome of blind adherence, mindless indoctrination, or coercion, but rather an active and dynamic process of engagement with ideals of good life and personhood (Farquhar 2016, 8), rendering it as much a search for identity as a religious experience or orientation. As has been noted with respect to Wahhabism, although that identity is rooted in clear doctrine and an ongoing quest for purity, in practice, Salafis do make some compromises with life in the contemporary world, such as adopting new technology or making doctrinal concessions for the sake of the economy.

Despite these parallels between Salafism and Wahhabism, there nevertheless remain significant differences. One is that Salafism is not necessarily or inherently connected to Saudi Arabia or any other particular location, even if its origins are usually placed in Egypt (Lacroix 2009; Lauzière 2016). A second is that, while both claim roots in the foundational era of Islam and a direct return to scripture, Salafis tend to be more intentionally rejectionist of the use of reason (ʿaql) as a matter of creed (ʿaqida) and therefore more literalist than Wahhabis in their understandings of scriptures and replication of the behavior of the pious forebears (Meijer 2009b, 4). A flashpoint in this regard is *hadith* authentication. Whereas Ibn ʿAbd al-Wahhab authenticated *hadith* by cross-referencing content against the Qurʾan, Salafi methodology, exemplified by al-Albani, limits such critique to formalities of linguistic or grammatical criticism, retaining the historical focus on the chains of transmission (*isnad*) rooted in the morality and reliability of the transmitters (Lacroix 2009, 65).

Third, Salafis have a different set of priorities than Wahhabis. Although both share the end goal of a reformed society, they do not necessarily agree on how to get there. Salafis debate whether political power, as a human construct, can ever be accepted by a person seeking to live in full accordance with *tawhid* due to the religious obligation to recognize God's singular status and authority over and above obedience or allegiance to a ruler or a state. Salafis thus debate— among themselves and with others—whether political power is ultimately rooted in a given ruler's personal piety and adherence to Islamic law, accompanied by questions about the obligations of believers in the event of a deviation, whether on the part of the ruler or broader society, with opinions ranging from offering correction and advice to refusing to engage at any level and even overthrowing the offending regime. There are also many Salafis who deny any political ambitions whatsoever, although Meijer argues that, whatever the rhetoric, they retain ideas with political dimensions due to their public implications, such as loyalty and disavowal (*al-wala' wa-l-bara'*) and commanding good and forbidding wrong (*al-amr bi-l-ma'ruf wa-l-nahy 'an al-munkar*), which can lead to coercion and violence (Meijer 2009, 18–19). This stands in marked contrast to Wahhabism's more pragmatic stance of accepting political leadership as a necessity, albeit one that is inherently imperfect and in constant need of religious guidance and advice. Official Saudi state *'ulama* encourage drawing a parallel between obedience to God and obedience to the ruler and, by extension, a wife giving obedience to her husband (Al Saud 2012, 60, 125).

For those Salafis with a political orientation, a fourth difference is the question of leadership. Whereas Wahhabis see political and religious leaders existing separately but symbiotically, politically oriented Salafis are often drawn to the model of the caliphate, a logical extension of their desire to replicate the early Islamic model. Salafis who are more "pietist-quietist" tend to eschew politics in favor of internal, personal transformation and are more likely to look for a teacher or guide—a model that generally escapes state notice (Meijer 2009, 9).

A fifth difference is that Salafis believe in outward displays of their beliefs— visible performativity through modes of dress and speaking the Arabic language as social markers and separators from non-Salafis (Haykel 2009, 36). This performativity showcases the personal transformation brought by faith as the humiliation, marginalization, discrimination, and political repression often associated with colonialism and postcolonial states are intentionally converted into a positive identity associated with a chosen sect (*al-firqa al-najiyya*) with privileged status, a distinct knowledge base, superior morality, and the ability to disrupt the dominant culture (Meijer 2009, 13; Lauzière 2016). Viewed in this way, the central issue is not so much about *da'wa* in terms of inviting others into this exclusive community and its accompanying strict mindset as it is about setting clear boundaries that are not to be transgressed. Although allegiance is pledged to the global ummah, it is nevertheless performed in local, specific spaces.

For all of the theological proximity between Salafism and Wahhabism, with attention to revival (*tajdid*), reform (*islah*), *da'wa*, upholding *tawhid*, rejecting *shirk* and *bid'a*, and returning to scripture, Salafis and Wahhabis nevertheless differ in orientations with respect to public life and performativity of faith.

Hybridizing Wahhabism and Salafism

These brief sketches of Wahhabism and Salafism are not intended to replace detailed historical studies. Rather, they point to orientations and how both Wahhabism and Salafism shape and are shaped by changing contexts and variables, including each other and other Islamic movements, to the point where some scholars argue that Wahhabis have become Salafis over time (Commins 2015). This reality makes it increasingly difficult to clearly identify an individual or movement as belonging exclusively to one group or the other, particularly where hybridization or cross-pollination occur. For example, AQAP founding ideologue Yusuf al-'Uyayri, a Saudi, received a Wahhabi education, but committed himself to Salafism and embraced jihad. His writings combined the terminologies of *tawhid*, purification, and intention with a sharp critique of reality, producing a jihadi strategy for change. Although he legitimated jihad within the boundaries of both Wahhabism and Salafism, he focused on militant jihad as the mechanism for achieving change, rather than offering "advice" or working for internal or personal transformation. It is not possible to assign a single label to him or his writings.

Similarly, in some instances, different groups and figures that appear to be similar nevertheless engage in sometimes vehement critique of each other. For example, Al-Qaeda and Islamic State (ISIS) harshly critique many Wahhabi institutions and leaders as inconsistent and insufficiently "pure" in their adherence to doctrine due to their failure to implement it absolutely (Voll 2009, 162). Ironically, these critiques are often couched in the terminology of *al-wala' wa-l-bara'*, a concept also central to both Salafism and post-eighteenth-century Wahhabism, although not necessarily manifested in the same way (Wagemakers 2012, 81, 84–87). Thus, while Wahhabis, Salafis, and even jihadis make use of the same phrases and concepts, the orientation as to how they are to be implemented varies considerably.

Finally, Wahhabis and Salafis each have their own genealogies based on their specific local circumstances and global developments (Al-Rasheed 2009, 302, 310). Yet they seem to feel an ongoing need to engage each other and point out presumed doctrinal or interpretational faults. Nowhere is this clearer than on the internet, where heated debates take place both across and among Wahhabis and Salafis. Salafis spend considerable time and energy on doctrinal disputes online, despite the purported transparency and evident nature of their doctrines, rooted as they are in literal interpretations of scripture. The prevalence of these debates about scriptural interpretation, *hadith*, accusations of misunderstanding, *bid'a*, and even questioning of scholarly credentials demonstrates ongoing engagement with the meaning and application of contemporary issues and mutual influence, even as they are rooted in scriptural and historical precedent. Examples of internal bickering among various Salafis include disagreements between Grand Mufti Bin Baz and Shaykh Muqbil bin Hadi al-Wadi'i over the presence of US troops on Saudi soil in the 1990–1991 Gulf War, and al-Wadi'i's criticism of Usama bin Laden, Abu Muhammad al-Maqdisi, and other jihadis for financing weaponry rather than mosques (Bonnefoy 2009, 336–337).

Although much of the disagreement occurs between Wahhabis and Salafis, they sometimes turn to a perceived common enemy—the Shi'ites—who serve variously as a convenient and semi-permanent "fifth column" threat, objects of religious derision, foils to "correct" beliefs and practices, and potential entry points for Iranian intervention in Saudi sovereign affairs (Steinberg 2009; Ismail 2016). Occasionally, gestures are made toward symbolic reconciliation or inclusion within the Saudi context, but these have yet to be implemented comprehensively or consistently (DeLong-Bas 2016).

Also caught between these two orientations is the Saudi state, which vacillates between trying to manage and control both to playing them against each other (Lacroix 2011; Mouline 2011), often resulting in the state finding itself in a defensive position, facing sharp critiques as having strayed from its religious roots through pragmatic concession and compromise for political purposes, rather than maintaining purity of doctrine (Lia 2009)—a critique that has been made repeatedly over the centuries. Open challenges to the state's legitimacy by Wahhabi-Salafi religious figures, from Juhayman al-'Utaybi, who orchestrated that takeover of the Grand Mosque in 1979, to Abu Muhammad al-Maqdisi, who has disavowed the Saudi monarchy for its interactions with "infidels" and has declared them subject to jihad (Meijer 2009, 10, 18), have pressured the Saudi state to position itself as a patron of "moderate" (*wasatiyya*) Islam. In this positioning, the Saudi state has variously silenced or jailed "radical" preachers, taken greater control over the production of religious knowledge, cut back on state funding and power for state religious organizations, and, most recently, curbed the power of the notorious CPVPV and the practice of *hisba*—the commanding of good and forbidding of wrong (*al-'amr bi-l-ma'ruf wa-l-nahy 'an al-munkar*)—espoused by both Wahhabis and Salafis and supported by the Saudi state as a mechanism for governing public morality.

One final point that should be noted on current analyses of Wahhabism and Salafism is that they are almost exclusively male-focused, addressing male leaders, male concerns, and male initiatives. On the rare occasions where women are mentioned, they tend to be referenced as objects of policy upon whom *da'wa* and its corrective expectations are to be visited, particularly where dress codes and modest behaviors are concerned (Al-Rasheed 2013). This could give the false impression that women are only acted upon by Wahhabism and Salafism, rather than being active participants in them. Yet women have served as protectors, networkers, teachers, and adherents since the foundation of Wahhabism, albeit with fluctuating levels of involvement (DeLong-Bas 2008, forthcoming; al-Harbi 2008). Although no women were admitted to the Islamic University of Medina until 2011 (Farquhar 2016, 115, 193), women have served as informal *da'iyat* since the 1970s, working to bring other women into the fold and educate them in Wahhabi and Salafi teachings and principles (Al Saud 2012; Makboul 2017).[8]

Although none have yet been included in official Saudi religious institutions, like their male counterparts, these women host and engage in Qur'an study circles (LeRenard 2012), hold advanced degrees, write exegesis (*tafsir*), engage in *ijtihad*, issue *fatwas*, demonstrate expertise at a variety of levels of Arabic, ranging from classical Arabic to local dialects (Al Saud 2012, 89), and, increasingly, are building a presence on the internet and social media (Makboul 2017). Also like their male counterparts, some have been imprisoned for their activism and for challenging, however gently, the official religious interpretation of the state. As such, they are transforming not only possibilities for fuller inclusion of women, but also what religious leadership looks like (Kalmbach 2015) and how religious orientation is to be understood for both women and men. Further study of these important contributions and how Wahhabi and Salafi orientations are embodied, performed, and transmitted by women is needed in order to fill a major gap in the literature.

Conclusion

Taking a big picture view of Wahhabism and Salafism demonstrates the interpenetration of ideas and fluidity of religious thought as multiple and competing religious agendas that contend for influence and as orientations in both private and public life across time and space. Although both are considered global phenomena, attention needs to be given to the specific local manifestations of these orientations and where they differ, their modes of discourse, their varying relationships to the state and modernity, and the relative importance assigned to politics and creed, as well as internal and external manifestations that may, but do not necessarily, include violence as a form of resistance. Ultimately, individuals must decide for themselves what to believe and how and where to express it, whether as a mode of dress, a personal search for meaning, an intellectual decision, or a political choice.

Notes

1. Valuable contributions of this type include Meijer 2009 and Hegghammer 2010. There are many other, far less academic and even polemical and politically driven studies designed to portray Wahhabis and Salafis simplistically, with an exclusive focus on their purported inherent violence and intolerance.
2. See the chapters on case studies in Part II of this volume.
3. See Chapter 6 by Nora Derbal in this volume.
4. See Chapter 3 by Christopher Anzalone and Yasir Qadhi in this volume.

5. For more on Wahhabi intrusions into the Bosnian context, see Chapter 14 by Harun Karčić in this volume.
6. For details on this topic, see Chapter 5 by Reinhard Schulze in this volume.
7. In this sense, Juhayman al-Utaybi and his Mahdi figure, Muhammad al-Qahtani, departed from both the Wahhabi and Salafi models.
8. Some of the most famous *da'iyat* include Sara al-Mas'ud, Ibtisam al-Sa'dun, Ruqayya al-Muharib, Nawal al-'Id, Asma al-Ruwayshid, and Dr. Fatima Nasif. In addition, Dr. Suhayla Zayn al-Abidin serves as a *mujtahid*.

References

Bonnefoy, Laurent. 2009. "How Transnational is Salafism is Yemen?" In *Global Salafism: Islam's New Religious Movement*, edited by Roel Meijer, 321–341. New York: Columbia University Press.

Commins, David. 2015. "From Wahhabi to Salafi." In *Saudi Arabia in Transition: Insights on Social, Political, Economic and Religious Change*, edited by Bernard Haykel, Thomas Hegghammer, and Stéphane Lacroix, 151–166. New York: Cambridge University Press.

Commins, David. 2016. *The Mission and the Kingdom: Wahhabi Power behind the Saudi Throne*, rev. ed. London: I. B. Tauris.

DeLong-Bas, Natana J. 2008. *Wahhabi Islam: From Revival and Reform to Global Jihad*, rev. ed. New York: Oxford University Press.

DeLong-Bas, Natana J. 2016. "Between Conflict and Coexistence: Saudi Shi'is as Subjects, Objects, and Agents in *Wasatiyya* and *Wataniyya*." *Journal of Islamic and Muslim Studies* 1(1): 47–64. doi: https://doi.org/10.2979/jims.1.1.04

DeLong-Bas, Natana J. Forthcoming. "The Role of Women in Solidifying 18th Century Revival and Reform Initiatives into Ongoing Mass Movements." In *Islam, Revival, and Reform: Redefining Tradition for the Twenty-First Century*, edited by Natana J. DeLong-Bas. Syracuse: Syracuse University Press.

Farquhar, Michael. 2016. *Circuits of Faith: Migration, Education, and the Wahhabi Mission*. Stanford, CA: Stanford University Press.

Firro, Tarik K. 2018. *Wahhabism and the Rise of the House of Saud*. Eastbourne: Sussex University Press.

Habib, John S. 1978. *Ibn Saud's Warriors of Islam: The Ikhwan of Najd and Their Role in the Creation of the Saudi Kingdom, 1910–1930*. Leiden: Brill.

al-Harbi, Dalal Mukhlid. 2008. *Prominent Women from Central Arabia*. Translated by Dr. Muhammad W. Abahsain and Dr. Mohammad A. al-Furaih. Reading, UK: Ithaca Press in association with the King Abdul Aziz Foundation for Research and Archives.

Haykel, Bernard. 2009. "On the Nature of Salafi Thought and Action." In *Global Salafism: Islam's New Religious Movement*, edited by Roel Meijer, 33–51. New York: Columbia University Press.

Hegghammer, Thomas. 2009. "Jihadi-Salafis or Revolutionaries? On Religion and Politics in the Study of Militant Islamism." In *Global Salafism: Islam's New Religious Movement*, edited by Roel Meijer, 244–266. New York: Columbia University Press.

Hegghammer, Thomas. 2010. *Jihad in Saudi Arabia: Violence and Pan-Islamism*. New York: Cambridge University Press.

Hegghammer, Thomas, and Stephane Lacroix. 2007. "Rejectionist Islamism in Saudi Arabia: The Story of Juhayman al-'Utaybi Revisited." *International Journal of Middle East Studies* 39: 103–122. doi: https://doi.org/10.1017/S002074380722255X

Hubbard, Ben. 2019. "Why Spy on Twitter? For Saudi Arabia, It's the Town Square." *New York Times*, November 7, 2019. https://www.nytimes.com/2019/11/07/world/mid dleeast/saudi-arabia-twitter-arrests.html (accessed September 7, 2020).

Ismail, Raihan. 2016. *Saudi Clerics and Shia Islam*. New York: Oxford University Press.

Kalmbach, Hilary. 2015. "Blurring Boundaries: Aesthetics, Performance, and the Transformation of Islamic Leadership." *Culture and Religion* 16(2): 160–174.

Kechichian, Joseph A. 1986. "The Role of the Ulama in the Politics of an Islamic State: The Case of Saudi Arabia." *International Journal of Middle East Studies* 18(1): 53–71. doi: https://doi.org/10.1017/S002074380003021X

Lacroix, Stéphane. 2009. "Between Revolution and Apoliticism: Nasir al-Din al-Albani and his Impact on the Shaping of Contemporary Salafism." In *Global Salafism: Islam's New Religious Movement*, edited by Roel Meijer, 58–80. New York: Columbia University Press.

Lacroix, Stéphane. 2011. *Awakening Islam: The Politics of Religious Dissent in Contemporary Saudi Arabia*. Translated by George Holoch. Cambridge, MA: Harvard University Press.

Lauzière, Henri. 2016. *The Making of Salafism: Islamic Reform in the Twentieth Century*. New York: Columbia University Press.

LeRenard, Amelie. 2012. "From Qur'anic Circles to the Internet: Gender Segregation and the Rise of Female Preachers in Saudi Arabia." In *Women, Leadership, and Mosques: Changes in Contemporary Islamic Authority*, edited by Masooda Bano and Hilary Kalmbach, 105–126. Leiden: Brill.

Lia, Brynjar. 2009. "'Destructive Doctrinarians?': Abu Mu'sab al-Suri's Critique of the Salafis in the Jihadi Current." In *Global Salafism: Islam's New Religious Movement*, edited by Roel Meijer, 281–300. New York: Columbia University Press.

Makboul, Laila. 2017. "Beyond Preaching Women: Saudi *Da'iyat* and Their Engagement in the Public Sphere." *Die Welt des Islams* 57: 303–328. doi: http://dx.doi.org/10.1163/15700607-05734p03.

Meijer, Roel. 2009. "Introduction." In *Global Salafism: Islam's New Religious Movement*, edited by Roel Meijer, 1–32. New York: Columbia University Press.

Mouline, Nabil. 2011. *Les Clercs de l'Islam: Autorite religieuse et pouvoir politique en Arabie Saoudite, XVIIIe–XXIe siècle*. Paris: Proche Orient.

Nahouza, Namira. 2018. *Wahhabism and the Rise of the New Salafists: Theology, Power and Sunni Islam*. London: I. B. Tauris.

Al-Rasheed, Madawi. 2006. *Contesting the Saudi State: Islamic Voices from a New Generation*. New York: Cambridge University Press.

Al-Rasheed, Madawi. 2009. "The Local and the Global in Saudi Salafi Discourse." In *Global Salafism: Islam's New Religious Movement*, edited by Roel Meijer, 301–320. New York: Columbia University Press.

Al-Rasheed, Madawi. 2013. *A Most Masculine State: Gender, Politics, and Religion in Saudi Arabia*. New York: Cambridge University Press.

Rashid, Ahmed. 2002. *Jihad: The Rise of Militant Islam in Central Asia*. New York: Penguin Books.

Rashid, Ahmed. 2000. *Taliban: Militant Islam, Oil, and Fundamentalism in Central Asia*. New Haven, CT: Yale Nota Bene, Yale University Press.

Rich, Ben. 2017. *Securitising Identity: The Case of the Saudi State*. Carlton, Australia: Melbourne University Press.

Rock-Singer, Aaron. 2019. "Leading with a Fist: A History of the Salafi Beard in the 20th Century Middle East." *Islamic Law and Society* 27(1–2): 1–18. doi: https://doi.org/10.1163/15685195-00260A06

Rundell, David H. 2020. *Vision or Mirage: Saudi Arabia at a Crossroads*. London: I. B. Tauris.

Al-Saif, Tawfiq. 2013. "Relationship between State and Religion in Saudi Arabia: The Role of Wahhabism in Governance." *Contemporary Arab Affairs* 6(3): 376–403. DOI: https://doi.org/10.1080/17550912.2013.822721

Al-Saud, Reem. 2012. "Female Religious Authority in Muslim Societies: The Case of the *Da'iyat* in Jeddah." Unpublished Ph.D. dissertation, St. Antony's College, University of Oxford.

Steinberg, Guido. 2009. "Jihadi-Salafism and the Shi'is: Remarks about the Intellectual Roots of anti-Shi'ism." In *Global Salafism: Islam's New Religious Movement*, edited by Roel Meijer, 107–125. New York: Columbia University Press.

Translation of the meanings of The Noble Qur'an in the English Language. 1999. Translation overseen by Dr. Muhammad Taqi ud-Din Al-Hilali, Formerly Professor of Islamic Faith and Teachings, Islamic University, Al-Madinah Al-Munawwarah, and Dr. Muhammad Muhsin Khan, Formerly Director, University Hospital, Islamic University, Al-Madinah Al-Munawwarah. Madinah, KSA: King Fahd Complex for the Printing of the Holy Qur'an.

Voll, John O. 2009. "The Impact of the Wahhabi Tradition." In *Religion and Politics in Saudi Arabia: Wahhabism and the State*, edited by Mohammed Ayoob and Hasan Kosebalaban, 149–167. Boulder, CO: Lynne Rienner.

Wagemakers, Joas. 2012. "The Enduring Legacy of the Second Saudi State: Quietist and Radical Wahhabi Contestations of *Al-Wala' wa-l-Bara'*." *Middle East Studies* 44: 93–110. doi: https://doi.org/10.1017/S0020743811001267

Wiktorowicz, Quintan S. 2006. "Anatomy of the Salafi Movement." *Studies in Conflict and Terrorism* 29(3): 207–239. doi: https://doi.org/10.1080/10576100500497004

Further Reading

Commins, David. 2006. *The Wahhabi Mission and Saudi Arabia*. London: I. B. Tauris.

Meijer, Roel, ed. 2009. *Global Salafism: Islam's New Religious Movement*. New York: Columbia University Press.

Al-Rasheed, Madawi. 2002. *A History of Saudi Arabia*. New York: Cambridge University Press.

Al-Rasheed, Madawi, ed. 2018. *Salman's Legacy: The Dilemmas of a New Era in Saudi Arabia*. New York: Oxford University Press.

3

From Dir'iyya to Riyadh

The History and Global Impact of Saudi Religious Propagation and Education

Christopher Anzalone and Yasir Qadhi

Introduction

One of the most discussed aspects of modern Islam is the rise of Salafism (and in particular the Wahhabi strain of Salafism) as a global transnational phenomenon. During the past half century, this movement has spread across the globe and has impacted every single aspect of the Islamic discourse. Even those who oppose the movement have had to reshape their thought in response to it and engage directly or indirectly with the tenets and appeal of Salafism. Saudi interpretations of Sunni Islamic theology, discourse, and education continue to play an integral role in the kingdom's domestic and foreign policies and intra-Muslim diplomacy and outreach globally. This chapter seeks to explore the rise of this movement and one of the main causes for its recent popularity, namely, the impact of the Islamic University of Medina, while also examining the ways in which the university and Saudi religious diplomacy and outreach are shaped not only by the kingdom's national interests but also local dynamics.

The Development of the Kingdom's Institutions and Programs of Religious Education

The Al Sa'ud and the Wahhabis of Najd

The origins of the alliance between the Al Sa'ud family and the Wahhabi movement of Najd dates back to 1744 during the lifetime of the latter's founder, Muhammad ibn 'Abd al-Wahhab (1703–1792), a Hanbali theologian and jurist who forged a working relationship with Muhammad ibn Sa'ud (d. 1765), the ruler of the Emirate of Dir'iyya in central Arabia, established in 1760, who

Christopher Anzalone and Yasir Qadhi, *From Dir'iyya to Riyadh* In: *Wahhabism and the World*. Edited by: Peter Mandaville, Oxford University Press. © Oxford University Press 2022. DOI: 10.1093/oso/9780197532560.003.0003 opposed Ottoman imperial rule in the Hijaz (Habib 2008; DeLong-Bas 2004; Commins 2006).

Coming from a scholarly family, Ibn 'Abd al-Wahhab preached against both what he saw as heretical innovations (*bid'a*) to Islam and the blind following (*taqlid*) of long-standing classical and medieval juridical interpretations and traditions, calling instead for a reinterpretation through independent reasoning (*ijtihad*), including a heavy reliance on the Qur'an and *hadith*. His views on polytheism (*shirk*) and absolute monotheism (*tawhid*) were not only religious but also profoundly political, serving as a call for his followers to mobilize to confront "unbelievers" (*kuffar*) and "polytheists" (*mushrikun*) not only in the realm of scholarly debate, but also with physical force, taking a much more militant stance than earlier Hanbali jurists like Ibn al-Jawzi (d. 1201) (Firro 2013, 771–772) and Ibn Taymiyya (d. 1328).

Wahhabism was "the product of processes of settlement and state formation" in Najd that had begun during the first half of the eighteenth century and this is distinctly shown in the universal scope of its message, its anti-nomadic themes, and support for the idea of a centralized state (al-Dakhil 2008, 33–34). Ibn 'Abd al-Wahhab and the early Wahhabis used religious learning, preaching, and *fiqh* to move toward the establishment of the first Saudi state before later harnessing the ideological power of the call to a "return" to *tawhid* as a tool to legitimize it and mobilize popular support (al-Dakhil 2008, 35).

The Kingdom of Saudi Arabia and Religious Education: The Islamic University of Medina and the Globalization of Wahhabi Da'wa

At the forefront of Saudi Arabia's international religious outreach is the Islamic University of Medina (IUM), which was established by royal decree in September 1961 and began operations in November of the same year (Islamic University of Medina 2019). The university previously focused almost entirely on religious studies such as *fiqh*, *usul al-fiqh*, *'aqida*, and *shari'a*, offering fully funded residential higher education to male Sunni Muslim students from around the world, but during the past several years has added new faculties and has required courses outside of the institution's original mandate, including courses in engineering, computers, and the sciences.

For much of its history the IUM primarily sought to attract non-Saudi students as part of the kingdom's foreign policy and soft power outreach, offering from its founding until 2002 over 28,000 student scholarships to successful applicants from around the world (Farquhar 2015a, 25–26). According to university statistics, 11,781 students graduated with bachelor's degrees as of 1997, and over 30,000 by 2010, according to IUM director Muhammad ʿAli al-ʿAqla (Farquhar 2015a, 26). These numbers only signify those who managed to complete the rigorous program (an average of six years for non-Arabic speakers: two years in learning Arabic, and four years in an undergraduate program of their choice). As for the actual number of students who joined the university but eventually dropped out before completion, it is not unreasonable to claim a few hundred thousand such students. Farquhar (2015a, 26) notes that a significant number of the IUM's first batch of students came from the same home countries as members of the university's founding advisory council, suggesting that recruitment was targeted at these countries through individual faculty and advisory council members' own interpersonal networks.

The university's founding came at a tense time for the Saudi state, which was then embroiled in a competition with pan-Arabist nationalists, including Egypt's popular president Gamal ʿAbd al-Nasser, for influence across the Middle East (Kerr 1967). The IUM and other official and parastatal nongovernmental organizations (NGOs) and organizations founded in the kingdom pushed forward Saudi diplomatic influence through an investment in religious soft power. These organizations included the Muslim World League (Rabitat al-ʿAlam al-Islami; MWL) founded in 1962 (Muslim World League 2010) and the World Assembly of Muslim Youth (WAMY) founded in 1972 (World Assembly of Muslim Youth 2020). Even after the decline of pan-Arabism, the IUM's mission has continued to spread Saudi Salafi (Wahhabi) interpretations of Sunni Islam globally, targeting not only non-Muslims but also—and arguably even primarily—non-Salafi Muslims. The university's graduates are expected to return to their home countries and preach Wahhabism in a bid to "return" errant Muslims to the "true" faith through daʿwa and other outreach activities (Farquhar 2015a, 21; 2017, Chapter 5). Through anecdotal sources, it appears that almost all graduates from specific countries were immediately sent out by WAMY as paid preachers on government stipends; this practice appears to have peaked in the 1970s and then fizzled out by the early 1980s.

The social processes at the university, however, were not unidirectional, but instead involved both the university and its curriculum influencing the institution's students as well as the global student body exerting influence on the university itself, with an estimated 80 or more percent of students coming from outside the kingdom (Farquhar 2015a, 22; 2015b, 702). The university was steered from its founding by the kingdom's religious establishment, headed by the grand mufti, with the late ʿAbd al-ʿAziz ibn Baz playing a particularly important role in the 1960s until 1975; he served as the university's president officially from 1970 to 1975 (Farquhar 2015a, 24), and also played an active role teaching throughout all of his years there. Students of this phase all recall that Ibn Baz would not just teach the students, but also played a fatherly role in many of their lives, mentoring them outside of the classroom and making sure they felt comfortable in their temporary home of Saudi Arabia (Qadhi 2020a, 2020b).

From its founding, the IUM employed a multiethnic and multinational faculty and staff, with a significant number being non-Saudis who had settled in the kingdom (Farquhar 2015a, 24; 2017, chapters 3 and 4). This might also be due to the fact that in the 1960s, there would not have been a large quantity of Saudi scholars qualified to teach in the disciplines offered at the university, especially the sciences of Qur'anic recitation (qira'at) and hadith. These included a number of prominent African 'ulama from the Sahel, including from Mali, Nigeria, and Mauritania (Ahmed 2015). Also represented were faculty and administrators associated with the Egyptian and Syrian Muslim Brotherhoods, Egypt's Salafi Ansar al-Sunna al-Muhammadiyya (founded in 1926 in Cairo), and the South Asian Ahl-i Hadith movement (Farquhar 2015a, 24–25; 2017, chapters 3 and 4; Lacroix 2011; Olidort 2015). The IUM's founding charter stated that advisory council members—who were tasked with supervising syllabi, setting and amending university administration and statutes, and overseeing the establishment of new faculties and departments—were to be multinational in order to secure a global reach, as well as to represent an array of areas of expertise (Farquhar 2015b, 707).

University advisory council members who attended its first meeting in 1962 included the Indian revivalist scholar-activists Abul A'la Mawdudi, founder of the Jamaat-e-Islami party, and Abul Hasan 'Ali al-Nadwi; Indian Ahl-i Hadith scholar Muhammad Dawud al-Ghaznawi; Yemeni Salafi scholar Muhammad Salim al-Bayhani; Egyptian Salafis 'Abd al-Razzaq 'Afifi (formerly head of Ansar al-Sunna al-Muhammadiyya) and the country's former grand mufti and Al-Azhar University scholar Hasanayn Muhammad Makhluf; Iraqi Muslim Brotherhood leader Muhammad Mahmoud al-Sawwaf; Iraqi Muhammad Bahjat al-Athari (formerly a student of the prominent Iraqi Salafi scholar Mahmoud Shukri al-Alusi); and Syrian Salafis Muhammad al-Mubarak (a co-founder of the Syrian Muslim Brotherhood) and Muhammad Bahjat al-Bitar (Farquhar 2015a, 25; 2015b, 708; Fattah 2003, 141). In the early 1980s, three-fifths of the university's faculty of around 400 were non-Saudis, over 130 of these being Egyptian nationals, with others coming from Sudan, Syria, Jordan, India, Iraq, Morocco, the Palestinian territories, Pakistan, South Yemen, Mauritania, and Australia (Farquhar 2015b,708).

Non-Saudi faculty occupied prominent positions within the university. They included Syrian Muslim Brotherhood member Muhammad al-Majdhub as a member of the editorial board of the IUM's journal and Egyptian Muslim Brotherhood member Sayyid Nazili as head of the university's program for student life (Farquhar 2015b, 708). Other faculty with family origins outside of Saudi Arabia included 'Abd al-Fattah al-Qari (b. circa 1911) from Uzbekistan's

Fergana Valley, who moved for studies to the Hijaz early in his life and whose son, 'Abd al-'Aziz al-Qari, later studied at the IUM and then joined its faculty, eventually serving as the dean of the Faculty of the Qur'an and Islamic Studies in the 1980s (Farquhar 2015b, 709). There were particularly close historical ties between South Asian Ahl-i Hadith scholars and Hijazi and Najdi 'ulama dating back to the eighteenth century. Najdi Wahhabi 'ulama, such as the prominent scholar Sa'd ibn 'Atiq, traveled to the Indian subcontinent to study with Ahl-i Hadith 'ulama (Farquhar 2015b, 711; Voll 1975; Nafi 2006). An Indian Ahl-i Hadith scholar, Ahmad ibn Muhammad al-Dihlawi from Delhi, even founded Medina's Dar al-Hadith institution, which was later subsumed within the IUM, and also cofounded a religious school in Mecca with Egyptian Ansar al-Sunna al-Muhammadiyya member 'Abd al-Zahir Abu al-Samih, a student of Rashid Rida's (Farquhar 2015b, 711; Ahmed 2015, chapter 4).[1]

Another influential figure in the development of Saudi religious education was 'Abd al-Rahman al-Ifriqi (d. 1957), who was born in Mali's Gao region during French colonial rule. He studied at Dar al-Hadith, later working as a teacher before receiving a Saudi government appointment as a Wahhabi missionary among the Bedouin in Yanbu al-Nakhl, 300 kilometers northwest of Jeddah (Ahmed 2015, 118; Triaud 2009). He then taught shari'a and hadith in Riyadh at the Ma'had al-Shari'a (Shari'a Institute) and the Ma'had al-'Ilmi (Scientific Institute), a college for teachers, (Triaud 2009). One of al-Ifriqi's preeminent students, the Fulani 'Umar Fallata, graduated in 1947 from Dar al-Hadith and later became a prolific lecturer and scholar of hadith and Qur'anic exegesis (tafsir) and fiqh, receiving a government teaching appointment at the Prophet's Mosque in Medina (Ahmed 2015, 119–120).

African Wahhabi 'ulama, including al-Ifriqi and Fallata, played a major role in the development and steering of Saudi religious education through institutions including Dar al-Hadith and the IUM. They were part of a historical line of West African Sunni Muslim pilgrims and students who traveled to the Hijaz, as well as others who were fleeing from European colonial rule in their home countries (Robinson 1987). Many later developed a more comprehensive dedication to Wahhabi views during their residencies and study in the kingdom (Ahmed 2015, chapters 1 and 2). Other prominent African faculty-'ulama who taught in Saudi religious schools, including the IUM, from the 1950s onward included Hammad al-Ansari (1925–1997), a Tuareg born in Ménaka, Mali (Ahmed 2015, chapter 3), into the clerical Kel Es Suq group who claim to be descended from the Prophet Muhammad's companions through a group led by 'Uqba ibn Nafi' (Hunwick and O'Fahey 2016); and Muhammad al-Amin al-Jakani al-Shinqiti (1907–1973), born in Mauritania's Kiffa region, who came to Mecca in 1947 as part of a hajj group and remained in the kingdom to teach in the Prophet's Mosque, Dar al-Hadith, and the Madrasa al-'Ulum al-Shar'iyya (School of Shari'a Sciences) after meeting with Saudi princes and regional governors of the Abha and Tabuk regions, respectively, Turki al-Sudayri and Khalid al-Sudayri, and then King 'Abd al-'Aziz (Ahmed 2015, 123-124).

Following the First Gulf War in 1991, the Saudi monarchy moved to replace faculty deemed too sympathetic to Islamist movements including the Muslim Brotherhood, promoting instead Salafi voices seen as being politically "quietist"—or at least more pliant to the government—including critic-turned-supporter of the Saudi rulers Rabi' ibn Hadi 'Umayr al-Madkhali (Farquhar 2015a, 25). Al-Madkhali and his "quietist Salafi" followers are heavily criticized today both by the Sahwa activist scholars, and also by Sunni militant Islamists in organizations like Islamic State (ISIS) and Al-Qaeda for "selling out" the religion in the interest of state patronage, and the moniker "Madkhalis" was used to derogatorily refer to Salafis who viewed support of the royal family as a part of their understanding of Wahhabism.

From the early 1990s onward, the university began an aggressive policy of "Saudiazation" among the faculty, purging almost the entirety of non-Saudis teaching there. By 1995, the university was effectively 100 percent Saudi in terms of professors (with a very few professors of Arabic linguistics and Qur'anic recitation that were kept because of lack of any Saudi replacement) (Farquhar 2015a, 25). By the end of the 1990s, politically active scholars like 'Abd al-'Aziz al-Qari were quietly shuffled away to administrative functions, while those who were heavily "quietist" (the methodology promoted by al-Madkhali and Muhammad Aman al-Jami) were given prominent posts and positions within all departments. This proved particularly useful, as they emphasized obedience to the ruler as a part of creedal purity, and shunned political activism/Islamism as heretical (Faruqhar 2015b, 715–716).

The Islamic University of Medina's Curriculum/Pedagogy, Student Life, Changes in Curriculum, and Related Issues

The IUM's teaching pedagogy was influenced by major shifts in religious education, including the adoption of more fixed schedules for students and faculty, examinations to determine knowledge acquisition and advancement, the modernization of the Saudi state, and counter-reactions to European colonialism and the infiltration of "un-Islamic" ideas into the education systems and social spheres of Muslim-majority countries (Faruqhar 2017, 110–112). Guided by members of its advisory council who warned against this "cultural invasion," including the Indian Ahl-i Hadith scholar Abul Hasan 'Ali Nadwi, the university followed what Faruqhar (2017, 113) terms an "activist approach" to religious education, with the end goal of producing graduates who learned to act upon their knowledge as missionary preachers (da'i; plural: du'at) of the Wahhabi da'wa. One IUM senior administrator, 'Abd al-Muhsin al-'Abbad, described the mission of graduates as "the stage of struggle" (marhalat al-jihad) and graduates collectively as "battalions of the [Wahhabi] da'wa" (Faruqhar 2017, 114, 116–119). For most of its history this mission of da'wa was seen by IUM administrators, faculty, and advisers as being primarily a male affair, with women expected to play a role in the private sphere (Faruqhar 2017, 114).

The IUM, influenced by advisers including Mawdudi and other Islamist scholars and intellectuals, did not advocate for a return to previous ("traditional") modes of Islamic religious education, but instead adopted a reformist program to better equip graduates to operate in a changing world (Faruqhar 2017, 115).[2] Mawdudi and other IUM-affiliated revivalists argued against a passive form of learning that blindly accepted the positions of past religious scholars and instead pushed for an activist method in which contemporary scholars and students developed new forms of knowledge and interpretation to meet modern-day challenges (Faruqhar 2017, 115–116).

When the university first opened in 1962, there was only one department. This original department then became the College of Shari'a (Islamic Law) when, in 1967, the College of Da'wa was formed, followed in 1974 by the College of Qur'anic Sciences, and in 1975 both the College of Arabic Language and the College of Hadith Science. For the next thirty years, these five Islamic colleges would be the backbone of the university—the entire campus was religiously oriented, with a galaxy of specialists in all fields, from all over the world. Given that the campus was located outside the city and all students resided within its premises, surrounded by religious clergy, it is difficult to overemphasize the effects of the atmosphere and impact that such an ambience had on a student, especially one coming from a non-Muslim-majority Western country. Even the city of Medina itself—regarded as a holy city by millions of pilgrims—seemed somewhat impure and polluted, with all of its bazaars and shopping malls and the intermixing of the sexes, compared to the pristine, ultra-religious world inside the walls of the campus (Qadhi 2020a, 2020b).

The curriculum of these five colleges largely overlapped. As a rough estimate, perhaps 70 percent of all the courses were of a similar nature. In all colleges, students studied theology (based primarily on the works of Ibn 'Abd al-Wahhab and Ibn Taymiyya); Arabic grammar, morphology, and rhetoric; Qur'anic exegesis; hadith books and sciences; Islamic law and the principles of deriving law; heresiology; homiletics; and other subjects. The emphasis in each college would be on its specialty, so, for example, while students in the College of Shari'a would only have one year on the science of hadith (mustalah) and four years in the sciences of deriving fiqh (usul al-fiqh); students in the College of Hadith had specialized courses in *mustalah* during all four years, and only one course on *usul al-fiqh*. Students in the College of Qur'an were the only students who specialized in the various recitations (*qira'at*) of the Qur'an; all other colleges only required partial memorization of the Qur'an (Qadhi 2020a, 2020b).

In addition to their daily academic coursework, students also participated in faculty and staff-led extracurricular activities and excursions based around Islamic history and supplementing their classroom religious education. These extracurricular activities included visiting famous battlefields from the days of the Prophet Muhammad and attending and participating in seminars where poetry was recited, lectures were given about the dangers of Marxism and other *kufr* ideologies, and the Islamic sciences and social concepts were discussed (Faruqhar 2017, 122).

Non-Arabic-speaking students typically were also required to complete a two-year Arabic diploma course in order to prepare for undergraduate studies, which were conducted in Arabic. Admitted students already fluent in Arabic were enrolled directly in one of the five Islamic studies colleges; this was before the recent introduction of secular tracks like engineering (Qadhi 2020a, 2020b). Courses included both mid-term and final examinations; students who failed even one final examination in a single course were required to repeat the entire year since the curriculum was considered to be a set, comprehensive program of study (Qadhi 2020a, 2020b). This was a particularly rigorous system of study, as the curriculum from the 1970s to 2005 mandated, on average, the study of around ten subjects per year, with some core subjects being taught by multiple teachers, and the equivalent of a twenty-five-hour course load (Qadhi 2020a, 2020b).

Students' official coursework was supplemented by regular attendance at open seminars and traditional learning circles (*halaqat*) held inside the Prophet's Mosque on various topics. Medina was also the home of numerous 'ulama, many of them affiliated with the IUM, and it was common for many of these scholars to host private classes in their homes or the homes of specific students, thus creating a complex web of interrelated cliques and persuasions (Qadhi 2020a, 2020b). Students who might sympathize with one trend (say, the Madkhalis, or the Sahwa scholars) would invariably find teachers of a similar persuasion. At times, the partisan politics of such divisions become ugly, with factions forming, "warning" other students of the "deviations" of other strands. The university administration tolerated such differences (as long as no violence occurred—a rare but occasional occurrence on campus); however, there were limits to that toleration (Qadhi 2020a, 2020b).

Despite the popular image of the IUM as a bastion of Wahhabism, not all students at the university sympathized with or adhered to the Wahhabi religious current and there were small pockets of students affiliated with other religious trends who kept to themselves and did not publicize their disagreements with the official religious ideology of the kingdom. To publicly criticize Salafi/Wahhabi theology would be grounds for expulsion—a not infrequent occurrence (Qadhi 2020a, 2020b).

Along with divisions based on religious trends, there were also divisions based on ethnicity and nationality and nationalities (Qadhi 2020a). Because of the IUM's heavy emphasis on attracting foreign students, students at the university, once in the country, would naturally gravitate toward other students from their home country, creating informal cliques. Since students were admitted based on a quota system, and the number of applicants varied exponentially from country to country, some nationalities (for example, Nigeria and Indonesia) had far more students than others (for example, the Nordic countries). Hence, depending on the size of a subgroup, it was possible to expand the informal fraternity to include students from other similar countries. For example, due to their small size, throughout much of the 1980s and 1990s students from the United States, the United Kingdom, Canada, and Australia all tended to socialize together, frequently gathering at each other's houses, and attending the same circles. However, by the early 2000s, as the number of students increased, it was possible to separate these countries more precisely based on nationality, and social gatherings became more politically demarcated (Qadhi 2020a, 2020b).

The Global Impact of the Islamic University of Medina and Localizing Wahhabism

Thousands of Muslims from around the world have circuited through the IUM and other Saudi Wahhabi religious institutions, many of them obtaining university and graduate degrees in the Islamic religious sciences. Upon returning to their home countries, non-Saudi graduates have gone on to found religious organizations, mosques, and other institutions and further indigenize Salafi movements in their home countries. In many of these countries, like Yemen, these graduates and their indigenous Salafi currents have played off of discontent with dominant socio-religious power structures, such as powerful preexisting religious hierarchies. While drawing on what Thurston terms a common "canon" of religious texts and Salafi learning obtained during their studies at the IUM (Thurston 2016, chapter 1), graduates also adapt their specific da'wa to local contexts. This section highlights the international influence of the IUM's graduates, with particular focus on Africa, the Middle East, and East Asia. Noorhaidi Hasan, Harun Karčić, James Dorsey, and Emil Nasritdinov and Mametbek Myrzabaev discuss, respectively, Indonesia/Southeast Asia, the Balkans/Europe, South Asia, and Kyrgyzstan/Central Asia in their chapters in this volume.

Yemen

Muqbil ibn Hadi al-Wadi'i, who was born into a non-*sayyid* Zaydi family in the Wadi'a tribe in the Sa'da region of northern Yemen, is credited with introducing an "ideologically structured" Salafi movement (Bonnefoy 2012, 54) to modern Yemen in the early 1980s. Though Salafism had existed in parts of Yemen, including in the southern port city of Aden (Reese 2012), for decades, al-Wadi'i was at the helm of its rapid expansion and organization into a defined socio-religious movement. Not being from a family of *sada* (singular: *sayyid*; descendants of the Prophet Muhammad's family, the Ahl al-Bayt), al-Wadi'i was looked down upon by Yemeni Zaydi elites and, he later claimed, was prevented from advancing socially and in the religious scholarly hierarchy (Bonnefoy 2012, 54–55). He worked and studied in Saudi Arabia for many years, starting in the 1950s, with a long period of residence following the start of the North Yemen Civil War in 1962 (Bonnefoy 2012, 55–56). Once attracted to the Muslim Brotherhood, he gradually distanced himself from the movement and later renounced them as being "worldly" instead of truly religious and began his advanced studies at the IUM, attending lectures by Nasir al-Din al-Albani and 'Abd al-'Aziz ibn Baz and graduating in 1976 with a master's degree in *hadith* sciences (Bonnefoy 2012, 56).

Returning to Yemen after being briefly imprisoned in and then expelled from Saudi Arabia over allegations relating to his connection to messianic militant Juhayman al-'Utaybi, whose small group seized control of the Grand Mosque in Mecca in November 1979 (Hegghammer and Lacroix 2007), al-Wadi'i went on to found, in the early 1980s with financial backing from wealthy Saudi businessmen of Yemeni descent, the preeminent institution of Salafi learning in Yemen, Dar al-Hadith, in Dammaj in the Sa'da region (Bonnefoy 2012, 57–58), which is also the home region of the country's powerful Houthi family and their tribal Islamist movement (Brandt 2017). By the late 1990s, Dar al-Hadith had a student body of nearly 1,000 resident and funded students, with a teaching mission aimed at furthering the spread of Salafism and combating *bid'a* (Bonnefoy 2012, 59). In an interview with the *Yemen Times* in the late 1990s, al-Wadi'i said that the institute had students from the United States, Britain, Germany, and France, as well as from majority-Muslim countries (Yemen Times, n.d.)

Al-Wadi'i's success in spreading Salafism in Yemen, and particularly in the historically Zaydi strongholds in the country's north, built on preexisting local resentment of the entrenched and hierarchical Zaydi social order and tenets of faith in Sa'da (Weir 1997, 22). By the mid-1980s, following al-Wadi'i's return from Saudi Arabia and the founding of Dar al-Hadith, sectarian competition and conflict between Sa'da's Zaydis and newly converted Salafis had started after the latter began to open their own schools, mosques, and institutions and also were appointed to state schools, thanks in large part to higher degrees of literacy among them (Weir 1997, 22). The new Yemeni Salafi movement also received tacit support from some of the region's tribal leaders, who approved of its anti-*sayyid* position due to long-standing rivalries between tribal and *sayyid* leaders (Weir 1997, 22–23). The *sada* and their supporters accused the Salafis of being driven by Saudi money and Wahhabi thought, importing a "foreign" creed into Yemen (Weir 1997, 23). Salafis made a point of entering Zaydi mosques and praying according to Sunni ritual practices which, in some regards, are recognizably different from the Zaydi method, and the former criticized Zaydi celebrations marking ʿEid al-Ghadir, the day when Shiʿi Muslims believe the Prophet Muhammad designated ʿAli ibn Abi Talib as his successor (Weir 1997, 23).

West Africa and the Sahel

The introduction and spread of Salafism in Africa—and indeed in other world regions—was not dictated or universally controlled by Saudi Wahhabi institutions, but rather evolved according to unique sets of dynamics specific to individual localities, countries, and regions. "Salafism" broadly conceived, though based on a common core set of tenets and methodologies, was subject to the agency of local, indigenous actors (Østebø 2015). African students and ʿulama also played a significant role in shaping the religious curricula at the IUM and other Saudi Wahhabi institutions of learning (Ahmed 2015, chapter 6). Like in Yemen, local Salafi entrepreneurs, many educated at the IUM and other Saudi institutions, utilized Salafism in part to contest the dominance of other social groups and hierarchies of power, including entrenched and often elitist Sufi orders. The adoption and spread of indigenous forms of Shiʿi Islam in parts of Africa occurred for similar reasons (Leichtman 2015, chapter 5).

In Nigeria, graduates from the IUM, forming a new "Salafi" identity based on a canon of scholastic and juridical works studied in Medina, established a firm foothold for Salafism by developing a set of normative practices and beliefs for the country's Salafis. Despite the historical dominance in northern Nigeria of Sufi orders, Nigerian Salafism enabled locals from humbler social backgrounds to challenge the dominance of Sufi elites for communal leadership, with Salafi graduates accelerating this process as they began to return home in the 1990s and early 2000s (Thurston 2016). Upon their return, IUM graduates began an aggressive proselytization campaign based on core Salafi principles drawn from the Qurʾan, *hadith*, and key juridical texts and commentaries, targeting other Muslims and challenging the continued societal and political authority of preexisting familial and Sufi power structures (Thurston 2016, chapters 4–6). Nigerian Salafis utilized new forms of media and technology in their *daʿwa* campaigns to debate rivals and critics and to broaden their own outreach capabilities and penetration among the Nigerian Muslim public and national society more broadly (Thurston 2016, chapter 5).

Non-Saudi Salafi students, graduates, and scholars in Saudi Arabia were at the forefront of contesting the continued authority and presence of Sufism and "heretical" Sufi ritual practices and beliefs in their home countries. The Malian 'Abd al-Rahman al-Ifriqi, for example, castigated the beliefs of the Tijani Order, one of the largest and most powerful Sufi orders in West Africa and the Sahel, in his book, *Al-Anwar al-Rahmaniyya li-Hidayat al-Firqa al-Tijaniyya* (The Divine Lights to Save the Tijaniyya Sect). Addressing Tijani Sufis themselves, he critiqued popular religious practices and beliefs that he said contradicted the core Islamic concept of *tawhid* and entered into *shirk* and *bid'a* (Ahmed 2015, 57–79). West African and Sahelian Salafis are also not united and have engaged in internal debates and splits due to disagreements on a range of issues, from methods of proselytization and combating what they see as *shirk* and *bid'a* to the permissibility of pursuing "Western-style" education and jihadi militancy (Thurston 2015).

Two of the most influential IUM-associated *'ulama* were the late Abubakar Gumi and his son, Ahmad Gumi. The former headed the "Yan Izala" movement (Jama'at Izalat al-Bid'a wa Iqamat al-Sunna; Society for the Removal of Heretical Innovation and Implementation of the Prophet's Tradition), which was also active along the border with Benin (Brégand 2007, 126; Clarke 1988) and influenced the Muslim Student Association of Nigeria's reformism, which was critical of Sufism (Umar 1993). The senior Gumi was awarded Saudi Arabia's highest honor, the King Faisal International Prize for Service to Islam, in 1987 for translating the Qur'an into Hausa (King Faisal Prize 2020) and also served in advisory roles for the IUM, MWL, and the King Faisal Bank (Jangebe 2015, 178; Brégand 2007, 126). His activism and preaching were also financially supported by the Saudi Islamic Relief Organization, which also backed other northern Nigerian Muslim leaders, including Gumi's rivals, like the sultan of Sokoto, to push against Sufism in the country's north (Brégand 2007, 126). Ahmad Gumi, a medical doctor, followed in his father's footsteps as a Salafi-learning religious scholar, completing a BA in *shari'a*, an MA in *fiqh*, and a PhD in *usul al-fiqh* at Mecca's Umm al-Qura University.

In Ghana, students from the north began to travel to study at the IUM in 1971, aided by scholarships (Iddrisu 2009, 167–168). Wahhabism, however, had been a part of Saudi diplomatic relations with Ghana since 1961, and the Saudi embassy in Accra included a religious affairs desk affiliated with the Saudi Ministry of Religious Affairs, Da'wa, and Guidance (Dumbe 2011, 54). The embassy's religious affairs desk, headed by Indian national Kamali Khalid, began sponsoring Islamic studies instruction at Accra's Central Mosque beginning in 1967, which was then built upon by Umar Ibrahim, born to a family from Benin and an IUM graduate who founded the Islamic Research and Reformation Centre (IRRC) in 1969 (Dumbe 2011, 54). Ibrahim studied at the Saudi Dar al-Hadith in Mecca beginning in 1959 and entered the IUM in 1964, graduating in 1968 with a degree in *shari'a* (Dumbe 2011, 55). The IRRC included members from Ghana's traditional *'ulama* opposed to the dominance of the Tijani Fayda movement (Dumbe 2011, 55, 57–58), as well as Western-educated Muslims with extensive experience in national politics, the latter serving as capable administrators for the new organization (Dumbe 2011, 55).

Recruitment to the IUM in the 1980s targeted Ghanaian students who excelled in the study of Arabic (Iddrisu 2009, 168). Returning graduates, such as Afa Seidu, who completed a BA from the IUM and an MA from King Saud University, where he wrote a thesis on the differences between Sufism and Salafism (Iddrisu 2009, 172), later played prominent roles in establishing indigenous Salafi movements, like the Munchere community, and *da'wa* projects aimed at undermining Sufi power structures (Kobo 2015). Graduates also brought back with them key texts they had studied in Saudi Arabia, including works by the fourteenth-century Hanbali jurist Ibn Taymiyya, Muhammad ibn 'Abd al-Wahhab and his successors, and the Indian subcontinent revivalist scholar Mawdudi (Iddrisu 2009, 173).

Ghanaian Salafis preached against local practices they said contradicted "pure" Islam, including popular wedding and funeral rituals, moonsighting, naming ceremonies, and local methods of prayer and Ramadan fasting (Iddrisu 2009, 174; Kobo 2015). In 1985, Ghanaian Salafis founded the Supreme Council for Islamic Call and Research (SCICR) to further the spread of Salafism in the country, bringing together graduates from Saudi, Kuwaiti, and Bahraini universities and institutions of learning, an initiative pushed by the Saudis who sought an organization through which to coordinate the activities of their graduates in Ghana (Dumbe 2011, 60–61). In 1997, another Salafi organization, the Ahlus-Sunnah Wal-Jama'ah, was formed after religious and power disputes within the SCICR, including the desire of local Salafi *'ulama* who had not studied in Saudi Arabia or elsewhere in the Middle East to attain positions of authority (Dumbe 2011, 64–69; Kobo 2015). Ghanaian Salafis, in addition to establishing educational and religious institutions and organizations, also engaged in humanitarian activities, in part aided by the Saudi Fund for Development (Dumbe 2011, 72–88).

Egypt

Saudi-influenced Salafism took root in Egypt, particularly in Alexandria, during the 1970s as Egyptian workers returned from jobs in the kingdom. For decades

the country's main Salafi groups, including the Da'wa Salafiyya, focused on quietist, apolitical preaching, but Salafis, supported by Saudi money, formed political parties following the 2011 ouster of President Hosni Mubarak. The Ansar
al-Sunna al-Muhammadiyya movement, founded in 1926, had close ties with
Saudi Wahhabi institutions, including the IUM, and also took a more political
and anti-Sufi stance, calling *shari'a* the only legitimate basis of government for
reforming Muslim societies (Gauvain 2010, 812–813; Høigilt and Nome 2014,
37–38). With a frequently fluctuating relationship with the Egyptian Muslim
Brotherhood under President Muhammad Morsi, the Salafi parties aligned
themselves not with their fellow Islamists but with the military coup that toppled
the Morsi government in 2013 (Karagiannis 2019; Al-Anani and Malik 2013;
Brown, 2011).

Jordan and the Palestinian Territories

One of the founders of the contemporary Salafi movement in Jordan, Muhammad
Ibrahim Shaqra (b. 1933), gradually adopted Salafism while teaching as a professor in Arabic at the IUM in the early 1960s and after meeting prominent Saudi
Wahhabi *shaykh*s, including bin Baz (Wagemakers 2016, 97–99). Jordanian
Salafis were also heavily influenced by the presence of Nasir al-Din al-Albani, another faculty alumnus from the IUM, during the many years he lived and taught
in Jordan (Wagemakers 2016, 100–109). Saudi funding also enabled Jordanian
Salafi scholars to devote their lives to research, writing and publishing, and
preaching (Wagemakers 2016, 110). The politically "quietist" leanings of most
Jordanian Salafis, though it existed before and independently from Saudi financial support, was seen by the Saudi monarchy as attractive in the 1990s and early
2000s when the kingdom saw the rise of a politically activist trend, the "Islamic
Awakening" (*Sahwa Islamiyya*), a loose collective of 'ulama (Wagemakers 2016,
110–114).

'Isam al-Barqawi, better known as Abu Muhammad al-Maqdisi, the prominent Jordanian-Palestinian "jihadi-Salafi" ideologue, also spent time in Medina,
though his ties to the IUM and official Saudi institutions are much more tenuous.
While in the kingdom he met Juhayman al-'Utaybi and members of his group
before they invaded the Grand Mosque in November 1979, the members of
which, interestingly, found some of al-Maqdisi's views too extreme (Wagemakers
2009, 285).

In the Palestinian territories, Palestinian graduates from Saudi universities,
who began returning home in the 1970s, spread Salafism on university campuses,
led at first by Shaykh Salim Sharab (Hroub 2008, 158, 162). Yasin al-Astal, an
IUM graduate, founded the Majlis al-'Ilmi li-l-Da'wa al-Salafiyya fi Filastin

(Scientific Council for the Salafi Call in Palestine; SCSMP) in Gaza in 1975, a hub for preaching and publishing (Hroub 2008, 161–162). At the IUM, he studied under al-Albani and bin Baz (Hroub 2008, 162). His predecessor, Sharab, whom al-Astal credits with introducing the Salafi *da'wa* in Gaza, had been an active member of the Al-Azhar Religious Institute and later the Islamic University of Gaza located there (Hroub 2008, 162).

Conclusion

Since its founding by Ibn Sa'ud in 1932, religion—and specifically the Salafi/Wahhabi interpretation of Sunni Islam—has been at the center of the kingdom's domestic and foreign policies, shaping the self-legitimization strategies of the ruling family and influencing its diplomacy in both the Muslim world and further afield in non-Muslim-majority countries. Though its dominant religious current later became indelibly linked, at least in the public mind, with the Wahhabi current of Salafism, the founding history of the Islamic University of Medina complicates this simplistic picture. It instead illustrates how multiple Sunni Islamic theological, interpretative, and political trends worked to shape Saudi religious education and soft power diplomacy. The spread of localized forms of Salafism by non-Saudi graduates of the IUM and other Saudi universities—as evidenced by the histories of local Salafisms in Yemen, West Africa and the Sahel, Jordan, the Palestinian territories, Egypt, and other countries—also succeeded as much, if not more so, because of local social, political, and class dynamics as they did from external funding from Saudi state and parastatal institutions.

Saudi Wahhabism, which became a magnet for international, mostly negative attention following the September 11, 2001, Al-Qaeda attacks in the United States, has profoundly influenced the contours of modern Sunni Islam. Even its critics, through their reactions to Salafi religious propagation and Saudi public religious diplomacy, have been shaped and changed by Wahhabism. The influence of Wahhabism could also arguably be said to have shaped aspects of contemporary Shi'ism, in particular the ways in which some Shi'i groups have developed specific sets of discourses meant to counter Salafis/Wahhabis and other Sunnis they see as hostile (Anzalone 2016). The same is true of anti-Salafi Sunni groups, including many popular Sufi preachers and movements—as well as popular commentators and analysts—who found in Saudi Salafism a convenient target to blame as the "root cause" of all problems in contemporary Muslim societies and communities (Kabbani 1997 and n.d.; Armstrong 2014).

The transnational impact of the Islamic University of Medina rests in its substantial pool of graduates who have come from around the world, from nearly every continent and both Muslim-majority and non-Muslim-majority countries. Despite their reputation as being bastions of Wahhabism, the university and Saudi religious parastatal *da'wa* and humanitarian organizations are not immune to political challenges and change, particularly following the "reformist" project of the new Saudi crown prince, Muhammad bin Salman (Hubbard 2017; Ulrichsen and Sheline 2019). Crackdowns on Saudi *'ulama* alleged by the state to be "dissidents" or "extremists" have shaken the kingdom's religious establishment, and it remains to be seen how the continued rise of the kingdom's new heir apparent will impact the contours of Saudi religious discourse both internally and internationally.

Notes

1. Al-Dihlawi had lived in Saudi Arabia since 1926 and was a supporter of the royal family, teaching in the Prophet's Mosque (*Masjid al-Nabawi*) in Medina. In Medina, al-Dihlawi taught students from around the Muslim world including many from West Africa such as 'Abd al-Rahman al-Ifriqi (d. 1957), who would later become a prominent religious scholar in his own right and go on to teach other multinational Wahhabi *'ulama* including 'Umar ibn Muhammad Fallata (1926–1998), a born-Meccan whose family was from Macina in south-central Mali but who had emigrated to Gombe in northern Nigeria.
2. Mawdudi himself was influenced by a variety of different sociopolitical and economic ideologies spreading in South Asia during his lifetime, including Marxism and ethnic and secular nationalism, as well as Islamic reformism and revivalism.

References

Ahmed, Chanfi. 2015. *West African 'Ulama' and Salafism in Mecca and Medina: The Response of the African*. Boston: Brill.

Al-Anani, Khalil, and Maszlee Malik. 2013. "Pious Way to Politics: The Rise of Political Salafism in Post-Mubarak Egypt." *Digest of Middle East Studies* 22(1): 57–73. https://doi.org/10.1111/dome.12012.

Anzalone, Christopher. 2016. "In the Shadow of the Islamic State: Shi'i Responses to Sunni Jihadist Narratives in a Turbulent Middle East." In *Jihadism Transformed: Al-Qaeda and Islamic State's Global Battle of Ideas*, edited by Simon Staffell and Akil Awan, 157–182. New York: Oxford University Press.

Armijo, Jackie. 2008. "Muslim Education in China: Chinese Madrasas and Linkages to Islamic Schools Abroad." In *The Madrasa in Asia: Political Activism and Transnational Linkages*, edited by Farish A. Noor, Yoginder Sikand, and Martin van Bruinessen, 169–189. Amsterdam: Amsterdam University Press.

Armstrong, Karen. 2014. "Wahhabism to ISIS: How Saudi Arabia Exported the Main Source of Global Terrorism." *New Statesman*. November 27, 2014. Available at: https://

www.newstatesman.com/world-affairs/2014/11/wahhabism-isis-how-saudi-arabia-exported-main-source-global-terrorism.

Bonnefoy, Laurent. 2012. *Salafism in Yemen: Transnationalism and Religious Identity.* New York: Oxford University Press.

Brandt, Marieke. 2017. *Tribes and Politics in Yemen: A History of the Houthi Conflict.* New York: Oxford University Press.

Brégand, Denise. 2007. "Muslim Reformists and the State in Benin." In *Islam and Muslim Politics in Africa*, edited by Benjamin F. Soares and René Otayek, 121–136. New York: Palgrave Macmillan.

Brown, Jonathan. 2011. *Salafis and Sufis in Egypt.* Report. Washington, DC: Carnegie Endowment for International Peace.

Clarke, Peter. 1988. "Islamic Reform in Contemporary Nigeria: Methods and Aims." *Third World Quarterly* 10(2): 519–538.

Commins, David D. 2006. *The Wahhabi Mission and Saudi Arabia.* New York: I. B. Tauris.

Al-Dakhil, Khalid S. 2008. "Wahhabism as an Ideology of State Formation." In *Religion and Politics in Saudi Arabia: Wahhabism and the State*, edited by Mohammed Ayoob and Hasan Kosebalaban, 23–38. Boulder, CO: Lynne Rienner.

DeLong-Bas, Natana J. 2004. *Wahhabi Islam: From Revival and Reform to Global Jihad.* New York: Oxford University Press.

Dumbe, Yunus. 2011. *Islamic Revivalism in Contemporary Ghana.* Huddinge: Södertörn University.

Farquhar, Michael. 2015a. "The Islamic University of Medina since 1961: The Politics of Religious Mission and the Making of a Modern Salafi Pedagogy." In *Shaping Global Islamic Discourses: The Role of Al-Azhar, Al-Madinah and Al-Mustafa*, edited by Masooda Bano and Keiko Sakurai, 21–40. Edinburgh: Edinburgh University Press.

Farquhar, Michael. 2015b. "Saudi Petrodollars, Spiritual Capital, and the Islamic University of Medina: A Wahhabi Missionary Project in Transnational Perspective." *International Journal of Middle East Studies* 47(4): 701–721. https://doi.org/10.1017/S002074381500094X.

Faruqhar, Michael. 2017. *Circuits of Faith: Migration, Education, and the Wahhabi Mission.* Stanford, CA: Stanford University Press.

Fattah, Hala. 2003. "'Wahhabi' Influences, Salafi Responses: Shaikh Mahmud Shukri and the Iraqi Salafi Movement, 1745–1930." *Journal of Islamic Studies* 14(2): 127–148. https://doi.org/10.1093/jis/14.2.127.

Firro, Tarik K. 2013. "The Political Context of Early Wahhabi Discourse of Takfir." *Middle Eastern Studies* 49(5): 770–789. http://dx.doi.org/10.1080/00263206.2013.811648.

Gauvain, Richard. 2010. "Salafism in Modern Egypt: Panacea or Pest?" *Political Theology* 11(6): 802–825. https://doi.org/10.1558/poth.v11i6.802.

Habib, John S. 2008. "Wahhabi Origins of the Contemporary Saudi State." In *Religion and Politics in Saudi Arabia: Wahhabism and the State*, edited by Mohammed Ayoob and Hasan Kosebalaban, 57–73. Boulder, CO: Lynne Rienner.

Hartung, Jan-Peter. 2014. *A System of Life: Mawdudi and the Ideologisation of Islam.* New York: Oxford University Press.

Hegghammer, Thomas, and Stéphane Lacroix. 2007. "Rejectionist Islamism in Saudi Arabia: The Story of Juhayman al-'Utaybi Revisited." *International Journal of Middle East Studies* 39(1): 103–122. https://doi.org/10.1017/S0020743807002553.

Høigilt, Jacob, and Frida Nome. 2014. "Egyptian Salafism in Revolution." *Journal of Islamic Studies* 25(1): 33–54. https://doi.org/10.1093/jis/ett056.

Hroub, Khalid. 2008. "Salafi Formations in Palestine and the Limits of a De-Palestinised Milieu." *Holy Land Studies* 7(2): 157–181. https://www.euppublishing.com/doi/abs/10.3366/E1474947508000206.

Hubbard, Ben. 2017. "Saudi Prince, Asserting Power, Brings Clerics to Heel." *New York Times.* November 5, 2017. https://www.nytimes.com/2017/11/05/world/middleeast/saudi-arabia-wahhabism-salafism-mohammed-bin-salman.html (accessed April 3, 2020).

Hunwick, John O., and R. S. O'Fahey, eds. 2016. "Scholars of the Kel al-Suq." In *Arabic Literature of Africa Online.* http://dx.doi.org/10.1163/2405-4453_alao_COM_ALA_40004_4 (accessed April 13, 2020).

Iddrisu, Abdulai. 2009. *Contesting Islam: "Homegrown Wahhabism," Education and Muslim Identity in Northern Ghana, 1920–2005.* PhD Dissertation. University of Illinois, Urbana-Champaign.

Islamic University of Medina. 2019. *About.* https://enweb.iu.edu.sa/site_page/20975 (accessed April 5, 2020).

Jangebe, Huzaifa Aliya. 2015. "Islamic Reform in Nigeria: The Contribution of Sheikh Abubakar Mahmud Gumi." *International Journal of Humanities and Social Science* 5(9): 176–181. http://www.ijhssnet.com/journals/Vol_5_No_9_September_2015/19.pdf.

Kabbani, Muhammad Hisham. 1997. *The "Salafi" Movement Unveiled.* n.p.: As-Sunnah Foundation of America. https://naqshbandi.org/wp-content/uploads/2018/11/ShaykhHishamKabbani-SalafiUnveiled.pdf (accessed December 13, 2020).

Kabbani, Muhammad Hisham. n.d. "200 Years of New Kharijism: The Ongoing Revision of Islam." http://aoislam.com/yahoo_site_admin/assets/docs/200_years_of_Kharijitism.221111806.pdf (accessed July 17, 2020).

Karagiannis, Emmanuel. 2019. "The Rise of Electoral Salafism in Egypt and Tunisia: The Use of Democracy as a Master Frame." *The Journal of North African Studies* 24(2): 207–225. https://doi.org/10.1080/13629387.2017.1417124.

Kerr, Malcolm. 1967. *The Arab Cold War, 1958–1967: A Study of Ideology in Politics,* 2nd edition. New York: Oxford University Press.

King Faisal Prize. 2020. "Shaikh Abu Bakr Mahmoud Gumi." https://kingfaisalprize.org/shaikh-abu-bakr-mahmoud-gumi/ (accessed April 23, 2020).

Kobo, Ousman Murzik. 2015. "Shifting Trajectories of Salafi/Ahl-Sunna Reformism in Ghana." *Islamic Africa* 6(1–2): 60–81. https://doi.org/10.1163/21540993-00602003.

Lacroix, Stéphane. 2011. *Awakening Islam: The Politics of Religious Dissent in Contemporary Saudi Arabia.* Cambridge, MA: Harvard University Press.

Leichtman, Mara. 2015. *Shi'i Cosmopolitanisms in Africa: Lebanese Migration and Religious Conversion in Senegal.* Bloomington: Indiana University Press.

Al-Madinah (newspaper). 2019. "Al-Yatimi: Accepting 3,500 Students from 200 Countries and Territories at the Islamic University." https://www.al-madina.com/article/631994/%D9%85%D8%AD%D9%84%D9%8A%D8%A7%D8%AA/%D8%A7%D9%84%D9%8A%D8%AA%D9%8A%D9%85%D9%8A-%D9%82%D8%A8%D9%88%D9%84-3500-%D8%B7%D8%A7%D9%84%D8%A8-%D9%85%D9%86-200-%D8%AF%D9%88%D9%84%D8%A9-%D9%88%D8%A5%D9%82%D9%84%D9%8A%D9%85-%D8%A8%D8%A7%D9%84%D8%AC%D8%A7%D9%85%D8%B9%D8%A9-%D8%A7%D9%84%D8%A5%D8%B3%D9%84%D8%A7%D9%85%D9%8A%D8%A9 (accessed June 15, 2020).

Muslim World League. 2010. *About MWL.* https://www.themwl.org/en/MWL-Profile (accessed April 7, 2020).

Nafi, Basheer M. 2006. "A Teacher of Ibn 'Abd al-Wahhab: Muhammad Hayat al-Sindi and the Revival of Ashab Al-Hadith's Methodology." *Islamic Law & Society* 13(2): 208–241.

Olidort, Jacob. 2015. "Why Are Salafi Islamists Contesting Egypt's Election?" *Washington Post.* November 12, 2015. https://www.washingtonpost.com/news/monkey-cage/wp/2015/11/12/why-are-salafi-islamists-contesting-egypts-election/ (accessed April 9, 2020).

Østebø, Terje. 2015. "African Salafism: Religious Purity and the Politicization of Purity." *Islamic Africa* 6(1–2): 1–29.

Qadhi, Yasir. 2020a. Personal observations from studies in Islamic University (years of study: 1995–2005).

Qadhi, Yasir. 2020b. Interviews with students at the Islamic University (multiple interviews with different students, from January to June 2020).

Reese, Scott S. 2012. "Salafi Transformations: Aden and the Changing Voices of Religious Reform in the Interwar Indian Ocean." *International Journal of Middle East Studies* 44(1): 71–92. https://doi.org/10.1017/S0020743811001255.

Robinson, David. 1987. "The Umarian Emigration of the Late Nineteenth Century." *The International Journal of African Historical Studies* 20(2): 245–270.

Thurston, Alexander. 2015. "Ahlussunnah: A Preaching Network from Kano to Medina and Back." In *Shaping Global Islamic Discourses: The Role of Al-Azhar, Al-Madinah and Al-Mustafa,* edited by Masooda Bano and Keiko Sakurai, 93–116. Edinburgh: Edinburgh University Press.

Thurston, Alexander. 2016. *Salafism in Nigeria: Islam, Preaching, and Politics.* New York: Cambridge University Press.

Triaud, Jean-Louis. "'Abd al-Rahman al-Ifriqi." In *Encyclopaedia of Islam, Three,* edited by Kate Fleet, Gudrun Krämer, Denis Matringe, John Nawas, and Everett Rowson. http://dx.doi.org/10.1163/1573-3912_ei3_COM_23182 (accessed April 13, 2020).

Ulrichsen, Kristian C., and Annelle R. Sheline. 2019. "Mohammed bin Salman and Religious Authority and Reform in Saudi Arabia." Report. Houston: Rice University's Baker Institute for Public Policy.

Umar, Muhammad Sani. 1993. "Changing Islamic Identity in Nigeria from the 1960s to the 1980s: From Sufism to anti-Sufism." In *Muslim Identity and Social Change in Sub-Saharan Africa,* edited by Louis Brenner, 154–178. Bloomington: Indiana University Press,.

Voll, John. 1975. "Muhammad Hayya al-Sindi and Muhammad ibn 'Abd al-Wahhab: An Analysis of an Intellectual Group in Eighteenth-century Madina." *Bulletin of the School of Oriental and African Studies* 38(1): 32–39.

Wagemakers, Joas. 2009. "A Purist Jihadi-Salafi: The Ideology of Abu Muhammad al-Maqdisi." *British Journal of Middle Eastern Studies* 36(2): 281–297. https://doi.org/10.1080/13530190903007327.

Wagemakers, Joas. 2016. *Salafism in Jordan: Political Islam in a Quietist Community.* New York: Cambridge University Press.

Weir, Shelagh. 1997. "A Clash of Fundamentalisms: Wahhabism in Yemen." *Middle East Report* 204: 22–23, 26.

World Assembly of Muslim Youth. 2020. http://wamy.org/ (accessed April 7, 2020).

Yemen Times. n.d. "Shaikh Muqbil bin Haadi'ee Interview with Hassan al-Zayidi of The Yemen Times." Salafi Publications. http://www.spubs.com/sps/downloads/pdf/MSC060013.pdf (accessed April 17, 2020).

Further Reading

Al-Rasheed, Madawi. 2015. "Saudi Religious Transnationalism in London." In *Transnational Connections and the Arab Gulf*, edited by Madawi Al-Rasheed, 149–167. New York: Routledge.

Amghar, Samir. 2012. "The Muslim World League in Europe: An Islamic Organization to Serve the Saudi Strategic Interests?" *Journal of Muslims in Europe* 1(2): 127–141. https://doi.org/10.1163/22117954-12341234.

Amin, Husnul. 2017. "Moderate Salafism and the Challenge of De-Radicalization: The Case of Pakistan." *Romanian Journal of Political Science* 17(1): 62–90.

Andraoui, Mohamed-Ali. 2020. *Salafism Goes Global: From the Gulf to the French Banlieues*. New York: Oxford University Press.

Birt, Jonathan. 2015. "Wahhabism in the United Kingdom: Manifestations and Reactions." In *Transnational Connections and the Arab Gulf*, edited by Madawi Al-Rasheed, 168–184. New York: Routledge.

Blengsli, Bjørn Atle. 2009. "Muslim Metamorphosis: Islamic Education and Politics in Contemporary Cambodia." In *Making Modern Muslims: The Politics of Islamic Education in Southeast Asia*, edited by Robert W. Hefner, 172–204. Honolulu: University of Hawai'i Press.

Bonnefoy, Laurent. 2008. "Salafism in Yemen: A 'Saudisation'?" In *Kingdom Without Borders: Saudi Arabia's Political, Religious and Media Frontiers*, edited by Madawi Al-Rasheed, 245–262. New York: Oxford University Press.

Bowen, Innes. 2014. *Medina in Birmingham, Najaf in Brent: Inside British Islam*. London: Hurst.

Cavatorta, Francesco. 2015. "Salafism, Liberalism, and Democratic Learning in Tunisia." *The Journal of North African Studies* 20(5): 770–783. https://doi.org/10.1080/13629 387.2015.1081464.

Chaplin, Chris. 2014. "Imagining the Land of the Two Holy Mosques: The Social and Doctrinal Importance of Saudi Arabia in Indonesian Salafi Discourse." *Austrian Journal of South-East Asian Studies* 7(2): 217–236.

Damir-Geilsdorf, Sabine, Mira Menzfeld, and Yasmina Hediger. 2019. "Interpretations of al-wala' wa-l-bara' in Everyday Lives of Salafis in Germany." *Religions* 10(2). https://doi.org/10.3390/rel10020124.

de Graaf, Beatrice. 2010. "The Nexus between Salafism and Jihadism in the Netherlands." *CTC Sentinel* 3(3): 17–22.

Diederich, Mathias. 2015. "Indonesians in Saudi Arabia: Religious and Economic Connections." In *Transnational Connections and the Arab Gulf*, edited by Madawi Al-Rasheed, 128–146. New York: Routledge.

Dumbe, Yunus. 2011. "The Salafi Praxis of Constructing Religious Identity in Africa: A Comparative Perspective of the Growth of the Movements in Accra and Cape Town." *Islamic Africa* 2(2): 87–116. https://doi.org/10.5192/21540993020287.

Elmasry, Shadee. 2010. "The Salafis in America: The Rise, Decline and Prospects for a Sunni Muslim Movement among African-Americans." *Journal of Muslim Minority Affairs* 30(2): 217–236. https://doi.org/10.1080/13602004.2010.494072.

Hammond, Andrew. 2017. "Salafi Thought in Turkish Public Discourse since 1980." *International Journal of Middle East Studies* 49(3): 417–435. https://doi.org/10.1017/S0020743817000319.

Hasan, Noorhaidi. 2002. "Faith and Politics: The Rise of Laskar Jihad in the Era of Transition in Indonesia." *Indonesia* 73: 145–169. https://doi.org/10.2307/3351472.

Hasan, Noorhaidi. 2007a. "Salafi Madrasahs and Islamic Radicalism in Post-New Order Indonesia." In *Islamic Studies and Islamic Education in Contemporary Southeast Asia*, edited by Kamaruzzaman Bustamam-Ahmad and Patrick Jory, 93–112. Kuala Lumpur: Yayasan Ilmuwan. http://dspace.fudutsinma.edu.ng/jspui/bitstream/123456 789/1358/1/IslamicStudiesandIslamicEducation%20%281%29.pdf#page=123.

Hasan, Noorhaidi. (2007b) "The Salafi Movement in Indonesia: Transnational Dynamics and Local Development." *Comparative Studies in South Asia, Africa and the Middle East* 27(1): 83–94. https://doi.org/10.1215/1089201x-2006-045.

Hasan, Noorhaidi. 2008. "The Salafi Madrasas of Indonesia." In *The Madrasa in Asia: Political Activism and Transnational Linkages*, edited by Farish A. Noor, Yoginder Sikand, and Martin van Bruinessen, 247–274. Amsterdam: Amsterdam University Press.

Hasan, Noorhaidi. 2010. "The Failure of the Wahhabi Campaign: Transnational Islam and the Salafi Madrasa in Post-9/11 Indonesia." *South East Asia Research* 18(4): 675–705. https://doi.org/10.5367/sear.2010.0015.

Hefner, Robert W. 2009. "Islamic Schools, Social Movements, and Democracy in Indonesia." In *Making Modern Muslims: The Politics of Islamic Education in Southeast Asia*, edited by Robert W. Hefner, 55–105. Honolulu: University of Hawai'i Press.

Islamic Foundation for Development. 2017. *Study in Madinah—2018/2019*. http://www.iffd-mw.org/education/bursary/study-in-madinah-20182019/ (accessed April 6, 2020).

Islamic University of Medina. 2019. *Required Documents*. https://admission.iu.edu.sa/RequiredDocuments.aspx?Id=100. (accessed April 5, 2020).

Islamic University of Medina. 2019. *University Vision and Mission*. https://enweb.iu.edu.sa/site_page/20987 (accessed April 6, 2020).

Ismail, Raihan. 2016. *Saudi Clerics and Shiʿa Islam*. New York: Oxford University Press.

Kaag, Mayke. 2007. "Aid, Umma, and Politics: Transnational Islamic NGOs in Chad." In *Islam and Muslim Politics in Africa*, edited by Benjamin F. Soares and René Otayek, 85–102. New York: Palgrave Macmillan.

Kaag, Mayke. 2011. "Connecting to the Umma through Islamic Relief: Transnational Islamic NGOs in Chad." *International Development Planning Review* 33(4): 463–474. https://doi.org/10.3828/idpr.2011.24.

Karčić, Harun. 2010. "Globalisation and Islam in Bosnia: Foreign Influences and Their Effects." *Totalitarian Movements and Political Religions* 11(2): 151–166. https://doi.org/10.1080/14690764.2010.511467.

Karčić, Harun. 2010. "Islamic Revival in Post-Socialist Bosnia and Herzegovina: International Actors and Activities." https://doi.org/10.1080/13602004.2010.533450.

Köni, Hakan. 2012. "Saudi Influences on Islamic Institutions in Turkey beginning in the 1970s." *The Middle East Journal* 66(1): 96–109. https://noi.org/10.3751/66.1.15.

Kourgiotis, Panos. 2016. "Salafism as a Tool of Post-Arab Spring Saudi Arabian Diplomacy." *Hemispheres* 31(1): 13–21. https://search.proquest.com/docview/1812376 283/fulltextPDF/9EC92A3929404B71PQ/1?accountid=14541.

Kraince, Richard G. 2009. "Reforming Islamic Education in Malaysia: Doctrine or Dialogue?" In *Making Modern Muslims: The Politics of Islamic Education in Southeast Asia*, edited by Robert W. Hefner, 106–140. Honolulu: University of Hawai'i Press.

Kroessn, Mohammed R., and Abdulfatah S. Mohamed. 2008. "Saudi Arabian NGOs in Somalia: 'Wahhabi' Daʿwah or Humanitarian Aid?" In *Development, Civil Society and Faith-Based Organizations: Bridging the Sacred and the Secular*, edited by Gerard Clarke and Michael Jennings, 187–213. London: Palgrave Macmillan.

Liow, Joseph Chinyong. 2009. "Islamic Education in Southern Thailand: Negotiating Islam, Identity, and Modernity." In *Making Modern Muslims: The Politics of Islamic Education in Southeast Asia*, edited by Robert W. Hefner, 141–171. Honolulu: University of Hawai'i Press.

Marchal, Roland, and Zakaria M. Sheikh. 2015. "Salafism in Somalia: Coping with Coercion, Civil War and Its Own Contradictions." *Islamic Africa* 6(1–2): 135–163.

Mårtensson, Ulrika. 2014. "Norwegian Haraki Salafism: 'The Saved Sect' Hugs the Infidels." *Comparative Islamic Studies* 8(1–2): 113–138. https://doi.org/10.1558/cis.v8i1-2.113.

McKenna, Thomas M., and Esmael A. Abdula. 2009. "Islamic Education in the Philippines: Political Separatism and Religious Pragmatism." In *Making Modern Muslims: The Politics of Islamic Education in Southeast Asia*, edited by Robert W. Hefner, 205–236. Honolulu: University of Hawai'i Press.

Merdjanova, Ina. 2016. *Rediscovering the Umma: Muslims in the Balkans between Nationalism and Transnationalism*. Oxford: Oxford University Press.

Morrison, Kenneth. 2008. *Wahhabism in the Balkans*. Defence Academy of the United Kingdom. https://www.files.ethz.ch/isn/50179/2008_March_Wahabism.pdf.

Musa, Mohd Faizal. 2018. "The Riyal and Ring-git of Petro-Islam: Investing Salafism in Education." In *Islam in Southeast Asia: Negotiating Modernity*, edited by Norshahril Saat, 63–90. Singapore: ISEAS—Yusof Ishak Institute.

Orkaby, Asher. 2017. *Beyond the Arab Cold War: The International History of the Yemen Civil War, 1962–68*. New York: Oxford University Press.

Østebø, Terje. 2011. *Localising Salafism: Religious Change among Oromo Muslims in Bale, Ethiopia*. Leiden: Brill.

Pall, Zoltan. 2018. *Salafism in Lebanon: Local and Transnational Movements*. New York: Cambridge University Press.

Pall, Zoltan, and Martijn de Koning. 2017. "Being and Belonging in Transnational Salafism: Informality, Social Capital and Authority in European and Middle Eastern Salafi Networks." *Journal of Muslims in Europe* 6(1): 76–103. https://doi.org/10.1163/22117954-12341338.

Petersen, Marie Juul. 2012. "Trajectories of Transnational Muslim NGOs." *Development in Practice* 22(5–6): 763–778. https://doi.org/10.1080/09614524.2012.685876.

Petersen, Marie Juul. 2016. *For Humanity or for the Umma?: Aid and Islam in Transnational Muslim NGOs*. London: Hurst.

Redissi, Hamadi. 2008. "The Refutation of Wahhabism in Arabic Sources, 1745–1932." In *Kingdom without Borders: Saudi Arabia's Political, Religious and Media Frontiers*, edited by Madawi Al-Rasheed, 157–182. New York: Oxford University Press.

Sadouni, Samadia. 2007. "New Religious Actors in Southern Africa: The Example of Islamic Humanitarianism." In *Islam and Muslim Politics in Africa*, edited by Benjamin F. Soares and René Otayek, 103–118. New York: Palgrave Macmillan.

Saggiomo, Valeria. 2011. "From Charity to Governance: Islamic NGOs and Education in Somalia." *The Open Area Studies Journal* 4: 53–61.

Salem, Zekeria Ould Ahmed. 2007. "Islam in Mauritania between Political Expansion and Globalization: Elites, Institutions, Knowledge, and Networks." In *Islam and Muslim Politics in Africa*, edited by Benjamin F. Soares and René Otayek, 27–46. New York: Palgrave Macmillan.

Salih, M. A. Mohamed. 2004. "Islamic N.G.O.s in Africa: The Promise and Peril of Islamic Volunteerism." In *Islamism and Its Enemies in the Horn of Africa*, edited by Alex de Waal, 146–181. Bloomington: Indiana University Press.

Saudi Arabia Scholarships. 2014. *Islamic University of Madinah Application for Scholarship Enrollment in the Bachelor's Degree, for the Academic Year 2015–2016.* https://www.facebook.com/ksascholarships/posts/islamic-university-of-madinah-application-for-scholarship-enrollment-in-the-bach/728359633907414/ (accessed April 6, 2020).

Shiozaki, Yuki. 2015. "From Mecca to Cairo: Changing Influences on Fatwas in Southeast Asia." In *Globalising Islam: Al-Azhar, Al-Medina and Al-Mustafa*, edited by Masooda Bano and Keiko Sakurai, 167–189. Edinburgh: Edinburgh University Press.

Souleimanov, Emil, and Maya Ehrmann. 2013. "The Rise of Militant Salafism in Azerbaijan and its Regional Implications." *Middle East Policy* 20(3): 111–120. https://doi.org/10.1111/mepo.12037.

Spannaus, Nathan. 2018. "Evolution of Saudi Salafism." In *Modern Islamic Authority and Social Change*, Volume 1: *Evolving Debates in Muslim Majority Countries*, edited by Masooda Bano, 150–171. Edinburgh: Edinburgh University Press.

Telci, Ismail Numan, and Aydzhan Yordanova Peneva. 2019. "Turkey and Saudi Arabia as Theo-political Actors in the Balkans: The Case of Bulgaria." *Insight Turkey* 21(2): 237–260. https://doi.org/10.25253/99.2019212.14.

Torelli, Stefano M., Favio Merone, and Francesco Cavatorta. 2012. "Salafism in Tunisia: Challenges and Opportunities for Democratization." *Middle East Policy* 19(4): 140–154. https://doi.org/10.1111/j.1475-4967.2012.00566.x.

van Bruinessen, Martin. 2008. "Traditionalist and Islamist Pesantrens in Contemporary Indonesia." In *The Madrasa in Asia: Political Activism and Transnational Linkages*, Edited by Farish A. Noor, Yoginder Sikand, and Martin van Bruinessen, 217–245. Amsterdam: Amsterdam University Press.

Wagemakers, Joas. 2012. "The Enduring Legacy of the Second Saudi State: Quietist and Radical Wahhabi Contestations of Al-Wala' wa-l-Bara'." *International Journal of Middle East Studies* 44(1): 93–110.

Wahid, Din. 2014. *Nuturing Salafi Manhaj: A Study of Salafi Pesantren in Contemporary Indonesia.* PhD thesis summary, *Wacana* 15(2): 367–376. https://doi.org/10.14764/10.ASEAS-2014.2-6.

Wehrey, Frederic, and Anouar Boukhars. 2019. *Salafism in the Maghreb: Politics, Piety, and Militancy.* New York: Oxford University Press.

Wiktorowicz, Quintan, and Suha Taji Farouki. 2000. "Islamic NGOs and Muslim Politics: A Case from Jordan." *Third World Quarterly* 21(4): 685–699. https://doi.org/10.1080/01436590050079065.

Woodward, Mark. 2017. "Resisting Salafism and the Arabization of Indonesian Islam: A Contemporary Indonesian Didactic Tale by Komaruddin Hidayat." *Contemporary Islam* 11: 237–258. https://doi.org/10.1007/s11562-017-0388-4.

Yizraeli, Sarah. 2012. *Politics and Society in Saudi Arabia: The Crucial Years of Development, 1960–1982.* London: Hurst.

4

Salafi Publishing and Contestation over Orthodoxy and Leadership in Sunni Islam

Andrew Hammond

Salafi publishing today is the outcome of a struggle over normativity within Sunni Islam that has characterized print culture since the late nineteenth century. This battle over orthodoxy played out among four constituencies: the modernist reform movement of Muhammad ʿAbduh (1849–1905) and Jamal al-Din Afghani (1838–1897); the Muslim Brotherhood and others who produced from the Islamic tradition a political ideology ("political Islam," or *al-islam al-siyasi*); the self-described Salafis who upheld the theology of Ibn Taymiyya and developed a radical critique of the premodern legal and theological culture of Cairo and Istanbul; and traditionalists who defended that system against the Salafi and modernist rebellions. This chapter will examine the origins of this conflict and its evolution to understand the nature of the contemporary struggle for the Muslim mainstream and Salafi Wahhabism's role within it.

Definitions

The problem of how to define Salafism is related to the broader question of the genesis of Sunni normativity in the classical period, especially on issues of creed, and the reification of the originalist principle that "earliest Islam is true Islam" and, furthermore, knowable. The term *ahl al-sunna* was first adopted by the ninth-century traditionist *hadith* movement associated with Ahmad ibn Hanbal (d. 855) to denote a specific program in law, theology, and devotion, centered on the claim to methodological supremacy of prophetic *hadith* in establishing this certain knowledge (Melchert 2002). Although the terminology was a polemical marker of separation in the sectarian milieu of the early Abbasid period, Sunnism came to be adopted by most groups except the Shiʿites as an umbrella term expressing a broad consensus underpinning divergence in law and theology.

Andrew Hammond, *Salafi Publishing and Contestation over Orthodoxy and Leadership in Sunni Islam*
In: *Wahhabism and the World*. Edited by: Peter Mandaville, Oxford University Press. © Oxford University Press 2022.
DOI: 10.1093/oso/9780197532560.003.0004

In this context, disputes came to be framed in terms of who represented the *salaf* more than others.

The word itself is rare in the earliest source material. It appears once in the Qur'an (43:56) to refer to Pharaoh's people who in drowning "we made a *salaf* [thing of the past] and an example to *al-akhirin* [those who came later]" (Melchert 2016, 34). Of the six canonical *hadith* collections, it comes once in the *Sahih* of Bukhari (d. 870) with the apparent meaning of companions of the Prophet (no. 5,423, titled "food, meat and other items the *salaf* would store in their houses and on journeys"), elsewhere referring to cash loans and advance payment for goods. Over 200 years later, Ghazali (d. 1111) says in *Iljam al-'Awamm 'an 'Ilm al-Kalam* (Restraining the Populace from Creedal Discussion) that he is writing to refute the claim that literal understandings of Qur'anic text describing God's powers in human terms (*tashbih*), a position that evolved in traditionist circles, represent the views of the *salaf* (*madhhab al-salaf*) (Ghazali 2017, 21–22). Another two centuries later, the Damascus Hanbali scholar Ibn Taymiyya (d. 1328) asserts once more that the traditionist program—untouched by Aristotelian logic, Neoplatonic philosophy, or the complex of Sufi and Shi'ite practices rooted in the notion of post-revelation divine charisma—reflects the position of the *salaf* (Ibn Taymiyya 1996, 141–166; 1972, 25).

With the spread of Ash'arism, Maturidism, and Sufism in the Ottoman arena, as well as Safavid Shi'ism, traditionist theology acquired a minority status in the post-classical world; Ibn Taymiyya himself became a somewhat marginal figure within Hanbalism (Melchert 2013). Following the Wahhabi movement's adoption of his ideas in the mid-eighteenth century, Arab scholars in the metropolitan centers of Damascus and Baghdad would rediscover him in a new struggle over normativity, this time in the context of modernity (Ahmed 2016, 92–97; Waardenburg 1979). Before the twentieth century there was no movement that used the name *salafi* as its prime designation or was recognized as such by others. In 1902, likely at the instigation of his acolyte Rashid Rida (1865–1935), 'Abduh used the term to describe a theological faction within Sunnism alongside Ash'arism (*ahl al-sunna, salafiyyin wa-asha'ira*) ('Abduh 1988, 27). While in describing these Salafis as "those who follow the creed of the *salaf*" (*al-akhidhin bi-'aqidat al-salaf*) 'Abduh appeared to validate traditionist claims, he did not describe himself as such a Salafi. After several decades of semantic competition over who could claim the mantle of *salafiyya*, the Syrian scholar Nasir al-Din al-Albani (1914–1999) decisively seized the term to denote his innovative and radical manifesto: an amalgam of Ibn Taymiyyan theology and excavation of an originalist law predating the formation of the classical schools and thus emanating in unmediated fashion from the Qur'an and prophetic *hadith* (al-Albani 1999, 142–144). This latter idea emerged from the long tradition critiquing *taqlid* (precedent within the corpus of a school's legal writing) and advocating *ijtihad* (direct access to earliest sources) (Ibrahim 2016). Having won widespread acceptance, al-Albani's term is often backdated to refer to Ibn Taymiyya's thought or Hanbalism more generally, though such usages are ahistorical.

While 'Abduh's ideas overlapped with those of Ibn Taymiyya's followers on some points—notably in his rejection of both adherence to the legal school and necessity of belief in the miraculous powers of saints (*karamat al-awliya*) ('Abduh 1994, 181–183)—his modernist agenda was of a fundamentally different nature. Responding to the challenge of European rationalist philosophy, 'Abduh and Afghani hoped to constitute an efficient scripture-based modern religion from the multiplicity of the Islamic tradition, and through this Reformation—a term used explicitly by Afghani (Afghani 1915, 65–66)—in order to help Muslim society attain the technical progress and political strength of the West. With the fall of the Ottoman Empire and its replacement with a radical secular-nationalist regime rejecting religious faith, practice, and institutions, the center of gravity in the western Islamicate shifted to Egypt, where this modernism (or renewal, *tajdid*) was, in the early decades of the twentieth century, ascendant. On the one hand, it produced a socially, politically, and economically liberal reformism that reframed Islam as a calque on Enlightenment religion, and on the other, it led to ideological movements such as the Muslim Brotherhood working within the paradigm of modern political systems (*shari'a* courts with parliaments, nation-states with caliphate, etc.). The success of the Saudi Wahhabi movement in securing an internationally recognized state by 1932 created a productive zone for the elaboration of Ibn Taymiyya's thinking, and Rashid Rida's interest in centering his discourse of Arab-Islamic revival around Ibn Taymiyya provided Wahhabism with a path to respectability after long being considered a fanatical outlier in cosmopolitan Arab culture.

Cairo: The First Battleground

Pro–Ibn Taymiyya publishing was centered around publishing houses which engaged in a combination of reproducing classical texts and issuing new works that both discussed those texts and addressed contemporary debates. These included *al-Manar*, established by Rida; the Kurdistan al-'Ilmiyya printing press of Faraj Allah al-Kurdi (d. 1940), a Kurdish emigre in Cairo; the Salafiyya publishing house established in 1909 by Rida's Syrian colleague Muhibb al-Din al-Khatib (1886–1969); and the publishing arm of the Egyptian Ansar al-Sunna al-Muhammadiyya organization of Muhammad Hamid al-Fiqi (1892–1959) (Khan 2016, 63, 93). Rashid Rida tried hard to marry 'Abduh's modernism with Ibn Taymiyya's system. Rida's footnotes to 'Abduh's signature work *Risalat al-Tawhid* rebuked him for not citing "the great renewer" (*al-mujaddid al-'azim*) in his survey of Muslim theology ('Abduh 1942, 26) and removed 'Abduh's section containing the traditional Ash'ari-Maturidi description of the written Qur'anic text, its vocalized recitation, and auditory reception as "created" (*makhluq*), since that was to veer from Ibn Taymiyya's traditionist thesis of the Qur'an as the uncreated word of God ('Abduh 2003, 53–55).

The Saudi entry into this field began in the 1920s once 'Abd al-'Aziz had completed his territorial expansions in the Hijaz, giving him access to pilgrim revenues. Both Rida and al-Fiqi's publishing activities received financial support from the Saudi state (Redissi 2008, 175–176), al-Fiqi was appointed to head government publishing in Mecca (al-Tahir 2004, 91), and the Syrian '*alim* Muhammad Bahjat al-Baytar, another of the Damascus scholars interested in Ibn Taymiyya, was invited to head a short-lived Islamic Institute (al-Ma'had al-Islami) in Mecca (Mouline 2014, 9, 111). In 1927 the Cairo Salafiyya publishing network opened a store and printing press in Mecca and in Multan in British India. A key figure to emerge at this time was the Jeddan notable Muhammad Nasif (1885–1971), who collaborated with al-Baytar and later al-Albani in publishing their work under the banner of Salafism (Commins 2015, 159–161).

'Abduh-inspired *tajdid* blossomed in the period between the end of the First World War and military coup of 1952, acquiring a hegemonic position in public space through the support of leading scholars at al-Azhar, print media, and intellectuals generating a reform literature known as *Islamiyyat* (Gershoni and Jankowski 1995). Thus, 'Ali 'Abd al-Raziq lost his status as both judge and credentialed Azhari '*alim* over his book *al-Islam wa-Usul al-Hukm* (Islam and the Foundations of Governance, 1925), which advanced Islamic justifications for a secular-nationalist political order with neither caliph nor *shari'a* court, but later served as minister of religious endowments in the period 1947–1949. Similarly, Taha Husayn became dean of Fuad (Cairo) University's faculty of arts years after *Fi-l-Shi'r al-Jahili* (On Jahili Poetry, 1926) saw him dismissed from the same university for suggesting that early Arabic poetry had been falsely backdated to pre-Islamic times. This era also saw Mustafa al-Maraghi, *shaykh* of al-Azhar in the periods 1937–1929 and 1935–1945, argue that it was unreasonable (*min ghayr al-ma'qul*) for legal texts of the early Islamic period to apply today (Sabri 1981, 285, 359); Shaykh Mahmud Shaltut, *shaykh* of al-Azhar from 1958 to 1963, question elements of the Qur'anic resurrection (Shaltut 1942, 515–517); and the writers Muhammad Husayn Haykal and 'Abbas al-'Aqqad try to normalize understandings of the Prophet as merely a genius among men, following the example of Afghani and 'Abduh (Afghani and 'Abduh 2002, 152–153). Theologically this project was as grand as it was doomed to failure with the turn toward religious conservativism following the collapse of the Arab nationalist project in the 1960s (though it continued through the liberal and progressive

Islam projects of figures such as Fazlur Rahman, Leonard Binder, Nasr Hamid Abu Zayd, and others in Western academia). It had sought no less than loosening the notion of God as the immediate cause of all things, aligning the Qur'an with empiricism and European science through rethinking miracles and prophethood ('Abduh 1906, 334–335), and asserting free will over predetermination (Afghani and 'Abduh 2014, 81–88). Muhammad Farid Wajdi, editor of *Majallat al-Azhar*, even introduced new vocabulary such as *i'tiqadiyyun* as an alternative to *mu'minun*, a calque on the English/French *believer/croyant* (Wajdi 1945, 57–60); and, following the path of Turkish Kemalism and Soviet communism, some writers openly embraced atheism (Adham 1937; al-Qasimi 1946).

By the late 1940s, the Muslim Brotherhood had established an extensive publishing network, including the outlets *al-Da'wa* and *al-Muslimun*, and short-lived experiments bringing together leftist and Islamist writers such as *al-Fikr al-Jadid* (January–March 1948), owned by Muhammad Hilmi al-Minyawi, a member of the Brotherhood's consultative assembly, and published by Brotherhood-linked publishing house Dar al-Kitab al-'Arabi (Sabaseviciute 2018). The face of Brotherhood publishing changed dramatically after the Islamist turn of Sayyid Qutb (1906–1966) and his prolific output via journals such as *al-Thaqafa*, *al-Risala*, and *Majallat al-Ikhwan al-Muslimin*, and his well-known series of books beginning with *al-'Adala al-Ijtima'iyya fi al-Islam* (Social Justice in Islam, 1949).

Brotherhood discourse typically made appeals to all sides in the disputes of the era, accepting a looser approach to the legal school but avoiding the minutiae of debate over creed. This was the intent behind al-Banna's statement of purpose at the Fifth Conference in 1939: the Brotherhood was not only a Salafi calling, but a Sunni *tariqa* and a Sufi truth (al-Banna 1965, 248). In this spirit, al-Banna also established links with the traditionalists who opposed these challenges to premodern Islamic epistemology and its institutions. In the 1940s he took as an advisor the late Ottoman mufti Mustafa Sabri (1869–1954) (Munir 2019), Ataturk's most implacable foe among the 'ulama, who fled Istanbul in 1922 and settled in Egypt in 1930. Al-Banna paid for the publication of Sabri's refutation of the modernists, *al-Qawl al-Fasl bayn Alladhina Yu'minun bi-l-Ghayb wa-Alladhina La Yu'minun* (The Definitive Word on Those Who Believe in the Unseen and Those Who Don't, 1942), and the small cohort of Turkish students in Sabri's circle were all followers of al-Banna and the Brotherhood (Düzdağ 2007, 249–296; Cenkçiler 2005, 25, 40–41, 91, 116, 118, 127).

Traditionalists Push Back against the Salafis and Modernists

The strongest challenge to the aggressive propagandization of Ibn Taymiyya came from Sabri's deputy in the Istanbul, Zahid Kevseri (1879–1952), or al-Kawthari as he was known in Arabic. In his Egyptian exile, al-Kawthari gathered classical manuscripts from libraries in Cairo, Damascus, and Jerusalem that responded to traditionist creed, publishing them with critical commentary. Al-Kawthari's prolonged engagement with the discourse of Salafism helped shape how al-Albani came to define and contextualize Salafism from the 1960s. Al-Kawthari's concerns were threefold: the normalization of the theology of Ibn Taymiyya after centuries of marginalization (El-Rouayheb 2010); radical rejection of the legal school, a trend he dubbed *la-madhhabiyya*, much to al-Albani's irritation (al-Buti 1970, 15–26); and the claim to the imprimatur of *salafiyya* with its implicit conferral of legitimacy upon those positions. Informed by the Hanafi law and Maturidi creed of Ottoman intellectual culture, al-Kawthari derided these views as the "false Salafism" (*salafiyya za'ifa*) (al-Kawthari 2005, 40) of *mutasallifun*— amateurs unfit for the '*alim*'s task of guarding the great tradition of Muslim knowledge (al-Kawthari 1990, 105).

The three creedal positions of Ibn Taymiyya that troubled al-Kawthari and by which Salafism would define itself were: rejection of intercession (*tawassul*); rejection of delayed judgment on faith (*irja*) and the related requirement for continuous proof of faith through actions; and anthropomorphic understandings of God. Al-Kawthari's first extant work, *Irgham al-Murid* (The Discipline of the Sufi Disciple, 1910), was intended as a repudiation of the anti-Sufi discourse emanating from Ibn Taymiyya's followers in Damascus and Baghdad. Early on in the work al-Kawthari set himself the task of refuting Ibn Taymiyya and celebrating faith as curated by Sufism, before elaborating on the history of the Gümüşhanevi line of the Khalidi Naqshbandi order to which his family belonged (al-Kawthari 2000c, 5–6). Al-Kawthari rejected the validity of two *hadith*s (nos. 969, 970) from the canonical collection of Muslim Nishapuri (d. 875) in which companions cite prophetic practice to justify destroying the shrines of Sufi saints. His logic was that since most Muslim communities over the centuries had not considered the *hadith*s as engendering a requirement to shun intercessionary practices, that cannot have been their intent (al-Kawthari 2000a).

Regarding *irja*, broad principles for accepting that a Muslim had truly attained faith (*iman*) while leaving ultimate judgement to God were upheld by Abu Hanifa, eponymous founder of the Hanafi school, but were rejected by the traditionist Hanbalis. Much to al-Kawthari's consternation, partisans of Ibn Taymiyya, including al-Fiqi and Nasif, managed to publish in Egypt and India with Azhari approval a classical text, *Tarikh Baghdad* (The History of Baghdad) by the preacher al-Khatib al-Baghdadi (1002–1071), containing criticism of Abu Hanifa on this point. Al-Kawthari's rebuttal, *Ta'nib al-Khatib* (Rebuking al-Khatib, 1941), attacked the credibility of the *hadith* reports in question (al-Kawthari 1990, 105, 83–103, 131–134, 319–320). In one, Abu Hanifa responds in the affirmative when asked if a man who kills his father, drinks from his skull, then fornicates with his mother should be considered a believer (*mu'min*) (al-Kawthari, 1990, 85–87). Al-Kawthari said the *hadith* must be a partisan fabrication because no transmitter of good character would have related such an absurd incident, but he added that despite the extremity of the case the basic principle holds that the established faith of Muslims cannot be invalidated by circumstantial acts, and were it not for the widespread acceptance of this principle over the centuries, it would have been possible "to declare the mass of fallible Muslims unbelievers" (al-Kawthari 1990, 91). Al-Kawthari was challenging the system of Ibn Taymiyya, which posits a state of godliness above *iman* called *ihsan* that through the constant test of actions, which could include jihad against *kuffar* (Ibn Taymiyya 1996), provides a better guarantee of salvation.

On the third point, Ibn Taymiyya said that allegorical interpretation (*ta'wil*) placed limits on God's will and power, and drew on the writings of 'Uthman bin Said al-Darimi (d. 893/894), a student of Ahmad ibn Hanbal, to argue that the revealed text intended man to understand God's powers in terms of movement exactly as written. While to al-Kawthari and other scholars in the Ottoman world this was rank anthropomorphism (*tajsim*), Ibn Taymiyya's point was a nominalistic one that rejected the Aristotelian language of universals and particulars and more broadly the prism of Greek thought through which scholars in the Ash'ari-Maturidi tradition viewed Islam. God has no like, no universal to which he can be compared; thus, the language used to describe Him in scripture is to be taken at face value without speculation (von Kügelgen 2013).

Al-Albani's Formulation of Salafism

Al-Kawthari came to function as the organizing Other in al-Albani's construction of *salafiyya* as the original Islam before the paradigmatic grip of law, theology, and philosophy inflicted their epistemic violence (Olidort 2015, 193–199). Al-Albani's claim was that it is necessary for a Muslim, freed from the legal *madhhab* and guided by the creed of Ibn Taymiyya, to declare his *manhaj* as *salafi*, meaning to have certitude of living by Qur'an and *hadith*-sourced original Islam (Hadi 2013). To this program al-Albani added rejection of the Muslim Brotherhood's choice to accept basic elements of Western liberal democracy (Pierret 2013, 107).

By 1960 al-Albani had begun prosecuting his case for Salafism outside Syria. During a visit to Cairo that year, he was introduced at a lecture in the offices of Ansar al-Sunna al-Muhammadiyya as *al-shaykh al-salafi* who had gained renown for his *salafiyya*, and his method in law and creed was described as emulation of the Prophet alone. In his talk he denounced intercession and defended the theory of God's movement, referring to Muslims who uphold these positions as *salafiyyun*, with the clarifying moniker *muhammadiyyun* (al-Albani 1960). In 1961, he was among many scholars invited by Saudi Arabia to teach at the new Islamic University of Medina. Despite his view that legitimate rulers of Muslim society need not come from the clan of Quraysh, his suggestion that Ibn 'Abd al-Wahhab wasn't fully *salafi* because of his attachment to Hanbali law stirred unease among Wahhabi scholars, leading to his abrupt departure in 1963. He was also criticized for equivocating on the status of faith, suggesting a believer could be forgiven neglect of proscribed prayer or visiting shrines if unaware of the error (Hadi 2013, 79), and arguing the licit nature of attire that leaves a woman's face uncovered (viz. his book *Hijab al-Mar'a al-Muslima fi-l-Kitab wa-l-Sunna*, 1952). But al-Albani won lasting admirers in the country. His supporters included 'Abd al-'Aziz ibn Baz (1910–1999), whom King Fahd appointed in 1992 to the chairmanship of both the Council of Senior Scholars (Majlis Hay'at Kibar al-'Ulama) and its Permanent Committee for Scholarly Research and Fatwas (Lacroix 2009; Olidort 2015, 169–202); and in 1966 his Saudi disciples established an informal group they called the al-Jama'a al-Salafiyya al-Muhtasiba (the Salafi Hisba Group, or Salafi Group for Promoting Virtue and Preventing Vice).

Al-Albani first mentions al-Kawthari in print in 1954, faulting him for having authenticated a *hadith* sourced to 'Ali ibn Abi Talib's mother in which the Prophet approves intercession (al-Albani 1954, 657–664; al-Kawthari 2000b, 350). The intent was to assert Salafism's claim to a superior methodology in *hadith* establishing certain knowledge of divine truth, rather than the biases he saw in the approach of scholars in the Cairo-Istanbul nexus (although al-Albani was accused of a similarly cavalier attitude toward *hadith*) (Melchert 2016, 43–51). In 1966, al-Albani attached himself to the anti-Kawthari activities of the Jeddan publisher Nasif, authoring the introduction to the second edition of *al-Tankil Bima fi Ta'nib al-Kawthari min al-Abatil* (Vituperation of the Nonsense in al-Kawthari's *Ta'nib*, 1966), a refutation of al-Kawthari's *Ta'nib al-Khatib* by 'Abd al-Rahman al-Mu'allimi, a Yemeni *hadith* scholar based in Mecca, that Nasif first published in 1949.

Accusing al-Kawthari (incorrectly) of rejecting single-source (*ahad*) reports tout court, he expanded the attack in a third edition, published in Cairo in 1968 (al-Albani 1999, 143; al-Albani 1986, 171–175). This war of the scholars continued with the 1971 imprint of al-Albani's commentary on the tenth-century creedal work of the jurist Abu Ja'far al-Tahawi (d. 933) known as *al-'Aqida al-Tahawiyya* (The Tahawi Creed), a Hanafi text conciliatory toward Hanbali theology and the new normal of *hadith*–based *fiqh* (Melchert 1997, 116–123). Al-Albani's long introduction described al-Kawthari as an irredeemably fanatical Hanafi (*hanafi halik fi-l-ta'assub*) who denies God's attributes (*jahmi mu'attil*) (al-Albani 1971, 44–5), and attacked 'Abd al-Fattah Abu Ghudda—a student of al-Kawthari who later served as head of the Syrian Muslim Brotherhood—for choosing loyalty to al-Kawthari over the Salafism of Ibn Taymiyya and Ibn ʿAbd al-Wahhab (al-Albani 1971, 47). He was particularly outraged at al-Kawthari's reasoning on the construction of shrines (al-Albani 1971, 32–33), and revisited these arguments in the preface to his abridged edition of al-Dhahabi's *Al-ʿUluww li-l-ʿAliyy al-Ghaffar* (The Elevated Location of God), a theological work by the well-known student of Ibn Taymiyya (al-Albani 1981, 15).

Al-Kawthari became the Salafis' bête noire. On the one hand, in his account of membership in the Salafi Hisba Group, a faction of which under Juhayman al-ʿUtaybi launched the failed Mecca insurrection in 1979, Nasir al-Huzaymi recounts how al-Albani was the centripetal figure of their Salafi movement and al-Kawthari was its enemy (al-Huzaymi 2011, 14–15, 169). On the other, there are the numerous anti-Kawthari works published by figures in the Salafi-Wahhabi orbit over the years, the most prominent of which include writings by judge Bakr Abu Zayd (1944–2008), a member of the Council of Senior Scholars and permanent *fatwa* committee, such as *Baraʾat Ahl al-Sunni min al-Waqiʿa fi ʿUlama al-Islam* (Absolving Sunnis of Guilt in Slandering Islam's ʿUlama, 1987). Published by the Saudi Ministry of Information, this book included a preface from the head of the government publication arm known as the combined directorates of religious research, *fatwa*-giving, preaching, and guidance, established in 1971 (al-Yassini 1985, 71), that condemned al-Kawthari as a "sinful criminal" (*al-mujrim al-athim*) and Abu Ghudda for his attachment to him (Abu Zayd 1987, 3). Other notable books in this tradition include Sadiq bin Salim bin Sadiq's *Takhil al-ʿAyn bi-Jawaz al-Suʾal ʿan "Allah Ayn?"* (Refinement Attained Through the Question of "Where Is God?", 2007), a Saudi Salafi attack on al-Kawthari's Maturidi creed and anti-Salafi polemics; Moroccan *shaykh* Ahmad al-Ghumari (d. 1960)'s *Bayan Talbis al-Muftari Muhammad Zahid al-Kawthari* (Clarification of al-Kawthari's Deceits, 1993), accusing him of Hanafi bias and printed posthumously through the efforts of Bakr Abu Zayd; and *Tanbih al-Bahith al-Sirri ila Ma Fi Rasaʾil wa-Taʿaliq al-Kawthari* (A Warning about al-Kawthari's Letters and Commentaries, 1948) by Muhammad al-ʿArabi ibn al-Tabbani (d. 1970), an Algerian who taught at the mosque schools in Mecca and Medina.

Saudi Arabia and Global Salafi Publishing

Spurred by al-Albani's work, Saudi Arabia became the center for a vast publishing enterprise applying the Salafi label to three broad groups of people: Ibn Taymiyya and theologians sharing his views on intercession, God's movement, Qurʾanic hermeneutics, the question of faith and action, and the primacy of prophetic *hadith*; al-Albani and scholars around the region who studied under him; and contemporary Wahhabi lights such as Ibn Baz and Muhammad ibn Salih al-ʿUthaymin (1925–2001). The project proceeded despite ambivalence about the term *Salafism* among the official organs of Saudi Islam. The Mecca-based World Muslim League's Islamic Fiqh Council issued a resolution in 1987, and republished in its journal in 2005, condemning both *la-madhhabiyya* and excessive attachment to the legal school (*al-taʿassub al-madhhabi*) (*Majallat al-Majmaʿ* 2005, 383–6). The default Wahhabi position was that since Muhammad Ibn ʿAbd al-Wahhab was merely a renewer (*mujaddid*) of normative Sunni faith and practice, his mission was above terminological innovation. Between 1960 and 2000, more than 300 classic Hanbali works were edited and published in Saudi Arabia, suggesting that official Wahhabism was more interested in establishing itself as the heir of classical Hanbalism than in appropriating Salafism (Mouline 2014, 45). For many years the government also promoted the works of Brotherhood thinkers like Qutb, until it soured on political Islam in the early 2000s.

From the 1980s, Saudi foreign policy weaponized Saudi Islam under the banner of Salafism to meet three challenges that emerged in the period 1979–1980: the Wahhabi insurrection in Mecca, the Iranian Revolution, and the Soviet invasion of Afghanistan. King Fahd ordered the publication of a new edition of the Qurʾan for global distribution through the King Fahd Complex for Printing the Holy Qurʾan, the first such undertaking since al-Azhar published its version in 1926 following the dissolution of the Ottoman caliphate. Government funding for its ʿulama-run coercive apparatus known as the Committee for Enjoining Virtue and Forsaking Vice more than doubled between 1979 and 1985, and in 1994 the organization launched the journal *Majallat al-Hisba*, reasserting the state's monopoly in the policing of public morality *contra* the volunteerism implicit in Salafism (Mouline 2014, 213). Huge budgets were made available to numerous Islamic institutions, including the Council of Senior Scholars; and the Saudi government worked with its US counterpart to facilitate the activities of Afghan mujahidin fighting the Soviet occupation. Salafism was also a convenient label for Saudi Islam in the context of Wahhabism's demonization in Western media after the Al-Qaeda attacks of September 11, 2001. Two examples illustrate how the term acquired common usage in English: in *Globalized Islam: The Search for a New Ummah* (2004), Olivier Roy substituted Salafism for what he previously called neo-fundamentalism, and the 2015 edition of Raymond Hinnebusch's *The International Politics of the Middle East* (2003), a standard work in the field, included a discussion of what he termed as Saudi state support for Salafi networks in Egypt and Syria (Hinnebusch 2015, 84).

The most important outlet for al-Albani's work in the 1960s and 1970s was the al-Maktab al-Islami. This was a publication house established in 1957 in

Damascus and Beirut by his collaborator Zuhayr al-Shawish (1925–2013) with funding from the *amir* 'Ali ibn 'Abdullah Al Thani (d. 1974) of Qatar, where Wahhabi Hanbalism had official sanction. Qatar also paid for the distribution of al-Maktab al-Islami's books in Jordan, India, and Pakistan (al-Ahmari 2019). This was part of a Qatari project to disseminate Salafi-Wahhabi works managed by Shaykh 'Abdullah Ibrahim al-Ansari (al-Ansari 2019), head of the Department for Islamic Affairs, who had studied in Mecca under another *shaykh* who authored an anti-Kawthari text (Hamza 1950). As a smaller state, Qatar could be more flexible than Saudi authorities in printing al-Albani's controversial works (Olidort 2015, 120), though his books were also published in Kuwait by Dar al-Arqam and in Egypt by Matba'at al-Taraqqi (Olidort 2015, 120). The arrangement effectively came to an end with Qatar's mass propagation of Muslim Brotherhood thought via Al Jazeera from 1996, but Saudi Arabia had already become the linchpin of a vast publishing enterprise, some of it government sponsored, some of it private, and some of it occupying territory in between.

Islamic institutions in Saudi Arabia produced many scholars who took the Salafi-Wahhabi brand to other countries. For example, Iraqi Turkmen 'Abdullah ibn 'Abd al-Hamid (b. 1958) established the Guraba publishing house in Istanbul in 1992, using his Turkish name Abdullah Yolcu, after studying in Saudi Arabia with Ibn Baz, al-'Uthaymin, Salih al-Fawzan (b. 1933), and others (Yolcu 2020), with the aim of countering the Hanafi-Maturidism of Ottoman-Turkish Islam and its Sufi practices (Yolcu 2017). Guraba publishes the works of al-Albani and these Saudi scholars in Arabic and translated into Turkish, as well as Yolcu's books, which were originally published in Saudi Arabia with government and private publishers. For example, Yolcu's *Self-i Salihin Akidesi* (Creed of the Pious Ancestors) was first published by the Turkish Islamist newspaper *Akit* in 1999 and then by Guraba in 2011, based on an Arabic original published by Guraba in 1997, and later by the Saudi Islamic affairs ministry in 2002 as *al-Wajiz fi 'Aqidat al-Salaf al-Salih*. Yolcu's *Ehl-i Sünnet ve'l-Cemaat'e Göre İman* (Faith According to the Sunni Tradition, 2014) is the translation of an Arabic original published by Saudi private publisher Madar al-Watan in 2003, *Al-Iman: Haqiqatuhu, Khawarimuhu, Nawaqiduhu 'ind Ahl al-Sunna wa-l-Jama'a*. These publishing activities expanded in the era of the Turkish Justice and Development Party (AKP) after it came to power in 2002, and further still from 2011 with the influx of Syrian refugees from civil war (Köni 2012; Hammond 2017). The overarching message of Yolcu's works is that Turkey is a nominally Muslim society on the edge of *kufr* in both its secular and Muslim culture.

Saudi publishers will often brand modern theoretical works as well as classical texts with the Salafi label, even if their authors did not use such language. For example, Muhammad Sultan al-Ma'sumi (1880–1960), a Tajik *shaykh* who settled in Mecca, published a book in Cairo in 1949 advocating direct access to

Qur'an and *hadith* titled *Hal al-Muslim Mulzam bi-Ittiba' Madhhab Mu'ayyan min al-Madhahib al-Arba'a?* (Is the Muslim Required to Follow One of the Four Schools?). The 1984 imprint, published in Riyadh by the Center for Studies on the Salafi Method (Markaz al-Dirasat al-Manhajiyya al-Salafiyya), appends the honorific title *al-salafi* to his surname. Al-Albani's followers such as Muqbil al-Wadi'i (1993–2001) and 'Abd al-Rahman 'Abd al-Khaliq (1939–2020) made Jordan, Kuwait, and Yemen notable regions for spreading his ideas in print, and Amman houses the Imam al-Albani Studies Centre (https://www.alalbany.org/). Some figures such as Rabi' al-Madkhali and Muhammad Aman al-Jami developed his ideas on quietist accommodation with Muslim rulers who deserve some level of opprobrium (Lacroix 2009, 74–76; Haykel 2009, 49), while others such as Abu Muhammad al-Maqdisi (b. 1959) developed insurrectionary views of Muslim rulers, including the Al Sa'ud and *'ulama* who defend their legitimacy (al-Maqdisi 1989). This ambiguous stance on questions of quietism and resistance—the broad range of opinions as well as the liminal position of some scholars (viz. al-Albani's contacts with Juhayman's faction, the Egyptian Jama'at al-Muslimin of Shukri Mustafa, and the Egyptian al-Jama'a al-Islamiyya)—is reflected in groups such as ISIS that operate broadly within Salafi-Wahhabi lines and include *irja* near the top of their list of theological heresies. So just as there are different views within Wahhabism regarding the Salafi project, Salafism has its own variety of opinions regarding Wahhabism. Yet the agreements between Salafism and Wahhabism are greater than their disagreements, and while most literature bearing the Salafi imprint would find approval among Saudi scholars, most Saudi religious literature could be considered Salafi even if it does not expressly declare itself so.

One important forum for the dissemination of this Salafi-Wahhabi literature is the *hajj* pilgrimage. *Hajj* is the occasion for distributing dozens of short booklets to hundreds of thousands of pilgrims in Arabic, English, Urdu, Malay, French, Turkish, and other languages of major pilgrim groups. These will be abridged works on faith and pilgrim rituals by, mainly, Ibn Taymiyya, Ibn 'Abd al-Wahhab, and Ibn Baz, issued by both Saudi private publishers and the government. Pilgrims, expatriates, and Saudis visiting the bookstores of Mecca, Riyadh, and other cities will find annotated versions of classical works of *tafsir, fiqh,* and *'aqida* in the Salafi-Wahhabi pantheon such as Ibn Kathir, Ibn Qudama, Ibn Hazm, Ibn al-Qayyim, Ibn Taymiyya, and Ibn 'Abd al-Wahhab, or glosses by modern scholars such as Ibn Baz, al-'Uthaymin, and al-Albani, as well as the canonical *hadith* collections and reworkings of them that al-Albani Salafism made its forte. A genre of note in the Saudi literature is that of life guidance, which merges *hadith* material on manners, conduct, and ethics with the self-help genre popular among Western reading publics. In the former category belongs al-Albani's abridged version of Ibn Taymiyya's *al-Kalim al-Tayyib*

(The Goodly Word), published by al-Maktab al-Islami and widely available in Saudi bookstores, and to the latter belong ʿAʾid al-Qarni's books *La Tahzan* (Don't Despair, 2002) and *Asʿad Imraʾa fi-l-ʿAlam* (The Happiest Woman in the World, 2003), both of which have sold millions of copies in many languages. Like Ottoman ʿalim Said Nursi's mid-twentieth-century *Risale-i Nur* series, al-Qarni's books set as their task the repudiation of non-Islamic Western systems in which the modern Muslim could mistakenly seek refuge from the anguish and dejection caused by what al-Qarni calls *ilhad* (atheism) and Nursi calls *maddiyya* (materialism) (al-Qarni 2007, 10; Nursi 1994, 221).

So Salafi publishing around the world is in one way or another an extension of publishing activities in Saudi Arabia and neighboring countries. One of the most prominent is Darussalam, founded in 1986 by a private individual in Riyadh, with branches all over the world, including London and Houston. The nodal point for a network of Islamic publishers, Darussalam is an online source for translations in English, Urdu, Hindi, Farsi, Spanish, Bengali, Indonesian, and many other languages of works in the Salafi-Wahhabi canon, including generic material such as Qurʾan and *hadith* collections. Among its bestsellers are Ibn ʿAbd al-Wahhab's *Kitab al-Tawhid*, al-Qarni's *La Tahzan*, al-ʿUthaymin's commentary on Ibn Taymiyya's *al-ʿAqida al-Wasatiyya*, Qurʾan translations, and Bukhari's *Sahih* (the UK site is https://darussalam.com/; the US site is http://dar-us-salam.com/).

Another notable online publisher is the Salafi Bookstore of Birmingham in England, which has a similar but smaller collection of materials in English and Arabic (https://salafibookstore.com/). However, the fact is that all manner of Islamic materials in Arabic, both classical and contemporary, excluding the most recent works, can be accessed via free download from a plethora of websites. This is a consequence of both the parlous state of intellectual copyright across the Arabophone world and the desire among Muslim scholars and their followers to spread Islamic knowledge as widely as possible, a desire as much philanthropic as it is driven by the conflict over establishing normativity in Sunni Islam.

Conclusion

Publishing was a field of intense contestation throughout the modern period in which several trends vied for status, legitimacy, and influence. It was an integral part of Salafi Wahhabism's successes in the Sunni public sphere, successes attained despite the absence of major change in the officially sanctioned legal and creedal rites of most Muslim countries. Print and latterly internet and transnational television have had huge impacts on Salafi Wahhabism's reach among Muslim populations at large and their views of certain beliefs and practices, even seeping into the ideology of rival movements such as the Muslim Brotherhood (Tamam 2010). That which is today defined as Salafi acquired this predominant position through the sponsorship of the Saudi state, the increasing resources it could devote to disseminating religious discourse, and the intellectual exertions of figures such as al-Albani and those he inspired. More broadly, through the discourse of Salafism, creedal and behavioral orthodoxy, scriptural authority versus the multiplicity of tradition, and the *shari'a* of the *'ulama* and *ma'rifa* of the Sufis as incompatible paths to God—these became critical issues defining Muslim religion in the modern era.

References

'Abduh, Muhammad. 1906. "Bab Tafsir al Qur'an al-Hakim." *al-Manar* 9(5): 334–335.

'Abduh, Muhammad. 1942. *Risalat al-Tawhid*, edited by Rashid Rida. Cairo: al-Manar.

'Abduh, Muhammad. 1988 [1905]. *Al-Islam wa-l-Nasraniyya fi-l-'Ilm wa-l-Madaniyya*. Beirut: Dar al-Hadatha.

'Abduh, Muhammad. 1994. *Risalat al-Tawhid*, edited by Muhammad 'Imara. Cairo: Dar al-Shuruq.

'Abduh, Muhammad. 2003. *Risalat al-Tawhid*, edited by Mahmud Abu Rayya. Cairo: Dar al-Ma'arif.

Abu Zayd, Bakr. 1987. *Bara'at Ahl al-Sunna min al-Waqi'a fi 'Ulama al-Islam*. Riyadh: Wizarat al-I'lam.

Adham, Ismail. 1937. *Limadha Ana Mulhid*. Alexandria: Matba'at al-Ta'awun.

Afghani, Jamal al-Din. 1915 [1886]. *Al-Radd 'ala al-Dahriyyin*, translated by Muhammad 'Abduh and 'Arif Efendi. Cairo: Matba'at al-Jamaliyya.

Afghani, Jamal al-Din, and Muhammad 'Abduh. 2002 [1904]. *Al-Ta'liqat 'ala Sharh al-'Aqa'id al-'Adudiyya*. Cairo: Maktabat al-Shuruq al-Dawliyya.

Afghani, Jamal al-Din, and Muhammad 'Abduh. 2014. *Al-'Urwa al-Wuthqa*. Cairo: Hindawi.

Al-Ahmari, Muhammad. 2019. Interview with Saudi intellectual. Doha, November 12.

Ahmed, Shahab. 2016. *What Is Islam?: The Importance of Being Islamic*. Princeton, NJ: Princeton University Press.

Al-Albani, Nasir al-Din. 1954. "Silsilat al-Ahadith al-Da'ifa: 3." *Al-Tamaddun al-Islami* 21: 657–664.

Al-Albani, Nasir al-Din. 1960. Lecture. http://www.4shared.com/file/75693629/8f9c2cdd/albani-1960.html?dirPwdVerified=4f3514e1 (accessed April 26, 2019).

Al-Albani, Nasir al-Din al-Albani. 1971. *Sharh al-'Aqida al-Tahawiyya*. Beirut: al-Maktab al-Islami.

Al-Albani, Nasir al-Din. 1981. *Mukhtasar al-'Uluww li-l-'Ali al-Ghaffar, Ta'lif al-Hafiz Shams al-Din al-Dhahabi*. Beirut: al-Maktab al-Islami.

Al-Albani, Nasir al-Din. 1986 [1965]. "Preface to al-Tankil," 2nd edition. In *Al-Tankil bi-ma fi Ta'nib al-Kawthari min Abatil*, by 'Abd al-Rahman ibn Yahya al-Mu'allimi. Edited by Nasr al-Din al-Albani, Zuhayr Shawish, 'Abd al-Razzaq Hamza, 171–175. Beirut: al-Maktab al-Islami.

Al-Albani, Nasir al-Din. 1992. *Hukm Tarik al-Salat*. Riyadh: Dar al-Jalalayn.

Al-Albani Nasir al-Din. 1999. "Preface to al-Tankil," 1st edition. In *al-Kawthari wa-Ta'addihi 'ala al-Turath wa-Bayan Halihi fi Mu'allafatihi wa-Mu'allaqatihi*, by Muhammad Bahjat al-Baytar, 142–144. Cairo: Dar al-Haramayn.

Amin, Kamaruddin. 2004. "Nāṣiruddīn al-Albānī on Muslim's Ṣaḥīḥ: A Critical Study of His Method." *Islamic Law and Society* 11(2): 149–176.

Al-Ansari, 'Abd al-Hamid. 2019. Interview with former Dean of Islamic Law at Qatar University; Doha, November 14.

Al-Banna, Hasan. 1965. *Majmu'at Rasa'il al-Imam al-Shahid Hasan al-Banna*. Beirut: Dar al-Andalus.

al-Buti, Sa'id Ramadan. 1970. *Al-Lamadhhabiyya Akhtar Bid'a Tuhaddid al-Shari'a al-Islamiyya*, 2nd edition. Damascus: publisher unknown.

Cenkçiler, Ali Yakub. 2005. *Hatıra Kitabı*. Istanbul: Darulhadis.

Commins, David. 2015. "From Wahhabi to Salafi." In *Saudi Arabia in Transition: Insights on Social, Political, Economic and Religious Change*, edited by Bernard Haykel, Thomas Hegghammer, Stéphane Lacroix, 151–166. Cambridge: Cambridge University Press.

Düzdağ, M. Ertuğrul. 2007. *Üstad Ali Ulvi Kurucu Hatıralar*, vol. 2. Istanbul: Kaynak.

El-Rouayheb, Khaled. 2010. "From Ibn Hajar al-Haytami (d. 1566) to Khayr al-Din al-Alusi (d. 1899): Changing Views of Ibn Taymiyya among non-Hanbali Sunni Scholars." In *Ibn Taymiyya and His Times*, edited by Yossef Rapoport and Shahab Ahmed, 269–318. Karachi: Oxford University Press.

Ghazali. 2017. *Iljam al-'Awamm 'an 'Ilm al-Kalam*. Istanbul: Siraç Yayınevi.

Gershoni, Israel, and James P. Jankowski. 1995. *Redefining the Egyptian Nation, 1930–1945*. Cambridge: Cambridge University Press.

Hadi, 'Isam Musa. 2013. *Al-Da'wa al-Salafiyya: Ahdafuha wa-Mawqifuha min al-Mukhalifin Laha*. Amman: publisher unknown.

Hammond, Andrew. 2017. "Salafi Thought in Turkish Public Discourse since 1980." *International Journal of Middle East Studies* 49(3): 417–35.

Hamza, Muhammad 'Abd al-Razzaq. 1950. *Hawla Tarhib al-Kawthari bi-Naqd Ta'nibih*. Cairo: Maktabat al-Imam.

Haykel, Bernard. 2009. "On the Nature of Salafi Thought and Action." In *Global Salafism: Islam's New Religious Movement*, edited by Roel Meijer, 33–58. London: Hurst.

Hinnebusch, Raymond. 2015. *The International Politics of the Middle East*, 2nd edition. Manchester: Manchester University Press.

Al-Huzaymi, Nasir. 2011. *Ayyam ma' Juhayman: Kuntu ma' al-Jama'a al-Salafiyya al-Muhtasiba*. Beirut: Arab Network for Research and Publishing.

Ibn Taymiyya. 1966. *Al-Fatawa al-Kubra*, vol. 5. Cairo: Dar al-Kutub al-Haditha.

Ibn Taymiyya. 1996. *Kitab al-Iman*. Beirut: al-Maktab al-Islami.

Ibn Taymiyya. 1972. *Majmu'at al-Rasa'il wa-l-Masa'il*, edited by Rashid Rida. Beirut: Dar Ihya' al-Turath al-'Arabi.

Ibrahim, Ahmed Fekry. 2016. "Rethinking the Taqlīd-Ijtihād Dichotomy: A Conceptual-Historical Approach." *Journal of American Oriental Society* 136(2): 285–303.

Al-Kawthari, Zahid. 1990 [1941]. *Ta'nib al-Khatib 'ala Ma Saqahu fi Tarjamat Abi Hanifa min al-Akadhib*. Cairo: publisher unknown.

Al-Kawthari, Zahid. 2000a [1953]. "Bina' al-Masajid 'ala al-Qubur wa-l-Salah 'alayha." In *Maqalat al-Kawthari*, edited by Yusuf Banuri, 153–156. Cairo: Al-Tawfikia Bookshop.

Al-Kawthari, Zahid. 2000b [1953]. "Mahq al-Taqawwul fi Mas'alat al-Tawassul." In *Maqalat al-Kawthari*, edited by Yusuf Banuri, 339–356. Cairo: Al-Tawfikia Bookshop.

Al-Kawthari, Zahid. 2000c [1910]. *Irgham al-Murid*. Cairo: al-Azhariyya.

Al-Kawthari, Zahid. 2005 [1929]. *Saf at al-Burhan 'ala Safahat al-'Udwan*. Cairo: al-Azhariyya li-l-Turath.

Khan, Ahmad. 2016. "Islamic Tradition in an Age of Print: Editing, Printing and Publishing the Classical Heritage." In *Reclaiming Islamic Tradition: Modern Interpretations of the Classical Heritage*, edited by Elisabeth Kendall and Ahmad Khan, 52–99. Edinburgh: Edinburgh University Press.

Köni, Hakan. 2012. "Saudi Influence on Islamic Institutions in Turkey Beginning in the 1970s." *Middle East Journal* 66(1): 97–110.

Lacroix, Stephane. 2009. "Between Revolution and Apoliticism: Nasir al-Din al-Albani and His Impact on the Shaping of Contemporary Salafism." In *Global Salafism: Islam's New Religious Movement*, edited by Roel Meijer, 59–82. New York: Columbia University Press.

Majallat al-Majma' al-Fiqhi al-Islami. 2005. "Bi-Sha'n al-Khilaf al-Fiqhi bayn al-Madhahib wa-l-Ta'assub al-Madhhabi." *Year 4*, 2nd edition, 383–386. Mecca: Muslim World League.

Al-Maqdisi, Abu Muhammad. 1989. *Al-Kawashif al-Jaliyya fi Kufr al-Dawla al-Sa'udiyya*. Amman: Minbar al-Tawhid wa-l-Jihad.

Melchert, Christopher. 1997. *The Formation of the Sunni Schools of Law, 9th–10th centuries C.E.* Leiden: Brill.

Melchert, Christopher. 2002. "The Piety of the Hadith Folk." *International Journal of Middle East Studies* 34(3): 425–439.

Melchert, Christopher. 2013. "The Relation of Ibn Taymiyya and Ibn Qayyim al-Jawziyya to the Hanbali School of Law." In *Islamic Theology, Philosophy and Law: Debating Ibn Taymiyya and Ibn Qayyim al-Jawziyya*, edited by Alina Kokoschka, Birgit Krawietz, Georges Tamer, 146–161. Berlin: De Gruyter.

Melchert, Christopher. 2016. "Muhammad Nasir al-Din al-Albani and Traditional Hadith Criticism." In *Reclaiming Islamic Tradition: Modern Interpretations of the Classical Heritage*, edited by Elisabeth Kendall and Ahmad Khan, 33–51. Edinburgh: Edinburgh University Press.

Mouline, Nabil. 2014. *The Clerics of Islam: Religious Authority and Political Power in Saudi Arabia*. New Haven, CT: Yale University Press.

Munir, Ibrahim. 2019. Interview with deputy general guide of the Muslim Brotherhood, London.

Nursi, Said. 1994 [1920]. *Al-Mathnawi al-'Arabi al-Nuri, edited by Ihsan Qasim al-Salihi*. Istanbul: Sözler.

Olidort, Jacob. 2015. *In Defense of Tradition: Muhammad Nāṣir Al-Dīn Al-Albānī and the Salafi Method*. PhD thesis, Princeton University.

Pierret, Thomas. 2013. *Religion and State in Syria: The Sunni 'Ulama' from Coup to Revolution*. Cambridge: Cambridge University Press.

Al-Qarni, 'A'id. 2007. *As'ad Imra'a fi-l-'Alam*, 7th edition. Riyadh: Obeikan.

al-Qasimi, 'Abdullah. 1946. *Hadhihi Hiya al-Aghlal*. Cairo: Maṭba'at Misr.

Redissi, Hamidi. 2008. "The Refutation of Wahhabism in Arabic Sources, 1745–1932." In *Kingdom without Borders: Saudi Arabia's Political, Religious and Media Frontiers*, edited by Madawi Al-Rasheed, 157–181. London: Hurst.

Sabaseviciute, Giedre. 2018. "Sayyid Qutb and the Crisis of Culture in Late 1940s Egypt." *International Journal of Middle East Studies* 50(1): 85–101.

Sabri, Mustafa. 1981 [1949]. *Mawqif al-'Aql wa-l-'Ilm wa-l-'Alam min Rabb al-'Alamin wa-Rusulihi*, vol. 4. Beirut: Dar Ihya al-Kutub al-Arabiyya.

Shaltut, Mahmud. 1942. "Raf 'Isa." *Al-Risala* 10(462): 515–517.

Al-Tahir, Ahmad Muhammad. 2004. *Jama'at Ansar al-Sunna al-Muhammadiyya*. Riyadh: Dar al-Fadila.

Tamam, Husam. 2010. *Tasalluf al-Ikhwan: Ta'akul al-Utruha al-Ikhwaniyya wa-Su'ud al-Salafiyya fi Jama'at al-Ikhwan al-Muslimin*. Alexandria, Egypt: Bibliotheca Alexandrina/Future Studies Unit.

Von Kügelgen, Anke. 2013. "The Poison of Philosophy: Ibn Taymiyya's Struggle for and against Reason." In *Islamic Theology, Philosophy and Law: Debating Ibn Taymiyya and Ibn Qayyim al-Jawziyya*, edited by Alina Kokoschka, Birgit Krawietz, Georges Tamer, 253–328. Berlin: De Gruyter.

Waardenburg, Jacques. 1979. "Official and Popular Religion as a Problem in Islamic Studies." In *Official and Popular Religion: Analysis of a Theme for Religious Studies*, edited by Pieter H. Vrijhof and Jacques Waardenburg, 357–365. The Hague: Mouton.

Wajdi, Muhammad Farid. 1945. "Al-Din fi Mu'tarak al-Shukuk." *al-Risala* 13(602): 57–60.

Al-Yassini, Ayman. 1985. *Religion and State in the Kingdom of Saudi Arabia*. Boulder, CO: Westview Press.

Yolcu, Abdullah. 2017. Interview with Zad TV, January 24. https://www.youtube.com/watch?v=c4AQZeoY1c4 (accessed May 25, 2020).

Yolcu, Abdullah. 2020. Public biography. https://www.facebook.com/pg/%C5%9Eeyh-Abdullah-Yolcu-286162341432970/about/ (accessed May 25, 2020).

5

Transnational Wahhabism

The Muslim World League and the World Assembly of Muslim Youth

Reinhard Schulze

Introduction: The Social and Cultural Setup of the Muslim World League

After the Second World War, the social and cultural conditions under which the Wahhabi scholars of Saudi Arabia exercised their religious influence changed drastically. On average, about 60,000 pilgrims visited Mecca every year until 1946, of whom at least half came from the Arabian Peninsula (Miller 2006). After 1947, the number of pilgrims from abroad increased gradually (see Figure 5.1). In 1950, 107,000 foreign pilgrims attended the *hajj*; in 1954 the number rose to 164,000, in 1959 to 204,000, and in 1962 to 216,000.[1]

This growth posed a challenge to the scholars: they were forced to communicate their puritanical interpretation of Islam to a broader Islamic public. After all, the kingdom was concerned that the pilgrims returned home with a positive image of the country. After Wahhabism had been recognized by the Islamic public as a legitimate religious order in Saudi Arabia, the Wahhabi scholars now sought to make their interpretation of Islam more comprehensible and acceptable through marketing their own publications.

After centralizing existing institutions and creating new institutions of social norm control and of legal and judicial administration[2] in which the Wahhabi scholars played a decisive role, the field of education even deepened their social influence on Saudi society.[3] But this new prestige was at the price of strengthening the state's surveillance of the Wahhabi order. Depending on political circumstances, the regime could now use the Wahhabis to assert state interests. Crown Prince Faysal, to whom King Saʿud had delegated the executive power in 1958, brought this surveillance to perfection.

Reinhard Schulze, *Transnational Wahhabism* In: *Wahhabism and the World*. Edited by: Peter Mandaville, Oxford University Press. © Oxford University Press 2022. DOI: 10.1093/oso/9780197532560.003.0005

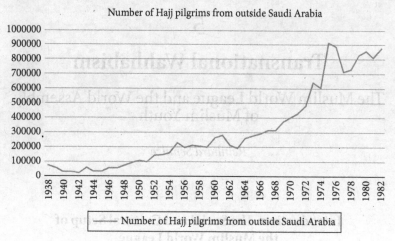

Figure 5.1. Number of *hajj* pilgrims from outside Saudi Arabia.

The Foundation of the Muslim World League

On May 18, 1962, 111 participants from 33 countries whom Faysal had invited to that "Islamic Conference" decided to found a "League of the Islamic World" (*Rabitat al-'Alam al-Islami*); the official English name was the Muslim World League (MWL) from 1963 onward (Schulze 1990, 181; Umm al-Qura 1920 (21.12.1381/25.5.1962), 1, 8).[4] Though the organizers tried to present the conference as a true "international gathering," the great majority of the participants came from Saudi Arabia. At least eight Wahhabi scholars from Najd, including four from the Al al-Shaykh family, participated in the conference. The prominent scholars included Muhammad ibn Ibrahim Al al-Shaykh and 'Abd al-'Aziz bin Baz (who at that time was vice president of the Islamic University of Medina).

The plan had been to set up a Constituent Council (*majlis ta'sisi*), which was implemented at the Islamic Congress in 1962. Twenty-one Muslim celebrities were appointed members of the Council; among them there was only one Wahhabi, the mufti of Saudi Arabia, who acted as "president of the Constituent Council." Later, the number of the Council's members steadily increased until it reached 60 in 1985–1986. During that period, about 12 percent of those who had become members of the Council came from Saudi Arabia. Seven of them can be classified as belonging to the Wahhabi tradition: the mufti, Ibn Baz (appointed in 1963), 'Abdullah bin Ibrahim al-Ansari (1966), 'Abdullah bin Humayd (1971), Salih 'Abd al-Rahman al-Husayn (1975), Muhammad al-'Alwani (1980), and

Salih bin Muhammad al-Luhaydan (1986). The five other Saudis came from the Hijaz, whose families were not embedded into the old puritanical socio-moral milieus but belonged to the very active merchant class.

Though many scholars who were members of these Hijazi families adopted Wahhabism as some modus to address Islamic issues, they had only superficially accepted the Wahhabi habitus. Through their international contacts, these families helped to ensure that the League could be integrated into a broad network of social and cultural relations. Faysal, who had been able to find a power base among these merchant families, ensured that all offices in the League were filled by members of these families: Muhammad ʿAli al-Harkan (appointed to the Constituent Council in 1963), a jurist from Medina who, after having retired from his position as minister of law in 1975, would become the secretary-general of the MWL; Muhammad Salih Qazzaz (1964), who would become second secretary-general in 1972; Amin Muhammad al-Shaybi (1975); ʿAbd al-ʿAziz Ahmad al-Sibaʿi (1986); and Muhammad ʿAbduh Yamani (1986). The Hijazis had the privilege of occupying the position of secretary-general right from the beginning: the first in office was the merchant, poet, and publisher Muhammad Surur as-Sabban (1898–1972). Only one out of ten MWL officials were educated as Wahhabi scholars, namely Muhammad Nasir al-ʿAbbudi (born 1926), born and raised in Burayda, whose principal teacher was Ibn Humayd. Later he taught at the Islamic University of Medina and served as deputy secretary-general of the MWL from 1983 onward.

Wahhabism now actively cooperated with its allies among Salafi scholars who numerically dominated the Constituent Council in its early days and with prominent members of the neo-salafiyya. They had even managed to win over the Pakistani leader of the Jamaat-e-Islami, Abu'l al-Aʿla Mawdudi, as a comrade-in-arms. He now sat at least once a year on the occasion of the meeting of the Council at the same table with the Indian scholar Abu al-Hasan Ali al-Nadwi, the Wahhabi mufti, and the (ex-)muftis from Jordan, Egypt, and Jerusalem such as Amin al-Husayni. This extraordinary alliance was essentially kept together by the patronage of Faysal, who had been proclaimed Saudi king in 1964.

The Wahhabi influence in the MWL was particularly evident in the activities of its Constituent Council, whereas the Hijazis focused on administration, press relations, and organizational policy. The room for maneuvering was initially limited. The MWL's budget was rather small: in 1962 the Saudi government provided the MWL with about 1 million riyals (then about US$200,000); in 1972 it was always about US$1.7 million, and even in 1979 it was just over US$13 million.[5]

The MWL, the Wahhabis, and the Muslim Brothers

In the early 1960s everything still looked like a harmonious integration of the Muslim Brotherhood into Saudi Arabian religious policy. For Faysal, the Brothers were a great help in his program of "Islamic modernization," of which the creation of a centralized education system was considered to be the most important part. It was certainly Faysal's intention to create a counterweight to the Wahhabi establishment, whose loyalty he could never be sure of, by nationalizing education.

Thus, right from the beginning, the MWL was successful in promoting Faysal's vision of Islamic transnationalism which was based on implementing the model of Saudi-Wahhabi dualism in the transnational Islamic public. As the MWL was conceived as a transnational institution claiming legitimacy that its members "represent the Muslim world with respect to dogmas and faith," Saudi Arabia lobbied for the foundation of a new intergovernmental Islamic organization which should supplement Islamic transnationalism and which was supposed to secure the position of Saudi hegemony, which became evident at the end of the Arab cold war in the early 1970s. In the MWL's charter of December 1962, it had been stated: "We will overcome all difficulties that stand against the creation of a league of the Islamic world (jami'at al-'alam al-Islami)" (Muslim World League 1963, 8).

In accordance with its self-image, the MWL conceived its—today we would say—transnational character with the term rabita ("bond") in order to express its ambition to act as an avant-garde for the formation of an international Islamic body of states (jami'a). The term rabita had formerly been used as a term for a logical or semantic connection (copula) and as a connecting element between two expressions or facts. In Ottoman usage, the term was also related to designate a cavalry unit that was deployed at the border, and hence it was common to understand rabita concretely as a factual bond between persons. This may have given rise to the idea that a rabita is an institutionalized alliance of people working for a common cause. In the Egyptian magazine al-Hilal in 1896, the term was understood as a "link between readers of the Arabic and Turkish languages, as they are combined by Ottoman citizenship" (al-Hilal 1896, 162).

Whereas in earlier times the expression rabita had been used to refer to specific social groups such as artists or scientists, the "Islamic world" was now considered the MWL's point of reference. The leaders of the MWL used this then still young expression (Vehbi 1884, vol. 3, 9; Kamil 2012 [1898], 18, with reference to Scawen Blunt)[6] as part of their attempt to define Islam as a feature of a global bloc. The "Islamic world" was now defined as the counterpart of any "world religion" (Christianity, Judaism), of "civilizations" (the West, the East), and of political blocs (nationalism, communism).

All these connotations now formed the semantic frame of the term *rabita*, which the Saudi government employed to define the future task of the MWL. In fact, in 1969 Faysal was able to enforce the establishment of such an international Islamic organization, and in 1972, his plans became true with the official foundation of the Organization of the Islamic Conference[7] (since renamed the Organization of Islamic Cooperation) to which 57 states worldwide have joined to date.

With the end of the Arab cold war, a first reorganization of the MWL took place in 1972–1973: its representatives now emphasized the Islamic character of the organization, diversified its tasks, and founded a multitude of sub-organizations. As for its Islamicity, however, there was a need for adjustments due to the fact that the MWL was built on an alliance of four Islamic social fields: Wahhabism, Hijazi culture, classical Salafi scholars, and neo-Salafi intellectuals.

Of course, the MWL has never been an ecumenical organization: it has never been concerned with uniting the existing plurality of Islamic interpretations in one large forum for debate. But that does not mean that the MWL merely reproduced Wahhabi teachings. Rather, it accepted the four sociocultural fields on which it has been based since its foundation in 1962. The Islam that the MWL presented was thus a mixture of standards that were dominant in these four fields. Of course, Wahhabism acted as an agency empowered to govern the MWL's Islamic policy through a nihil obstat regime. But owing to the fact that former Muslim Brothers, Salafi scholars, and members of the Hijazi elites brought in their specific worldviews, the MWL broadened the fields of cultural and religious intervention beyond traditional Wahhabi jurisprudence and its puritan traditionalism.

The secretary-general of the MWL's *gründerzeit*, the entrepreneur and publisher Muhammad Surur as-Sabban,[8] died in 1972; thus this most important office of the MWL, namely the secretary-general, could be newly filled, and the first steps to broaden the institutional basis of the League were undertaken. The objective of the MWL now concentrated on its missionary activities among Muslim communities and strengthening its ties with Saudi Arabian religious policy. Now particular attention was paid to "Muslim minorities."[9]

In essence, the MWL became a replica of the Saudi-Wahhabi order, which reproduced the dualism of state power and social authority. The representatives of the MWL saw themselves as being empowered to assert Islam as a social moral order and to define the rules of control. In return, they confirmed their loyalty to the Saudi royal house, which was recognized as the only legitimate political order safeguarding a transnational Islam. The missionary activities aimed at empowering local and regional Muslim organizations to exercise moral policy according to standards developed in Saudi Arabia and controlled by Wahhabi institutions. The MWL offered organizational, financial, and personal aid to fulfill this task and even mediated financial support to erect new mosques or cultural Islamic centers. In return, local Islamic leaders had to agree to allow their congregations to focus on an Islamic puritanical order and to prevent the emergence of a political orientation among Islamic organizations. Thus the "puritanization" of Muslim congregations coincided with strengthening the power position of the Saudi kingdom. The MWL acted as a transnational facsimile of the Saudi order of rule. In order to successfully implement this model, it was very helpful that the MWL integrated various contemporary Islamic milieus; it was not just a tool of Wahhabi religious politics. Rather, it reflected the diversity of religious orders still existing in Saudi Arabia, which, though being subordinated to the sovereignty of the Wahhabis, could nevertheless maintain cultural autonomy in some areas and respects. Above all, the milieus, such as the merchant families in Hijaz, have had far-reaching networks that could now be used to benefit the MWL.

Daʿwa Politics

The Saudi regime took clear advantage of Islamic transnationalism. According to their idea, the MWL should not only be a bulwark against communism, socialism, and secular nationalism, but above all banish the still republican-minded neo-Salafi organizations and their political claim from the new Islamic public.

Initially, the MWL pursued a strategy of hierarchically staggering cooperation and coordination tasks via so-called country, regional, and continental councils. But such representative bodies proved to be less dynamic, too expensive, and too inflexible and were therefore gradually abolished. The MWL opened offices in Saudi Arabia itself and in various countries and set up special departments in some Saudi embassies to serve the purposes of the MWL. By 1986, a total of twenty-seven such offices had been established, plus up to eighteen Islamic centers, often linked to a mosque and other Islamic cultural institutions. Until 2019, the number of offices and centers has been reduced to eighteen and twelve, respectively, located in twenty-six countries.[10]

The main body for the MWL's missionary activities was the International Supreme Council of Mosques (al-majlis al-aʿla al-ʿalami li-l-masajid, 1975–2017) that at its height directed the work of some 1,000 conveners (duʿat) and supported selected Muslim places of worship worldwide. In addition, the MWL's Constituent Council founded, on the occasion of its twentieth meeting (October 1978), the International Islamic Relief Organization (IIRO, hayʾat al-ighatha al-ʿalamiyya al-Islamiyya), which took up work after having received royal approval in 1979. Some governments have suspected that this organization supported the financing of certain terrorist organizations. The government of Kenya, for instance, banned the IIRO along with other NGOs in September 1998 (Agence France-Presse 1998). In line with Saudi Arabian religious policy, the MWL also established institutions for Islamic religious education, which—outlined as Islamic education—referred to the Qur'an, above all to Qur'an memorization (tahfiz) and recitation (tajwid), to the Prophetic tradition (sunna), and to the biography of the Prophet (sira). Its educational patterns dominated for some time catechism classes in those congregations in which the MWL had gained a foothold. In the 1980s, the MWL would list up to 1,000 Islamic organizations that should have accepted its hegemony (Schulze 1990, 291). The level of detail of the grants cannot be estimated from official sources. However, the level of aid is likely to have been well below the expectations of most communities. Since the aid was never secured in the medium or long term, it only had a structuring effect in exceptional cases. If this was the case, it was mostly in the area of disaster relief (e.g., the establishment of health stations in West Africa).

In the context of the Bosnian War, the International Islamic Welfare Organization was suspected of also financing militant Islamic alliances; as early as 1996, American and French authorities accused it of supporting jihadi networks such as the Egyptian Islamic Community (al-Jama'a al-Islamiyya) and Usama bin Laden's Al-Qaeda network. In the course of the conflict of the Saudi ruling house with the Wahhabi elites and the Wahhabi militant dissidents in the 1990s, the International Islamic Welfare Organization changed its profile and then acted primarily as a civic organization for disaster relief in the Islamic world.

After the strategic realignment of 1973–1974, the MWL chose the area of law as another field of transnational policy. This initiative certainly went back to the Wahhabi establishment, which had reorganized itself through various regional and national institutions of law since the beginning of the 1970s.[11] In the context of constructing a transnational Islamic public sphere, Islamic jurisprudence had a multifaceted function: on the one hand, it was intended to help define an order of norms that subjected the local and regional communities in which the MWL exercised a certain influence to the same social and religious standard; on the other hand, jurisprudence also served to strengthen resistance against Western criticism of an Islamic legal order. And third, the legal discourse served to create autonomy within Islamic communities that corresponded to the ideals of the Wahhabis. Of course, tension arose almost inevitably in relation to the classical Islamic order of the schools of law. On the one hand, the MWL wanted to show that its authority also enjoyed recognition outside the Hanbali-Wahhabi milieus; to this end, the MWL had to try to attract prominent Muslim jurists who belonged to other schools of law. On the other hand, the Wahhabi members in particular wanted to use the MWL to enforce their interpretation of Islamic law outside Saudi Arabia.

The last impetus for the establishment of a legal organization of the MWL came from the Wahhabi scholars themselves: in November 1976, at a conference in Riyadh, they had called for the establishment of an Islamic Academy of Law which was designed to undermine the interpretive sovereignty that al-Azhar had previously claimed and to give Wahhabi jurists international recognition.[12] In fact, the Constituent Council of the MWL decided in the autumn of 1977 to establish an international body of jurisprudence called the Islamic Fiqh Academy (al-majma' al-fiqhi al-Islami). The MWL nominated twenty members, including a president and a vice president. Most of them were already members of the Constituent Council of the MWL; seven of the members of the Academy were Saudis; it was no wonder that Ibn Baz was elected president and the jurist and secretary-general of the MWL and al-Harkan the vice president.[13] In spite of its activities, the Academy was rarely able to compete with or to prevail internationally over other institutions of Islamic jurisprudence, especially the corresponding research institution in Kuwait, the OIC International Islamic Fiqh Academy (majma' al-fiqh al-islami al-duwali)[14] and Egypt's al-Azhar. The MWL Fiqh Council restricted its activities to select Wahhabi legal rulings, which were considered worth transferring to a broader Islamic public. Some eccentric Wahhabi rulings, such as those concerning the shape of the earth or the possibility of landing on the moon, were not considered by the MWL.

As noted, the MWL has been a result of Saudi Arabia's religious policy. Therefore, the most important framework in which the MWL has defined and interpreted Islam is the religious policy of the kingdom. But as there have been two rather different varieties of religious policy in the kingdom—that of the Saudi royal regime and its social allies and that of the Wahhabi establishment and its allies—the MWL was therefore subject to two religious patronage systems that were not always sympathetic to each other. Until his death, King Faysal had been able to balance the interests of these two blocs. But by 1972, the rift between these two policies deepened. At the Islamic University of Medina, the influence of Wahhabi puritan dissidents was growing gradually, gaining some support among younger Wahhabis in Riyadh and Qasim. Now the importance of the Wahhabi interpretation of Islam was increasing inside and outside the MWL. The Wahhabi religious policy in the country repeatedly dared to confront the royal house, especially in connection with the occupation of the Muslim sanctuary in Mecca by a Wahhabi eschatological sect in 1979. In various, sometimes bizarre debates, the Wahhabi factions of the MWL challenged the royal house. The loyalty of the Wahhabis to the regime fluctuated and faded, especially between 1979 and 1995. The MWL reflected this process by privileging Wahhabi positions in its public sphere and its institutions, especially under the presidency of the grand mufti, Ibn Baz, and under Secretary-General 'Abdullah bin 'Umar Nasif (acting from 1983 to 1994).

After the state crisis as a result of the First Gulf War in 1991 and the growing Wahhabi opposition to the regime (known as the Sahwa movement), the Saudi government made more efforts to reintegrate the MWL into their apparatus and to reduce its administrative autonomy. Under the new secretary-general, 'Abdullah bin Salih al-'Ubayd from Qasim, appointed in December 1996, the MWL clearly took sides with the royal house, which at that time still hoped for a restoration of the social pact with the Wahhabis. At the end of December 2000, al-'Ubayd was followed by the jurist 'Abdullah bin 'Abd al-Muhsin al-Turki, who acted as the second secretary-general coming from Najd and who headed the MWL until 2016 (al-Nimr 2005).

The World Assembly of Muslim Youth

The complicated religious-political situation in Saudi Arabia meant that the royal regime often doubled or tripled its policy when institutionalizing its interests. Thus, it founded two Islamic legal academies and likewise it linked the MWL to a twin organization, the World Assembly of Muslim Youth (WAMY, *al-nadwa al-'alamiyya li-l-shabab al-Islami*), founded in 1972. This institution also served to balance interests: unlike the MWL, whose apparatus was mainly based on elites from Hijaz, the WAMY was much more closely linked to the Wahhabi tradition. Its original purpose had been to function as a supervisory body with which the kingdom tried to keep authority over those Saudi students who had gone abroad mainly to Western countries (even though the former mufti, Ibn Baz, had ruled that studying in non-Muslim countries was "against Islam"). However, this also resulted in a division of tasks. The MWL was to become effective above all in the new Islamic diaspora communities, primarily in Europe and Southeast Asia, while the WAMY concentrated much more on the United States, Australia, and Egypt, countries in which a relatively large number of Saudi students lived.

In order to prepare Saudi citizens for a stay abroad, the Wahhabi scholars had held a world conference for the Islamic *da'wa* in Riyadh in December 1972. At this meeting, they voted for the governmental project to establish the World Assembly of Muslim Youth. The naming is notable. It was coined as a clear parallel to the Young Men's Christian Association (YMCA) that George Williams (1821–1905) had founded in London in 1844 and which had become a transnational association at its First World Conference in Paris in 1855.

The WAMY officials soon decided to establish regional bureaus in several parts of Saudi Arabia. Thus, in contrast to the MWL, the WAMY was primarily rooted in the context of the complex Saudi society. Obviously, the Wahhabi elite responded to the growing readiness of Saudi citizens to go to America and to

European countries for study. The initial aim of the WAMY was to offer assistance to Saudi students who had gone to a university in Great Britain or North America. The Wahhabi scholars feared that the students would be exposed to "secular ideas" and that there would be a risk that, after having returned to Saudi Arabia, they would help to spread these ideas and to undermine the religious-cultural cohesion of the country. In practice, one of the first tasks of the WAMY was to create an "Islamic space" for Saudi students in foreign countries, including the building of separate student hostels (Muslim World League 1973, 84–86).

The WAMY was one of the more successful foundations of transnational *da'wa* organizations. Currently the WAMY has thirty-eight local offices in Saudi Arabia and operates thirty-two bureaus for Central Asia, Central and South Africa, East Africa, Eastern Europe, Western Europe, North America, South America, and Australia. The WAMY was particularly successful in networking existing Muslim organizations in the United States and Australia. However, it is difficult to say whether the success of the WAMY was based on a carefully regulated policy or simply due to the use of existing personal relationships and networks. It is equally difficult to say whether the activities of the WAMY also contained the obligation of implementing a Wahhabi canon into the self-representation of local Muslim organizations.

The network of personal relations of the WAMY members was somehow confusing. The Supervisory Board consists of ten Wahhabi representatives from Saudi Arabia and twelve WAMY representatives abroad. In some cases, the WAMY cooperated with institutionalized offsprings of the Muslim Brothers or, as in the case of the Islamic Foundation in Leicester, with the tradition of the Pakistani Jamaat-e-Islami. It may be that the leaders of the WAMY considered the Muslim Brothers as useful allies, as David Commins wrote (Commins 2006, 153, citing Yassini 1985, 73):

> A notable aspect of the World Assembly of Muslim Youth is its publication list, which features Muslim Brother rather than classic Wahhabi works. The World Assembly of Muslim Youth figures as an important institution for distributing the works of Sayyid Qutb and another influential Muslim Brother author-martyr, Abd al-Qadir Awda.

This is a rather surprising observation, as already in the early 1980s prominent Wahhabi scholars had vehemently criticized the Muslim Brotherhood and in particular Sayyid Qutb, whose teachings they regarded as incompatible with that of a "true Islam." Nevertheless, some observers argued that the WAMY "might as well be called a Muslim brotherhood organisation" (Nielsen and Otterbeck 2016, 154).

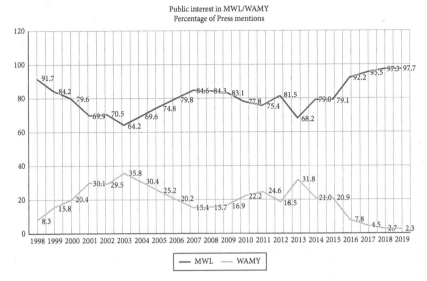

Figure 5.2. Public interest in MWL/WAMY Percentage of press mentions.

Note: The total number of annual references is based on a frequency count of all media stories in each year that mention either the MWL or the WAMY (the total number of annual references of both combined) and then expresses the figures as a percentage of this total number for both organizations.

Table 5.1 Book Publications on MWL or WAMY, 1970s to 2000s

Decade	1970s	1980s	1990s	2000s
MWL	48	109	214	581
WAMY	9	17	36	229

The WAMY could never attract as much public attention as the MWL. Based on a review of English press reports,[15] the distribution shown in Figure 5.2 can be assumed. Obviously, at the beginning of the twenty-first century, public interest in the WAMY grew, as the numbers of book publications that dealt with the WAMY or the MWL in some way prove (see Table 5.1).

The WAMY thus reflects the religious culture of Saudi Arabia much more closely than the MWL. In addition, as already mentioned, the regional reference areas differ. The MWL's main area of action is clearly Europe. About 50 percent of the MWL's activities refer to Europe. The WAMY, on the other hand, concentrates its activities on sub-Saharan Africa, South Asia and Southeast Asia, the Arab world and, of course, the

Map 5.1. Distribution of international representatives of MWL and WAMY, 2020

United States. Map 5.1 shows the distribution of the offices and branches of both organizations (as of 2020).

To date, neither the MWL nor the WAMY have provided information on their budgets or published reports on their activities. In public, both organizations give the impression that they mainly organize conferences that define specific thematic priorities and act as contact points for local Muslim communities. The MWL (and probably the WAMY as well) does not reveal how they act as brokers of relations with Saudi Arabia and its environment and how they manage to integrate local communities into a network of loyalty relations. After all, it is clear that the patronage, which the MWL has offered local communities, has increased the prestige of the communities until the beginning of the twenty-first century and has also brought them financial advantages. The border between the MWL and the WAMY is fluid, as both are located in a similar social setting. So, it is not surprising that the current president of the WAMY is the former minister of Islamic affairs, Salih bin ʿAbd al-ʿAziz Al al-Shaykh, and that his deputy is the former secretary-general of the MWL, Nasif. However, it can be assumed that due to its Wahhabi profile the WAMY is closer to the center of power in Riyadh than the MWL with its more Hijazi base. Besides, the WAMY used the publishing house of the MWL in Mecca in order to distribute its own writings, including those of its secretary-general Salih ibn Sulayman al-Wuhaybi.[16]

There is no reliable information on the level of financial support granted from Saudi Arabia to institutions of the MWL and of the WAMY. Gilles Kepel's remark (2002, 72) that the MWL "opened new offices in every area of the world where Muslims lived" and that Saudi Arabia had planned and financially supported the foundation of about 1,500 mosques worldwide since the death of King Faysal until 2000 is certainly exaggerated.

A Time of Standstill

With the beginning of the twenty-first century, the MWL was threatened with a massive loss of influence on Muslim communities abroad. Increasingly, those responsible did not meet the financial commitments they had made to individual Muslim communities. At the same time, the image of the MWL deteriorated for several reasons: First, after the attacks of September 11, 2001, the MWL—and in particular some departments of the Islamic Relief Organization—was suspected, not only by the Western public, of being a fundraiser of terrorism. Second, the MWL was suspected of being the tip of the Saudi spear for exporting Wahhabism. Third, the MWL was seen as nothing more than an instrument of religious power for the Saudi royal house. Fourth, Wahhabism was regarded as an ideological platform and ideological breeding ground for jihadi terrorism.[17]

In the two decades of the secretary-generals from Najd (1996–2016), for example under al-'Ubayd and al-Turki, the MWL had followed closely the Wahhabi tradition and thus had adopted the unclear attitude of the Wahhabi establishment toward the challenges that had arisen as a result of the emergence of post-Wahhabi extremism. The internal conflict over the preservation or reform of the Wahhabi tradition was not new; it had already taken shape in the period after 1973. But from 2003 it has become evident that the Wahhabi tradition was losing its sovereignty of interpretation over Islamic puritanism and unitarianism.

In these two decades, the structural crisis at the MWL was clearly noticeable. At first, it became apparent that the MWL had overstretched its structure by far. In its heyday, the MWL had twenty-one sub-organizations, which referred to Islamic education and upbringing, welfare and relief, law and jurisprudence, as well as media and science. The entire administrative apparatus was far too bloated and could hardly react with any flexibility to upcoming challenges. The MWL's strategic orientation was no longer discernible. Nor were there any instruments that could have contributed to overcoming the Wahhabi legitimacy crisis. This crisis had already begun in 1973, when two very contradictory networks of critics of the existing Saudi religious order were formed: The hub of the first network, which was soon to be called the *ahl al-hadith*, was Nasir al-Din al-Albani; at the center of the second network, which would later become known as the Sahwa, were the two immigrant teachers to the kingdom, Muhammad Surur and Muhammad Qutb. This crisis reached its first climax with the formation of the puritanical eschatological sect of al-Juhayman 'Utaybi and Muhammad al-Qahtani that seized control of Mecca's Grand Mosque in 1979.

King Fahd's decision on August 7, 1990, to call American troops into the country to ward off possible aggression by the Iraqi army fueled the debate about the legitimacy of the pact between the royal house and the Wahhabi establishment, which is part of the founding myth of the kingdom. Some scholars, especially those who belonged to the Wahhabi Sahwa movement with its pro–Muslim Brotherhood stance, wanted to subject the system of rule completely to a system of norms they controlled. The MWL, on the other hand, under its new secretary-general, al-Turki, stood behind the royal regime and vehemently defended the pact, even when Saudi religious politics intervened in the Wahhabi order of ethical and legal social norms. This had clearly contributed to a loss of legitimacy of the MWL, which Mufti Ibn Baz, who was at least sympathetically supportive to the Sahwa movement, could not compensate for.[18] Until 1994–1995, the conflict between old Wahhabi scholars, Wahhabis loyal to the state, and puritans critical of the regime was still open. At the same time, however, new ultra-Islamic alliances were emerging, especially in Algeria, which fused political and ritual action in jihad and referred to a Wahhabi canon. Ultra-militant preachers such as Abu Muhammad al-Maqdisi argued similarly. Until 1995, the old Wahhabi scholars had still set the tone in the MWL, including Ibn Baz, Muhammad Ibn 'Uthaymin, Salih Ibn Fawzan, and 'Abd al-Rahman al-Barrak. They pleaded for the maintenance of the pact between the royal house and the Wahhabi scholars, but insisted that the regime should leave them alone to control the norms of society.[19] They also wanted to retain the privilege of being consulted on crucial issues such as the deployment of foreign troops in the country. The royal house reacted by strongly promoting the quietist Wahhabi tradition of Rabi' bin Hadi al-Madkhali (b. 1931). They used his argument that the ruler (wali al-amr) had to be followed unconditionally in order to secure religious worship. In al-Madkhali's view, Islamic scholars and jurists should never claim to make political decisions; in return, the state must ensure the orthodox lifestyle of the puritans.

The MWL did not officially take sides in either of these two schools of thought. However, their leaders continued to show a preference for the old Wahhabi tradition and their advocates. Al-Madkhali has not been mentioned—as far as I can see—in the MWL's publications since 2016.[20] Likewise, the MWL now abstained from any statement that could be read as an endorsement of the jihadi alliances, for example of Al-Qaeda. After the attacks in 1995 in Saudi Arabia, the 1998 US embassy bombings in Dar es Salaam and in Nairobi, and especially after September 11, 2001, the MWL became completely subject to the state's religious policy.

About two weeks after the terrorist attacks of September 11, 2001, American newspapers reported that the IIRO and the MWL were under investigation for possibly delivering financial aid to Al-Qaeda. Shortly before, the then-secretary-general of the MWL, al-Turki, had declared: "We condemn any possible retaliation attacks against Muslim nations or minorities. [. . .] If investigations indicate that Islamic organisations or groups were involved the Muslim World League will call for a fair public trial for those responsible" (Agence France-Presse 2001).

But already in the summer of 2000, investigations had revealed that bin Laden is said to have transferred funds to the jihadi group of Abu Sayyaf via his brother-in-law Muhammad Jalal Khalifa, who acted as a representative of the MWL and the IIRO in Manila in the Philippines (Agence France-Presse 2000; Ottaway and Morgan 2001). Since then, the voices suspecting the MWL of being part of a financing network of Al-Qaeda have not fallen silent. The network of the MWL, which was certainly difficult to understand even by Saudi Arabian authorities, was becoming more and more of a problem. The sub-organizations of the IIRO were, in particular, suspected of having provided financial aid to jihadi groups. A 2006 UN Security Council resolution designated the IIRO offshoots in the Philippines and Indonesia as Al-Qaeda support organizations. The MWL succeeded after 2009 in getting its sub-organizations removed from the "suspected terror list," but the stigma remained with the MWL. The MWL was only able to counter this by submitting itself even more closely than before to the supervision of the kingdom's governmental authorities. For the state, the suspicions were an additional argument to finally abolish the MWL's institutional autonomy.

Thus after 2003, the MWL's scope for an autonomous Islamic policy had become smaller and smaller. In fact, it had finally turned into a Saudi state agency. This meant that for a long time the MWL served to reject accusations that the kingdom had supported terrorism. In January 2002, in a statement issued after a six-day meeting, a group of scholars affiliated with the MWL spelled out their definition of terrorism, saying it applied to "any unjustified attack by individuals, groups or states against a human being" (Agence France-Presse 2002; Doney 2002).

Since then, terrorism and extremism have dominated as subject of the MWL's publications. Initially, the term *irhab* (terrorism) referred only to members of jihadi groups and federations, but after 2010 the scope of the term was greatly expanded. Islamic State (IS/ISIS/ISIL) has been mentioned only once in the MWL's publications since 2016, in an interview with the Belgian-Moroccan Muslim theologian at the University of Ghent, Tijani Boulaouali (2017). As elsewhere, Boulaouali avoided seeing IS in an Islamic context; rather, he emphasized the connection between the problem of immigration and integration. This reflects the MWL's strategy of largely de-Islamizing Islamic extremism. This also applies to the terminology used by the jihadis themselves. The term "jihad," for example, was now increasingly used to refer to the "spiritual purification" of the believer; for a long time, the West had been accused of falsifying the Qur'an with its reading of the term "jihad" (Muslim World League 2005, 5). This same accusation was now made against the jihadis. This discourse allowed the MWL to directly reproduce Saudi religious policy. After 2011, the royal house made no secret of its hostility toward the Muslim Brotherhood. For the MWL, this meant a crucial test for its institutional coherence, because there were still individual personalities in the apparatus of the MWL who were close to the Muslim Brotherhood or who were even acting as spokespersons for the Muslim Brotherhood. The most famous among them was Yusuf al-Qaradawi, who was a member of the Islamic Fiqh Academy. After 2010, all references to the Muslim Brotherhood disappeared from the MWL's journalism and, in early June 2017, the membership of al-Qaradawi in the Islamic Fiqh Academy was suspended (Al-Rabita 2017).

A New Beginning?

The reform process heralds the vision of a post-Wahhabi society that is to create a new form of national affiliation in Saudi Arabia.

This new Saudi religious policy, which tries to turn Wahhabi scholars into "Saudi scholars," demanded a profound reform of the MWL itself. The reorganization of MWL, which began in 2014, was not completed in 2021. The first step was the renaming of the Constituent Council to the Supreme Council, which is to have a maximum of sixty members.[21] In addition, a new association was founded under the name of the International Commission of Jurists (al-hay'a al-'alamiyya li-l-huquqiyin) in November 2018 (al-'Ukaz 2018), which is intended to help align international legal standards with Islamic legal norms. The MWL condensed its complex apparatus to five organizations in two steps, greatly reduced its staff, closed some of its offices worldwide, and restructured the areas of religious politics. On the one hand, this reorganization was intended to counteract the institutional proliferation, but, on the other hand, the Saudi regime was certainly also concerned with maintaining hegemony over the network of the MWL and even strengthening its hegemony by tightening this network. Today, apparently only the following five sub-organizations of the MWL are still active:

- International Organization for the Holy Qur'an and Immaculate Sunna
- International Organization for Relief, Welfare, and Development (Muhammad Abd al-Karim al-'Isa as CEO)
- International Organization for Muslim Scholars (founded in 2006)
- Islamic Fiqh Council
- International Commission of Jurists

The formerly powerful World Supreme Council for Mosques ceased to exist in 2016–2017, though the MWL's website still mentions this body.[22]

The Quest for a New Strategy

It remains to be seen whether the change of course in Saudi Arabia will actually lead to a post-Wahhabi order and thus change the foundations of the MWL. Many Islamic critics are convinced that the Saudi regime has formed an alliance with the tradition of the Madkhaliyya (or *madakhila*, also called Jamiyya). This tradition, which demands strict obedience by Muslims to those in power and sees the Muslim Brotherhood as heretics who want to eradicate every basis of Islam, is of perfect benefit to the regime. There is evidence that the Madkhali tradition is indeed courted by the royal house, but, so far, there is no indication in the MWL and WAMY media that the regime explicitly refers to this tradition.

Meanwhile, the Saudi press has also reviewed the MWL's relations with the cofounders of ultra-Islamic jihad alliances. For example, it is mentioned that 'Abdullah 'Azzam had been closely connected to the MWL in 1981 and 1984 in Saudi Arabia before he went to Peshawar and founded the "Services Bureau" there in 1984 (Al-Arabiya.net 2015).

With all this, the MWL also had to make major concessions. Thus, it was claimed that the Muslim Brotherhood had been closely associated with the Shi'a since the 1930s. Therefore, it was reported that in 1938 Hasan al-Banna had received the young Ruhollah Khomeini in Cairo, who, for his part, had praised the successes of the Muslim Brotherhood. It was also pointed out that in 1964 Sa'id Ramadan had reported in his Geneva magazine *al-Muslimun* how the MWL had organized in the same year in Mecca a symposium on the caliph Abu Bakr, in which Khomeini had taken part (al-Jarida 2019). And the WAMY was now criticized, too: it was said that the WAMY, which in 1973, as one of its first official activities, gave the Muslim Brotherhood, who were able to travel to the *hajj* again after the amnesty in Egypt in 1971, the opportunity to reactivate their transnational network. One is almost tempted to say that the Saudi Arabian press today portrays the WAMY as the midwife of the international networks of the Muslim Brotherhood after the 1971 amnesty.

This also required the MWL to reassess its own history. After all, at the beginning of its history it was precisely those personalities who were now considered personae non gratae in Saudi Arabia and whose names have not been mentioned in public by the MWL since 2016 that were important. The most recent references to Sayyid Qutb in the Arabic monthly journal of the MWL can be found in an article by the Syrian jurist 'Uthman Jum'a Dumayriyya (2016) and in an article by the educator Hayat 'Abd al-'Aziz Muhammad Niyaz (2017). In 2018, the Saudi Arabian Ministry of Education declared that all teaching materials and curricula will now be rewritten to cleanse them from the influence of the Muslim Brotherhood. Mawdudi was last mentioned in a contribution of the English social worker Shajeda Islam (2017) and of the Indian educator Tauseef Ahmad Parray (2018). So far, however, the MWL has refrained from explicit criticism of its historical ties with the Muslim Brotherhood.

It is noticeable that since June 2017, the frequency in the use of the term *da'wa* in the Arabic publications of the MWL has decreased considerably. It is still too early to decide whether this decline is significant and whether it is due to another change in MWL strategy. However, it would be a logical continuation of the new Saudi religious policy if the MWL in the future saw itself far less as a platform for mission than it had done ten years ago. The League's new profile will depend to a large extent on the future course of the royal regime's religious policy.

Notes

1. Numbers partly taken from Long 1979, 128, and from official Saudi statistical records.
2. Permanent Committee for Scholarly Research and Ifta (al-Lajna ad-Da'ima lil-Buhut al-'Ilmiyya wal-Ifta, August 29, 1971), Council of Senior Scholars (Majlis Hay'at Kibar al-'Ulama, officially established August 29, 1972), the various stages of institutionalizing the Saudi magistracy and judiciary (esp. between 1959 and 1975).
3. In 1960, a Royal Pronouncement was issued to establish "The General Presidency for the Education of Girls."
4. The name "Muslim World League" had already been used in a report on the conference in *Muslim News International* (Karachi) 1 (1962), 31.
5. After 1979, the League did not publish any figures.
6. 'Abduh and Rida used the expression in al-Manar right from its beginning in 1898. A general discussion of the emergence of the idea of an Islamic World as part of Muslim discourses of the late nineteenth century is Aydın (2017). The English term "Islamic World" was first used as part of the Chicago World Exposition of 1893 and then was popularized by William Henry Abdulla Quilliam who accordingly named his monthly magazine *Islamic World* (May 1894). The far less meaningful expression "Moslem world" had been first used in the 1750s, substituting for the earlier notion "Mahometan world."
7. At the 38th Council of Foreign Ministers meeting in Astana, Kazakhstan (June 2011), the delegates decided to change its name from Organization of the Islamic Conference to its current name.
8. He was said to have edited and published the first "modern book" under Saudi rule, namely his *Adab al-Hijaz* published in Mecca in April 1926.

9. Only in the 1960s, the Islamic public started to use the expression "al-aqalliyya al-muslima" (Muslim minority).

10. In Austria, Nigeria, Denmark, the United Kingdom, and Bosnia, the League has been represented by an office and an Islamic center.

11. al-Lajna ad-Da'ima lil-Buhut al-'Ilmiyya wal-Ifta', Hay'at Kibar al-'Ulama', al-Majlis al-A'la li-l-Qada', etc.

12. In December 1973, the Secretary General of the Saudi Arabian Muslim World League, al-Qazzaz, had proposed the foundation of an Academy of Islamic Jurisprudence. He did not yet propose the academy to be a body of the League (Akhbar al-'Alam al-Islami 357 (23.11.1393/17.12.1973), 11, no. 24).

13. A summary of the Council's decisions up to 2006 was published in 2007: Muslim World League, Islamic Fiqh Council, 2007/2015. Decisions from 2007 to 2010 in: al-Majma' al-Fiqhi al-Islami, 2011, 483–540 (https://d1.islamhouse.com › data › single_010 › ar_qrarat_elmogama3_alfiqhy; accessed November 25, 2019).

14. http://www.iifa-aifi.org/. The establishment of the Islamic Fiqh Academy of the Organization of the Islamic Conference (OIC) was implemented pursuant to a resolution issued by the Third Islamic Summit Conference, which was held in Mecca in 1401 (1981). Its current president, Salih bin 'Abdullah ibn Humayd, is also imam at the Great Mosque in Mecca. His brother Ahmad has been member of the MWL *fiqh* council. Salih, born in Burayda in 1950, was also a member of the League's Mosque Council. The secretary-general has been the Jordanian jurist 'Abd al-Salam Dawud al-'Abbadi.

15. Factiva Corpus (https://global.factiva.com).

16. Al-Wuhaybi (b. 1950 in Riyadh), who had earned a PhD in Koranic studies from Indiana University in 1982, became WAMY's secretary-general in 2002. As late as 2015, the Saudi Arabian media mentioned that he was also a member of the General Assembly of the Academy for the Rapprochement between Schools of Thought in Tehran.

17. There is a long list of books, chapters, and articles in which the authors try to prove or to deny the MWL's support of terrorism. A typical example is Gold (2003).

18. Ibn Baz's attitude is unclear despite his many *fatwa*s and dictated texts. On the one hand, especially in the 1970s, he advocated a strict Wahhabi conservatism and resisted the "Islamic modernization" that Faysal had decreed for the kingdom. Ibn Baz had tried in vain in 1968 to enforce al-Albani's reappointment to a university in Saudi Arabia. In 1975 he was a newly appointed member of the Council of the Islamic University of Medina and thus was partially rehabilitated in Saudi Arabia.

19. For an overview of this conflict, see Schulze (2016, 350–354, 493–497).

20. Occasionally members of the MWL as individuals have been very critically to al-Madkhali. See, for example, Salih ibn Muhammad al-Luhaydan (b. 1932), president of the Supreme Court and member of the Organization of Great Scholars.

21. The Supreme Council has nominally 60 members, but currently only names of 44 members are mentioned (https://www.themwl.org/en/Supreme). It is not entirely clear when the renaming took place. In a report on the Fifteenth Islamic Conference of

the MWL in Mecca, the newspaper *al-Sharq al-Awsat* already mentions the Supreme Council of the League on September 30, 2014.
22. https://themwl.org/en/node/34252 (November 11, 2019); Saudi Press Agency, December 20, 2017. The periodicals of the MWL did not mention the Mosques Council after 2016.

References

Agence France-Presse. 1998. "Kenya's NGO Council protests ban on NGOs." September 11, 1998. https://global.factiva.com/ha/default.aspx#./!?&_suid=160586901159104786520327902588 (accessed November 20, 2020).

Agence France-Presse. 2000. "Bin Laden Supporting Hostage-Takers: Philippine Defence Chief." August 9, 2000. https://global.factiva.com/ha/default.aspx#./!?&_suid=16058696038930458170557449 1559 (accessed November 20, 2020).

Agence France-Press. 2001. "Muslim World League Condemns Possible US Reprisals." Agence France-Press. September 17, 2001. https://global.factiva.com/ha/default.aspx#./!?&_suid=16324060362250252286218 5053998 (accessed November 20, 2020).

Agence France-Press. 2002. "Muslim Scholars Define 'Terrorism' as Opposed to Legitimate Jihad." Agence France-Press. January 10, 2002. https://global.factiva.com/ha/default.aspx#./!?&_suid=163240656203002113616367 7344333 (accessed November 20, 2020).

Al-Arabiya.net. 2015. "Maraya baqaya 'Abdullah 'Azzam." September 17, 2015. https://www.alarab iya.net/ arab- and- world/ 2015/ 09/ 17/ عزام-بقايا-عبدا لله-عزام- مرايا (accessed November 20, 2020).

Aydın, Cemil. 2017. *The Idea of the Muslim World: A Global Intellectual History*. Cambridge, MA: Harvard University Press.

Boulaouali, Tijani. 2017. "With the Researcher and Islamic thinker Tijani Boulaouali, Winner of the Award for Best Journalistic Work in the League Magazine." *Al-Rabita* 612: 39–45. https://themwl.org/ar/file-download/download/public/2042.

Commins, David. 2006. *The Wahhabi Mission and Saudi Arabia*. London: I. B. Tauris.

Doney, James N. 2002. "Islamic Conference Issues Definition of Terrorism." *Wall Street Journal*. January 14, 2002. https://global.factiva.com/ha/default.aspx#./!?&_suid=16324057729130847656371469 8548 (accessed November 20, 2020).

Dumayriyya, 'Uthman Jum'a. 2016. "Islamic Landmarks in the Farewell Sermon." *al-Rabita* 599: 54–57. https://themwl.org/ar/file-download/download/public/1179.

Gold, Dore. 2003. *Hatred's Kingdom: How Saudi Arabia Supports the New Global Terrorism*. Washington, DC: Regnery.

Niyaz, Hayat 'Abd al-'Aziz Muhammad. 2017. "The Approach of the Noble Qur'an in the Development of Cognitive Mental Processes." *al-Rabita* 605: 42–46. https://themwl.org/ar/file-download/download/public/1669.

al-Hilal. 1896. "Muhammad Namiq Kemal Bey." *Al-Hilal* 5(5): 16–167.

Islam, Shajeda. 2017. "Comparative Analysis of the Western Ethics and Islamic Ethics." *Journal Muslim World League* 46(3): 45–50. https://themwl.org/downloads/The-MWL-Journal-2017-December.pdf.

al-Jarida. 2019. *al-Jarida*. May 8, 2019. https://storage.googleapis.com/jarida-cdn/pdfs/1557239930708726600/1557239960000/file.pdf.

Kamil, Mustafa. 2012 [1898]. *Al-mas'ala al-sharqiyya*. Cairo: Hindawi.

Kepel, Gilles. 2002. *Jihad: The Trail of Political Islam*. Translated by Anthony F. Roberts. Cambridge, MA: The Belknap Press of Harvard University Press.

Long, David E. 1979. *The Hajj Today: A Survey of the Contemporary Pilgrimage to Makka*. New York: State University of New York Press.

al-Majma' al-Fiqhi al-Islami. 2011. *Qararat al-majma' al-fiqhi al-islami fi dawrati al-'ishrin (1398–1423/1977–2010)*. Mecca: MWL. https://d1.islamhouse.com › data › single_010 › ar_qrarat_elmogama3_alfiqhy (accessed November 25, 2019).

Miller, Michael B. 2006. "Pilgrims' Progress: The Business of the Hajj." *Past & Present* 191: 189–228.

Muslim World League. 1963. *Majallat rabitat al-'alam al-islami* 1.

Muslim World League. 1973. *Majallat rabitat al-'alam al-islami* 10.

Muslim World League. 2005. *Al-'Alam al-Islami* 1884. April 11, 2005.

Muslim World League. Islamic Fiqh Council, 2007/2015. *Resolutions of Islamic Fiqh Council, Makka Mukarrama: From 1st to 18th Sessions during 1398–1427H (1977–2006)*. Mecca: MWL, 2007. Part I. https://web.archive.org/web/20151213231604/http://themwl.org/downloads/Resolutions-of-Islamic-Fiqh-Council-1.pdf, December 13, 2015), Part II via https://web.archive.org/web/20170110195617/http://themwl.org/downloads/Resolutions-of-Islamic-Fiqh-Council-2.pdf (accessed January 10, 2017).

Nielsen, Jørgen S., and Jonas Otterbeck. 2016. *Muslims in Western Europe*. Edinburgh: Edinburgh University Press.

al-Nimr, Khalaf Bin Sulayman. 2005. *Isham rabitat al-'alam al-islami fi bina' iqtisad islami. Bahth muqaddam li-l-mu'tamar al-alami al-thalith li-l-iqtisad al-islami* (Mecca, 23.–26.4.1426/31.5.–3.6.2005). Mecca: RAI.

Ottaway, David B., and Dan Morgan. 2001. "Two Muslim Charities under Scrutiny; Saudi-Funded Groups Deny Ties to Terrorist Networks but Cite Vulnerability." *Washington Post*, September 30, 2001. https://www.washingtonpost.com/archive/politics/2001/09/30/two-muslim-charities-under-scrutiny/6173a614-a1a2-4b41-a827-76183722d864/ (accessed August 26, 2021).

Parray, Tauseef Ahmad. 2018. "Thematic Studies of the Qur'an: An Assessment." *Journal Muslim World League* 46(7): 52–55. https://www.themwl.org/downloads/The-MWL-Journal-2018-Apr.pdf.

Al-Rabita. 2017. "The Muslim World League Condemns the Terrorist Attack in London." *Al-Rabita* 609: 9. https://themwl.org/ar/file-download/download/public/1858.

Schulze, Reinhard. 1990. *Islamischer Internationalismus im 20. Jahrhundert. Untersuchungen zur Geschichte der islamischen Weltliga*. Leiden: Brill.

Schulze, Reinhard. 2016. *Geschichte der islamischen Welt. Von 1900 bis zur Gegenwart*. München: Beck.

Al-Ukaz. 2018. "Al-'alam al-Islami: Insha' hay'a 'alamiyya li-l-huquqiyin." *Al-Ukaz*. November 10, 2018. https://www.okaz.com.sa/local/na/1684904 (accessed November 29, 2020).

Vehbi, Hamid. 1884. *Meşahir-i Islam. I–III*. Istanbul: Mihran Matba'ası.

al-Yassini, Ayman. 1985. *Religion and State in the Kingdom of Saudi Arabia*. Boulder, CO: Westview Press.

6

Humanitarian and Relief Organizations in Global Saudi *Da'wa*?

Nora Derbal

On October 10, 2019, one of the headlines of *Arab News* warned: "Overseas Aid from Saudi Arabia Must Go Through KSRelief" (SPA 2019a).[1] In the article, the spokesperson of KSRelief, Dr. Samer Al-Jetaily, reminded his audience of "the royal order[2] stipulating that any donations for humanitarian or charitable overseas aid—whether from government or civilian sources—must be made through KSRelief." KSRelief is the acronym for the King Salman Humanitarian Aid and Relief Center (*Markaz al-Malik Salman li-l-Ighatha wa-l-Aʿmal al-Insaniyya*), which opened in May 2015 in Riyadh, shortly after King Salman ascended the throne in January 2015. Since 2015, the Saudi Press Agency (SPA) has issued numerous alerts in not only English-language media like *Arab News*, but also local Arabic newspapers such as *Al-Riyadh* (SPA 2020), repeating the narrative that donations made outside of KSRelief are illegal. Through the following analysis, I explain how KSRelief has become a symbol of a fundamental reorientation of the Saudi humanitarian landscape. This reorientation manifests the control of the Saudi state over international aid flows but it also—less visibly—reorients the role of religion in Saudi humanitarianism.

This chapter examines the relationship between Saudi aid and religion, between relief work and proselytization. Saudi aid organizations are strongly associated with missionary activity and the propagation of Wahhabi Islam. Particularly with regard to *da'wa* practices, KSRelief marks a drastic turning point for Saudi humanitarianism. In the following analysis, I show how KSRelief promotes Saudi humanitarianism as "universal" aid, void of religion. With the establishment of KSRelief, the Saudi government has assumed authority over the humanitarian landscape and centralized humanitarian aid flows, to an unprecedented extent. Traditionally, Saudi aid has been channeled through a multitude of actors, including private charities, royal foundations, and public campaigns, as well as bilateral and multilateral aid through regional and international organizations. In order to understand Saudi humanitarianism *abroad*, it is important to recognize this complex *domestic* relationship between public, private, and royal entities involved in the field of aid, which the following analysis unfolds. It is not

Nora Derbal, *Humanitarian and Relief Organizations in Global Saudi Da'wa?* In: *Wahhabism and the World*. Edited by: Peter Mandaville, Oxford University Press. © Oxford University Press 2022.
DOI: 10.1093/oso/9780197532560.003.0006

surprising that "Saudi assistance is, at once, humanitarian and deeply political" (El Taraboulsi-McCarthy 2017, iii; see also Lowi 2019). Foreign aid and development assistance have long been understood as soft power that can help political actors achieve strategic interests (Escobar 1995; Mitchell 2002). Yet, how has the state's encroachment and reorganization of the humanitarian landscape affected the religious dimension of Saudi humanitarianism?

I argue that Saudi Arabia's political leadership today aims to sideline Islam from humanitarianism in order to add international recognition and visibility to a new image of the state—a post-Wahhabi Saudi state. This is part of a larger political trajectory, manifest in the country's national development strategy, "Vision 2030." The ambitious socioeconomic reform initiative, proclaimed by Crown Prince Muhammad bin Salman in April 2016, aims at reviving the staggering Saudi economy through its diversification, foreign direct investment, and—implicitly—social and moral reform. Vision 2030 promotes Islam as a "way of life" (*manhaj haya*) (KSA 2017, 16). Few, selective references to the sayings and deeds of the Prophet Muhammad (*ahadith*) offer "guidance on the values of hardwork, dedication, and excellence" (KSA 2017, 16). This novel version of Saudi state Islam as a "generic Islam"—to borrow a phrase from Dale Eickelman (1992, 650–51)—which stands for universal values like moderation, tolerance, and discipline, and which marginalizes the authority of Saudi Arabia's traditional religious leaders, is a far cry from previous versions of Saudi-state Islam.

Since Saudi Arabia maintains one of the largest humanitarian aid budgets in the world, any attempt to discuss the role of religion in Saudi humanitarianism draws inevitably a selective picture. The kingdom has emerged as one of the largest donors of humanitarian assistance outside the Western states. Official statistics show Saudi Arabia's foreign aid between 1996 and 2018 as US$86.7 billion, spent in eighty countries (KSRelief 2019d, 6–8). As of March 2019, KSRelief claims to have spent a total of US$3.25 billion on 996 projects in forty-four beneficiary countries (KSRelief 2019d, 17).

In this context, it is important to differentiate between the representation of humanitarian action and the actual practice—or rather practices—in the field. At the heart of the analysis presented in this chapter is a shift in official representations away from an emphasis on "Islamic solidarity" and the ummah toward a global humanitarian paradigm that stresses "impartiality" in the name of a shared "humanity" (for a critical deconstruction of this paradigm, see De Waal 1989; and Fassin 2011; in historic perspective, Davies 2012). The analysis is based on documentations produced by humanitarian actors, such as annual reports, press releases, and websites. The documentations express official, negotiated representational discourse. In other words, the documentations represent, above all, how these organizations want to provide aid, or how they think one *ought* to provide aid. In order to move beyond the level of representation and to probe into the effects that the shift in representation has had on the role of religion in actual practice, this chapter draws on interviews with Saudi humanitarian workers and representatives of the organizations discussed here, conducted in Riyadh in January and March 2020, as well as observations gathered at the second "Riyadh International Humanitarian Forum" held in the Saudi capital in March 2020.[3]

Charity, *Da'wa*, and the Wahhabi Mission

Whereas sociocultural and political traditions of the Global North tend to differentiate between humanitarianism, relief, charity, and development as separate fields of engagement, in the Saudi context these boundaries are often blurred. In the cultural history of the Middle East, ideas of relief and Islamic charity are intimately intertwined, not only rooted in religious traditions of philanthropy and communal self-help practices, but also reflecting the colonial experience of the region (Moussa 2014; Framke and Möller 2019). Jasmine Moussa's linguistic study (2014) highlights that the Arabic language itself has no single accepted term equivalent to "humanitarianism." Only in the second half of the twentieth century did the term *insaniyya* (and its masculine adjective *insani*) emerge to denote "humanitarian" action. Rather than assuming a universal definition of humanitarianism, this chapter pays attention to the conditions in which Islamic charity (*khayr*) and relief (*ighatha*) have come to be represented in the language of humanitarianism.

Da'wa is an intrinsic aspect of Islamic charity. The concept goes back to the Arabic root of the term *da'a*, meaning to call and to invite; commonly, *da'wa* describes practices aimed at winning non-Muslims to the cause of Islam. This comprises acts of outward proselytization. *Da'wa* also takes on subtler forms, especially where it is directed at Muslims to become more "devout" in their religious practice. Both charity and *da'wa* have deep roots in Islamic doctrine and practice and often appear entangled in multiple ways. This is highlighted by the *zakat*, the obligatory annual alms, which are considered one of the five pillars of Islam. In the Qur'an, the so-called verse of *zakat* (Q 9:60) specifies that alms are "for those whose hearts have been won over" (*al-mu'allafat qulubuhum*), commonly assumed to refer to converts, and alms shall also be spent "for the cause of God" (*fi sabil Allah*).[4]

The spread of a Saudi Islam through the country's humanitarian mission has raised concerns not only in the West, but also in Muslim societies of the Global South. Throughout the twentieth century, the dominant Islam of Saudi Arabia was widely regarded as Wahhabi Islam. Wahhabism began as a theological reform movement ignited by the preacher Muhammad ibn 'Abd al-Wahhab

(1703–1792) in central Arabia's Najd region (DeLong-Bas 2004). A historic alliance with the Al Saʿud family, formed in 1744, helped spread the puritanical reform movement's message throughout Arabia. In return, the Al Saʿud dynasty benefited from an elevated status, which Ibn ʿAbd al-Wahhab's teachings grant the ruler who ensures that the Muslim community lives in accordance with God's word (Commins 2006). Wahhabism promotes a literalist understanding of the Qurʾan. Followers of the movement do not want to be understood as "Wahhabis"; instead, they describe themselves rather as *muwahhid* (one who professes God's unity) or "Salafi," which denotes the Islam of the pious ancestors (*al-salaf al-salih*) (Haykel 2009). Muhammad ibn ʿAbd al-Wahhab and his followers believed it a religious obligation to spread the call (*daʿwa*) for a restoration of pure monotheistic worship. With its aim of a "return" to "correct" Islamic belief and practice, the distribution of religious materials, such as copies of the Qurʾan and religious commentary, as well as religious education and preaching, has become a hallmark of the Wahhabi mission. Ideas of *daʿwa*, charity, and Islamic relief (*ighatha islamiyya*) stood behind the emergence of Saudi Arabia's largest and most (in)famous humanitarian organizations, such as the International Islamic Relief Organization (IIRO), the Al-Haramain Islamic Foundation, and Al-Waqf al-Islami.

The proliferation of Islamic relief in the 1970s and 1980s rested on an understanding of "Islamic solidarity" (*tadamun* or *taʿawun islami*), but it was also motivated by political rivalry. In an attempt to counter Gamal ʿAbd al-Nasser's secular pan-Arabism, King Faisal (r. 1964–1975) promoted the idea of (pan-) "Islamic solidarity," which portrayed all Muslims as one people with an obligation to support one another. Beneficiaries of aid were represented as fellow "Muslim brothers and sisters" and the work of humanitarian organizations framed as a contribution toward "strengthening the ummah," the community of believers.[5] However, neither "Islamic solidarity" nor the ummah mirrors natural facts or mechanical equations. As social constructs, they reflect an understanding of belonging to a specific historic moment, which can equally be the result of the mobilization of governments or particular group interests (Mandeville 2001; Schulze 1990, 47–86, 104–48). Saudi transnational Islamic relief organizations, like the IIRO, helped compensate the weak legitimacy of Wahhabi Islam at critical moments. The legitimacy of the Saudi religious-political project was questioned *domestically* by a group of militants around Juhayman al-ʿUtaibi, who seized the Grand Mosque of Mecca in 1979, and later during the First Gulf War years, 1990–1991; and *internationally* by the Iranian Revolution of 1979, which fueled Sunni-Shiʿite rivalries over religious and political hegemony in the region.

At that time, a number of transnational Islamic relief organizations, which largely originated from private initiatives at first, were not only tolerated but indeed encouraged by the Al Saʿud ruling family, for they helped further the political and strategic interests of the Saudi state. The IIRO traces its origins to a group of wealthy Saudi individuals, who started organizing shipments of food and clothes to people in the Horn of Africa in 1978 (Petersen 2015, 65). In January 1979, the IIRO was recognized as a subsidiary organization of the Muslim World League (MWL) and subsequently appeared as the long arm of the Saudi government. Annual reports of the IIRO showcase the royal government in support of "the poor and needy" and, more specifically, "Muslim brothers and sisters," in Asia, Africa, and Europe. The activities of the IIRO, one of the largest Islamic charity organizations of the mid-1990s, ranged from emergency relief to social welfare programs. It included education, healthcare, the construction of mosques and wells, and a "Holy Qur'an and Da'wa Program," which taught the Qur'an and "shari'a sciences." Another case in point is the Al-Haramain Islamic Foundation, which was established in 1989 in the city Peshawar by 'Aqil 'Abd al-'Aziz al-'Aqil, who previously worked for the Saudi Red Crescent (Bokhari et al. 2014). Al-Haramain's activities combined the distribution of the Qur'an and religious education alongside relief and development work in some forty countries. Similarly, the charity organization Al-Waqf al-Islami, established in 1986–1987 with an emphasis on religious education of youth, particularly second- and third-generation Muslim migrants to Europe, shows an understanding of humanitarianism that is tied to proselytization and the religious establishment of Saudi Arabia. Among the founders of the organization, for instance, is Shaykh 'Abdullah bin Sulayman al-Manea, today a member of the Saudi Council of Senior Scholars.

Yet, it would be wrong to conflate the Wahhabi mission with the Saudi humanitarian mission. Some humanitarian organizations, like the IIRO, Al-Haramain, and Al-Waqf al-Islami, are indeed notorious for their missionary and Wahhabi zeal; yet, many other Saudi charities and humanitarian organizations have distanced themselves from these groups. I want to stress that—instead of religion—many Saudi charities have for some time promoted ideas of development, empowerment, and capacity building, thus resonating with and promoting global trends in humanitarian practice among Saudi charity organizations, most prominently among them the Society of Majid bin 'Abd al-'Aziz for Development and Social Services in Jeddah, the King Khalid Foundation in Riyadh, and Alwaleed Philanthropies under the aegis of the Saudi billionaire Prince Alwaleed bin Talal. Rather than assuming one monolithic Saudi humanitarian mission, I have suggested elsewhere that we should understand the Saudi field of aid as a contested field in which a multiplicity of actors—sometimes with competitive agendas, sometimes highly critical of each other, often in cooperation—have historically found one of the rare spaces for engagement within the authoritarian frame of the Saudi state (Derbal 2019, 2017).

The Saudi Aid Landscape

Throughout the twentieth century, the Saudi state has had an interest in supervising and regulating charitable practices, though with limited success. As early as 1925, state-founder Ibn Sa'ud made the payment of the zakat mandatory for all his subjects in Najd and Al-Ahsa (Toth 2012, 66). Before the discovery of oil, zakat was an important source of revenue given the scarce budget of the young state, but it also fulfilled important symbolic functions as a demonstration of allegiance. In April 1951, Ibn Sa'ud stipulated the collection of zakat from all individuals and companies holding Saudi citizenship at a rate of 2.5 percent.[6] In May 1951, a ministerial resolution established the Department of Zakat and Income Tax (DZIT) within the Ministry of Finance (MoF).[7] In other words, the Ministry of Finance disposes of zakat money. The Ministry of Finance channels zakat money toward social welfare programs in Saudi Arabia and abroad through the Ministry of Social Affairs and the Ministry of Islamic Affairs.

In 1961, the Ministry of Labor and Social Affairs was established in order to oversee communal engagement, particularly charity associations (jam'iyyat khayriyya). With few exceptions, all charity organizations in Saudi Arabia have had to register with the Ministry of Social Affairs. In 1976, legislation banned charities from collecting donations without explicit permission from the ministry, permission which was only granted to organizations registered with the Ministry of Social Affairs.[8] Charity associations in many ways represented a continuation of traditional individual, charitable practices, which have a long history on the Arabian Peninsula, by feeding the poor and needy, through soup kitchens and the care of orphans. Yet, the notion of charity also expanded in this new collective format, for instance, in the Penny for Palestine Society (Jam'iyyat Qirsh li-l-Filistin), founded in 1935, in order to raise funds to support the Palestinian struggle, or the National Medical Ambulance Society (Jam'iyyat al-Is'af al-Tibbi al-Watani), founded in 1934 by a group of social activists from the Hijaz, who provided humanitarian aid to the victims of the Saudi-Yemeni war along the southern borders of the new nation-state. In 1963, this latter initiative was turned into the Saudi Red Crescent Society (al-Hilal al-Ahmar, SRC), which then became one of the state's major agencies for overseas relief. In April 2016, the Ministry of Social Affairs counted 736 registered charity associations (ICNL 2017). The spectrum of engagement of these charity organizations is wide and includes medical services, education, poverty relief schemes, food banks, artisanal training, and campaigns for environmental awareness (Derbal 2014).

Charities, which engage in religious propagation and proselytization, on the other hand, traditionally fell under the jurisdiction of the Ministry of Islamic Affairs, Da'wa, and Guidance. Established in 1993, it has overseen, for instance, the numerous charities of the Holy Qur'an Memorization Association (Jam'iyyat

Tahfith al-Qur'an al-Karim). According to the Ministry of Islamic Affairs, Saudi Arabia counted 163 charities of the Holy Qur'an Memorization Association in 2012–2013 (1434–1435 h.) with a total of 729,713 students (Ministry of Islamic Affairs, Da'wa, and Guidance 2019).[9] The numbers increased toward a total of 1,060,179 students by 2016–2017 (1438–1439 h.) (Ministry of Islamic Affairs, Da'wa, and Guidance n.d.).[10] In the context of *da'wa*, the King Fahd Complex for the Printing of the Qur'an, under the auspices of the Ministry of Islamic Affairs, is of particular significance. This government institution publishes every year about 10 million copies of the Qur'an, translated into thirty-nine languages for distribution around the globe—as an act of charity. The books are explicitly marked on the cover as "endowment for Allah's sake" (*waqf Allah*). The copies give a distinct "Wahhabi flavor" to the holy book of Islam.[11] For instance, a very recent publication of the King Fahd Complex translates one of the most controversial verses on women in the Qur'an, Sura al-Nisa (The Women, Qur'an 4:35), as follows:

> Men are the protectors and maintainers [*qawwamun*] of women, because Allah has made one of them to excel the other, and because they spend (to support them) from their means. Therefore the righteous women are devoutly obedient [*qanitat*] (to Allah then to their husbands), and guard in the husband's absence what Allah orders them to guard (e.g. their chastity, their husband's property). As to those women on whose part you see ill-conduct [*nushuz*], admonish them (first), (next), refuse to share their beds, (and last) beat them (lightly, if it is useful); but if they obey you, seek not against them means (of annoyance). (Taqi-ud Din al-Hilali and Khan 1441 h. (2019–2020), 145)

Sanctioned by the Saudi religious establishment, this verse conflates translation with commentary. The English translation thereby leaves out the controversial debate about terms such as *nushuz*, *qanitat*, and *qawwamun*, which invite a considerable degree of interpretation (Ali 2006, 117–126; Abdel Halim 2011). In short, the patriarchal reading conflates obedience to God and obedience to husbands, which—to put it mildly—is highly problematic.

For the Ministry of Islamic Affairs, as well as religious charities, things have changed drastically under King Salman. The Ministry of Islamic Affairs continues to oversee mosques and the training of preachers, who work inside Saudi Arabia and abroad. However, in a highly controversial move upon ascending the throne, King Salman announced the establishment of a General Authority for Endowments under the auspices of Ahmad bin Sulayman al-Rajhi, who became minister of Social Affairs in 2018. Until 2015, the Ministry of Islamic Affairs oversaw the country's Islamic endowments (*awqaf*), which arguably represented the wealth of the ministry. Similarly, the new NGO law, issued in 2015 by royal decree of King Salman, elevated the Ministry of Labor and Social Affairs as the responsible authority (*al-sulta al-mas'ula*, §4) for all civic organizations, including religious associations.[12] The new laws reduce the role of the Ministry of Islamic Affairs to one of "technical supervision" (*ishraf fanni*, §5)—at least in theory. Other decrees have similarly marginalized the role of the religious establishment in the recent past. For instance, in a widely reported move attributed to Crown Prince Muhammad bin Salman, the Saudi government curbed the powers of the so-called religious police, the Committee for the Promotion of Virtue and the Prevention of Vice (in short: *al-Hay'a*), who are no longer permitted to roam the streets to denounce those whom they deem in conflict with Islamic precepts. Those popular Saudi clerics with a history of criticizing government policies—often former supporters of the Sahwa movement with alleged sympathies to the Muslim Brotherhood, such as Salman al-'Awda and Muhammad al-'Arifi—have been arrested in 2017 and 2018, respectively. These restraints on the religious establishment in the widest sense support the stellar rise to power of Muhammad bin Salman and the centralization of power around the royal court.

Controlling the Flow of Overseas Aid

In the absence of a ministry of international development or cooperation, overseas aid from Saudi Arabia has been administered through various channels. Royal and non-royal Saudi individuals have historically established charity organizations with a global humanitarian agenda. Today one of the world's largest private foundations is based in Saudi Arabia: Alwaleed Philanthropies, established in 1980, with an estimated annual budget of around US$200 million, totaling US$750 million in value (Dickinson 2017). The Saudi state, on the other hand, has been (and continues to be) active in a number of multilateral regional aid organizations, including the Arab Gulf Program for Development (AGFUND) and the Islamic Development Bank, and in global multilateral organizations such as the International Monetary Fund, the OPEC Fund for International Development, UN organizations, and the World Bank. In 1974, the Saudi government established the Saudi Fund for Development (SDF) in Riyadh, charged primarily with providing long-term loans for infrastructural support programs to Arab states. Until today, the SDF holds Saudi Arabia's largest aid budget by far. Since 2010, the SDF spent on average US$800 million per year, with a peak of US$2.4 billion in 2016, whereas KSRelief has spent an annual average of US$350 million since 2015 (KSRelief 2019b). This distribution of resources is an important aspect in understanding the function of KSRelief. Rather than a new funding institution, one of the functions of KSRelief is to oversee and regulate the multiplicity of Saudi actors and organizations in the field of overseas aid.

The September 11, 2001, terrorist attacks, which involved fifteen Saudi nationals, cast a long shadow over Saudi humanitarianism. Following 9/11, the IIRO, Al-Haramain, and Al-Waqf al-Islami were accused of supporting Al-Qaeda and other terrorist networks, either through money laundering or through the propagation of a militant Islam. While most of the allegations could not be proven (Lacey and Benthall 2014; Benthall 2016), the accusations did highlight that the Saudi government could not control or had no intention of controlling the flow of overseas money. With international pressure mounting, in 2002 the Saudi embassy in Washington, DC, announced a total shutdown of private and national Saudi charities sending funds outside of the kingdom unless it was in coordination with the Ministry of Foreign Affairs (Bokhari et al. 2014, 210). In 2002, the government also announced the creation of a High Commission for Oversight of Charities, which was established in 2004 by royal decree as the Commission on Relief and Charity Work Abroad—but it seems to have never become fully operational. Following Al-Qaeda attacks within Saudi Arabia in 2003, the Saudi government tightened its regulations on the financial sector at large, effectively banning charity associations from handling cash and from sending money overseas, as well as banning cash collections throughout Saudi Arabia, including donations made at mosques. As of 2003, a Financial Investigation Unit (SA-FIU) of FATF—the global Financial Action Task Force—was invited to operate in the kingdom, which classified the country's charities to be "high-risk" and requiring "increased levels of due diligence" (§ 379, in MENAFATF 2010, 83–84). These measures had a devastating effect on Saudi charities. Until today, charity organizations like the King Khalid Foundation in Riyadh stress the financial exclusion placed upon Saudi nonprofit organizations through anti-money-laundering and anti-terrorism legislation (King Khalid Foundation 2018). In the words of a female social activist (interviewed in Riyadh, January 27, 2020), these regulations have "crippled" the nonprofit sector for a long time to come.

The King Salman Humanitarian Aid and Relief Center (KSRelief)

Through its mandate, KSRelief not only restructures the Saudi landscape of aid, it is effectively reorienting humanitarian practices toward a single, unified approach that resonates with the dominant paradigm of "the global moral community" with its "expectations of universality" (Fassin 2011). In other words, instead of Islamic solidarity, KSRelief stresses "impartiality" for the sake of "humanity." I suggest that we should understand this major overhaul of Saudi humanitarianism as a reaction to continued international pressure, as well as a strategy through which the new ruling elite seeks to relocate the Saudi state visibly among the "international community" (an aspiration that is visible, for instance, in Saudi Arabia's presidency over the G20 in the year 2020; the importance of other, historic alliances, such as the Arab League, appear to be of subordinate significance to the new leadership). In the context of aid, the "international community" as a new frame of reference speaks to the major "secular," "humanitarian," and "international" organizations, represented and governed by a body of transnational institutions situated in the Global North, which Alex de Waal has critically coined the "Humanitarian International" (de Waal 1989).

KSRelief headlines, such as those cited earlier, thus also appear as a message directed at the "international community," namely that the Saudi state has finally taken steps to control the flow of overseas aid. Almost on a daily basis, since its inception in 2015, KSRelief has been a topic in the English press from Saudi Arabia. Given the highly circumscribed freedom of the press, this should be read as a reflection of the will of the state to propagate the center among a global audience, whose dominant language of communication is English. On the other hand, the fact that the Saudi Press Agency continues to issue frequent warnings, which criminalize donations that do not go through KSRelief, can also be read as an indication of a continuing struggle of authority over the flow of aid. The lack of public outcry over KSRelief's absolutist claim should not be mistaken to equal a general approval of these drastic measures by Saudi society. In light of the general lack of freedom of expression, the risk involved in openly criticizing the government has increased considerably during King Salman's reign (Human Rights Watch 2019).

"Cooperation" and "partnership" with humanitarian actors of the Global North are a key aspiration of KSRelief. The center lists on its website some fifteen humanitarian organizations as partner organizations, including the United States Agency for International Development (USAID), the International Committee of the Red Cross (ICRC), and the UN Office of the High Commissioner for Human Rights (OHCHR), to whom it extends office space under the roof of the center. In 2018, KSRelief launched its own "International Humanitarian Forum" (*Muntada al-Riyadh al-Duwali al-Insani*), inviting some one thousand "global experts," "professionals and key-decision makers from across the international humanitarian community" (KSRelief 2018, n.p.). The conference program listed more than twenty speakers of well-known agencies such as UNRWA, USAID, and the ICRC. Yet, the program did not include one representative with a background in an Islamic relief organization (KSRelief 2019c), although it appears that the new chief of International Islamic Relief Organization of Saudi Arabia (IIROSA), Hassan Shahbar, participated in the meeting (*Saudi Gazette* 2018).

With the shifting frame of reference, the representation of Saudi aid has changed considerably. Today, the official motto of Saudi aid abroad is propagated by the website and brochures of KSRelief as "Towards an Unrestricted

Humanity" (*Nahu insaniyya bi-la hudud*). KSRelief stands for humanitarianism and humanitarian action, and no longer for Islamic relief, Islamic solidarity, or Islamic charity. Humanitarian aid, translated as *a'mal insaniyya* (literally meaning "humanitarian action"), is adopted by the name of the center. From its inception, the center broke with Islamic traditions that favor secrecy in giving. A full-fledged, bilingual website offers information on the center's projects in English and Arabic (including images and stories about its beneficiaries). The king's opening speech, translated into English, explains that the "primary goal is to operate this center solely on the basis of humanitarian need and without any other motive." The original Arabic speech uses the term "human dimension" (*al-bu'd al-insani*) (KSRelief 2019a, n.p.). The first message on KSRelief's website stresses that "our primary goal is to operate this center solely on the basis of humanitarian need and without any other motive." This self-identification in the negation of "other motives" (instead of a positive affirmation of certain [religious] principles) reflects the extent of allegations previously raised against Saudi humanitarianism.

In May 2019, KSRelief launched an online donation portal, which showcases the new, government-sanctioned humanitarianism and the exclusions which this discourse produces. Through the website, donors are given the choice to donate to twenty-one countries from Asia and Africa. Prominently missing from the list are Egypt and Yemen. Donors can alternatively choose to support a specific program authorized by KSRelief and executed by local and international partners in the respective regions. KSRelief does not itself execute any programs abroad. During the second International Humanitarian Forum in Riyadh, a lower-ranked representative of KSRelief (interviewed on March 2, 2020) explained the function of the center as merely conducting "security checks." All "approved humanitarian programs" went through KSRelief's security check, which according to the employee, was "very difficult to pass." The sanctioned programs address medical and health issues, food security, water, sanitation, and education. The e-donation portal does not list any program with an explicitly religious content, such as religious or spiritual education, the distribution of religious materials, or the building of mosques. After operating for seven months, in November 2019, the e-donations portal only counted 1,445 donors and donations totaling SAR 1,024,414 (approx. US$273,000); after one year, in September 2020, the number stood at 42,674 donors and SAR 13,844,022 (US$3.7 million) (KSRelief n.d.).

KSRelief is based on a "Code of Ethics" (*qawa'id al-suluk wa-akhlaqiyyat al-'amal*), which is void of religious reference. The eighteen-page document, subtitled "Working with Integrity and Humanity," defines KSRelief's "Core Values (§6)" to be "complete neutrality, transparency," "professionalism," and "strong international partnerships" (KSRelief 2017, 9). It further elaborates on the motto of KSRelief, "Towards an Unrestricted Humanity (§7)": "KSRelief shall only seek to promote humanity . . . whose only purpose is the human being everywhere without any discrimination" (KSRelief 2017, 9). This entails a set of principles, above all:

1. The humanitarian imperative comes first;
2. Aid is given regardless of adverse distinction or discrimination of any kind. Aid priorities are calculated based on need alone;
3. Aid will not be used to further a particular standpoint;
4. We shall respect culture and customs.
   (KSRelief 2017, 10)

The fourth principle in particular is a stark departure from the Wahhabi missionary impulse and religious proselytization.

This does not, however, mean that Saudi aid has necessarily become void of religion. Although Islam as a point of reference is missing from KSRelief's website, the king's opening speech refers to Islam as a source of motivation. King Salman himself—in whose name the center operates—has an outstanding record of Islamic relief and service, which earned him in 2001 the King Faisal Prize (KFP 2001). When I asked Dr. Samer Al-Jetaily, spokesperson of KSRelief, during an interview conducted on January 29, 2020, if Islam no longer plays a role in Saudi humanitarianism, he suggested that

[i]t would not be appropriate to talk about Islamic solidarity. We work in an International Community. . . . We do not only help Muslims, we would help non-Muslims. But we all know that it is a sad truth that the most, many of our beneficiaries, of the poorest people around the world and the people in crisis are Muslims. We don't like to have religion promoting our projects, we promote a humanitarian agenda. We aim at reaching the human being, despite his or her race or religion. (S. Al-Jetaily, personal communication, January 29, 2020)

Al-Jetaily suggested that Islamic charity played an important role in financing the center. According to Al-Jetaily, KSRelief was free to spend donations received in the form of *sadaqa* (voluntary alms) on everyone in need, including non-Muslims. *Zakat*, on the other hand, which KSRelief received would have to be spent on Muslims only, since this, according to Al-Jetaily's reading, was mandated by the "verse of *zakat*" (Qur'an 9:60). Yet, later in the interview, Al-Jetaily clarified that 95 percent of KSRelief's budget came from the Saudi government, with private charity currently only making a small contribution. The center was working on plans, however, to increase the contribution of private charity. Only at the very end of our interview, Al-Jetaily added with emphasis: "I'm a Muslim, and that's why I help. It's my obligation." Islam as a source of motivation is a thread through Al-Jetaily's biography, which drove him to volunteer as an active board member in several Saudi charity associations (*jam'iyyat khayriyya*) and one charity foundation (*mu'assasa khayriyya*), and motivated him to volunteer as a dentist in Syria, when the civil war in that country broke out in 2011.

What does KSRelief mean for other actors in the field of Saudi humanitarianism? The impact has been mixed. Jonathan Benthall suggests that by April 2017, the IIRO had been reduced to a small office in Jeddah, forbidden from raising funds for overseas aid (Benthall 2018, 1). The Saudi Red Crescent Society (SRC), which in the past functioned as one of the main humanitarian players from Saudi Arabia, is now represented merely as a national "charity body" (UNDP et al. 2016, 23) with no activity outside of Saudi Arabia. Today, the Saudi Red Crescent only operates a national ambulance service, although it was represented at the second Humanitarian Forum in Riyadh. When I inquired about these changes with an employee of the Saudi Red Crescent Society in Riyadh (personal communication, March 1, 2020), he became visibly uneasy and ended the interview abruptly, stating "Let's not talk politics." Rather than confronting existing humanitarian players, KSRelief appears to sideline organizations by assuming center stage: When the president of the International Committee of the Red Cross (ICRC) met King Salman in October 2019, Saudi newspapers seized the opportunity to showcase statistics of KSRelief while not mentioning the Saudi Red Crescent at all (*Arab News* 2019). Only a two-sentence statement issued by the Saudi Press Agency suggested that the ICRC president also met with the new president of the Saudi Red Crescent (SPA 2019b). The schedule of the second Riyadh International Humanitarian Forum in March 2020—yet again—did not include speakers from internationally operating Saudi humanitarian organizations other than KSRelief. Only the last panel, which was sparsely attended by members of the "international community," offered a platform to national charity organizations, which offer alternative health services in Saudi Arabia. The fact that all those organizations that were once considered major, global Saudi humanitarian players count new chiefs, like IIROSA and the Saudi Red Crescent as well as the Muslim World League (MWL)—headed since 2016 by Muhammad Al-Issa, who is known to be a close ally to Crown Prince Muhammad bin Salman (Feuer 2019)—is itself an indication of the restructuring of the field of aid. The Saudi Aid Platform, a database administered by KSRelief, "to reflect all of the Kingdom's foreign aid efforts," does not include the IIRO, Al-Waqf al-Islami, or other nongovernmental charities.[13] The aid statistics presented by the Saudi Aid Platform illustrate that KSRelief has seized considerable resources: while the SDF leads the statistics with a total funding of US$16.4 billion (spent since 1975), KSRelief can count a funding of US$3.5 billion. The Saudi Red Crescent is listed with US$42.8 million in the period 2000–2015, with no budget after the year 2015.

Old Wine, New Bottles?

In contemporary Saudi Arabia, the official discourse of humanitarianism has shifted away from notions of Islamic solidarity with an emphasis on religious proselytization, toward a "universal" humanitarianism that is described as impartial, needs-based, and void of discrimination. Since the 1980s, many Islamic relief organizations have undergone a process of professionalization with the effect of adapting "universal" standards of aid, a process that accelerated in the wake of 9/11, with international pressure mounting on Islamic charities. With its inception in 2015, KSRelief has emerged as the central state authority that regulates and controls the flow of overseas aid from Saudi Arabia, but its function is also to produce and sell an image of Saudi humanitarianism as "universal" aid, and thereby to broker the Saudi position within the "international community." Although the discourse in which Saudi humanitarianism is presented today no longer emphasizes Islamic solidarity, the aid statistics of KSRelief continue to show a strong concentration on Arab and Muslim states. In 2019, for instance, KSRelief executed projects in eleven countries, chief among them Yemen and Syria, with only one country (Mauritius) not being a Muslim-majority society (KSRelief 2019). The King Fahd Complex for the Printing of the Qur'an under the auspices of the Ministry of Islamic Affairs continues to distribute every year millions of copies of the Qur'an that perpetuate a distinct Wahhabi reading of the scripture. Religion continues to play an important role for many Saudis involved in humanitarian organizations, who draw their motivation to engage for the poor and needy from an Islamic imperative to engage in charity and beneficence.

The reorientation of the Saudi aid landscape has had a devastating effect on some of those humanitarian organizations, which were once the pride of the Saudi state but no longer match the strategic, political interest of the new political elite, such as the Saudi Red Crescent and the IIRO, both of which appear barely operational today. The militant history of a comparatively small number of Saudi charity organizations and their association with da'wa activism form the backbone for KSRelief and the reform program of the Saudi government, which has mobilized the "threat of abuse" and "terrorism" to legitimize the encroachment of the state over autonomous forms of charity. The reorientation of the aid landscape comes at the cost of freedom of organization and a loss of the multiplicity of values, which the field of humanitarianism historically represented.

Notes

1. I thank Peter Mandeville and the participants of the authors' workshop "Wahhabism in the World" in December 2019 in Washington, DC, for their insightful comments

on an earlier draft of this chapter and Christopher Anzalone for his help with bringing the text in shape. Special thanks go to Yasmine Farouk for her help with the research.

2. Royal order (*amr malaki*) no. 55871, dated 9.11.1436 h. (August 25, 2015), see "EDonation Portal," King Salman Humanitarian and Relief Center, 2019, https://don ate.ksrelief.org/ (accessed November 10, 2019).

3. I thank the King Faisal Center for Research and Islamic Studies for hosting me as a research fellow in January 2020 and Dr. Fahad Alsharif for sharing his insights.

4. The full verse reads, "Voluntary alms are for the poor and wretched, for those who collect them, for those whose hearts have been won over, for slaves to buy their freedom, for those in debt, for the cause of God and for the needy wayfarer" (Khalidi 2009).

5. *Ummah* is a complex term with deep religious roots; in the Qur'an, *ummah* appears 62 times, where it refers to communities "sharing a common religion" (Denny 2015).

6. Royal decree no. 17/2/28/8634, dated 29.06.1370 h. (April 7, 1951).

7. Ministerial resolution no. 394, dated 7.08.1370 h. (May 14, 1951).

8. La'ihat Jam' al-Tabarru'at li-l-Wujuh al-Khayriyya (Regulations for Collecting Donations for Charitable Purposes), by ministerial resolution (*qarar majlis al-wuzara'*) no. 547, dated 30.3.1396 h. (March 31, 1976); see Ministry of Social Affairs, *Lawā'iḥ wa-Anẓimat Wizārat al-Shu'ūn al-Ijtimā'iyya* [Rules and Regulations of the Ministry of Social Affairs], 5th edition, Riyadh 2009, 277–284.

9. This number comprises 359,762 male students and 369,951 female students.

10. It is interesting to note that the sharp increase reflects an increase in female students (681,812), while the number of male students has remained relatively stable (378,367).

11. I thank Natana DeLong-Bas for bringing this up.

12. Nizam al-Jam'iyyat wa-l-Mu'assasat al-Ahliyya (Statute Governing Civic Associations and Foundations), royal decree (*marsum malaki*) no. M/8, dated 19.02.1437 h. (December 1, 2015). Lower-ranked regulations (*la'ihat*), which address further procedures, were passed in March 2016. The statute is available on the website of the Bureau of Experts at the Council of Ministers: https://laws.boe.gov.sa/BoeL aws/Laws/LawDetails/37e0768f-8e3c-493a-b951-a9a700f2bbb1/2.

13. The Saudi Aid Platform was issued by royal decree no. 41555, dated 10.09.1438 h. (June 5, 2017), according to the description of the website; see https://data.ksrelief. org/Pages/About (accessed September 23, 2020).

References

Abdel Halim, Asma M. 2011. "A Home for Obedience: Masculinity in Personal Status forMuslims Law." *Journal of Women of the Middle East and the Islamic World* 9(1–2): 194–214. doi: https://doi.org/10.1163/156920811X578467.

Ali, Kecia. 2006. *Sexual Ethics and Islam. Feminist Reflections on Qur'an, Hadith, and Jurisprudence.* Oxford: OneWorld.

Arab News. 2019. "King Salman Receives International Committee of the Red Cross President," October 16, 2019. https://www.arabnews.com/node/1569536/saudi-arabia.

Benthall, Jonathan. 2016. *Islamic Charities and Islamic Humanism in Troubled Times.* Manchester: Manchester University Press.

Benthall, Jonathan. 2018. "The Rise and Decline of Saudi Overseas Humanitarian Charities." 20. Occasional Paper. Qatar: Georgetown University. https://repository.library.georgetown.edu/bitstream/handle/10822/1051628/CIRSOccasionalPaper20JonathanBenthall2018.pdf?sequence=1&isAllowed=y

Bokhari, Yusra, Nasim Chowdhury, and Robert Lacey. 2014. "A Good Day to Bury a Bad Charity: Charting the Rise and Fall of the Al-Haramain Islamic Foundation." In *Gulf Charities and Islamic Philanthropy in the "Age of Terror" and Beyond*, edited by Robert Lacey and Jonathan Benthall, 199–230. Berlin: Gerlach Press.

Commins, David. 2006. *The Wahhabi Mission and Saudi Arabia*. London: I. B. Tauris.

Davies, Kathrine. 2012. "Continuity, Change and Contest: Meanings of 'Humanitarian' from the 'Religion of Humanity' to the Kosovo War." *HPG Working Paper*. London: Overseas Development Institute. https://www.odi.org/publications/6737-continuity-change-and-contest-meanings-humanitarian-religion-humanity-kosovo-war.

Denny, F. M. 2015. "Umma." In *Encyclopaedia of Islam*, 2nd edition, edited by P. J. Bearman, T. Bianquis, C. E. Bosworth, E. J. van Donzel, and W. P. Heinrichs. Leiden: Brill (1960–2015). doi: http://dx.doi.org/10.1163/1573-3912_islam_COM_1291 (accessed June 21, 2020).

de Waal, Alex. 1989. *Famine That Kills*. Oxford: Clarendon Press.

DeLong-Bas, Natana J. 2004. *Wahhabi Islam: From Revival and Reform to Global Jihad*. Oxford: Oxford University Press.

Derbal, Nora. 2014. "Domestic, Religious, Civic? Notes on the Institutionalized Charitable Field in Jeddah, Saudi Arabia." In *Gulf Charities and Islamic Philanthropy in the "Age of Terror" and Beyond*, edited by Robert Lacey and Jonathan Benthall, 145–168. Berlin: Gerlach Press.

Derbal, Nora. 2017. "Charity for the Poor in Jeddah, Saudi Arabia, 1961–2015 (Microfiche)." DPhil. dissertation. Freie Universität Berlin.

Derbal, Nora. 2019. "Saudi Arabia, Humanitarian Aid and Knowledge Production: What Do We Really Know? #MUHUM." *AllegraLab* (blog). July 5, 2019. https://allegralaboratory.net/saudi-arabia-humanitarian-aid-and-knowledge-production-what-do-we-really-know-muhum-5/.

Dickinson, Elizabeth. 2017. "Exclusive: Inside Alwaleed Philanthropies' New Global Strategy." Devex. October 3, 2017. https://www.devex.com/news/sponsored/exclusive-inside-alwaleed-philanthropies-new-global-strategy-91161.

Eickelman, Dale F. 1992. "Mass Higher Education and the Religious Imagination in Contemporary Arab Societies." *American Ethnologist* 19(4): 643–55.

El Taraboulsi-McCarthy, Sherine. 2017. "A Kingdom of Humanity? Saudi Arabia's Values, Systems and Interests in Humanitarian Action." HPG Working Paper. London: Overseas Development Institute. https://www.odi.org/sites/odi.org.uk/files/resource-documents/11741.pdf.

Escobar, Arthuro. 1995. *Encountering Development, the Making and Unmaking of the Third World*. Princeton, NJ: Princeton University Press.

Fassin, Didier. 2011. *Humanitarian Reason: A Moral History of the Present*. Berkeley: University of California Press.

Feuer, Sarah. 2019. "Course Correction: The Muslim World League, Saudi Arabia's Export of Islam, and Opportunities for Washington." Washington, DC: The Washington Institute for Near East Policy. https://www.washingtoninstitute.org/policy-analysis/view/course-correction.

Framke, Maria, and Esther Möller. 2019. "From Local Philanthropy to Political Humanitarianism: South Asian and Egyptian Humanitarian Aid during the Period of

Decolonisation." ZMO Working Papers. Berlin: Zentrum Moderner Orient. https://d-nb.info/1185449493/34.

Haykel, Bernard. 2009. "On the Nature of Salafi Thought and Action." In *Global Salafism: Islam's New Religious Movement*, edited by Roel Meijer, 33–57. London: Hurst.

Human Rights Watch. 2019. "The High Cost of Change: Repression under Saudi Crown Prince Tarnishes Reforms." https://www.hrw.org/report/2019/11/04/high-cost-change/repression-under-saudi-crown-prince-tarnishes-reforms.

ICNL. 2017. "Civic Freedom Monitor: Saudi Arabia." The International Center for Not-for-Profit Law. January 10, 2017. http://www.icnl.org/research/monitor/saudiarabia.html.

KFP. 2001. "The Saudi Arabian High Commission for Donations to Bosnia-Herzegovina." King Faisal Prize. 2001. https://kingfaisalprize.org/the-saudi-arabian-high-commission-for-donations-to-bosnia-herzegovina/.

Khalidi, Tarif, trans. 2009. *The Qur'an*. Penguin Classics.

King Khalid Foundation. 2018. "Financial Inclusion in Saudi Arabia. Reaching the Financially Excluded." Riyadh. https://kkf.org.sa/media/ipuh5olx/2-financial-inclusion-in-saudi-arabia-2018.pdf.

Kingdom of Saudi Arabia (KSA). 2017. "Vision 2030." Kingdom of Saudi Arabia. https://vision2030.gov.sa/sites/default/files/report/Saudi_Vision2030_EN_2017.pdf.

KSRelief. 2017. "Code of Ethics." https://www.ksrelief.org/UploadData/About/CODEOFETHICSEnglish.pdf.

KSRelief. 2018. "Global Experts to Attend First International Humanitarian Forum in Saudi Arabia. 26–27 February 2018." Press release. https://www.dropbox.com/s/x1w716vn1ms6sjx/Press%20Release%20-%201st%20Riyadh%20International%20Humanitarin%20Forum%2026-27%20February%202018%20FINAL%20ENGLISH%20Int.docx?dl=0.

KSRelief. 2019. "General Statistics about KSRelief Projects (Complete–Ongoing) until 31 October 2019." https://www.ksrelief.org/Statistics/YearDetails/2019.

KSRelief. 2019a. "Establishment." https://www.ksrelief.org/Pages/AboutDetails/300d3cf9-ccb2-4263-b133-9aacf35a3004.

KSRelief. 2019b. "Saudi Donors Entities." Saudi Aid Platform. 2019. https://data.ksrelief.org/Projects/Sponsors.

KSRelief. 2019c. "Speakers." Riyadh International Humanitarian Forum. 2019. https://rihf.ksrelief.org/en/Speakers.aspx.

KSRelief. 2019d. "Kingdom of Saudi Arabia Humanitarian and Relief Overview." https://www.ksrelief.org/Doc/PDF/6.

KSRelief. n.d. "EDonation Portal." https://donate.ksrelief.org/ (accessed September 13, 2020).

Lacey, Robert, and Jonathan Benthall, eds. 2014. *Gulf Charities and Islamic Philanthropy in the "Age of Terror" and Beyond*. Berlin: Gerlach Press.

Lowi, Miriam R. 2019. "Charity as Politics 'Writ Small' in Gulf Petro-Monarchies." *Journal of Muslim Philanthropy and Civil Society* 3(2): 26–59.

Mandeville, Peter. 2001. *Transnational Muslim Politics: Reimagining the Umma*. London; New York: Routledge.

MENAFATF. 2010. "Anti-Money Laundering and Combating the Financing of Terrorism. Kingdom of Saudi Arabia." Mutual Evaluation Report. Middle East and North Africa (MENA) Financial Action Task Force (FATF). http://www.fatf-gafi.org/publications/mutualevaluations/documents/mutualevaluationofthekingdomofsaudiarabia.html.

Ministry of Islamic Affairs, Da'wa, and Guidance. 2019. "Numbers [sic] of Mosques and Its Employees, Charities and Call Centers and Offices." Open Data (al-Bayanat al-Maftuha). July 2019. https://data.gov.sa/Data/en/dataset/numbers_of_mosques_and_ its_employees-_charities_and_call_centers_and_offices.

Ministry of Islamic Affairs, Da'wa, and Guidance. n.d. "Al-Kitab al-Ihsa'i li-l-'Am al-Mali 1438-1439 h. (2016–18)." https://www.moia.gov.sa/Statistics/Pages/Details.aspx?ID=9 (accessed November 29, 2019).

Ministry of Social Affairs. 2009. *Lawāʾiḥ wa-Anẓimat Wizārat al-Shuʾūn al-Ijtimāʿiyya* [Rules and Regulations of the Ministry of Social Affairs]. 5th edition. Riyadh.

Mitchell, Timothy. 2002. *Rule of Experts: Egypt, Techno-Politics, Modernity.* Berkeley: University of California Press.

Moussa, Jasmine. 2014. "Ancient Origins, Modern Actors: Defining Arabic Meanings of Humanitarianism." HPG Working Paper. Overseas Development Institute: Humanitarian Policy Group. https://www.odi.org/publications/9019-anci ent-origins-modern-actors-defining-arabic-meanings-humanitarianism.

Petersen, Marie Juul. 2015. *For Humanity or for the Umma? Aid and Islam in Transnational Muslim NGOs.* London: Hurst.

Saudi Gazette. 2018. "IIROSA Chief Participates in Riyadh Humanitarian Forum," February 28, 2018. http://saudigazette.com.sa/article/529479.

Schulze, Reinhard. 1990. *Islamischer Internationalismus im 20. Jahrhundert*. Leiden: Brill.

SPA. 2019a. "Overseas Aid from Saudi Arabia Must Go through KSRelief, Spokesman Reiterates." *Arab News*, October 10, 2019. https://www.arabnews.com/node/1567026/ saudi-arabia.

SPA. 2019b. "President of Saudi Red Crescent Authority Receives President of ICRC." October 15, 2019. https://www.spa.gov.sa/1982521?lang=ar&newsid=1982521.

SPA. 2020. "'Ighatha al-Malak Salman' al-Jiha al-Wahida al-Mukhawwala bi-Tasallum al-Tabarru'at wa-Isalaha li-l-Kharij ['King Salman Relief' Is the Only Agency Authorized to Receive Donations and Channel Them Abroad]." *Al-Riyadh*, April 20, 2020. http:// www.alriyadh.com/1818557.

Taqi-ud Din al-Hilali, Muhammad, and Muhammad Muhsin Khan. 1441 h. (2019–2020). *Translation of the Meaning of the Nobel Qurʾan into the English Language.* Medina: King Fahd Glorious Qurʾan Printing Complex.

Toth, Anthony B. 2012. "Control and Allegiance at the Dawn of the Oil Age: Bedouin, Zakat and Struggles for Sovereignty in Arabia, 1916–1955." *Middle East Critique* 21(1): 57–79.

UNDP, Ministry of Finance, The Saudi Fund for Development, King Salman Humanitarian Aid and Relief Center, and Ministry of Foreign Affairs. 2016. "Partnership in Development and South-South Cooperation." http://www.sa.undp.org/content/saudi _arabia/en/home/library/human_development/KSA_ODA_report.html.

PART II
COUNTRY CASE STUDIES

7

Salafism, Education, and Youth

Saudi Arabia's Campaign for Wahhabism in Indonesia

Noorhaidi Hasan

Recently I had a discussion with Abu Nida, one of the early proponents of the Wahhabi campaign calling for a return to the purity of belief and the exemplary practices of the first generation of Muslims, who are collectively known as *Salaf al-Salih* (pious predecessors), in Indonesia. Under the banner of Salafism, he began to actively organize *halqas* (workshops) and *dauras* (study circles) in the areas around university campuses in Yogyakarta in the mid-1980s. His main targets were young Indonesian Muslims, particularly university students who had been zealously seeking authenticity and purity while actualizing themselves amid the political pressures posed by Suharto's New Order authoritarian regime at that time. Owing to the support of Ahmad Faiz Asifuddin, Aunur Rafiq Gufron, and Yazid Abdul Qadir Jawwas, among other friends and colleagues who had also finished their studies in Saudi Arabia, Abu Nida succeeded in gaining prominence among the students. His pioneering effort to spread Salafism inspired Abdul Hakim Abdat, Ahmad Farid Oqbah, Yusuf Usman Baisa, Ja'far Umar Thalib, Muhammad Umar As-Sewed, Lukman Baabduh, and Dzulqarnain Muhammad Sunusi, to mention but a few, to likewise develop their own Salafi *da'wa* activities and recruit membership. As a result, Salafis' Islamic study circles and enclaves of members sprang up in different cities of Indonesia and even reached remote areas of the countryside.

Abu Nida proudly told me that Jamilurrahman, the first Salafi teaching center he had established in the outskirts of Yogyakarta, has evolved into the Bin Baz Islamic Center, an integrated center of education, *da'wa*, and health services, managing Islamic formal schools at all levels of education from kindergarten to primary and secondary that adopt national curriculums. The center also manages two community colleges—a college for Islamic education, and a college for health sciences—plus a hospital built six miles (ten kilometers) away from the center. Interestingly perhaps, like other students in Indonesia, students in his schools were obsessed with continuing their secondary and undergraduate educations at their favorite universities, undertaking medicine, engineering, social sciences, and the arts, he told me. Abu Nida insisted that

Noorhaidi Hasan, *Salafism, Education, and Youth* In: *Wahhabism and the World*. Edited by: Peter Mandaville, Oxford University Press. © Oxford University Press 2022. DOI: 10.1093/oso/9780197532560.003.0007 being Salafi does not mean taking away from the open society around them or standing in opposition to the state. He further argued that Salafism is basically a system (*manhaj*) that teaches us how to live in a dynamic way, yet in accordance with the exemplary practices set by the Prophet Muhammad and the first generation of Muslims.

Abu Nida's view represents a recent shift in the development of Salafism in Indonesia. In changing circumstances following the national campaign against radicalism and terrorism after 9/11, the movement moved to the center, undergoing a process of adaptation and appropriation. Salafis' distinctive lifestyle can still be strikingly seen in the appearance of young men wearing long, flowing robes (*jalabiyya*), turbans (*imama*), trousers right to their ankles (*isbal*), and long beards (*lihya*), as well as women wearing a form of enveloping black veil (*niqab*). Yet this distinctive lifestyle is not followed by an ambition to be set apart from the national system and modern life. Employing a more accommodative approach, Salafi preachers now have more of a following—not only those following a Salafi lifestyle, but also Muslims from diverse backgrounds, including artists and celebrities. They successfully have used various social media platforms—including Facebook, Twitter, WhatsApp, Instagram, Line, and YouTube—to expand their networks, articulate their ideas, and promote their identities.

This chapter examines how Salafism has evolved and has exerted its religious influence among Indonesian Muslims. It focuses on the agencies that shared similar global linkages to Saudi Arabia and played a significant role in introducing Salafism among Indonesian Muslims. As a broad, transnational, multilayered, and multistranded social movement that encapsulates a variety of different actors, institutions, and foundations, Salafism is sustained not through any singular organizational structure. It is rather through a variety of agents active in producing lived experiences, divergences, and sometimes heated debates in relation to certain meanings of religious doctrines and practices, and multiple ways in which it is "enacted" within a given locality, that Salafism exists (Chaplin 2014; Hasan 2018a). Within this context it is also of interest to look at the extent to which Salafism has taken on local characteristics through some adaptations of its doctrine or theological character to better suit prevailing Indonesian religious norms. Moving beyond the existing literature on Salafism that emphasizes the ideological and transnational aspects of its spread around the world, this chapter will also examine the strategy deployed by Salafi authorities in accumulating religious, cultural, social, and economic capitals by producing Islamic knowledge. Through the establishment of educational institutions and the publication of books, magazines, pamphlets, cassettes, CDs, radio and TV programs, and YouTube *da'wa* content, they disseminated and contextualized the Salafi thoughts which have increasingly moved toward what can be called "post-Salafi Islam."

Historical Trajectory

Despite the fact that the call for Islamic purification arose during the early nineteenth century—as marked by the eruption of the Padri movement in West Sumatra—the efflorescence of the Salafi movement constitutes a relatively new phenomenon in Indonesia. It can be seen against the background of Saudi Arabia's attempt to position itself as the center of the Muslim world following the defeat of united Arab forces led by Egypt in the 1967 War against Israel. Bolstered by its permanent status as *khadim al-haramayn* (guardian of the two holy sanctuaries), the position at the center of the Muslim world was considered crucial to ensure the acquiescence of Muslim-majority countries to Saudi leadership and to boost its domestic legitimacy (Fraser 1997; Kepel 2002; Al-Rasheed 2007; Lacroix 2011).

Saudi Arabia believed that the way to achieve this goal was by exporting Wahhabism, whose doctrines are politically conservative, as emphasized by its official clerical body, known as the Council of Senior 'Ulama (Majlis Hay'at Kibar al-'Ulama). Led by 'Abdullah Bin Baz, this council insistently eschewed public dissent or open challenge to the government (Maher 2017, 9). They referred to the opinion of the classical Salafi thinkers, such as Taqi al-Din Ahmad Ibn Taymiyya (1263–1328), who argued that it is impermissible from a theological point of view to rebel against any existing legitimate Muslim ruler (Malkawi and Sonn 2011). Belonging to scholars of the *madhhab al-salaf* in classical Islam, who called for strict monotheism while espousing the need to return to the Qur'an and the Sunna, Ibn Taymiyya inspired Muhammad ibn 'Abd al-Wahhab (1703–1792) to launch Wahhabism in the eighteenth century.

The skyrocketing of world oil prices during the 1970s provided the opportunity for Saudi Arabia to campaign for the Wahhabization of the Muslim ummah. The Rabitat al-'Alam al-Islami (Muslim World League, MWL), an organization established in 1962 following a conference of Muslim scholars in Mecca, was urged to act as its philanthropic agent in the liberal distribution of money for the construction of mosques, Islamic schools, and social facilities, as well as to fund *da'wa* activities for Islamic organizations all over the world—in collaboration with local agents. In this way, Salafism was exported and spread (Al-Rasheed 2007, 2008). The campaign for Salafism was intensified following the Iranian Revolution in 1979 that challenged Saudi Arabia's dominant geopolitical and geostrategic position in the Muslim world.

Nevertheless, Saudi Arabia's campaign for Salafism soon backfired. Muslim Brotherhood activists, who solicited political protection from the Saudi government following Egypt's policy to pursue and arrest them, used the campaign for their own political interests. They actively promoted the

Brotherhood ideology among Saudi activists. This activism resulted in the rise of al-Sahwa al-Islamiyya (Islamic Awakening) movement, which soon became a central element of the Saudi social fabric (Lacroix 2011, 37–38). Inspired by the Sahwa, Juhayman al-'Utaybi led a group to seize control over Mecca's Grand Mosque (*Masjid al-Haram*) in 1979 (Hegghammer and Lacroix 2007). Due to this event, Saudi Arabia learned quickly about the danger of Salafism when it is infiltrated by the Brotherhood ideology. As a response, Saudi Arabia developed a policy of advertising its commitment to Islamic purification while suppressing the radical ideology of the Brotherhood. A new variant of Salafism—whose concern is more on seemingly trivial, superficial issues, such as *jalabiyya*, *niqab*, *lihya*, and *isbal*—has since proliferated as a result of this policy.

Home to the world's largest Muslim population, Indonesia saw the impact of Saudi Arabia's campaign for Salafism as early as the mid-1970s. Muhammad Natsir, former prime minister during Sukarno's era and Masyumi leader who failed to revive his banned Islamic party when Suharto came to power in 1966, decided to work more closely with Saudi Arabia by establishing the Indonesian Council for Islamic Proselytizing (DDII, Dewan Dakwah Islamiyah Indonesia) in 1967. This organization soon appeared to be the primary agent of the campaign in Indonesia, distributing Saudi money through such channels as the MWL, Hay'at al-Ighatha al-Islamiyya al-'Alamiyya (International Islamic Relief Organization), al-Majlis al-'Alami li-l-Masajid (World Council of Mosques), al-Nadwa al-'Alamiyya li-l-Shabab al-Islami (World Assembly of Muslim Youth), and Lajnat Birr al-Islami (Committee of Islamic Charity).

Saudi Arabia's considerable financial support allowed DDII to underwrite a variety of *da'wa*, education, and social activities, plus the construction of new mosques, orphanages, and hospitals, the founding of Islamic schools, the distribution of free copies of the Qur'an and books, and preacher training. This control over resources led the organization to assume a central position among Islamic organizations in Indonesia (Hasan 2006; Chaplin 2018). Within the framework of the Muslim preacher-training project, DDII entered into cooperation with the Majelis Ulama Indonesia (the Council of Indonesian 'Ulama)—a semi-governmental body of representative 'ulama from different Muslim organizations—by launching a *da'i transmigrasi* program. Through this program, hundreds of Muslim preachers were sent to remote transmigration areas. Moreover, it came to act as an important conduit in the distribution of grants provided by the kingdom for Indonesian youth wanting to study Islam in Saudi Arabian universities. Between 1975 and 1985, DDII received twenty-five grants every year to be distributed among the Muslim organizations' young cadres.

Through DDII, which served as a bridge in negotiations for financial support, Saudi Arabia's money flooded a number of Indonesian Muslim organizations, particularly those from the modernist end of the spectrum. These included Muhammadiyah, al-Irsyad, and Persis, which had lost their vitality in conjunction with the marginalization of Muslim politics under Suharto. In spite of its very different doctrine and certain animosity toward Wahhabism, the same held true for the Nahdlatul 'Ulama, Indonesia's largest traditionalist Muslim organization, known for its accommodation of local cultures. The kingdom's generous financial aid also flooded some leading *pesantren*s, traditional Islamic boarding schools where students studied Arabic and Islamic subjects using *kitab kuning* (classical Arabic texts) with the *kyai* (traditional *'ulama* in Java) as their central recipients. In exchange, Saudi agents were allowed to recruit talented *pesantren* students to study at either Imam Muhammad ibn Saud University or the Islamic University of Medina. The opportunity to study in Saudi Arabia remained a privilege for many *pesantren* graduates, who would be expected to strengthen the authority of the *pesantren*s when they returned home.

To intensify its campaign, Saudi Arabia established the Institute for the Study of Islam and Arabic (LIPIA, Lembaga Ilmu Pengetahuan Islam dan Bahasa Arab) in Jakarta in 1981. Directly affiliated with Imam Muhammad ibn Saud University in Riyadh, this institute was established by Saudi Decree No. 5/N/26710 as the Lembaga Pengajaran Bahasa Arab (Institute of Arabic Teaching, LPBA). Its first location was at Jl. Raden Saleh, Central Jakarta, before it moved to Jl. Salemba Raya, also in Central Jakarta. Its current location is at Jl. Buncit Raya, South Jakarta. To pave the way for the establishment of LIPIA, the then-Saudi ambassador to Indonesia, Bakr 'Abbas Khamis, played an enormously important role in initiating diplomatic steps with the Indonesian government. The institute was the first foreign educational institution in Indonesia (Kovacs 2014; Muhtarom 2019).

In its first three years, LIPIA was concerned with teaching the Arabic language to candidates recruited by DDII to study in Saudi Arabia. LIPIA offered regular programs of Arabic courses, including a one-year non-intensive course and a two-year pre-university course. Because of the important position of LIPIA in the eyes of Saudi Arabia, a number of high functionaries of the kingdom visited this institute during the 1980s and 1990s: Prince Sultan ibn 'Abd al-'Aziz, Prince Sa'ud al-Faysal, Prince Sultan ibn Salman ibn 'Abd al-'Aziz, Prince Turki al-Faysal, Khalid bin Muhammad al-Anqari, 'Abdullah ibn 'Abd al-Muhsin al-Turki, Usama Faysal, 'Abdullah al-Hijji, 'Abdullah ibn Salih al-'Ubayd, and Ibrahim al-Akhdar (Hasan 2006). In tandem with its strengthening foothold, LIPIA recruited more *pesantren* and madrasa graduates, some of whom had the chance to continue their studies at Saudi universities, particularly the Islamic University of Medina.

The Rise of Salafi Authorities

The role of DDII as the main local agent for spreading Wahhabism in Indonesia declined in tandem with the return of the alumni who had finished their studies in Saudi universities. Abu Nida, Ahmad Faiz Asifuddin, Yazid Abdul Qadir Jawwas, Aunur Rafiq Ghufron, and Yusuf Usman Baisa were among the alumni who soon tapped into a network of university campus da'wa initiated by DDII in urban centers such as Yogyakarta, Bandung, Makassar, Solo, Surabaya, and Jakarta. Owing to their broad knowledge of Salafi Islam—evidenced in their ability to refer to the works of both classical and modern Salafi authorities such as Ibn Taymiyya, Ibn Qayyim al-Jawziyya, Muhammad ibn 'Abd al-Wahhab, 'Abd al- 'Aziz 'Abdullah bin Baz, and Muhammad bin Salih al-'Uthaymin—they quickly became a popular attraction for university students. For the students, Salafism presented an original, authentic, and ideal Islam that Muslims badly needed to deal with uncertain situations confronting their lives.

Enthusiastic responses from the students urged Abu Nida and his friends to be more active in organizing da'wa activities. Gradually they emerged as the key actors in the spread of Salafism, who worked more independently from DDII (Hasan 2006; Machmudi 2018). In fact, they can be distinguished from their predecessors—older DDII cadres who likewise had the opportunity to complete their studies in Saudi Arabia in the 1970s and adopted a more political haraki type of Salafism. They were more committed to adopting an apolitical quietist approach as they believed that the struggle for purifying Muslim belief and practice should be prioritized over everything else. They were likewise more sympathetic to Saudi Arabia's shifting policy of reducing Muslim Brotherhood elements in Salafism. In their eyes, the kingdom was not simply a source of educational sponsorship but also, more importantly, a source of religious authority and social ideals (Hasan 2006; Chaplin 2014). The proliferation of their da'wa activities served as a catalyst for the establishment of Salafi foundations and madrasas in many parts of Indonesia.

Owing to his experiences as an administrative staff member at the MWL central office in Jeddah, Abu Nida successfully positioned himself as the most trusted individual local agent of the Salafi campaign. Generous support for his campaign came from the Mu'assasat al-Haramayn al-Khayriyya (Haramayn Charitable Foundation), a Saudi-based institution which was backed by the Saudi religious establishment. It operated under the supervision of the Saudi Ministry of Islamic Affairs, Endowments, Da'wa, and Guidance before it came under scrutiny by the US government in the aftermath of the 9/11 Al-Qaeda attacks. Abu Nida also succeeded in gaining considerable support from the Kuwaiti-based Jam'iyyat Ihya al-Turath al-Islami (Reviving of Islamic Heritage Society), set up in 1981 under the supervision of the Kuwaiti government and the

Saudi religious establishment, evidenced in a letter sent by Bin Baz to its founder, Tariq Samiy Sultan al-'Aishiy. This foundation operated with generous support from wealthy Kuwaiti merchants (Pall 2018, 43). Aware of the considerable trust he had obtained from the foundations, in 1994 Abu Nida established his own foundation, the Majlis Ihya al-Turats al-Islami, which served as a sponsor for the construction of mosques and madrasas, as a distribution point for Salafi books, and as the organizer of various Salafi da'wa activities.

Nevertheless, the rapid proliferation of Salafism was accompanied by increasing tension among its protagonists due to competition for the position of the movement's legitimate representatives. The first serious tension occurred between Abu Nida and Ja'far Umar Thalib, whom the former had invited to join the Salafi campaign. Thalib finished his studies at the Mawdudi Islamic Institute of Lahore before joining the Jamilurrahman-led Jamaat al-Da'wa ila al-Qur'an wa Ahl al-Hadith Salafi faction of Afghan mujahidin, and also briefly studied with a leading Yemeni Salafi authority, Muqbil ibn Hadi al-Wadi'i. These experiences gave him the credential as an 'alim who had not only broad knowledge of Islam, but also the bravery to venture to the frontlines of battle. Supported by his excellent oratorical skill, he was prolific in explaining his understanding of Salafi religious doctrines and why every other approach should be rejected. It is understandable, therefore, that Thalib quickly gained fame among the participants of the Salafi halqas and dauras. This fame facilitated his claim to be the leading authority among Salafis, usurping the leadership of Abu Nida. Inevitably, rivalries flared between them.

As rivalries intensified, Thalib accused Abu Nida and other quietist leaders, such as Yusuf Usman Baisa, Abdul Qadir Jawwas, and Ahmad Faiz Asifuddin, of being Sururis, followers of Muhammad bin Surur al-Nayif Zayn al-'Abidin (Hasan 2009), one of the main critics of Saudi Arabia's decision to invite foreign troops onto Saudi soil during the First Gulf War. Saudi Salafi clerics had different opinions pertaining to that decision. A group of clerics, including Salman al-'Awda, Safar al-Hawali, 'Aid al-Qarni, and Bin Surur, harshly criticized the policy. Others, especially those close to 'Abd al-'Aziz 'Abdullah bin Baz, the head of the Committee of Senior Clerics, defended the king. Bin Surur was condemned as a proponent of the takfir doctrine. This doctrine considers that a regime is necessarily apostate if it does not follow the shari'a and that violence can be used to topple such a regime and replace it with a true Islamic state. Abu Nida responded to Thalib's harsh criticism by emphasizing his commitment to the main Salafi mission of purifying Muslim belief and practices through da'wa and education.

In his rivalry against Abu Nida, Thalib garnered support from the alumni of the Islamic University of Medina, including Usamah Faisal Mahri and Abu Munzir Zul Akmal, who were obsessed with the thoughts of Muhammad Nasir al-Din al-Albani, a university professor teaching at the Faculty of Hadith Studies. Emphasizing the need to apply *hisba*, or the commanding of right and forbidding of wrong, and to revitalize the *hadith* as the main reference for Muslims' religious practice, al-Albani's thought later grew into the Jamaʿah Salafiyya Muhtasiba, a movement that very much informed the religious and political dynamics occurring in Saudi Arabia during the 1980s and 1990s (Lacroix 2011). The alumni requested *fatwas* from their Saudi mentors, such as Rabiʿ ibn Hadi al-Madkhali, Muhammad ibn Hadi al-Madkhali, and ʿAbd al-Razzaq ibn ʿAbd al-Muhsin al-ʿAbbad, and other of al-Albani's students who were persistent in criticizing *haraki* and jihadi trends within Salafism.

Thalib used the issue of *takfir* to likewise discredit the followers of the homegrown Darul Islam (DI/TII) rebellion for an Islamic state that later transformed into the Negara-Islam Indonesia (NII) movement. This movement adopted the Salafi jihadi ideology through the engagement of its leaders, especially Abdullah Sungkar and Abu Bakar Baʾasyir, with the ideals of ʿAbduAllah ʿAzzam, Abu Muhammad al-Maqdisi, and other Salafi jihadi thinkers. Thalib criticized the followers of NII for labeling the Indonesian government *taghut* (tyrants) for imposing Pancasila as the state ideology. Spurred by his confrontationist approach, many of NII's followers, who had felt exhausted being active in a clandestine movement which was under close surveillance by intelligent agents, decided to join quietist Salafism. Abdullah Sungkar and Abu Bakar Baʾasyir themselves escaped to Malaysia in 1985 to avoid arrest. Losing membership at home, both sought to recruit new membership, expand networks, and further develop the NII's militancy and radicalism (Abuza 2003). From 1985 to 1990 they succeeded in dispatching some 200 members to Afghanistan to participate in military training (*iʾdadashkari*) at Harby Pohantum founded by Shaykh Rasul Sayyaf (Solahudin 2013, 132–134). The purpose was to acquire military knowledge and skills for jihad against the Indonesian government. In Afghanistan, these militants became acquainted with jihadi teachings, arguing that it is necessary to aggressively fight jihad against Islam's enemies (Pavlova 2007; Solahudin 2013, 144–145). Later, they established Jemaah Islamiyah (JI), which was responsible for a series of bombing attacks in Southeast Asia.

Rivalry and Conflict

Thalib's loyalty to his apolitical stance met a real challenge when skirmishes between local Muslims and Christians erupted in Maluku in the aftermath of the fall of the Suharto regime in May 1998. In response to the skirmishes, which soon escalated into full-blown communal conflict in the islands (Hasan 2006; Sidel 2006; van Klinken 2007), he issued a resolution calling on Indonesian

Muslims to perform jihad and mobilized his quietist followers by establishing the Laskar Jihad in December 1999. Naming himself the group's commander, he also requested *fatwa*s from Salafi clerics in the Middle East. In response, al-'Uthaymin, Salih bin Fawzan al-Fawzan, al-Madkhali, and al-Wadi'i, for instance, stated that there was a reason to fight jihad in Maluku since Muslims were under attack by belligerent Christians (Hasan 2005, 2006). Under the auspices of the Laskar Jihad, thousands of Salafis participated in the jihad against Christians. Until its disbanding in October 2002, the Laskar Jihad reportedly dispatched more than 7,000 fighters to Maluku (Hasan 2006, 196).

The call for jihad in Maluku facilitated further tensions among the Salafi authorities. Figures like Ayip Syafruddin, Muhammad Umar As-Sewed, Lukman Ba'abduh, Dzulqarnain, Abu Munzir zul Akmal, Qamar Suaidi, and Abu Turab al-Jawi, who were initially involved in the jihad operation, felt disappointed with Thalib, whom they alleged had sold Laskar Jihad out for his own political interest. As a result, they led opposition against Thalib by requesting *fatwa*s from Saudi Salafi authorities, particularly al-Madkhali. Despite the fact that he had no a real base in Saudi Arabia, al-Madkhali had a significant following all over the world, including in Indonesia, particularly thanks to his generous attention and closeness with his students. In response, al-Madkhali issued a *fatwa* recommending that Laskar Jihad disband. Following this revolt against Thalib's leadership, a new network of the quietist group was born. Known as Madkhali Salafis (followers of al-Madkhali), they sought to uphold a commitment to Salafi principles and with the necessity—they believed—of obeying existing rulers (Sunarwoto 2020). Among their leaders were Lukman Ba'abduh, Dzulqarnain, and Abu Turab al-Jawi, who themselves competed with one another for leadership of the Indonesian Madkhali Salafis.

Lukman Baabduh built a base in Ma'had As-Salafi in Jember, East Java. In his competition with Dzulqarnain and his like-minded followers, he managed to draw into his orbit other former Thalib followers, including Muhammad Umar as-Sewed, Ayip Syafruddin, Qamar Suaidi, Abu Hamzah Yusuf, and Abdurrahman. In response to Lukman Baabduh's maneuvers, Dzulqarnain strengthened his Ma'had al-Sunnah in Makassar and built an alliance with Dzul Akmal and Jauhari, the founders of Ma'had Ta'dhim As-Sunnah in Pekanbaru Riau and al-Madinah in Solo, Central Java, respectively. They have been active in attacking the maneuvers of what they called the Lukmaniyun Group to rebuild their credentials as the true Salafis. Often referred to sarcastically as RMS (Riau, Makassar, and Solo) by their opponents, the Dzulqarnain Group even managed to maintain an exclusive access to Bin Fawzan al-Fawzan, a leading Salafi authority in Saudi Arabia, and successfully maintained trust and support from Saudi religious institutions, such as Hay'at Kibar al-'Ulama and the Lajnat al-Da'ima, as well as influential authorities in the Saudi government and universities. Exclusive access to Bin Fawzan al-Fawzan is crucial to ensure continued support from Saudi Arabia and, more importantly, to validate their credentials as Salafi authorities in Indonesia.

In contrast to Dzulqarnain, Lukman Ba'abduh and his group apparently did not succeed in convincing Bin Fawzan al-Fawzan to maintain his patronage with them. Their access to the Saudi cleric ended. Disappointed with this situation, Ba'abduh discredited the Dzulqarnain group as *mutalawwinun*, *la'ibun*, and *makirun* (being chameleons, just making fun, and rebellious in character). Despite this conflict, all of them interestingly came to actively engage in countering violent jihadism by publishing pamphlets and books condemning it. In their attempts to position themselves as the main supporters of the government in this particular concern, the Madkhalis were even more extensively involved in producing anti-jihadism books than those produced by Salafis of other persuasions.

While tensions and conflict continued to occur among the Indonesian Madkhalis, Abu Nida was relatively successful in maintaining the cohesiveness of his network. Instead of supporting Thalib's call for jihad in Maluku, Abu Nida consistently worked for *da'wa* and education. In his opinion, there was no legitimate reason for Muslims to fight jihad in the islands since they were under the control of the Indonesian government. He worked very hard to develop the Bin Baz Islamic Center, which was established in 1993 on one hectare of land donated by Yogyakarta's governor and king of Yogyakarta's court, Sultan Hamengkubowono X. Generous financial support to build study rooms, a mosque, office, dormitories, and teachers' houses was provided by Kuwaiti and Saudi donors, as demonstrated by the inscriptions on their walls. The then-Kuwaiti ambassador to Indonesia attended the launch of the center.

The dynamics of Salafism in Indonesia therefore cannot be regarded as solely the result of the Saudi campaign for Wahhabism. It is obvious that its proliferation occurred through the personal and intellectual connections the Indonesian students had built with their Salafi mentors who propagated certain trends of religious thought. Utilizing this thought, they constructed an imaginary of the ideal Islam in Indonesia, a form of Islam they believed had lost its vitality in the face of Suharto's policy of marginalizing Muslim politics. Balancing a historical Islamic past with a modernist religious present and future, Salafism indeed boosted Saudi Arabia's image as a model for a society that was both pious but also knew how to adeptly deal with contemporary issues—separate from the kingdom's capacity to serve as a source of educational and financial sponsorship. Despite the challenges of local cultural sensibilities and preexisting conceptions and practices of Indonesian Islam, the Salafis have more than enough capital to propagate a religious discourse linked to scholars and educational institutions in Saudi Arabia that they believe emulate the *Salaf al-Salih*. Nevertheless, the extent to which Salafi ideals were accepted was very much contingent upon the dynamics of Indonesia's domestic politics. Salafism is indeed a perfect example of how transnational Islam has intertwined with domestic politics.

Knowledge Production

Despite the rivalry and conflict among its protagonists, Salafism remains a movement that has successfully attracted a significant following, especially among the younger generations of Indonesian Muslims. The key success of the Salafis in attracting a strong following can be explained by their ability to instill habitus through a certain mode of knowledge production (Bourdieu 1995). The Salafis produce religious knowledge in a broad sense to include not only theology, morality, *fiqh*, and in general Islamic reasoning, but also all kinds of non-discursive ritualized, performative, and embodied forms of knowledge production, such as prayer, ritual, and bodily practices that denote worship and religiousness. In tandem with their ultimate concern with a purification of Muslim belief and practice in accordance with the Qur'an and the Sunna, as well as the example set by the *Salaf al-Salih*, the Salafis emphasize the teaching of *tawhid*, or more precisely Wahhabi doctrine, in their practices of knowledge production (Hasan 2010). Meaning to accept and believe in the oneness of God and His absolute authority, *tawhid* is considered by the Salafis to be the central pillar of Muslim creed. Total submission to God entails a person's sincere determination to implement all of His commands and scrupulously avoid all of His prohibitions.

Tawhid is taught through the main subject in its curriculum, i.e., Islamic theology ('*Aqida*). For this subject, Salafis read works such as *al-Qawl al-Mufid fi Adillat al-Tawhid* (The Useful Opinion on the Evidence of the Oneness of God), which is a summary of *Kitab al-Tawhid* (the Book on the Oneness of God) by Muhammad ibn 'Abd al-Wahhab. In some of the Salafi teaching centers, students are obliged to memorize this text by heart as a precondition before continuing on to study other books. The understanding of fundamental doctrines provides the foundation for the Salafis to study other subjects, including Qur'anic exegesis, the Prophetic traditions, Islamic legal theory, jurisprudence, and *da'wa* methodology.

Initially, the Salafi madrasas emerged as institutions that rejected anything tainted with the corrupting influence of Western culture. They were generally set up as the node of an informal social network for the purpose of propagating Salafi ideology in remote areas of Indonesia, which were perceived to be the "red" areas imbued with syncretic, communist influences. The ability of the Salafi madrasas to exert their influence at the grassroots was largely ineffective, however, owing to the Salafis' exclusivist and self-limiting character (Hasan

2018a). Though generally located in areas of urban or semi-urban settlement, these madrasas appeared to be enclaves that drew a firm distinction from the "anything goes" open society around them.

The rigid Salafi religious doctrines and exclusivist lifestyle taught in the Salafi madrasas attracted only a small number of villagers and thus have not brought about significant change in the larger Muslim population as a whole. Young Muslim recruits to Salafism were those disaffected youth who were eager to feel a sense of empowerment and declare their independence from village elders. Other Indonesian Muslims remained skeptical of the Salafis' claim to promote authentic Islam and their criticism of local religious practices. Instead, the proliferation of Salafi madrasas compelled villagers to further practice Islamic and traditional rituals in an attempt to decontextualize and combat the Salafi call for purifying Muslim beliefs and practices.

This was the course of events in Batikan, Muntilan, a village located several kilometers from Borobudur, where the Madrasa Minhaj al-Sunnah was established with the financial support of a local businessman and owner of a network of restaurants in Central Java. No doubt, the presence of this madrasa inspired more villagers to attend Friday prayers and the daily congregational prayers and more women to wear headscarves. Nonetheless, they also have been very active in attending *selamatan*, *barzanzi*, and *hadrah*, traditional rituals and practices deemed *bid'a* (religiously unacceptable "innovation") by the Salafis. These performative events have been organized as a cultural strategy employed by the villagers to resist Salafism. They believe that there is no need for the Salafis' promotion of a strict, literalist version of Islam since it only disturbs their village conviviality and harmonious life.

In response to the growing cultural resistance and difficulties confronting Salafism after 9/11, some of the Salafi madrasas have demonstrated their readiness to accommodate calls for reform and a movement toward the Islamic mainstream. For instance, they did not hesitate to undertake a review of their school curricula and to incorporate both religious and secular knowledge into course syllabi. Accordingly, the curricula adopted in their madrasas help to bridge the educational dualism that has characterized Muslim education for almost two centuries. Yet the main character of the madrasas is maintained—they are principally Islamic teaching centers that aim to train a new generation of Muslims rooted in and committed to the dissemination of the Salafi faith (Wahid 2014). Interestingly, with this reformed system and relatively modern management requiring students to pay tuition fees and living costs, the madrasas have apparently facilitated the mobility of Salafi teachers and students in Indonesia. Those madrasas apparently have succeeded at creating a system that enables them to operate independently, without Saudi money (Hasan 2018a).

Some of the madrasas took this a step further by adopting the education system developed by the country's Ministry of Religious Affairs. This is particularly the case with the madrasas under the control of Abu Nida and his group. Other madrasas, such as those under the control of Dzulqarnain, developed into the so-called integrated Islamic schools which are identical to the Muslim Brotherhood–inspired Tarbiyya movement. Since the late 1990s the movement's activists have attempted to develop their distinctive education system while remaining in the framework of the national education system. This strategy of working within the state system fits well with the desire of the Tarbiyya activists to Islamicize society through a gradual, peaceful, long-term process, rather than pursuing the largely failed revolutionary campaign for establishing an Islamic state. The integrated Islamic schools have rapidly evolved to become one of the fastest-growing trends in Islamic education in contemporary Indonesia (Hasan 2012). Although there are no exact data, their expansion is clearly visible and active across the country.

Apart from the Bin Baz Islamic Center, Abu Nida established Al-Athari Islamic Education Foundation in 2007. Supported by young *ustadh*s (teachers) in his circle, he wanted his *da'wa* to reach broader audiences, not only those in the Salafi circles, but also Muslims from diverse backgrounds. They published *At-Tauhid* Friday Bulletin, spread weekly among Friday congregations in hundreds of mosques. Aware of the strength of information technology, they migrated online to offer online *da'wa* services by setting up www.muslim.or.id and www.muslimah.or.id. These platforms provided the opportunity for audiences to communicate with them and raise diverse questions. Next, they established Muslim Radio, a radio station active in contextualizing Salafi *da'wa* to larger audiences. More importantly perhaps, they founded Yufid Group in 2009, a kind of holding company to manage all their online business activities.

Manned by Abu Nida's followers who have IT educational backgrounds, the Yufid Group moved a step further by introducing Yufidia.com, an online search engine for Islamic information; Yufidedu.com, online courses in Arabic, mathematics, and physics; and Yufid TV and Rodja TV, TV stations producing short videos of Salafi *ustadh*s' religious talks, further disseminated through YouTube and iPhone, iPad, and Android devices (Sunarwoto 2016; Chaplin 2018). The positive responses they received from viewers and audiences encouraged them to establish the Association of Indonesian Muslim Entrepreneurs (PPMI), aimed at bridging the business interests of the Salafis.

Inspired by Abu Nida's success in expanding their *da'wa* and education activities through various online channels, the Madkhalis similarly sought to migrate online to spread their *da'wa*. Lukman Ba'abduh's group set up Tukpencarianalhaq.com, and Dzulqarnain's group launched pelitaalhaq.com. Luqman Ba'abduh claimed to gain support from both al-Jabiri and al-Madkhali.

Similarly, Dzulqarnain invited Salafi *'ulama* like Al-'Umayri to give lectures in Islamic gatherings they organized, including in Ma'had Al-Madinah, Surakarta. The latter intensified their campaigns by forging an alliance with Rodja TV and Yufid TV, as well as radio stations established by Abu Nida's followers (Sunarwoto 2016). To justify their support for Rodja TV and Yufid TV, they disseminated *fatwas* on the permissibility of displaying photos of living beings. They are also not reluctant to wear *peci*, the typical Indonesian black hat. Both the display of photos of living beings and the wearing of *peci* remain rejected by Lukman Baabduh.

Salafism and Youth

Despite its waning influence and adaptation to local context, Salafism is a social movement that has a solid ideology. It holds that Islam has lost its vitality because Muslims fell into *bid'a* (heretical innovation) and *shirk* (infidelity). Returning to the Qur'an and Sunna, based on the exemplary model and practice of the first generation of Muslims, is the only choice if Muslims want to revive their glory which was lost during the *khilafat* (caliphate) era. Within this context, Salafi ideology offers young people a framework to articulate injustice and at the same time provides a dream of future glory (Hasan 2016). This millenarian character of Salafi ideology even serves as a banner for rebellion against the ruling class, especially among youth who feel frustrated by their surrounding circumstances. They desire to be seen as powerful and capable of doing something for the betterment of the entire situation surrounding their life.

Aware of the importance of the ideology they are struggling for, as I have argued elsewhere (Hasan 2020), the Salafis worked very hard to extend their influence beyond Salafi circles, reaching students at senior high schools and colleges. One remarkable impact of the Salafi expansion among students can be seen from the shifting theological discourse in the Islamic literature used in school and university education from the Ash'arites, who were very popular in Indonesia, to the Salafi theology. According to the Ash'arite doctrine of *tawhid* popularized by Abu Hasan al-Ash'ari (d. 935 or 936) and Abu Mansyur al-Maturidi (d. 944), God is one, unique, eternal, existent Being; He is not a substance, not a body, not an accident, not limited to any direction, and not in any space. He possesses attributes such as knowledge, power, life, will; He is hearing and seeing and has speech. This theology is especially popular among Indonesian traditionalist Muslims.

The shift occurred when Ash'arite theology was challenged by the concept of *tawhid* that refers to the doctrines developed by Ahmad ibn Hanbal and Ibn Taymiyya, and later elaborated upon further by Ibn 'Abd al-Wahhab. This concept divides *tawhid* into three branches: *tawhid 'ubudiyya* (unity of worship); *tawhid rububiyya* (unity of lordship); and *tawhid al-asma wa'l-sifat* (unity of Allah's names and attributes). It is a kind of strict monotheism, which implies not only the belief in the existence of one god, but also that God must be the only deity that is worshipped and that other objects of veneration, such as saints and holy men, should be rejected entirely. Within this context, the refusal to speculate on God's names and attributes is deemed an integral part of the doctrine (Wagemakers 2020).

More and more books used for Islamic education courses at schools and colleges are adopting the concept of the so-called *tawhid 3*, for example, textbooks for Islamic education courses used in the Islamic University of North Sumatra, Andalas University of West Sumatra, and Muhammadiyah University of Mataram. The idea to incorporate the *tawhid 3* into the curricula of universities and other schools has grown since 2007. The initiator was, among others, Muhaimin, a professor of Maulana Malik Ibrahim State Islamic University of Malang, who argued that the teaching of theology among students should touch their hearts and feelings (Suhadi 2018). For him, insight into the Oneness of God, as explained in the concept of *tawhid 3*, is essential to provide a foundation for students to have a correct understanding of their faith, one that influences their attitude, behavior, and everyday lifestyle.

In my recent research on Islamic literature used in school and university education in sixteen Indonesian provinces, the topics about purification of faith, the discourse of revitalization of the prophetic tradition, and exemplary *Salaf al-Salih* are imbued in textbooks and Islamic literature spread among the students. The popularity of the Salafi books discussing these topics, which is second only to the so-called popular Islamist and *Tarbawi* literatures, goes hand in hand with the growing acceptance of the ideological books of the Salafis, such as Ibn 'Abd al-Wahhab's *Kitab al-Tawhid* and *Fath Majid* by 'Abd al-Rahman bin Hasan Al al-Shaykh (Hasan 2018b). These books serve as the main references used widely by authors of Islamic textbooks for students. *Kitab al-Tawhid* contains the doctrine of monotheism which is strictly defined by Ibn 'Abd al-Wahhab as belief in the Only Almighty God, consequently rejecting any forms of polytheism (*shirk*) and Sufism. The definition of *shirk* in *Kitab al-Tawhid* includes the practice of prayer in accordance with the exemplary practice of the *Salaf al-Salih*. Within this context, submitting to religious leaders, seeking blessings of inanimate objects, and asking for help from those other than God are considered anathema to Islam.

The Prophetic traditions (*hadith*) also receive particular attention from the authors of textbooks and Islamic literature used at schools and in university education. It is not difficult for the authors to explore more about *hadith*, as Salafi teaching centers, campuses, and publishers provide abundant references to *hadith*. Imam al-Shafi'i College for Islamic Studies in Jember, for instance, is known for its focus on the study of *hadith*. In fact, canonical *hadith* books such as Sahih al-Bukhari, Sahih Muslim, Al-Adab al-Mufrad, Nayl al-Awtar, al-Arba'in al-Nawawiyya, Riyad al-Salihin and Bulugh al-Maram, to mention but a few, constitute the core references and the backbone of the Salafi discourse of Islam. These books have been widely read by the participants in the Islamic Study Unit (Rohis) and university-based Islamic Missionary Unit (LDK). Among the Salafi publishers active in publishing such books are Solo-based Al-Ghuroba, Zamzam, and al-Qalam, plus Al-Qamar Media (Yogyakarta), Pustaka Umar (Bogor), Pustaka At-Taqwa (Bogor), Darul Haq (Jakarta), and Imam Adz-Dzahabi (Bekasi).

Most of these books belong to the category of canonical works that are also standard Islamic references used by traditionalist Muslims as well as Salafis. But the books published by the Salafis include the annotations of leading Salafi scholars, such as al-'Uthaymin, al-Albani, and Bin Fawzan al-Fawzan. In the annotations, particular emphases are put on the need to abide by the Salafi doctrines as interpreted by the clerics. Some Indonesian Salafi proponents have also emerged as the leading annotators, including Yazid bin Abdul Qadir Jawwaz (Ikhwan 2018). Referring to al-'Uthaymin and al-Albani, Jawwas in his *Sharh Ahl al-Sunna wa'l Jama'a [Explanation of the Followers of the Sunna and the Community of the Prophet]* (2017) explains that the intention in prayer should not be pronounced out loud. This opinion is intended to refute the followers of the Shafi'i school of thought.

Toward a Post-Salafi Islam

The Salafis understand well that the growth of new modes of interactive communication, such as satellite television, the internet, cell phones, and social media, has become one of the most crucial factors in shaping the recent dynamics of Islam all over the Muslim world, including in Indonesia. New modes of piety which conceal a clear shift from the earlier emphasis of Islamism on creating an Islamic state to a new focus on personal piety have arisen out of this context. Supported by the expansion of the new media, performative religious programs have attracted the attention of a diverse range of Indonesian Muslims, including youth and the emerging middle class, which thrived as a result of the government's mass education program, enabling a large number of Indonesians to pursue a higher education. They belong to the category of new religious audiences who are not interested in an Islamist agenda that seeks to reform and reshape Islam and society totally while demanding the replacement of the existing governmental system with one based on the *shari'a*.

Built on individual choice and freedom, the so-called post-Islamist piety (Bayat 2005, 2007) presents Islam in a ready-to-use standard directly correlated with the interests and lifestyles of the new religious audiences who need practical references about the way to understand and apply religious messages, yet do not want to sacrifice their status as members of the (upper) middle class. Such references are normally not found in long homilies of the 'ulama, who used to hold a monopoly on the right and duty to make sure that all major developments in politics and society were in conformity with God's commands, predicated on the grounds that they were most knowledgeable in the sciences of the Qur'an and the traditions of the Prophet (Zaman 2007). These practical references are now available in booklets, pamphlets, colorful magazines, mailing lists, videos, and WhatsApp and Instagram conversations—they are no longer the exclusive purview of the 'ulama. In contrast to the long-winded sermons of the 'ulama, these materials appear to be an interactive communicative means whereby the new Muslim intellectuals might foster Islam as part of a global, modern culture.

The rise of post-Islamist piety has paralleled the mushrooming of motivational books and self-help manuals which approach Islam more from the perspective of popular culture. Instead of demonstrating Islam as an alternative system, these manuals are more concerned with delivering practical messages about the way to live in harmony and reconciling Islam with modern life, dealing with diverse issues which often come up among Muslims, including fashion, teenage romance, emotional intelligence, and Islamic banking. These manuals contain practical guidelines to cope with daily problems. Readers are not forced to put their worldly ambitions aside in order to seek religious rewards.

One example of such a manual is *La Tahzan* (Don't Be Sad), a book by the popular Saudi Salafi scholar 'Aid al-Qarni. Translated into Bahasa Indonesia in the early 2000s, this book became very popular among Indonesian Muslim readers, eclipsing in popularity any other Islamic book. The book's main message is that readers should not give up trying to do what they really want to do in life. Wherever and whenever there are loved and motivated, they can survive any challenges and constraints, and thus will eventually realize their dreams. The popularity of the book has inspired some Indonesian celebrity preachers to write similar books. Abdullah Gymnastiar, more commonly referred to as Aa Gym, a celebrity preacher pioneering humorous television sermons on the practicalities of everyday life (Hoesterey 2016, 68) published *Menggapai Qolbun Saliim: Bengkel Hati Menuju Akhlak Mulia* (Reaching Peaceful Heart: Spiritual Workshop toward Fine Attitude). Muhammad Arifin Ilham followed in his steps by publishing *Menzikirkan Mata Hati* (Clean up Heart's Eye). The fame of the book has also inspired Salafi-leaning young writers, including Asma Nadia, Cahyadi Takariawan, Ahmad Rifa'i Rif'an, and Abu Al-Ghifari. They wrote *La Tahzan for Hijabers* (Don't Be Sad for Veiled Women), *Keluarga Sakinah*

(Wonderful Family), *Man Shabara Zhafira: Success in Life with Persistence* (Whoever Is Patient Will Be Lucky; Success in Life with Persistence), and *Kudung Gaul: Berjilbab tapi Telanjang* (Cool Veiling: Veiled but Naked), respectively (Schmidt 2017, 77–88; Kailani 2018).

Salafi preachers themselves lost no time in producing Islamic self-help books and popular *da'wa* contents. One such example is Firanda Andirja, a young Salafi preacher who graduated from the Islamic University of Medina. Being close with Saudi clerics, including 'Abd al-Razzaq ibn 'Abd al-Muhsin al- 'Abbad, Bin Fawzan al-Fawzan, Ibrahim bin Amir, and Ibrahim al-Ruhaili, he actively organized religious gatherings and soon achieved a credential as a Salafi religious authority. In contrast to other Salafi preachers, he preferred to put himself forward as a celebrity preacher close to the millennial generation of Indonesian Muslims. He appeared trendy and colorful and used television and the internet as the main media for his *da'wa* to propagate a sort of post-Salafi Islam. He himself was involved in the establishment of two Salafi television channels, Rodja TV and Yufid TV.

Through these two television channels, the influence of young Salafi preachers like Firanda goes beyond their respective domains to reach broader audiences of Indonesian Muslims from different generations. The main target audiences are young Muslims seeking a sense of being embedded in religious tradition, on the one hand, while also being attached to globalization, on the other hand. The mastery of classical knowledge of Islam is no longer a dominant factor in shaping their public profile, which is determined more by their ability to perform before the camera and communicate with audiences through the multiplicity of religious programs they offer. TV stations will reconsider the sustainability of a program based on its ratings and if and when its viewership declines. In this context, in collaboration with creative media workers, new Salafi *'ulama* are required to offer and package fresh religious programs on television.

The rise of Firanda as a Salafi celebrity preacher unleashed a storm of critiques from the older Indonesian Salafis. Critiques were particularly directed to the use of TV as a channel for *da'wa*, as recorded in online debates involving some Salafi preachers. Dzulqarnain, for instance, warned Indonesian Muslims and particularly his fellow Salafis of the danger of Salafi *da'wa* on TV. Deemed to be a form of heretical innovation, TV is believed to have potentially led Muslims away from the Salafi system. Another criticism came from Lukman Ba'abduh, who considered Firanda to be an unauthoritative Salafi preacher, particularly because of his ignorance of the prominence of al-Madkhali's method of *da'wa* (Sunarwoto 2020). Anticipating the unexpected consequences of such critiques, Firanda came to visit Bin Fawzan al-Fawzan to request a *fatwa* on this particular issue. He also explained that the Salafi TV stations have contributed a great deal to Salafi *da'wa*, through which *fatwa*s by leading Salafi *'ulama* could be disseminated to larger audiences. Owing to the TV channels as well, Firanda even claimed that he was able to mobilize between 100,000 to 130,000 participants to attend religious speeches by Saudi Salafi *'ulama* such as Abd al-Razzaq al-'Abbad and Ibrahim al-Amir. In response to this report, Bin Fawzan al-Fawzan promised to ask Dzulqarnain to clarify his criticism against Firanda (Dzulqarnain 2020; Firanda 2020; Abusalma 2020).

Conclusion

The spread of the Salafi religious influence in Indonesia went hand in hand with the rise of a new type of Islamic activism and new religious authorities. The story began with the dispatching of a dozen Indonesian students to study in the Salafi teaching centers in the Middle East. Upon returning home, they organized *halqa*s and *daura*s and established Salafi madrasas across Indonesia. In so doing, they recruited loyal followers and sympathizers into their circles. Salafi teaching centers and madrasas had grown into small Salafi communities and networks in which the Salafi creed constituted an integral element of the Salafis' habitus and everyday life. The production, development, authorization, and dissemination of Islamic knowledge in these networks created specific modes of bonding and community building.

Salafis are often claimed to have a monolithic Islamic worldview, one which undermines the diversity of local religion and culture. But the Salafi movement that proliferated in Indonesia is far from monolithic. For the last couple of decades, Indonesian Salafis have been divided into various groups that were involved in rivalries and conflict around some doctrinal and ideological issues. Some, especially Salafi jihadis, remain opposed to the state, while other Salafis (especially the quietists) have become critical of the jihadis' doctrine and stood at the frontline to refute the former's ideological position. But this contestation is somehow productive. Many Indonesian Salafi authorities have arisen out of this context, publishing books and pamphlets defending their respective positions.

It is important to note that the influence of Salafism has expanded beyond Salafi circles through the role played by Salafi preachers and authorities both in producing Salafi literature and in contextualizing and appropriating the Salafi message into the country's schools and universities. More and more books used for Islamic education courses in Indonesian educational institutions follow the doctrinal and ideological concepts of the Salafis, including the *tawhid* 3, the re-vitalization of the Prophetic tradition in teaching Islam, and full commitment to follow the exemplary practices set by the *Salaf al-Salih*. More importantly perhaps, the Salafis went a step further by establishing radio and TV stations to further disseminate Salafi messages to larger audience. Some Indonesian Salafis, such as Firanda, transformed themselves into celebrity preachers. Aware that their audiences are primarily composed of younger generations of Indonesian Muslims who need a solid reference to Islam and, at the same time, have a strong attachment to globalization, these new Salafi preachers do not hesitate to offer a more youth-friendly, post-Salafi Islam.

References

Abusalma. 2013. "Komentar-terhadap-surat-ustadz-dzulqarnain-kepada-al-allamah-asy-syaikh-shalih-al-fauzan-hafidhahullah." https://abusalma.net/2013/11/25/komen tar-terhadap-surat-ustadz-dzulqarnain-kepada-al-allamah-asy-syaikh-shalih-al-fau zan-hafidhahullah-b (accessed on February 25, 2020).

Abuza, Zachary. 2003. *Militant Islam in Southeast Asia: Crucible of Terror*. Boulder, CO: Lynne Rienner.

Bayat, Asef. 2005. "What Is Post-Islamism." *ISIM Review* 16: 5. https://openaccess.leidenu niv.nl/bitstream/handle/1887/17030/ISIM_16_What_is_Post?sequence=1.

Bayat, Asef. 2007. *Making Islam Democratic Social Movements and the Post-Islamist Turn*. Stanford, CA: Stanford University Press.

Bourdieu, Pierre. 1995. *Outline of a Theory of Practice*. Stanford, CA: Stanford University Press.

Chaplin, Chris. 2014. "Imagining the Land of the Two Holy Mosques: The Social and Doctrinal Importance of Saudi Arabia in Indonesian Salafi Discourse." *ASEAS: Austrian Journal of South-East Asian Studies* 7(2): 217–235. doi: https://doi.org/10.14764/10.ASEAS-2014.2-6.

Chaplin, Chris. 2018. "Salafi Activism and the Promotion of a Modern Muslim Identity: Evolving Mediums of Da'wa amongst Yogyakartan University Students." *South East Asia Research* 26(1): 3–20. doi: https://doi.org/10.1177/0967828X17752414.

Commins, David. 2006. *The Wahhabi Mission and Saudi Arabia*. London: I. B. Tauris.

DeLong-Bas, Natana J. 2004. *Wahhabi Islam, from Revival and Reform to Global Jihad*. London: Oxford University Press.

Dzulqarnain, M. Sanusi. 2013. "Membela-dakwah-salafiyah-dan-ulama-umat-dari-kenistaan-pemikiran-firanda." https://dzulqarnain.net/membela-dakwah-salafiyah-dan-ulama-umat-dari-kenistaan-pemikiran-firanda-bagian-pertam.html (accessed on February 25, 2020).

Firanda, Andirja. 2013. "Ada-apa-dengan-radio-rodja-rodja-tv-bag-8." https://firanda.com/961-ada-apa-dengan-radio-rodja-rodja-tv-bag-8-gelaran-gelaran-indah-ustadz-dzulqarnain.html (accessed February 25, 2020).

Fraser, Cary. 1997. "In Defense of Allah's Realm: Religion and Statecraft in Saudi Foreign Policy Strategy." In *Transnational Religion and Fading States*, edited by Susanne Hoeber Rudolph and James Piscatori, 226–234. Oxford: Westview Press.

Hasan, Noorhaidi. 2005. "Between Transnational Interest and Domestic Politics: Understanding Middle Eastern Fatwas on Jihad in the Moluccas." *Islamic Law and Society* 12(1): 73–92. https://www.jstor.org/stable/3399293.

Hasan, Noorhaidi. 2006. *Laskar Jihad: Islam, Militancy and the Quest for Identity in Post-New Order Indonesia*. Ithaca, NY: Southeast Asia Program, Cornell University.

Hasan, Noorhaidi. 2009. "Ambivalent Doctrine and Conflict in the Salafi Movement in Indonesia." In *Global Salafism: Islam's New Religious Movement*, edited by Roel Meijer, 223–243. New York: Columbia University Press.

Hasan, Noorhaidi. 2010. "The Failure of the Wahhabi Campaign: Transnational Islam and the Salafi Madrasa in Post-9/11 Indonesia." *South East Asia Research* 18(4): 675–705. https://www.jstor.org/stable/23750964.

Hasan, Noorhaidi. 2012. "Education, Young Islamists and Integrated Islamic Schools in Indonesia." *Studia Islamika* 19(1): 77–112.

Hasan, Noorhaidi. 2016. "Violent Activism, Islamist Ideology, and the Conquest of Public Space among Youth in Indonesia." In *Being Young and Growing up in Indonesia*, edited by Kathryn Robinson, 223–243. Leiden: Brill.

Hasan, Noorhaidi. 2018a. "Salafism in Indonesia: Transnational Islam, Violent Activism, and Cultural Resistance." In *Routledge Handbook of Contemporary Indonesia*, edited by Robert W. Hefner, 246–256. London: Routledge.

Hasan, Noorhaidi. 2018b. "Penutup: Gagalnya Jihadisme di Kalangan Generasi Milenial." In *Literatur Keislaman Generasi Milenial: Transmisi, Apropriasi, dan Kontestasi*, edited by Noorhaidi Hasan, 267–280. Yogyakarta: Pascasarjana UIN Sunan Kalijaga Press.

Hasan, Noorhaidi. 2020. "Salafism, Knowledge Production and Religious Education in Indonesia." In *The New Santri Challenges to Traditional Religious Authority in Indonesia*, edited by Norshahril Saat and Ahmad Najib Burhani, 131–150. Singapore: ISEAS Yusof Ishak Institute.

Hoesterey, James Bourk. 2016. *Rebranding Islam Piety, Prosperity and a Self-Help Guru.* Stanford, CA: Stanford University Press.

International Crisis Group. 2008. "Indonesia: Jemaah Islamiyah's Publishing Industry." Report no. 147. Brussels: International Crisis Group. https://www.crisisgroup.org/asia/south-east-asia/indonesia/indonesia-jemaah-islamiyah-s-publishing-industry

Hegghammer, Thomas, and Stéphane Lacroix. 2007. "Rejectionist Islamism in Saudi Arabia: The Story of Juhayman al-'Utaybi Revisited." *International Journal of Middle East Studies* 84(4): 103–122. https://www.jstor.org/stable/4129114

Hegghammer, Thomas. 2009. "Jihadi-Salafis or Revolutionaries? On Religion and Politics in the Study of Militant Islamism." In *Global Salafism: Islam's New Religious Movement*, edited by Roel Meijer, 244–266. New York: Columbia University Press.

Ikhwan, Munirul. 2018. "Produksi Wacana Islam(is) di Indonesia: Revitalisasi Islam Publik dan Politik Muslim." In *Literatur Keislaman Generasi Milenial: Transmisi, Apropriasi, dan Kontestasi*, edited by Noorhaidi Hasan, 63–108. Yogyakarta: Pascasarjana UIN Sunan Kalijaga Press.

Kailani, Najib. 2018. "Perkembangan Literatur Islamisme Populer di Indonesia: Apropriasi, Adaptasi dan Genre." In *Literatur Keislaman Generasi Milenial: Transmisi, Apropriasi, dan Kontestasi*, edited by Noorhaidi Hasan, 143–207. Yogyakarta: Pascasarjana UIN Sunan Kalijaga Press.

Kepel, Gilles. 2002. *Jihad, the Trail of Political Islam.* Cambridge, MA: Belknap Press.

Kovacs, Amanda. 2014. "Saudi Arabia Exporting Salafi Education and Radicalizing Indonesia's Muslims." *German Institute for Global and Area Studies Focus* 7: 1–5. https://www.files.ethz.ch/isn/184727/gf_international_1407.pdf.

Lacroix, Stéphane. 2011. *Awakening Islam: Politics of Religious Dissent in Contemporary Saudi Arabia*, trans. George Holoch. Cambridge, MA: Harvard University Press.

Lauziére, Henri. 2016. *The Making of Salafism Islamic Reform in the Twentieth Century.* New York: Columbia University Press.

Machmudi, Yon. 2018. "The Middle East Influence on the Contemporary Indonesian Campus Islam." In *Islam in Southeast Asia Negotiating Modernity*, edited by Norshahril Saat, 91–111. Singapore: ISEAS.

Maher, Shiraz. 2017. *Salafi-Jihadism: The History of an Idea*. London: Hurst.

Malkawi, Banan, and Tamara Sonn. 2011. "Ibn Taymiyya on Islamic Governance." In *Islam, the State and Political Authority: Middle East Today*, edited by Asma Afsaruddin, 111–127. New York: Palgrave Macmillan.

Meyer, Birgit. 2006. *Religious Sensations: Why Media, Aesthetics and Power Matter in the Study of Contemporary Religion* (inaugural lecture). VU University: Amsterdam.

Muhtarom, Ali. 2019. *Ideologi dan Lembaga Pendidikan Islam di Indonesia: Kontestasi, Aktor dan Jaringan*. Yogyakarta: Zahir.

Pall, Zoltan. 2018. *Salafism in Lebanon: Local and Transnational Movement*. Cambridge: Cambridge University Press.

Pavlova, Elena. 2007. "From a Counter-Society to a Counter-State Movement: Jemaah Islamiyah According to PUPJI." *Studies in Conflict and Terrorism* 30(9): 777–800. doi: https://doi.org/10.1080/10576100701501984

Rajan, V. G. Julie. 2015. *Al Qaeda's Global Crisis: The Islamic State, Takfir, and the Genocide of Muslims*. London: Routledge.

Al-Rasheed, Madawi. 2007. *Contesting the Saudi State: Islamic Voices from a New Generation*. Cambridge: Cambridge University Press.

Al-Rasheed, Madawi. 2008. "Introduction: An Assessment of Saudi Political, Religious and Media Expansion." In *Kingdom without Borders: Saudi Arabia's Political, Religious and Media Frontiers*, edited by Madawi Al-Rasheed, 1–38. London: Hurst.

Schmidt, Leonie. 2017. *Islamic Modernities in Southeast Asia: Exploring Indonesian Popular and Visual Culture*. London; New York: Rowman and Littlefield.

Sidel, John. 2006. *Riots, Pogroms, Jihad: Religious Violence in Indonesia*. Ithaca, NY: Cornell University Press.

Solahudin. 2013. *The Roots of Terrorism in Indonesia: From Darul Islam to Jema'ah Islamiyah*, trans. Dave McRae. Ithaca, NY: Cornell University Press.

Suhadi. 2018. "Menu Bacaan Pendidikan Agama Islam di SMA dan Perguruan Tinggi." In *Literatur Keislaman Generasi Milenial: Transmisi, Apropriasi, dan Kontestasi*, edited by Noorhaidi Hasan, 29–62. Yogyakarta: Pascasarjana UIN Sunan Kalijaga Press.

Sunarwoto. 2016. "Salafi Dakwah Radio: A Contest for Religious Authority." *Archipel* 91: 203–230. https://journals.openedition.org/archipel/314.

Sunarwoto. 2020. "Negotiating Salafi Islam and the State: The Madkhaliyya in Indonesia." *Die Welt des Islams* 60: 205–234. doi: https://doi.org/10.1163/15700607-06023P03

Sunesti, Yuyun, Noorhaidi Hasan, and Najib Azca. 2018. "Young Salafi-Niqabi and Hijrah: Agency and Identity Negotiation." *Indonesian Journal of Islam and Muslim Societies* 8(2): 173–190.

Van Bruinessen, Martin. 2003. "Making and Unmaking Muslim Religious Authority in Western Europe." Paper presented to *the Fourth Mediterranean Social and Political Research Meeting*, Robert Schuman Centre for Advanced Studies, European University Institute, Florence, March 19–23.

Van Klinken, Gerry. 2007. *Communal Violence and Democratization in Indonesia, Small Town Wars*. London: Routledge.

Wagemakers, Joas. 2012. *A Quietist Jihadi: The Ideology and Influence of Abu Muhammad al-Maqdisi*. New York: Cambridge University Press.

Wagemakers, Joas. 2020. "Salafism: Generalisation, Conceptualisation and Categorisation." In *Contextualising Salafism and Salafi Jihadism*, edited by Magnus Ranstorp, 21–36. Copenhagen: Danish Center for Prevention of Extremism.

Wahid, Din. 2014. *Nurturing the Salafi Manhaj: A Study of Salafi Pesantrens in Contemporary Indonesia*. PhD thesis, Utrecht University.

Zaman, Muhammad Qasim. 2007. *The Ulama in Contemporary Islam: Custodians of Change*. Princeton, NJ: Princeton University Press.

8

Saudi Influence in Kyrgyzstan

Beyond Mosques, Schools, and Foundations

Emil Nasritdinov and Mametbek Myrzabaev

Introduction

This chapter analyzes the influence of Saudi Arabia and Salafism on the religious situation in Kyrgyzstan—the former Soviet Union republic in the heart of Central Asia. The country has been independent for nearly three decades and there are plenty of historical developments to review to make such an analysis. The chapter aims to describe the history of Saudi engagement with the Kyrgyz state and local population, to review the mechanisms of engagement and demographics of affected groups, and to study the local perception of Saudis and Saudi *da'wa*. The chapter begins by setting the scene, describing Kyrgyzstan's policy toward religion in general, and discussing the methodology of approaching such a subject.

Kyrgyzstan is known as a country with the most liberal policy toward religion in Central Asia. The first serious attempt to regulate religious life was introduced only in 2005 when the Law on the Freedom of Religion was developed, while the more serious attempts to formulate a proper religious policy were only made in 2013–2014. Prior to that, Kyrgyzstan was a fairly welcoming home for all kinds of religious movements; many were able to establish their roots and acquire followings. Not only Muslims, but also a large number of Christian Evangelical churches used this opportunity to preach, and many became quite popular.

Even when the new policy was developed in 2014, Kyrgyzstan still maintained a much more liberal and less repressive policy toward religion compared to other Central Asian countries and Russia. Until now, it has a number of groups that are banned in neighboring countries but are legal in Kyrgyzstan, like Khizmet, which is tied to the Turkish religious figure Fethullah Gülen, and the Tablighi Jamaat. Some see this situation as a matter of security concern, while many other experts believe that the relative freedom of religion that Kyrgyzstan has is the best guarantee of stability in the country.[1] On the one hand, when the government is

Emil Nasritdinov and Mametbek Myrzabaev, *Saudi Influence in Kyrgyzstan* In: *Wahhabism and the World*. Edited by: Peter Mandaville, Oxford University Press © Oxford University Press 2022. DOI: 10.1093/oso/9780197532560.003.0008 not repressive toward religion, it does not give grounds for radical and extremist groups to attack the secular regime. On the other hand, the legal presence of more peaceful Islamic groups creates strong competition and an obstacle for the development of more radical ideologies.

The government rhetoric on religion, however, is far from homogenous. There are many secular politicians who regularly make populist statements about the dangers of growing religiosity, about the foreignness of various religious teachings and styles of dress, about the replacement of Kyrgyz traditions with Islamic or Christian traditions, and about the need to ban the wearing of the hijab in schools and public places (Kutueva 2014; Yalovkina 2014). At the same time, there are a number of politicians, such as Torobai Zulpukarov and Tursunbai Bakir Uulu, who stand up to defend Islamic values and practices. So, one could say that while the majority of politicians retain a more neutral stand on religious questions, there is a strong contrast, as well as opposition, between the smaller secular and the religious camps.

Kyrgyz society is divided similarly. The majority prefer a neutral ground, yet the anti-religious sentiment is quite strong (Kaleev and Maseitova 2019) and it responds to the visibly growing religiosity of the population, particularly among the younger generation of citizens. The conflict is more likely to take place on various social media platforms, such as Facebook. Face-to-face conflicts on the streets are not very common. The main group that does experience discrimination on the street and at the work/study places includes women wearing hijab and Islamic dress.

This chapter studies how Saudi Arabia was able to explore this relatively open environment and find its place among other religious influences in the country. Methodologically, this is not a very easy task. The distinction must be made between the influence of Saudi Arabia as a country, with its diplomatic mission in Kyrgyzstan, and the influence of Saudi religious doctrine—Salafism. Saudi officials and Saudi religious scholars invited by Kyrgyz government officials do not promote the doctrine. Instead, Salafism comes to Kyrgyzstan not only from Saudi Arabia but also, or even more so, from other countries.

While Saudi officials do not engage in open da'wa, various Saudi foundations do; yet they do not do it openly and they are also not easy to study. While the religious policy in Kyrgyzstan is liberal, Saudi foundations have experienced more pressure in the last five or six years than religious foundations from other countries. Often, they present themselves as institutions engaging only in charity or development projects.

Salafism came to Kyrgyzstan not only from Saudi Arabia but also, or even more so, from Russia and neighboring Kazakhstan. The Salafi doctrine originated in Saudi Arabia, but it was modified and adapted to local post-Soviet realities in these countries and it came to Kyrgyzstan in a filtered form. So, inferring links between Saudi Arabia and Salafism in Kyrgyzstan is not a straightforward exercise.

According to interviews with an expert, financial flows are even more difficult to trace.[2] This is partly because Saudi money mixes with money coming from Qatar and Kuwait. Once money comes to the region, there is strong competition for it, and many other groups that have little or nothing to do with Salafism might also receive and benefit from it. In addition, local foundations that receive Saudi money also receive money from other countries and transnational religious groups. As the money then is translated into specific forms of *da'wa* adopted by these groups, the ideological influence of Saudi Arabia also becomes even more ambiguous and difficult to trace.

Perhaps the only solid conclusion that can be made is about Kyrgyz students who have received religious education in Saudi Arabia. They are exposed to direct forms of Salafi teaching. Some embrace it and, upon return to Kyrgyzstan, teach it locally, while others do not or at least do not do so openly. Because of the significant amount of government pressure that Kyrgyz Salafis have experienced in recent years, many graduates of Saudi religious schools claim to follow the traditional Hanafi school of religious legal thought and deny connections to Salafism.

This chapter builds on interviews with Kyrgyz experts on religious issues, representatives of Saudi foundations, representatives of groups receiving money from such foundations, religious scholars, and local religious practitioners who follow the Salafi doctrine. Considering the sensitive nature of the topic due to the pressure from the state and potential retaliation from extremist groups, all sources of information for this project were confidential. We have excluded all references to personal names and instead have used such terms as "religious expert," "religious scholar," "local Salafi," etc.

Considering the great deal of secrecy surrounding this subject, there are many conspiracies about the activities of Saudis in Kyrgyzstan. While conducting this research, we came across many interesting statements that are impossible to verify or discredit. Thus, one of the very common words used by us in this chapter is "allegedly." We acknowledge from the very beginning that this chapter is to a large degree the representation of a local discourse on the role of Saudi *da'wa* in Kyrgyzstan, rather than the hard proof of it. Yet, we believe that, even as such, it has certain value for the volume, considering that the number of solid studies on the subject of Salafism conducted in the former Soviet space is very limited. We start this analysis by looking at the history of Saudi influence in Central Asia generally and then, specifically, in Kyrgyzstan.

History of Saudi Influence in Kyrgyzstan

Many perceive Salafism as a relatively recent post-Soviet influence in Central Asia. Yet, if we look deeper into history, we can see that it has much longer and older roots in the region. Two papers by Sebastien Peyrouse (2007) and Martha Brill Olcott (2007) provide us with a very interesting account of that. The following section summarizes some of the main historical developments highlighted by these scholars. It is followed by the review of post-Soviet developments.

Salafi Influence in Central Asia during the Pre-Soviet and Soviet Periods

Central Asia, being the almost homogeneously Islamic region in the Soviet Union, was home to all kinds of Islamic groups and ideologies throughout its history. Wahhabism appeared in the region not long after it became popular in its place of origin, Najd in the Arabian Peninsula, and it was often in conflict with the more traditional local forms of Islamic practice. Most of Central Asia follows the Hanafi *madhhab*, which allows Muslims to be ruled even by a non-believer or infidel if the latter allows Islamic religious practices. The fourteenth-century Central Asian ruler Timur (Tamerlane) used religion to keep his empire together and personally appointed the senior clerics and heads of Sufi *tariqa*s (orders) (Olcott 2007). This political practice of religious loyalty to the ruling regime continued until the nineteenth century, and not much changed when Central Asia was occupied by the Russian Empire: the Islamic Spiritual Administration established by the Russians had a similar function of being the middleman between local populations and the colonial administration. Such politically loyal religious establishments were always under attack by more politically radical groups, many of whom were Salafi. By the early twentieth century, such critics were perceived as "Wahhabis" (Olcott 2007). The tension between conservatives and fundamentalists was always a normal feature of religious life in Central Asia.

In the first years of Soviet rule until 1924, the relations between the Bolsheviks and Muslims were positive: the Soviets sought support among the imams to win over the hearts of people and gain influence. However, according to Erickson (2017), once Soviet power was firmly established, the repression started: mosques and madrasas were closed (out of 26,000 mosques before Soviet rule, only 1,000 remained by 1942) and many religious leaders were jailed, exiled, or killed. The Soviets also specifically targeted Central Asian Sufis in their repression because the latter traditionally had a strong influence on the population (Peyrouse 2017).

By doing so, the Soviet administration inadvertently supported more fundamentalist scholars, who criticized Sufi practices.

According to Peyrouse (2017), one such scholar who had strong influence on the future generations of preachers was Shami-domullah, who was Shafi'i Muslim, but whose ideas were very close to Salafism and whose students established the movement called Jamaat Ahl al-Hadith (People of the Hadith). In the 1940s, Stalin reduced the pressure on religious communities, and established the Spiritual Board of Muslims of Central Asia (SADUM) in 1943. The first mufti of SADUM was Ishan Badakhan, a member of the Jamaat Ahl al-Hadith, and he appointed his son, Ziauddin Babakhanov, as *qadi* (judge). Their religious views were also shaped by Salafi ideology, and they pulled many Jamaat Ahl al-Hadith members into positions of power in SUDUM in Tashkent and in other regions, who introduced many new practices from other *madhhabs*. Ziyauddin Babakhanov was sent by the Soviets to Al-Azhar University in Egypt, and he brought back a lot of literature from there about the Hanbali legal school of jurisprudence.

The SADUM criticized Sufism and Hanafism. It also controlled three main Soviet Central Asian institutions: Mir-i Arab in Bukhara, Baraq-Khan madrasa in Tashkent, and the Higher Islamic Institute in Tashkent. They also supported the clandestine system of learning throughout the country, and one particularly fruitful place for that was the Ferghana Valley. The Hanafi scholars were losing ground as fundamentalist Salafi ideas were supported and spread everywhere by the Babakhanovs' clan, who held the position of mufti for several decades: first Ziauddin, then his son, and then his grandson. The Babakhanovs were *khodjas* (descendants of saints), enjoying influential positions in society and, due to the strong patronage system and endogamy, they remained influential for a long period of time.

Both Olcott (2017) and Peyrouse (2017) describe how the main opponent of the Babakhanovs was Mullah Hindustani, who was a very strong supporter of the Hanafi school. He called the Babakhanovs "Wahhabis" and openly preached against their teachings. Hindustani's other major opponent was his own student, Mullah Hakimjon-Qori Morghilani, who was later called the "father of Wahhabis" in Central Asia. The radicalization progressed was even turned against Hakimjon-Qori when two of his own students, Rahmatullah Allama and Abduvoli-Qori Mirzoev, in the late Soviet period, criticized their teacher for refusing to commit to a more radical version of Salafism and to militant action. They both settled in Andijon and started preaching a militant political form of Islam: anti-communist and anti-Hanafi. Their influence spread through most of the Ferghana Valley. They had a large number of followers already in 1980s, and when the Soviet Union collapsed, they were quite serious in their support for the establishment of an Islamic state governed by *shari'a*. However, heavy repression by the new president of Uzbekistan, Islam Karimov, left very little of this fundamentalist Salafi vision of religion intact. It forced Salafis underground or out of the country, as happened with the Islamic Movement of Uzbekistan (IMU), established by Tohir Yuldashev and Juma Namangani, which relocated first to Tajikistan and then to Afghanistan and northwest Pakistan.

This brief historical overview shows that Salafism is much more local to Central Asia than is often perceived. It was in the region long before the Soviet Union and, paradoxically, not only did the Soviets not diminish its impact, on the contrary, they solidified it. The main area where Salafi influence spread during Soviet times was in the Uzbek Soviet Republic, but because the Soviet SADUM was responsible for all other Central Asian Soviet republics and because students from other republics studied in the Soviet madrasas controlled by the SADUM, Salafi influence spread significantly beyond the borders of Soviet Uzbekistan.

Many early post-Soviet scholars of Islam from Kyrgyzstan also obtained education in these Uzbek madrasas.[3] However, there is little record or evidence pointing to how much they were affected by the Salafi ideology taught there. There were no local scholars with big names in Kyrgyzstan who would preach Salafism in the 1990s. Considering that the number of Kyrgyz Islamic scholars was generally significantly lower than in Uzbekistan or Tajikistan, one could argue that when Saudi emissaries and foundations began to arrive in Kyrgyzstan in the 1990s, there was little local Salafi knowledge to work with, except in southern Kyrgyzstan where a large percentage of the population are ethnic Uzbeks, many of whom might have shared the more fundamentalist views popular in the Ferghana Valley in the 1980s and early 1990s. How has Salafism progressed in the country since then? The next section will look into three distinguishable periods.

Three Periods of Saudi Influence in Post-Soviet Kyrgyzstan

Nearly thirty years have passed since the Soviet Union broke up. While other Central Asian republics had fairly stable political regimes with very little or no turnover in leadership, Kyrgyzstan has had two revolutions, four presidents, and one interim president. Each president had his own perspectives on religious questions and relations with Saudi Arabia. This lack of consistency, reinforced by some major global events such as the wars in Chechnya and wars in Syria and Iraq, resulted in significant changes to the dynamics with regard to how the Saudi *da'wa* evolved in Kyrgyzstan. The analysis of these changes enables us to distinguish three main periods: (1) the establishment of roots and the emergence of local Salafi scholars, (2) an active period of open *da'wa*, and (3) problems with the state and switching to a "standby" mode. The following three subsections describe each period individually.

First Stage: Establishing Roots and Educating Local Scholars

In the early 1990s, when opportunities arose for Saudi Arabia to establish its presence in Central Asia, the Saudis were more interested in countries like Uzbekistan and Tajikistan because of their stronger Islamic legacies and in Uzbekistan and Kazakhstan because of their larger population and richer natural resources. Kyrgyzstan was not very attractive for them at first. Yet, Kyrgyzstan was one of the most open countries in the region and it had the most liberal policy concerning religion.

Kyrgyzstan's first president, Askar Akaev, established a multi-vector approach in his foreign policy and was open to cooperation with anyone who could bring money into the country. Saudi Arabia was one potential international partner—and a rich one—to work with. The Saudi kingdom established its embassy in the capital, Bishkek, to deal with all official exchanges, while for less formal dealings, the Saudis started establishing various foundations. One of the first such foundations was established in 1993, the Al-Wakf Al-Islamia. Its key figure was Shaykh Abu Hasan Muntasir, who was active in Kyrgyzstan for nearly twenty years until he was deported in 2010. One of the first projects of this foundation was the Kyrgyz Islamic University. Al-Wakf Al-Islamia provided financial support for the university and even paid salaries to local teachers. It also brought in teachers from Saudi Arabia.

A local representative of this foundation was Kylych Shambetov, who became Muntasir's right hand and who has been coordinating the work of this foundation for nearly thirty years. He was one of the main educators, and he brought up many influential local Salafi scholars, such as Ilyas Maksutov and Shamsuddin Abdykalykov.

The foundation also sent the first local students to obtain religious education in Saudi religious universities in Mecca and Medina. One of the most prominent figures was Chubak ajy Zhalilov, who later became a mufti and the most revered Kyrgyz scholar of Islam. It is claimed that when Chubak ajy went to Saudi Arabia, he presented himself as a Salafi and maintained that position for a number of years while he was there, but shortly before his return to Kyrgyzstan, he distanced himself from Salafism.[4]

Students like Chubak ajy received financial support both while in Saudi Arabia and even upon their return home. Over the last thirty years, more than 500 students have received Salafi-style educations in Saudi Arabia (Bulan Institute 2017). The Saudis also opened one of the first Kyrgyz madrasas, located in the village of Koi-Tash. Moldogazy Gaziev is their representative in this madrasa. He had quite traditional religious and even Sufi-style roots, but over the years, it is alleged, he became a Salafi.[5]

During the 1990s, a number of other Saudi foundations were created. Some of them bore their original Saudi names, while others became unique and locally registered foundations, though the latter still received financial support from Saudi Arabia.

In the 1990s, the way Kyrgyz perceived Salafis was not much different from the way they perceived other religious groups. People just did not know much about Salafism and perceived Salafis simply as Muslims. Often they even idealized them because everything that came from the land of the Prophet Muhammad was seen as authentic, and there was a naïve loyal appreciative attitude on all levels—from state officials to the average citizenry. People were hungry, both literally and spiritually, and Saudi religious and charitable foundations, like many other religious foundations, provided food for both. Also, as one of the interviewed local experts claims, these foundations did not have the goal of spreading Salafism during that period: they were driven by the ideas of Muslim solidarity and establishing the basic religious infrastructure where there was none—mostly through building mosques.[6]

This was the period when the level of religious knowledge among the first Kyrgyz Salafis was minimal and they were occupied with more primitive and often visual tenets of Salafism, like wearing pants above the ankles, growing long beards, and banning both music and *nashid*s (chants). In the 1990s, the world for those early Salafis, as for members of other Islamic and non-Islamic religious movements, was often black and white, without much care for nuances.

Thus, this first period of the 1990s can be seen as that of preparing the ground, establishing the institutional infrastructure, planting the seeds, and sprinkling them with the water of financial support. By the early 2000s, these efforts began bearing fruit.

Second Stage: Active Open *Da'wa*

The second stage began when students who had studied in Saudi Arabia started returning to Kyrgyzstan and began preaching and engaging in other activities at the local level. This was a very active and open stage when these scholars became well-known public figures, imams who started teaching in mosques, in madrasas, and from their homes. There were even moments when the preaching was done on state media channels. These Saudi-educated scholars also gained positions in the Kyrgyz Muftiyat (Spiritual Board of Muslims in Kyrgyzstan). Three examples of such scholars are Ilyas Maksutov, Shamsuddin Abdykalykov, and Umar Kulov. They became known as being very respectable religious leaders and their weekly lessons (*dars*) were very popular, including among the Russian-speaking urban youth and among women. Besides preaching, Salafi scholars also started publishing their own work.[7]

However, in the early 2000s, the local population's perception of Salafis was also partly shaped by the war in Chechnya. Russian media presence in Kyrgyzstan is very influential, particularly on TV, and as the conflict was escalating, Wahhabism came to be a strong negative concept spoken on the streets. This was when the earlier reverence and respect for Saudis began to be mixed with more critical and cautious attitudes toward them.

As the level of Islamic knowledge was increasing and Kyrgyz Salafis were learning about the world and other contexts, the simplified tenets of the 1990s became more complicated, while the black-and-white visions of the world were becoming more nuanced. The focus was shifting from the more visual aspects of Salafism to the questions of *aqida* (creed) and to more complicated visions of global politics. As this was happening, the composition of Kyrgyz Salafis was also becoming much less homogenous and more diverse. Also, if in the first stage Salafism was mostly popular in Bishkek and Osh, the two largest cities of Kyrgyzstan, in the second stage Salafis started establishing their presence in the country's other regions.

The peak of this active open period was reached after the revolution of 2005 when the first president, Askar Akaev, was ousted and Kurmanbek Bakiev took office. The rise of Salafi activity in 2005–2006 might have happened in the wave of mobilization created by the revolution. This is when local Salafi leaders began openly criticizing and conflicting with other religious groups, such as the Tablighi Jamaat, Khizmet, and traditional local Islam. Shamsuddin Abdykalykov published a two-volume book titled *Sabil wa Subul* (Road and Roads, or Source and Sources). Even its title implied distinction between the "one true Salafi way" and other misleading paths. The book was particularly critical of the Hanafi *madhhab* and the Maturidi school of Sunni theology. In this book, Abdykalykov compared the followers of the *madhhab*s to dogs following the orders of their owners. Salafi scholars also began establishing a presence in mass media and online by creating websites and TV channels, developing YouTube channels, and giving interviews to various media outlets. Shamsuddin Abdykalykov used to publish a newspaper, *Islam Nuru* (Light of Islam). Websites such as *Islam Jolu* (Islamic Way) were created and became popular.

The second Kyrgyz revolution of 2010, when President Bakiev was kicked out of office, created yet more momentum for Salafi groups and, this time, they activated the more radical *takfiri* groups. While *takfiri*s tried to gain some influence and criticized the state, the other groups and Salafi scholars that can be characterized as Madkhalis—Salafis who preach obedience to the ruler—cooperated with the government, and this reflected a significant division between more compliant and more radical Salafi groups. The Kyrgyz Madkhalis would engage only in religious and apolitical *da'wa* and some scholars, like Umar Kulov, even gave lessons to the officers at the State Committee on National Security. He was also working in the Muftiyat, being in charge of its foreign relations, particularly with Saudi Arabia.

The group that was between these two camps can be called Sururis—these were Salafis who had a strong political agenda and were oppositional to the state, but they were not as radical as *takfiris*. A similar group that can be placed in this middle ground includes Salafis influenced by the Ikhwan al-Muslimun (Muslim Brotherhood). This group has Egyptian origins, but the members who were active in Kyrgyzstan were also allegedly connected to the Brotherhood's Saudi branch and received financial support from Saudi Arabia. It was at this stage that the scholars representing more political and radical groups became quite critical of the state and started making open political statements.

Unlike in Kyrgyzstan, in the early 2000s, other countries in Central Asia began exerting more pressure on and even started closing Saudi foundations. As this was happening, many of such foundations allegedly migrated to Kyrgyzstan, which maintained a more liberal attitude toward religion in general and to the Saudis specifically. Since then, Kyrgyzstan acquired a particular significance for Saudi foundations. Experts claim that it became a home base for their broader Central Asian projects. The scheme was very simple: money came to Kyrgyzstan to the banks of local Kyrgyz Salafi foundations, and then it was transferred to other Central Asian countries and Afghanistan as money from Kyrgyzstan. Supposedly during this time, Kyrgyz Salafis established productive links with Salafis from other Central Asian countries and began forming a transnational Central Asian Salafi network.

We can describe the early 2000s as the most active stage for Central Asian Salafism, at the end of which, local Salafi scholars engaged in open *da'wa*, which was often critical of the state and other religious groups in the country. As a result, they started attracting the attention of and dislike from state officials, security agencies, traditional religious scholars, representatives of other religious groups, and the local population in general.

Third Stage: Problems with the State, Ideological Conflicts, Standby Mode of Operation

The result of the active open *da'wa* and critical political message of Salafi groups was that, by the end of first decade of the 2000s, Kyrgyz officials became quite concerned about the influence of Saudi Arabia and the growing popularity of Salafism. It was under the new Kyrgyz president, Almazbek Atambaev, that the policy toward religion in general started to take a more restrictive position and the state's attitude toward several religious groups began to change. In 2013, the Security Council, which was devoted completely to the questions of religion, met. The president formed a special task force consisting of experts, state officials, and security agents to update the official religious policy. By this time, local expertise on the questions of religion had become more advanced, including the understanding of Salafism and its complexity. Yet, there was still little consensus among the experts concerning whether Salafis were a security threat. Nonetheless, the traditional Hanafi *madhhab* was promoted almost to the level of the only formally approved version of Islam, while Salafism was labeled as dangerous, radical, and extremist.

This period coincided with the civil wars in Syria and Iraq, the formation of Islamic State (ISIS/ISIL) and Jabhat al-Nusra, and increasing evidence of Kyrgyz citizens joining these groups in the conflict zone. This further increased the concern of state officials about Saudi influence and Salafism. Shaykh Abu Hasan Muntasir was deported; Shamsuddin Abdykalykov was arrested for six months and his book *Sabil wa Subul* was banned as being extremist; Ilyas Maksutov was frequently detained for interrogation; Uzbek imam Rashot Kamalov, who openly called himself Salafi, was arrested in Kara-Suu and sentenced to seven years of imprisonment; and Umar Kulov was removed from the Muftiyat.

Ilyas Maksutov and Shamsuddin Abdykalykov were the first generation of local Salafi scholars. As they were silenced in the early 2010s, their students and representatives of younger Salafis began entering the stage, such as Arlen Bayzakov. They were more energetic and better educated (mostly in Saudi Arabia) and they had to operate in a very different and more hostile political environment. The result of the emergence of such new Salafi leaders was the development of an even stronger division among Kyrgyz Salafis. The more restrictive state policy led to some Salafis maintaining their less radical and apolitical stance, while it pushed others to adopt even more confrontationist political views. There were also Salafi groups that became quite radical, extremist, and even terrorist. The latter were banned and had to operate clandestinely.

Some Salafis suggested that the new president, Sooronbai Jeenbekov, who replaced Almazbek Atambaev in 2017 and was known to be more religious himself, would change the state of affairs and establish stronger links with Saudi Arabia. That did not happen, and the real decline of Salafi influence began after 2018. This was partly but not solely the result of more restrictive state policies. Some interviewed local experts explain that the decline also happened because of the reduction of financial flows from Saudi Arabia caused by the economic decline there.[8]

The religious scholars that come to Kyrgyzstan from Saudi Arabia via official channels (i.e., the Muftiyat) openly support the ideas of traditional Islam and the Hanafi *madhhab* and criticize the political versions of Islam. They are often invited to large Islamic conferences and the state uses them to support its policies. Under pressure, many local Salafis use the strategy of adjusting to local madhhabs. They issue fatwas that allow them to call themselves Hanafis, pray in the Hanafi way, and allow women to take off their full-face veils (niqabs).

Interestingly, the overall critical attitude toward Saudis is seen mostly only in official state discourse and in the populist statements of some (mostly less religious) politicians who raise alarms about the "Arabization" of Kyrgyz culture. In reality, over all these years, Saudis were able to establish strong linkages with and provided various kinds of support to many important politicians, and this helped the Saudis to maintain the status quo regarding their overall influence in the country. Thus, the official state position toward Saudi Arabia is one of loyalty and, allegedly, money is the main motivation for this. There is always hope to receive more Saudi funding. As explained by an expert, the religious aspect is more important for "simple people," but they do not have much direct contact with Saudis.[9]

As a result, the Kyrgyz national policy toward Saudi Arabia and Salafism at the moment is rather amorphous and not concrete. The policy is concrete only in regard to the extremist takfiri groups such as Jund al-Khalifat, Ansarullah, At-Taqfir wal-Hijrah, and others. The list of banned groups now has a couple of dozen names on it. These groups are banned and their members are arrested and given long prison sentences. As for moderate Salafi groups, the state still cannot formulate an appropriate policy, and many experts doubt whether such a policy can be created and properly implemented at all.[10]

At the local level, the relations between state officials and Saudi foundations are quite positive because these foundations provide financial assistance for the construction of mosques, schools, hospitals, roads, bridges, and other projects. They also give salaries to imams and financially support mosques and madrasas. In exchange, these foundations allegedly try to employ loyal imams and qadis and even try to secure positions for Salafis in the local territorial councils.[11]

At the beginning of the 2020s, Saudi influence in Kyrgyzstan is at its lowest, but the institutional infrastructure, financial channels, ideological foundation, and Salafi scholarship have been established. Being under pressure, they currently operate more in a standby mode, waiting for more favorable conditions to be reactivated. How soon such conditions can emerge, or whether they can emerge at all, is still an open question.

Mechanisms and Channels of Saudi Da 'wa

What Saudi Arabia is most well-known for in Kyrgyzstan is building mosques. Since independence, the number of mosques has increased by more than one hundred times—from approximately forty to more than 4,000. The exact percentage of mosques built with Saudi money is hard to trace, but most interviewed experts agree it is significant. Yet, as most interviewed experts also believe, with the exception of a few Salafi mosques, the mosques built by Saudis do not play a significant role in the spreading of Saudi da'wa.[12] Once built, they are used by local residents without Saudi connections and by members of other groups such as the Tablighi Jamaat. Instead of mosques, a number of other mechanisms and actors that make the spread of Saudi da'wa possible can be identified. These are summarized in the following.

Foundations

The main institutional actors involved with Saudi da'wa are various Saudi and local foundations. Main Saudi foundations or foundations that receive financial support from Saudi Arabia in Kyrgyzstan include the Al-Wakf Al-Islamia, World Assembly of Muslim Youth (WAMY), Ehsan Khairiya, As-Salam, As-Safa, As-Salabil, Nama, and Itar-Zharkyn Zhashtar.

Besides building mosques, these foundations actively engage in various kinds of social projects. Two experts suggest that today many foundations limit their engagement with religious issues because they are always under surveillance. Instead, they are mostly engaged with charity, development, and education.[13] Nearly seventy schools in the country were built by various Islamic foundations, including ones from Saudi Arabia. These schools are secular and do not teach religious subjects or promote Saudi ideology. Such social projects are seen as great contributions to local communities in Kyrgyzstan. These projects often involve some degree of local corruption, and part of the money is often stolen in the process of construction, but the end result is still very significant.

Earlier, we described the work of Al-Wakf Al-Islamia. Another very influential group is the World Assembly of Muslim Youth (WAMY), led by Sayyed Bayumi. The group is actively involved in the construction of mosques, schools, medical clinics, and other institutions. They financed the establishment of the Theological Faculty at Arabaev University and a prayer room inside the Kyrgyz parliament building. Together with As-Salabil, the WAMY funded forty-five secular schools in various regions of the country. In 2018–2019 alone, they built thirty-three small medical clinics.

It is claimed that Sayyed Bayumi's ideological stance is similar to that of Ikhwan al-Muslimun or Sururi Salafism, but he works with a lot with Saudi donors. He became a middleman who helps channel the financial flows. One expert claims that Bayumi has strong influence on Saudi donors and that he uses it to label certain local groups as Sufi and thus undeserving of financial support.[14]

When Saudi foundations began to be closed in other Central Asian countries in the early 2000s, the Saudis financed the creation of the As-Safa and As-Salam foundations, which are registered as local Kyrgyz entities. Now, as one expert claims, they use these Kyrgyz foundations to transfer money to organizations in other Central Asian countries and Afghanistan. This way, Kyrgyzstan might serve as a transit point for transferring money from Saudi Arabia to the Central Asian countries where Saudi Arabia cannot send money directly.[15]

When the Kyrgyz government became more suspicious of Saudi foundations and the money coming from Saudi Arabia, Saudi groups became reluctant to openly bring money into the country. Thus, the same expert claims, they adopted a different strategy. They started bringing money via foundations from countries like Qatar and Kuwait. Since diplomatic relations between Saudi Arabia and Qatar have worsened, they now work more with foundations from Kuwait. Both Qatar and Kuwait are perceived with less suspicion in Kyrgyzstan. For example, when Saudis organize cultural events, fewer politicians attend because many are afraid of affiliating themselves with Saudis, but for events organized by Qataris and Kuwaitis people come freely.[16]

Quite an important role was played by the Kyrgyz-Arab faculty created at the Kyrgyz State University of Construction, Transport, and Architecture in regard to Saudi influence. This faculty sponsored students from different programs: students received stipends and were taught Arabic. Dr. Fauz al-Dakhir was the dean of this faculty, which operated from 1996 to 2014 and was quite popular among students. It was closed in 2014 on the wave of state anti-Saudi sentiments.

There is competition between various foundations for the money that comes from Saudi Arabia, and foundations employ different strategies to secure funding. For example, the Itar-Zharkyn Zhashtar Foundation claims that it is the only openly Salafi foundation in Kyrgyzstan and that this entitles them to more financial support.[17]

Muftiyat, *Hajj*, and *Umrah*

The Kyrgyz Muftiyat (Spiritual Board of Muslims in Kyrgyzstan) has long-standing and productive relations with Saudi Arabia. The Muftiyat is in charge of all mosques and madrasas in the country and is always at least partially involved in the construction of new and the renovation of old religious facilities financed by Saudis, as well as in the distribution of Saudi financial support to madrasas.

In addition, the Muftiyat is dependent on Saudi Arabia because it is the main institution processing *hajj* pilgrims. At its highest (in 2019), 6,010 people from Kyrgyzstan were given visas to perform *hajj*. The number of people who perform the lesser pilgrimage (*umrah*) is also very high. Performing *hajj* and *umrah* provides Kyrgyz pilgrims with direct exposure to Saudi Arabia, its culture, and religion. They have opportunities to purchase literature and listen to Saudi *da'wa* while in the kingdom. Every year the Saudi embassy in Bishkek gives approximately 200 Kyrgyz citizens the opportunity to perform *hajj* for free, and these free placements are distributed via the Muftiyat and the State Committee on Religious Affairs. In addition, the Saudi embassy and Muftiyat regularly organize free trips to perform *umrah*. Often, these trips are given to politicians, state officials, and relatives of top officials. Thus, many of them return indebted to the Saudis. One expert claimed that free trips are also offered to Kyrgyz Salafis who join the groups of pilgrims in order to preach to them during the journey.[18]

The Kyrgyz mufti himself regularly travels to Saudi Arabia with organizational questions related to *hajj* and other matters. *Hajj* and *umrah* are also seen as a lucrative business, and in the past there were many public scandals in which the Muftiyat was accused of corruption in the distribution of *hajj* visas. Today, the process is much more open and corruption allegations are less frequent. Both the Muftiyat and the State Committee on Religious Affairs openly defend the Hanafi *madhhab* and traditional Islam, criticize Salafism, and mostly engage with Saudi Arabia through official state channels.

Finally, the Muftiyat has always had someone representing the Salafi school of thought, someone close to the Saudi embassy, or someone who is not openly Salafi but who would lobby for Salafi interests. Umar Kulov was one such scholar. He is a graduate of the Islamic University of Medina, where he studied *shari'a*. He is a Russian-speaking scholar and he preached at the mosque near Madina Bazaar in Bishkek attended by a large number of ethnic Uyghurs, many of whom are Salafis.[19] He was removed from the Muftiyat during the wave of repression toward Salafism.

Politics

One of other mechanism of Saudi influence involves working with Kyrgyz politicians. Experts claim[20] that Saudis try to "recruit" some current politicians or promote politicians who are supportive of the Saudi cause.[21] They do so by supporting such politicians financially and logistically, for example by offering them free trips to *hajj* and *umrah*, and helping them build mosques, schools, madrasas, kindergartens, and medical clinics so that these politicians can score politically with their local communities. Politicians see the Saudis as a source of real money. There are even non-religious politicians who are nonetheless open to Saudi collaboration and even accept invitations to perform *hajj* or *umrah*. Parliament deputy Torobai Zulpukarov is known to be religious and is seen as a politician with strong Saudi connections. He is from the Nookat region and, allegedly, quite a lot of Saudi money went to various social projects there. Another example is Ikrom Ilmiyanov, who was a driver and close friend of President

Atambaev and who had a great deal of political influence in the country. He allegedly helped appoint Salafis to important positions, for example the *qadi* of the Batken region. However, while many politicians have received support from Saudi foundations, they are also very careful with regard to how they position themselves toward Saudi Arabia nowadays: they try not to make such relations public because it might work against them, as the public attitude toward Saudi influence over the past decade has significantly worsened.

Universities in Saudi Arabia

There are several universities in Saudi Arabia that accept students from Kyrgyzstan. These include Umm al-Qura University in Mecca, the Islamic University of Medina, and King Saud University and Imam Muhammad ibn Saud Islamic University in Riyadh. According to the State Committee on Religious Affairs, cited in the report by the Bulan Institute (2017), the largest number of students from Kyrgyzstan receiving formal Islamic education abroad in the 2016–2017 academic year were studying in Saudi Arabia: 127 students (compared to 87 in Turkey, 26 in Egypt, 25 in Jordan, 24 in Russia, 9 in Pakistan, and 6 in Kuwait). These universities provided scholarships for students from Kyrgyzstan beginning from the early 1990s. The scholarship includes accommodation, airfare for two round trips a year for the entire family, and a stipend to live on while in Saudi Arabia (Bulan Institute 2017). Upon graduation and return to Kyrgyzstan, students are not forgotten. Many continue receiving financial support and maintain links with their alma mater. They are regularly invited to various events at the Saudi embassy and other foundations and are offered opportunities to make *da'wa*, including teaching in Salafi madrasas and becoming imams in Salafi mosques. Every year, approximately twenty to thirty students receive such scholarships, and over the past thirty years, nearly 500 students had an opportunity to study in Saudi Arabia. The Bulan Institute report (2017) describes how, in the past, many students went to study overseas via the Kyrgyz Mufiyat, but that, since 2014, the Muftiyat has stopped sending students to several countries, including Saudi Arabia, because of the civil wars in Syria and Iraq. So students make travel and study arrangements on their own.

Durus (Lessons)

In the early 2000s, *durus* (plural for *dars*, religious lessons) became one of the main ways to spread Salafi ideology. Such lessons were organized in mosques, madrasas, or in private homes. A number of local Salafi scholars were involved in teaching using the *dars* format. Some were extremely popular *and* very well attended. As explained by a Salafi who used to take such lessons, the *ustad*s (teachers) used to preach very tolerant forms of Salafism. However, he witnessed how the students were often significantly more radical; they would look for more radical interpretations elsewhere and have more radical discussions after classes. All *durus* were banned in the early 2010s, and no lessons haven taken place since then.[22]

Business

In other resource-rich countries like Kazakhstan, Saudi groups are usually associated with various oil and gas companies. In Kyrgyzstan, this connection is nonexistent because the country lacks these natural resources. However, Saudis engage with certain kinds of mining, for example coal. They buy mines or they try to put local Salafis in administrative positions in these mines. This happened in the mining towns of Kyzyl-Kiya and Min-Kush. The financial revenues generated by mines may help sustain local Salafi activities. In this way the local groups become less dependent on external sources of revenue.

Allegedly, Saudis also engage in distributing money for local Salafis to develop different kinds of businesses. For example, many local Salafis work in the sphere of IT: they open computer clubs, computer and phone shops, and give IT lessons. This is one niche that local Salafis have occupied. In addition, many Salafis work in currency exchange shops.[23]

Cultural Influence

The Saudi embassy organizes "Days of Saudi Arabia" and "Days of Arab Culture." These usually involve the demonstration of Arab food, clothing, and traditions. Many important politicians and state officials are invited to such events. Similarly, "Days of Kyrgyz Culture" are also organized in Saudi Arabia. Saudis also actively participate in the Nomadic Games organized in Kyrgyzstan, and they organize similar festivals in Saudi Arabia. In 2019, they paid for 500 participants from Kyrgyzstan to attend such games.

Another form of cultural/religious activity is organizing *iftar* dinners during Ramadan. The Al-Arabia restaurant, opened by the Saudi embassy together with Saudi businessmen, serves as a place for such celebrations.

Finally, Arabic language courses are quite popular today. Many of them are free or not very expensive. In these courses, students of different ages learn Arabic and Arab culture.

Media

Saudi foundations sponsor different kinds of Kyrgyz media channels. Two TV channels have received financial support: Marva TV and Echo of Manas. These channels mostly broadcast religious programs. Famous journalists like Myktybek Arstanbek have established their own programs on these channels, also with support from various Saudi foundations. These channels did not necessarily promote a strong Salafi message, but they did host Salafi scholars and their programs did reflect, to some degree, certain elements of Salafi ideology.

Different media channels and small companies are involved in the translation of books, booklets, video materials, etc. Saudis sponsored the translation of the Qur'an into Kyrgyz. However, most Salafi and, more generally, Islamic literature comes to Kyrgyzstan not from Saudi Arabia but from Russia, more specifically from Moscow and Kazan. There is some literature in Kyrgyz, but not much. Beginning in 2010, books began to be widely replaced by CDs, DVDs, flash drives, and the internet. In the south of Kyrgyzstan, there is more literature in Uzbek because of the large numbers of ethnic Uzbeks there.

Several websites were opened with Saudi support. The most popular ones are *Islam Zholu* (Islamic Way) and *Islam Nuru* (The Light of Islam). They publish in Russian and Kyrgyz, and their content has a strong Salafi orientation.

In addition, WhatsApp became a popular platform for spreading Salafi messages. There are many open and closed groups that include Salafis not only from Kyrgyzstan, but also from a much wider geographic area, mostly in the Russian-speaking space.

Finally, Salafis also use SMS services to send Islamic messages. One such number/account is 4040 and it regularly sends messages to a very extensive list of subscribers.

The abundance of various media and online materials creates fruitful platforms for self-Salafization. As claimed by one of the experts, today this is the main path toward Salafism. There is no need for *ustad*s and personal engagement with other Salafis or Saudi foundations with so much information available at people's fingertips on their phones.[24]

In this section, we have reviewed several mechanisms, instruments, and channels for spreading Saudi *da'wa*. There are a number of ways people in Kyrgyzstan can become exposed to Salafism. What kinds of groups are more likely to respond to the Saudi message and engage with it? This will be discussed in the following section.

Groups Affected by Saudi *Da'wa*

From the fairly wide spectrum of the Kyrgyz population who might become exposed to Saudi *da'wa*, we can identify three main groups that are more likely to respond: young Russian-speaking urbanites, ethnic minorities, and Kyrgyz-speaking youth from the regions who went to study in Saudi Arabia or were exposed to Salafi teachings in Kyrgyzstan. Each group has its own reasons and paths for joining Salafi groups. In addition, we want to look at the difference between men and women and at how Salafism affects members of criminal groups.

Russian-Speaking Urbanites

The capital, Bishkek, and other settlements in the Chuy Valley in northern Kyrgyzstan have a large number of ethnic Kyrgyz who attended Russian schools and often do not speak Kyrgyz. This phenomenon is a legacy of the Soviet education system. Most of the schools in the capital still teach in Russian. In contrast, out of nearly ninety madrasas in the country, there is no single madrasa that teaches Islamic subjects in Russian. With so many madrasas, Kyrgyzstan still does not produce a single Russian-speaking imam in one year. Thus, there is a strong linguistic divide between, on the one hand, locally produced Islamic knowledge in Kyrgyz and local Kyrgyz-speaking Islamic clergy who preach in the mosques and, on the other hand, a large segment of the general population who do not understand Kyrgyz. Currently in Bishkek there are more than forty congregational (*juma*) mosques where Friday prayers are performed, but in spite of the large Russian-speaking population, not a single one of these forty mosques performs Friday sermons in Russian because there are no local Russian-speaking imams (Nasritdinov, Urmanbetova, Murzakhalilov, and Myrzabaev 2019).

Usually, when young people become interested in Islam, the first time they go to the mosque is on Fridays. So, when Russian-speaking boys attend such Friday prayers, they do not understand the sermons performed in Kyrgyz and, not having access to Russian-speaking imams, they start looking elsewhere for religious guidance. This is when they gain exposure to Salafi books, most of which are published in Russian, online resources in Russian, and come across other local Russian-speaking Salafis.

One Salafi member claimed that education is an important factor: Russian-speakers are better educated and, having plenty of literature and online content available, they become more interested in the theory and meaning of Salafism, while for Kyrgyz-speaking Salafis, the ritual aspects of religious practice play a larger role.[25]

Many young Russian-speaking Salafis are also critical of the Muftiyat because it is almost completely Kyrgyz-speaking.

Ethnic Minorities

Another group susceptible to Salafi influence is ethnic minorities. Two groups that stand out are ethnic Uyghurs and ethnic Uzbeks. Experts claim that both groups have strong grievances: Uyghurs in regard to how unfairly they are treated in the Xinjiang province in China, and Uzbeks in regard to the violent and bloody ethnic clashes between Kyrgyz and Uzbeks in 1990 and 2010.[26] Also, since Soviet times, it was believed that Uyghurs were involved in drug trafficking and that is why police still regularly search their houses and arrest community members, and that too contributes to the sense of injustice. These grievances create a fertile ground for accepting the more justice-oriented political messages of Salafism.

In addition, as was described in the historical section of this chapter, ethnic Uzbeks were under the stronger influence of Soviet Salafism supported by the SADUM and had stronger exposure to more radical forms of Salafism that evolved in the Ferghana Valley, of which Osh and Jalal-Abad provinces in Kyrgyzstan are part and where the majority of the country's ethnic Uzbeks live. Some local Uzbek imams have preached the Salafi message, like the Kamalov brothers (one was arrested on extremism charges, one was killed by the security agencies), who were imams in the Kara-Suu mosque in southern Kyrgyzstan. Some experts claim that they were supported by Saudis, as were other Uzbek community leaders such as Kadyrzhan Batyrov and Ravshan Sabirov.[27] Such claims are difficult to prove, though.

One other expert explained that Uzbeks have better Arabic skills and they often find work with Saudi foundations, where they perform all the daily main duties, with Saudis themselves coming in once a day to check on the office and sign papers.[28] Finally, experts also claim that it is common for Uyghurs and Uzbeks to give their daughters in marriage to Saudi men, often as second or third wives. This way they become related by family and can have more secure access to Saudi money.[29]

Kyrgyz-Speaking Salafis

The third group that is affected by Saudi *da'wa* is Kyrgyz-speaking youth who travel to study in Mecca or Medina and those Kyrgyz who are later affected by their teaching once the former return home. Very often, the former group are the graduates of Koi-Tash Madrasa that has a strong Salafi orientation. This group does not have the limitations experienced by the Russian-speaking youth or the grievances of ethnic minorities. For them, exposure to Salafi thought is a result of an opportunity to study for free in Saudi Arabia. In Kyrgyzstan, Kyrgyz-speaking Salafis lag behind Russian-speaking Salafis mostly because of the shortage of literature and resources available in Kyrgyz. However, very few Russian-speakers travel to study in Saudi Arabia, so when Kyrgyz-speaking Salafis return, they possess much stronger and more grounded Islamic knowledge than Russian-speaking Salafis. Many become Salafis during the course of study and upon return from Saudi Arabia they preach in their mosques, madrasas, and among friends and relatives, thus becoming the agents of the Kyrgyz-speaking Salafi school in the country.

Criminal Groups

Finally, experts believe that Salafism is becoming popular among the criminal groups. Criminals are drawn to more Sururi versions of Salafism that justify certain criminal activities, comparing, for example, robbery to the spoils of war.[30] Many criminals become exposed to Salafi ideology inside prisons, where members of radical groups arrested on the charges of extremism are not separated from other inmates and they use their time in prison to preach radical messages. Inmates are often forced to seek protection among Salafis and that might eventually bind them to the group membership, ideology, and religious practice.

Gender

An interesting discussion emerges regarding how men and women are affected by Salafi ideology. An insider proposed the 70 percent (men) to 30 percent (women) composition and explained that one reason behind that is the lack of female teachers.[31] Some experts suggest that women are more likely to like Arabs and many would consider marrying wealthy Arab *shaykhs*.[32] At the same time, over the years it became a common notion that marrying a Salafi, especially the local ones, is undesirable because when men become Salafis they allegedly become very patriarchal and violent to their families and start imposing all kinds of limitations on women. An expert shared a story of a woman who ran away from Kazakhstan to Kyrgyzstan to get away from her Salafi husband who used to beat her and ban her from talking to her mother. In retaliation for her escape, the husband claimed that she was a terrorist and now there is a court case.[33]

This section described several groups that are more likely to be affected by Saudi ideology and become Salafis. We acknowledge that this is a rather simplified view that only reveals main trends, while, in reality, the demographic portrait of Kyrgyz Salafis is much more complex. To understand the influence of Saudis and Salafis in Kyrgyzstan, it is important to understand how they are perceived by representatives of other religious groups and by the general population.

Perception of Saudis and Salafis by Other Religious Groups

As pointed out in the introduction to this chapter, the relatively high degree of religious freedom and relatively liberal religious policy in Kyrgyzstan made it a home to a large number of Islamic and non-Islamic religious movements. So, Saudi da'wa faces a lot of competition on the ground, and this, over the past three decades, has shaped its relations with other groups. Relations between Salafis and other Muslim groups (jamaats) in Kyrgyzstan are complicated, but they never cross the line into open animosity. In comparison, in Kazakhstan the conflict between Salafi and non-Salafi Muslims is much stronger and the reason is the strong anti-Salafi state propaganda there that inadvertently legitimizes the conflict and negative attitude from other groups toward Salafis. In Kyrgyzstan, the state never bothered itself with making a strong criticism of Salafism and that makes Kyrgyz Salafi relations with other groups and with the general population better. There are a number of non-Salafi groups and other important transnational and local religious influences in Kyrgyzstan, and in this section we discuss six: the Ikhwan ul-Muslimun, Hizb ut-Tahrir, Khizmet, the Tablighi Jamaat, traditional imams, and the Tengirchiler. We have organized them according to the nature of their relations with Salafis, from more positive to more negative.

Ikhwan al-Muslimun and Hizb ut-Tahrir

The Ikhwan ul-Muslimun (Muslim Brotherhood) is a group founded in Egypt in 1928, but which has some of representatives in Kyrgyzstan who receive support from Saudi Arabia.[34] Thus, we can observe to some degree a merger and good relations between local Muslim Brothers and Saudis. This unification is particularly noticeable in the more political Sururi branches of Salafism. Hizb ut-Tahrir, which broke away from the Ikhwan ul-Muslimun in 1953, is a group that is banned in Kyrgyzstan. Hizb ut-Tahrir's members also share strong political visions of Islam's role in society and allegedly have good relations with Salafi Sururis.[35]

Khizmet

Khizmet groups are one of the major transnational influences in Kyrgyzstan. They are supported by the Turkish preacher Fethullah Gülen and they work mostly in the sphere of education through the system of so-called Turkish lyceums and one university. There is no open conflict between them and Salafis, but they do maintain distance. They try not to intervene in each other's affairs and they do not criticize each other openly. Khizmet is not an openly political movement, but they try to exert their influence on politicians and wealthy businessmen in Kyrgyzstan in the same way the Saudi Salafis do. This is where we see competition for influence between the two groups. For the political wing of Salafis, Khizmet is their main competitor. However, it is common to see local Kyrgyz politicians, like Torobai Zulpukarov, working with both Saudis and Khizmet. Such alliances, in some ways, force these two groups to cooperate and look for common ground. Yet, one expert claimed that influential Khizmet figures use their connections with Kyrgyzstan's security agencies to put pressure on Salafis.[36]

Tablighi Jamaat

The Tablighi Jamaat is a group that originated in India in the 1920s. It distances itself from any kind of overt politics and works mostly with the common folk on the ground. However, as its influence spreads from the bottom up, more and more Kyrgyz politicians have expressed sympathy for the Tablighi vision. Yet, this influence on politicians is relatively insignificant compared to that of Khizmet and the Salafis. The main Tablighi competition with Salafis happens on the ground at the level of everyday relations between mosque attendants. Salafis are critical of many Tablighi practices, which they portray as *bid'a* (innovation in Islam), and they criticize its apolitical stands and Sufi roots. Tablighis are critical of Salafis' political nature and their disregard for local *madhhab*s. The conflict is mostly ideological and does not lead to open fights, but the mutual dislike of each other is strong, as is the Tablighi-Salafi competition for influence on the ground. Up to this point in time, the Tablighis seem to have the upper hand in this on-ground competition.

Traditional Imams

Salafis have very complicated relations with local traditional imams. This conflict is based on purely ideological grounds. All imams in Kyrgyzstan are appointed by the Muftiyat, and the majority of them follow and preach the traditional Hanafi *madhhab*. Thus, it is common for them to criticize Salafism and Salafi religious teachings and practices for their disregard of the *madhhab*s. Such critical public statements, often made during Friday prayer sermons, are perceived by Salafis as direct attacks on them. Thus, they develop grievances against such imams and often engage in arguments and verbal conflicts with them.

Tengirchiler

Even harsher attitudes toward Salafis can be found among such groups as the Tengirchiler, who claim to follow the region's indigenous pre-Islamic religious traditions. They attack Salafism because Salafis attack Kyrgyz national traditions. Whereas Muslims who are more nationally minded also join this fight against Salafis on the same nationalistic grounds—against what they see as "Arabization"—the Tengirchilers' aggression is more generic: they are strongly against Islam, and many do not differentiate between Salafis and other Islamic groups.

While discussing relations with other groups, we must differentiate between people's attitudes toward Salafism and toward Saudi Arabia. While the former is mostly negative, the latter is more complicated. The majority-Muslim population of the country, particularly those who actively practice Islam, has a positive attitude toward Saudis because Arabs are the descendants of the Prophet Muhammad and because there is a clear instruction in the *hadith* about praising the legacy of the Arabs. In addition, Arabs are respected for all the charity and financial support they provide for the construction of mosques, schools, and other building projects. However, many secularists and nationalists still see Saudi Arabs in a negative light for the same reasons that they dislike Salafis. It is common to hear criticisms that Saudis are funding the "Arabization" of Kyrgyz culture and that Saudi *shari'a* is a threat to the secular regime in Kyrgyzstan.

Conclusion

In conclusion, we can try to give an assessment of the overall influence of Saudi Arabia and Saudi *da'wa* on the religious situation in Kyrgyzstan. We believe that over three decades this impact can be seen as quite significant. Saudis were able to significantly alter the religious landscape; they are seen as very serious players with a lot of money behind them. They formed and supported the emergence of the local Salafi *jamaat*, which is the third most influential transnational *jamaat* in the country after Khizmet and the Tablighi Jamaat. Yet, in comparison to these two, Saudi influence on Kyrgyz society is less significant. Most experts agree that Turkish influence is much stronger.[37] Turkish lyceums and universities produce a large number of graduates, Turkish businesses have a much larger presence in Kyrgyzstan, and aid from the Turkish government is also larger and directed toward all kinds of development projects, not only charity and mosque construction. In addition, today Erdoğan is more likely to be perceived as a hero of the Islamic world, as opposed to Saudi kings who are perceived as the United States' puppets. Similarly, the Tablighi Jamaat is more active and more influential on the ground. So, in comparison to these *jamaat*s, Saudi influence is less significant.

Perhaps the biggest impact of Saudi Arabia in Kyrgyzstan was in the creation of religious infrastructure and the building of mosques. Nowadays, almost every settlement in the country has at least one mosque, and many of them were built with Saudi money. Yet, once a mosque is built, it is given over to local residents and is not used to spread Salafism.

Saudis might not directly engage in politics, but they do have influence on many Kyrgyz politicians. They also found a particular place in the hearts of young people, especially those among the Russian-speaking urbanites and among ethnic minorities, such as Uzbeks and Uyghurs. They created the ideological doctrinal conflict with the traditional local Islamic school of thought. This conflict has led to tensions in society, both at the level of larger religious scholarship and in the everyday religious practices of Kyrgyz Muslims in the mosques.

We can distinguish the later part of the first decade of the 2000s as the peak of Saudi influence, which then declined after the state began exerting pressure on Saudi foundations and on Salafi scholars. Nowadays, also due to the economic decline in Saudi Arabia and shortage of financing, Saudi influence is at its lowest.

Notes

1. Personal interview with Indira Aslanova, Associate Professor, Religious Studies, Kyrgyz-Russian Slavonic University.
2. Personal interview with local expert on religion (name withheld for reasons of personal security), Bishkek, October 19, 2019.
3. Personal interview with Bilal Saipiev, the head of Dawah Department at the Kyrgyzstan's Muftiate, Bishkek, April 20, 2017.
4. Personal interview with local expert on religion (name withheld for reasons of personal security), Bishkek, October 10, 2019.
5. Personal interview with local expert on religion (name withheld for reasons of personal security), Bishkek, October 19, 2019.
6. Personal interview with local expert on religion (name withheld for reasons of personal security), Bishkek, October 10, 2019.

7. Personal interview with local Salafi member (name withheld for reasons of personal security), Bishkek, October 24, 2019. ·

8. Personal interview with local expert on religion (name withheld for reasons of personal security), Bishkek, October 5, 2019, and personal interview with local expert on religion (name withheld for reasons of personal security), Bishkek, October 19, 2019.

9. Personal interview with local expert on religion (name withheld for reasons of personal security), Bishkek, October 10, 2019.

10. Personal interview with local expert on religion (name withheld for reasons of personal security), Bishkek, October 10, 2019; personal interview with local expert on religion (name withheld for reasons of personal security), Bishkek, October 14, 2019; and personal interview with local expert on religion (name withheld for reasons of personal security), Bishkek, October 5, 2019.

11. Personal interview with local expert on religion (name withheld for reasons of personal security), Bishkek, September 20, 2019.

12. Personal interview with local expert on religion (name withheld for reasons of personal security), Bishkek, October 10, 2019, and personal interview with local expert on religion (name withheld for reasons of personal security), Bishkek, October 5, 2019.

13. Personal interview with local expert on religion (name withheld for reasons of personal security), Bishkek, October 10, 2019, and personal interview with local expert on religion (name withheld for reasons of personal security), Bishkek, September 20, 2019.

14. Personal interview with local expert on religion (name withheld for reasons of personal security), Bishkek, October 10, 2019.

15. Personal interview with local expert on religion (name withheld for reasons of personal security), Bishkek, October 19, 2019.

16. Personal interview with local expert on religion (name withheld for reasons of personal security), Bishkek, October 19, 2019.

17. Personal interview with local expert on religion (name withheld for reasons of personal security), Bishkek, September 20, 2019.

18. Personal interview with local expert on religion (name withheld for reasons of personal security), Bishkek, September 20, 2019.

19. Personal interview with local Salafi member (name withheld for reasons of personal security), Bishkek, October 24, 2019.

20. Personal interview with local expert on religion (name withheld for reasons of personal security), Bishkek, September 20, 2019.

21. Personal interview with local expert on religion (name withheld for reasons of personal security), Bishkek, September 20, 2019.

22. Personal interview with a local Salafi member (name withheld for reasons of personal security), Bishkek, September 24, 2019.

23. Personal interview with local expert on religion (name withheld for reasons of personal security), Bishkek, September 20, 2019.

24. Personal interview with local expert on religion (name withheld for reasons of personal security), Bishkek, October 5, 2019.

25. Personal interview with Salafi member (name withheld for reasons of personal security), Bishkek, October 21, 2019, and personal interview with local expert on religion (name withheld for reasons of personal security), Bishkek, October 5, 2019.
26. Personal interview with local expert on religion (name withheld for reasons of personal security), Bishkek, October 5, 2019, and personal interview with local expert on religion (name withheld for reasons of personal security), Bishkek, October 10, 2019.
27. Personal interview with local expert on religion (name withheld for reasons of personal security), Bishkek, September 20, 2019.
28. Personal interview with local expert on religion (name withheld for reasons of personal security), Bishkek, October 22, 2019.
29. Personal interview with local expert on religion (name withheld for reasons of personal security), Bishkek, October 22, 2019.
30. Personal interview with local expert on religion (name withheld for reasons of personal security), Bishkek, October 14, 2019.
31. Personal interview with Salafi member (name withheld for reasons of personal security), Bishkek, October 24, 2019.
32. Personal interview with local expert on religion (name withheld for reasons of personal security), Bishkek, October 14, 2019.
33. Personal interview with local expert on religion (name withheld for reasons of personal security), Bishkek, October 10, 2019.
34. It is hard for us to say if this still true after the Saudi crackdown on the Ikhwan and other Islamists in the kingdom.
35. Personal interview with local expert on religion (name withheld for reasons of personal security), Bishkek, October 19, 2019.
36. Personal interview with local expert on religion (name withheld for reasons of personal security), Bishkek, September 20, 2019.
37. Personal interview with local expert on religion (name withheld for reasons of personal security), Bishkek, October 5, 2019; personal interview with local expert on religion (name withheld for reasons of personal security), Bishkek, October 10, 2019; and personal interview with local expert on religion (name withheld for reasons of personal security), Bishkek, September 20, 2019.

References

Bulan Institute. 2017. "Obrazovanie grazhdan KR v zarubezhnyh islamskih uchebnyh zavedeniyah: situatcionnyi analiz" [Citizens of Kyrgyz Republic Studying in the Foreign Islamic Institutions: Situational Analysis]. https://prevention.kg/wp-content/uploads/2019/02/Report-Religious-Education-in-Russian.pdf (accessed September 14, 2021).

Erickson, A. 2017. "How the USSR's Effort to Destroy Islam Created a Generation of Radicals." *Washingtonpost.com*, January 5, 2017. https://www.washingtonpost.com/news/worldviews/wp/2017/01/05/how-the-ussrs-effort-to-destroy-islam-created-a-generation-of-radicals/ (accessed January 2, 2021).

Kaleev, U., and I. Maseitova. 2019. "Real and Perceived Islamophobia in Bishkek: A Quantitative and Qualitative Study." *Constructive Dialogues on Religion and Democracy*,

International Alert, Bishkek-2019. https://www.international-alert.org/sites/defa ult/files/Kyrgyzstan_ConstructiveDialogues_ENG_2019.pdf (accessed December 24, 2020).

Kostenko, Y. 2012. "Tursunbai Bakir uulu: Konstitutciya Kyrgyzstama ne zapreshaet noshenie. Hidjaba" [Tursunbai Bakir uulu: Constitution of Kyrgyzstan does not prohibit wearing hijab]. 24.kg, September 24, 2012. https://24.kg/archive/ru/community/ 137642-tursunbaj-bakir-uulu-konstituciya-kyrgyzstana-ne.html/ (accessed January 1, 2021).

Kutueva, A. 2014. "Mairamkul Tilenchieva: Khidzhab nikogda ne byl traditsionnoi odezhdoi kyrgyzov," [Mairamkul Tulebaeva: Hijab was never a part of Kyrgyz traditional culture]. 24.kg, September 12, 2014. https://24.kg/archive/ru/parlament/ 186330-majramkul-tilenchieva-xidzhab-nikogda-ne-byl.html/ (accessed January 1, 2021).

Nasritdinov, E., Z. Urmanbetova, K. Murzakhalilov, and M. Myrzabaev. 2019. "Vulnerability and Resilience of Young People in Kyrgyzstan to Radicalization, Violence and Extremism: Analysis across Five Sectors." Central Asia Program paper no. 213, January 2019, Elliot School of International Affairs, George Washington University. https://centralasiaprogram.org/wp-content/uploads/2019/02/CAP-paper-213-Emil-Nasritdinov.pdf (accessed December 24, 2020).

Olcott, M. 2007. "The Roots of Radical Islam In Central Asia." Carnegie Endowment for International Peace. https://carnegieendowment.org/2007/01/17/roots-of-radical-islam-in-central-asia-pub-18967 (accessed December 7, 2020).

Peyrouse, S. 2007. "The Rise of Political Islam in Soviet Central Asia." *Current Trends in Islamist Ideology*, May 23, 2007. https://www.hudson.org/research/9892-the-rise-of-political-islam-in-soviet-central-asia (accessed December 29, 2020).

Yalovkina, A. 2014. "Atambaev: Religioznye normy ne dolzhny zatmevat tcennosti kyrgyzov" [Atambev: Relighious norms should not replace Kyrgyz values]. Vechernii Bishkek, November 3, 2014. https://www.vb.kg/doc/292093_atambaev:_religioznye_ normy_ne_doljny_zatmevat_cennosti_kyrgyzov.html (accessed January 1, 2021).

9

Saudi Arabia

A South Asian Wrecking Ball

James M. Dorsey

An eclectic poet, philosopher, politician, and barrister, Sir Muhammad Iqbal, better known as Allama Iqbal, is widely seen as the political godfather of a country for Muslims in South Asia, even if he died before the state of Pakistan was carved out of British India in 1947 during partition (Iqbal Academy, n.d.).

Wittingly or unwittingly, Iqbal helped create the Muslim state and national identity most instrumental and receptive to Saudi Arabia's global support of ultra-conservative strands of Islam that propagate literal, ritualistic expressions of the faith to garner soft power. Ultra-conservatism offered Saudi Arabia a powerful antidote to interpretations of the faith as well as secular philosophies it either opposed on theological grounds or perceived as existential threats to the survival of the ruling Al Sa'ud family and its power-sharing arrangement with the kingdom's religious establishment. Nowhere has the global, decades-long Saudi religious soft-power campaign, aided and abetted by successive Pakistani governments and political and societal forces, written ultra-conservative Islam deeper into the DNA of society and wreaked greater havoc and fueled sectarianism than in Pakistan.

Iqbal employed the vocabulary of nationalism and the right of self-determination to argue in favor of partition, but framed its raison d'être in pan-Islamic terms. He envisioned an Islamic state in South Asia "as a step toward a larger Islamic community, a vehicle for the perfection of Islam" (Cohen 2004, 37). To him, territorial nationalism was a stepping stone for the unification of the global ummah, the community of the faithful, based on the notion that "political power was essential to the higher ends of establishing God's law" (Talbot 2000, 30). His vision of an independent Pakistan was not that of a Westphalian nation-state, but as a vehicle to liberate Islam from alien Hinduism and obsolescent Islamic encrustations (Cohen 2004, 30).

By imbuing Pakistan's identity with pan-Islamic attributes, Iqbal contributed to a national myth intended to provide a glue for the new country's multiple Muslim sects and religious minorities and ethnic groups, as well as the millions of *muhaijirs*, Muslim immigrants from what became independent

James M. Dorsey, *Saudi Arabia* In: *Wahhabism and the World.* Edited by: Peter Mandaville, Oxford University Press.
© Oxford University Press 2022. DOI: 10.1093/oso/9780197532560.003.0009

India. Pan-Islamism and the fact that Pakistan was the world's only country created to provide a home to Muslims as a religious group rather than a nation that emerged from colonialism, with a population that in majority adhered to Islam, nurtured notions of a nation—like Saudi Arabia, home to the faith's most holy cities—that had a responsibility toward the global ummah, rather than only its citizenry. It was a notion that in the minds of many Pakistanis put Pakistan as a Muslim state in the same category as Saudi Arabia. It was not just a Muslim state, it was a state for Muslims, even if it restricted immigration to those from what was British India.

Political scientist and historian Eqbal Ahmed recalled Pakistanis perceiving the founding of their state as the creation of a new Medina, a reference to one of the two holy cities in Saudi Arabia. "The Hijaz is sacrosanct for Muslims on the subcontinent. Religion dominated the slogans used for independence. References to Saudi Arabia lent legitimacy to the ruling elite," Ahmed noted, charting the history of Saudi-Pakistani relations (interview, 1991, Amsterdam). It is a perception that shapes Pakistan until today. A banner erected by vendors in Islamabad's Aabpara Market declared in 2017 that "any attack on Saudi Arabia is an attack on the Muslim world." Pakistani prime minister Imran Khan assumed office in 2018, declaring that he would reshape his country in the image of seventh-century Medina. "For Muslims there is only one model, and that is the Prophet created the state of Medina," Khan said (Council on Foreign Relations 2019, n.p.).

Shahnaz Wazir Ali, an articulate, fast-speaking president of a prestigious university and former minister in the government of Zulfikar Ali Bhutto, noted that "the connection between Pakistan and Saudi Arabia is conceptual. The aura in the minds of many Pakistanis harks back to Saudi Arabia as the custodian of the holy cities and the birthplace of the Prophet. It is spiritual, religious, emotional, physical and cognitive. Pakistanis are holier than the pope. If we would be against Saudi Arabia, we would be against our own religion. Nobody thinks of the Saudis and their hypocrisy, secret lives and barbaric practices" (interview, 2016, Islamabad).

A Union Waiting to Happen

As a result, the marriage of geopolitics and religion-driven Saudi ultra-conservatism and Pakistani political ambition was a union waiting to happen. Pakistan, established as a country for Muslims, and Saudi Arabia, a kingdom created by the union of the Al Sa'ud family and their army of tribal warriors backed by the aggressive, exclusionary theology of Muhammad ibn 'Abd al-Wahhab, shared a common understanding of themselves as states whose ethos positioned them as leaders of the Muslim world. It was a union in which Pakistan brought mass to the table, with a large population and strategic geography, while Saudi Arabia, even before the spiking of oil prices with the 1973 oil boycott of the United States and the Netherlands because of their support for Israel in that year's Israeli-Arab war, could offer funding. As the custodian of Islam's two most holy cities, Saudi Arabia moreover could enhance Pakistan's pan-Islamic credentials.

It was a marriage in which ultra-conservatism and latent radicalism were written into the DNA of the state in the years after Pakistan was carved out of British India as a separate state for Muslims. "The state and society were systematically injected with greater dozes [sic] of religious narrative especially in politics," said Pakistan scholar Ayesha Siddiqa (Siddiqa 2010; interview, 2016, Islamabad). A resolution by the Pakistani parliament adopted in 1949 that defined Pakistan as a religious entity confined to the principles of Islam has served as the basis for successive constitutions. Conservatives and ultra-conservatives defeated government efforts to establish a more tolerant and inclusive Islam, embodied in institutions like the Iqbal Academy, founded in 1950 in honor of the philosopher-politician. The academy challenged "reactionary clerics" and propagated "Islamic concepts of liberty, fraternity and equality" (Hakim 2006, n.p.) in publications distributed to military personnel ordered to put down ultra-conservative protests in Lahore in 1953 (interview, 2016).

The failure of more liberal forces meant that notions of pan-Islamism promoted by Islamist forces as well as Saudi Arabia, rather than providing an inclusive societal glue, created an environment conducive to sectarianism and polarization. They were aided and abetted by Pakistan's dependence on economic and financial aid; Pakistani willingness to accede to Saudi requests that hardened societal fault lines and geopolitical developments, including the perennial dispute with India over Kashmir; and the 1979 Iranian Revolution, as well as the Soviet invasion of Afghanistan. The momentous events of 1979 opened the floodgates to Saudi funding for the building of somewhere between 24,000 (The Economist 2016) and 30,000 madrasas (e-mail exchanges with Pakistani sources, 2016).

Tahir Ashrafi, the Saudi-aligned head of the Pakistan Ulema Council, asserts that 60 percent of the pupils at madrasas were "not involved in any training or terrorist activities." interviews, 2016–2017, Islamabad). In other words, 40 percent may be. "It's a very complex feeder system. All the remaining 40 percent are not involved in terrorism or terrorist training, but they could be sympathizers, they could funnel part of their funds to terror outfits, they could aid and abet in various ways," said Mahboob Mohammed, Pakistani lawyer, operator of an e-learning platform and author of an unpublished book on Islam (e-mail exchanges, 2016).

Who Is a Muslim?

Men like Syed Abu'l A'la Mawdudi—a philosopher, jurist, journalist, and imam who played a key role in the creation of pillars of the Saudi religious soft-power effort like the Muslim World League and the Islamic University of Medina (IUM) and led Jamaat-e-Islami, the Pakistani political party closely aligned with Saudi Arabia for the longest period of time—used Islam to foster exclusionary politics that created opportunities for the kingdom to enhance its influence in the country.

A billboard in a mosque built on the site where Mawdudi's original house of worship once was lists Saudi king Faysal, Islamist Turkish president Recep Tayyip Erdoğan, ousted Egyptian president Muhammad Morsi, and Tunisian Islamist leader Rashid Ghannouchi (both members of the Muslim Brotherhood), controversial Qatar-based *shaykh* Yusuf al-Qaradawi, former Hamas leader Khalid Mash'al, and Hasan al-Banna, the founder of the Muslim Brotherhood, as Mawdudi's protégés.

The 1953 riots that targeted Ahmadis, a sect widely viewed by conservative Muslims as heretics, were sparked by domestic political infighting and Jamaat-e-Islami's politicization of the question, "Who is a Muslim?" They further opened the door to Saudi-backed ultra-conservatism and paved the road for the adoption of restrictive, religiously motivated rule and laws under Prime Minister Zulfikar Ali Bhutto and the subsequent ultimate Islamization of Pakistani society and the state by the government of General Zia-ul-Haq.

The riots erupted after Sir Ghulam Muhammad, the governor-general of Pakistan, asked Mawdudi to write a book about the Ahmadis that would clarify their status as Muslims. The book, *The Qadiani Problem* (Mawdudi, n.d.), served to justify Mawdudi's arrest and subsequent conviction to death on charges that it had incited the violence (interview, 2017, Islamabad). Mawdudi's use of the derogatory term "Qadiani" to describe Ahmadis signaled Saudi theological influence on his thinking. Qadiani refers to the birthplace in northern India of Mirza Ghulam Ahmad, the founder of the sect. It contrasted starkly with Mawdudi's assertion fifteen years earlier in a handwritten letter, at a time when he first engaged with Saudi scholars, that Ahmadis were a "group (that) is included within Islam." Mawdudi at the time went on to say that "we cannot issue any fatwa (religious opinion) against them on the basis of the *shari'a* (Islamic law)" (The Lahore Ahmadiyya Movement 2017, n.p.). Mawdudi graduated to taking a stand against the Ahmadis under the pressure of Saudi-backed Indian Muslim scholar Maulana Husain Ahmad Madani and his Pakistani followers. Madani, a longtime resident of Mecca, forged close relations with 'Abd al-'Aziz bin Baz, the Saudi grand mufti, and Shaykh 'Abdullah bin Humayd, the kingdom's chief justice and imam of Mecca's Grand Mosque (Sikand 2007, 95–108).

Ultimately, it was Mawdudi's standing among Saudi scholars as a result of his writings, an exchange of letters with prominent members of the Al al-Shaykh family (descendants of Muhammad ibn 'Abd al-Wahhab, the founder of Wahhabism, the ultra-conservative strand of Sunni Islam prevalent in the kingdom), and his association with the Muslim Brotherhood that prompted Saudi King Sa'ud bin 'Abd al-'Aziz Al Sa'ud to persuade Pakistani authorities to cancel the death sentence against Mawdudi and release him on a legal technicality (interview, 2017, Islamabad). It was an intervention that would put a lasting mark on Pakistan as well as the Saudi soft-power campaign. Ahmadis were excluded in 2020 from a national commission created by the government to promote religious tolerance and counter persecution of minorities. Pakistan's religious affairs ministry barred inclusion of Ahmadis on grounds that they did not qualify as a minority and refuse to recognize the country's constitution (Hashim 2020).

Beyond allowing the kingdom to piggyback on Jamaat-e-Islami's efforts in Afghanistan to counter Kabul's support for Pashtun separatism in Pakistan in the decades prior to the anti-Soviet guerrilla insurgency (Hussein 2005), it positioned Mawdudi as an intellectual powerhouse, helping Saudi Arabia situate itself as a leader of the Muslim world. A constituent member of the Muslim World League (MWL), a key Saudi vehicle established in 1962 to distribute Saudi proselytization funds, Mawdudi was asked that same year by King Sa'ud to identify people and countries the MWL should target, as well as to develop the concept of an Islamic university in the holy city of Medina. Like the MWL, the IUM became a key node in the global expansion of religious Saudi soft power (Farquhar 2016).

Saudi Arabia's 1953 intervention cast a shadow over Pakistan that until today it has been unable and/or unwilling to remove. Encouraged by Saudi leaders and Islamic scholars, Pakistani leaders sowed the seeds of Sunni-Shi'ite sectarianism and the country's lurch toward debilitating ultra-conservatism by seeking, from the 1970s onward, to narrow the definition of who was a Muslim and to defeat the inclusive nature of a Muslim identity that was Pakistan's raison d'être. Needing to assuage Saudi king Faisal, who felt he was overshadowed by Bhutto, Palestine Liberation Organization chairman Yasir Arafat, Libyan leader Mu'ammar Qaddafi, and Bangladesh president Mujibur Rahman, during a Saudi-funded Islamic summit in Islamabad, persuaded the Pakistani leader to bow to Saudi and Islamist pressure to accept a constitutional amendment that would declare Ahmadis non-Muslims. The pressure involved multiple requests by Saudi king Faisal that Pakistan delegitimize the Ahmadis, including in a meeting with the prime minister on the sidelines of a Saudi-funded Islamic summit in Islamabad in February 1974, as well as calls by Mawdudi (Jalal 2014).

Under attack at the time by hardline Islamists, including Mawdudi, who demanded his resignation, Bhutto's concession was part of a wider Islamization of Pakistani society that was designed to garner favor with Gulf states and particularly Saudi Arabia (Akhtar 2018, 98). It involved making Friday the weekly holiday and banning alcohol, nightclubs, and other "un-Islamic" activities that were designed to garner favor with Arab Gulf states and particularly Saudi Arabia (Akhtar 2018, 98). Bhutto conceded after traveling the globe in the year before the amendment to raise funds for his government, whose coffers were empty in the wake of the 1971 India-Pakistan War. In Saudi Arabia, Faisal told him that Saudi clerics demanded that he ensure that Ahmadis would not travel to Mecca for the *hajj*. Bhutto rejected the king's suggestion that the government cancel Ahmadis' passports, saying he could not do so legally (interview, 1999, Islamabad). Nonetheless, the 1973 constitution opened the door to the anti-Ahmadi amendment by stipulating that Islamic law should be implemented in line with the precepts of ultra-conservative religious scholars. Bhutto started to cave to Saudi and Islamist demands by introducing an oath in which the president and the prime minister declared that they were Muslims who believed that Muhammad was the final and last prophet. The summit proposed by Bhutto was intended to give him the cover to support adoption of a constitutional amendment that would put Ahmadis beyond the pale by declaring them non-Muslims (Constitution of the Islamic Republic of Pakistan, n.d.). Two months after the amendment was adopted, the MWL called on all Muslim governments to excommunicate Ahmadis and bar them from holding sensitive government positions. "We were aware of Saudi moves in 1974. We knew something was brewing. There had been an upsurge in religious agitation against us," said Shahid A. Ata-Ullah, an Ahmadi elder in Lahore (interview, 2017, Lahore).

The concessions put an end to state-led efforts to counter Saudi-inspired pressure to ensure that Pakistan would be guided by ultra-conservatism rather than more liberal interpretations of the faith (Blood 1994), described by Pakistani cultural critic Nadeem F. Paracha as "Islamic Modernism." Reflecting on the defeat of the liberals, Paracha said in an article published in 2017: "One now wonders, would the state of the country have been better today had Islamic Modernism been allowed to evolve beyond the 1970s?" (Paracha 2017, n.p.).

The amendment made religious identity and the definition of who belonged to the community of the faithful a matter of public policy. It allowed Saudi-backed ultra-conservatives to take the concept of Pakistan's religiously infused nationalism to the next level by questioning whether Shi'ites were Muslims. The sectarian push energized by the 1979 Iranian Revolution and its subsequent Islamization under Ayatollah Ruhollah Khomeini in Pakistan's predominantly Shi'ite neighbor, Bhutto's acquiescence, and the promotion of ultra-conservatism by his successor, General Zia, constituted a response to the loss as a result of the 1971 India-Pakistan War of Eastern Pakistan. The emergence of Bangladesh as an independent state pointed a dagger at the heart of Pakistan's raison d'être: the partition of the subcontinent into a Hindu India and a single state, Pakistan, that would be home to Muslims of all stripes. Ethno-linguistic differences had defeated the notion of a common Muslim identity. Ultra-conservatism and sectarianism, aided and abetted by Saudi Arabia as well as post-revolutionary Iran, filled the ideological crater.

Opportunity Galore

In effect, the decade of the 1970s, bookended by Bangladeshi independence in the early years and the Soviet invasion of Afghanistan in 1979, opened vast new opportunities for Saudi soft-power diplomacy that allowed the kingdom and Wahhabis, as well as ultra-conservative Pakistani religious scholars, to significantly cement and expand their network beyond Mawdudi's Jamaat-e-Islami and the Ahl-i Hadith or the People of Tradition, a Saudi-inspired Salafi movement with semi-autonomous units that traces its roots to nineteenth-century northern India.

Jamaat-e-Islami's influence was evident in the creation or empowering of institutions like *shari'a* courts and the Council of Islamic Ideology, tasked with ensuring that legislation did not violate Islamic law. It also was apparent in moves to put 126,000 mosque officials on the government payroll and the hiring of 3,000 Islamic scholars in villages as part-time teachers (Ahmad 1997, 106). The effect of these moves, coupled with the fallout of Pakistani support for the US- and Saudi-backed Islamist mujahidin fighting Soviet occupation troops in Afghanistan and subsequent Pakistani support of the Taliban and other militants, was felt over time. "By the 1990s, the political and discursive fields had been transformed—a thoroughly Islamized idiom of politics had become virtually hegemonic," noted Pakistan scholar Aasim Sajjad Akhtar. Akhtar went on to say that "the long-term impact is plain to see. The state's security apparatus, along with foreign states such as Saudi Arabia, has empowered any number of sectarian/militant organizations" (interview, 2018, Singapore; Akhtar 2018, 99–100).

"Jamaatis are entrenched as ever. They run the academic associations and control the administration. Nobody can get hired without their approval. They provide cover to the shenanigans of the (religious right) whilst prohibiting activities of any students they suspect of harbouring progressive ideas. In principle, the government of the day appoints a university's vice-chancellor. In practice, it is the Jamaatis who decide who sits in the top office of the university," Akhtar added (interview, 2018, Singapore).

The Islamists' influence in academia was mirrored in their continued dominance of the labor movement and peasant collectives, both of which were once left-wing strongholds. Religion became the most powerful mobilizer.

Jamaat-e-Islami's ability to wield influence stemmed in part from its Communist Party–style cadre-based structure and its nationwide social services infrastructure. The party's operatives in student groups, trade unions, and professional organizations, as well as its media assets, positioned it as an ally for government and military officials who believed that Pakistan needed a religious anchor. The party's ability to facilitate Saudi influence in the military was enhanced by the fact that two of its Pakistani-army-trained militant groups, Al-Badr and Al-Shams, targeted Bangladeshi nationalists seeking independence from Pakistan in 1971.

The Council of Islamic Ideology, Pakistan's top Islamic advisory body, is made up of ten clerics and judges, who at times have included militants such as Maulana Ali Muhammad Abu Turab, a Balochistan-based leader of Ahl-i Hadith who was designated as a terrorist by the US Treasury on allegations that he raised funds for Al-Qaeda, and Hafiz Saeed, also Saudi-educated and similarly designated by the US Treasury and the United Nations with a $10 million US bounty, who is believed to lead the outlawed militant group Lashkar-e-Taiba (LeT), as well as Jamaat-ud-Dawa, an alleged LeT front, and is suspected of being the mastermind of the 2008 Mumbai attacks in which 166 people were killed.

Saeed was sentenced in 2020 to eleven years in prison in an effort to prevent an international anti-money laundering and terrorism finance watchdog, the Financial Action Task Force (FATF), from blacklisting Pakistan for failing to crack down on militants' funding. The conviction constituted the first time in twenty years of repeated arrests and releases from detention that Saeed was successfully charged and prosecuted. The US Treasury designated Abu Turab, an Islamic scholar of Afghan descent, in 2018 on a day that he was touring Saudi Arabia to raise funds for his string of madrasas along Pakistan's border with Iran and Afghanistan that are attended by thousands of students. Abu Turab's tour occurred at a time when Saudi and United Arab Emirates nationals of Baloch heritage were funneling large amounts to militant anti-Shi'ite and anti-Iranian Islamic scholars in Balochistan. It was not clear whether the fundraising had tacit government approval (Dorsey 2018).

The Council of Islamic Ideology's members have a long history of links to Saudi Arabia. Marouf Dualibi, an Islamic scholar with close ties to Saudi King Fahd, was dispatched by the kingdom to help General Zia introduce *hudud*, punishments for certain offenses mandated in Islamic law, as well as mandatory *zakat*, a charitable tax, and *ushr*, an agricultural levy that dates back to early Islam; he also persuaded the Pakistani leader to adopt anti-Shi'ite laws (Council of Islamic Ideology 1981).

Justice Afzal Cheema, Zia-ul-Haq's first appointed Council chairman, was given a position in the Saudi-funded, Karachi-based World Muslim Congress (Wasti 2009, 116). Cheema drafted the laws introducing the *shari'a* concepts of *qisas*, which gives the right of a murder victim's nearest relative or legal guardian to take the life of the killer with the approval of a court, and *diyya*, the principle of financial compensation paid to the victim or heirs of a victim in cases of murder, bodily harm, or property damage. The introduction sparked confusion in the Pakistani judiciary as well as the public, according to Pakistan-born Islamic legal scholar Tahir Wasti: "The law borrowed ideas, concepts and even technical terms from the tribal culture of the Hijaz (Saudi Arabia) while both the judiciary and Pakistani society were wholly unfamiliar with such 'traditional' mores, norms, values and technical terms" (Wasti 2009, 237).

The laws, particularly the one related to *diyya*, helped perpetrators of honor killings escape prison. The effect was a dramatic increase in the number of killings, while the number of related court cases dropped 100 percent with police encouraging parties to agree on blood money arrangements (Wasti 2009, 257–271). The spike in honor killings mirrored the jump in militant attacks on artists, writers, and journalists, not to mention the multiple suicide bombings that killed hundreds if not thousands across the country in past decades.

"The enemy within is not a fringe. . . . Large sections of society sympathize with these groups. They fund them, directly and indirectly. They provide them recruits. They reject the Constitution and the system. They don't just live in the 'badlands' but could be our neighbours. The forces . . . also . . . operate in the cities where hundreds, perhaps thousands form sleeper cells, awaiting orders or planning to strike," wrote Pakistani columnist Ejaz Haider (Haider 2016, n.p.).

"Pakistani society's tolerant disposition was converted into what it is today through the efforts of [the] Pakistani state system by socialising at least more than one generation into religious orthodoxy and militancy. The orthodox and hardline religious circles were pampered by the Pakistani state in cooperation with friendly foreign countries that had their own overlapping agendas to pursue," added Pakistani security analyst Hasan Askari Rizvi (Rizvi 2017, n.p.).

Repeated defeat of efforts to abolish the Council of Islamic Ideology illustrate the power of Saudi-backed ultra-conservatives and the obstacles this erects to Pakistani efforts to determine Islam's place in society. "The kind of space afforded to the Council of Islamic Ideology is symptomatic of the state's unresolved relationship with Islam. There's never been a consensus on the kind of Islam the state of Pakistan was meant to represent," said author Farzana Shaikh (interview, 2016, Singapore).

Ultra-Conservatism Meets Geopolitics

For its part, the Ahl-i Hadith movement was Wahhabism's earliest ally on the subcontinent. Relations dated back to the 1800s when Saudi Wahhabi missionaries traveled to far-flung places to forge alliances. The Ahl-i Hadith shared the

Wahhabis' rejection of any form of perceived innovation, including Shi'ite and Sufi practices. The alliance endured even if the Ahl-i Hadith, in line with multiple Salafi schools of thought and in contrast to Wahhabism's adherence to the Hanbali school of legal thought, rejected all legal schools as innovations. The Ahl-i Hadith insisted that only a literal interpretation of the Qur'an and the *hadith* was legally valid.

Despite being the smallest of the ultra-conservative sects on the subcontinent, the Ahl-i Hadith proved its value to the Saudis even before the kingdom or Pakistan had emerged as independent states. In the 1920s, at a time that many Muslims opposed and demonstrated against 'Abd al- 'Aziz ibn Sa'ud's conquest of Islam's holiest cities, Mecca and Medina, and his subsequent destruction of holy places considered innovations by the Wahhabis, Ahl-i Hadith activists defended his approach in public rallies and the publication of legal treatises that justified Saudi practice. 'Abd al- 'Aziz thanked the Ahl-i Hadith for its support in a series of letters published by the group's newspapers (Sikand 2010).

Relations between the Saudis and the Ahl-i Hadith were always both ideological and personal. That was as true in the 1800s as it was in the mid-twentieth century. Abdul Ghaffar Hasan al-Hindi, a leading Ahl-i Hadith scholar who left Jamaat-e-Islami because he favored education as opposed to the ballot box as the path to an Islamic state, taught *hadith* for fifteen years at the IUM in the 1960s and 1970s. Al-Hindi and Hafiz Mohammad Ghondalavi, the father-in-law of Ehsan Elahi Zaheer, a leading Ahl-i Hadith scholar, were invited to teach in Mecca by a Saudi delegation that visited Pakistan in 1964. Prominent Saudi scholars were among his students. Zaheer published a book written in Urdu and translated into Arabic and English in 1980 that denounced Shi'ism as heresy and Shi'ites as Zionist agents. The Saudi government distributed the book widely (Ghattas 2020, 159–160).

Al-Hindi's close ties to Bin Baz, the Saudi grand mufti, secured continued support from the kingdom for his Pakistani movement (Abou Zahab 2009, 128) including the founding of new madrasas in the North-West Frontier Province and southern Afghanistan (Rubin 1997, 187) and the creation of a publishing empire. The number of Ahl-i Hadith madrasas jumped 273 percent, from 134 in 1988 to 500 in 2008, or six percent of all religious seminaries in Pakistan, many of which were affiliated with the IUM. Some 34,000 students were studying in Ahl-i Hadith madrasas in 2008, compared to 18,800 in 1996 (Ahmed 2002; Abou Zahab 2009, 133). A study by the Norwegian Centre for International and Strategic Analysis (SISA) estimated in 2013 that the Ahl-i Hadith operated 1,400 religious seminaries (Zaidi 2013).

The Saudi government, as well as government-controlled nongovernmental organizations, also funded publication of anti-Shi'ite and anti-Sufi tracts, political texts that post-1979 denounced the Iranian Revolution as an un-Islamic conspiracy designed to establish Shi'ite hegemony, and literature holding the kingdom up as a model of Islamic governance, written by Ahl-i Hadith authors, as well as translations of Saudi *fatwa*s and other religious texts that often denounced other Sunni and non-Sunni schools of thought as heretical.

Expanding the Ahl-i Hadith's appeal was facilitated by the return of migrant workers who had been imbued with ultra-conservatism while in Saudi Arabia, as well as graduates from the IUM. The Afghan war and the increasing number of madrasas broadened its social base even if it remained one of the smaller ultra-conservative groupings in Pakistan. Prominent Pakistani journalist Khaled Ahmed identified seventeen groups in Pakistan that were associated with the Ahl-i Hadith, six of which engaged in politics while three others, including Jamaat-ud-Da'wa, were jihadi in nature. The majority focused on *da'wa* or pros-elytization and the running of madrasas (Ahmed 2002).

Like Saudi-backed writers, scholars, and opinion leaders across the globe, Ahl-i Hadith authors urged Muslims to have minimal contact with non-Muslims, contributing to an environment in which ultra-conservative communities risked becoming hotbeds of militancy. It also constituted an effort to reduce Islam's rich diversity to a debate primarily among Muslims whose ultra-conservative views, irrespective of whether they had affinity with Wahhabism, furthered Saudi Arabia's geopolitical goals.

Zaheer represented a new breed of ultra-conservative intellectuals who, in the wake of the Iranian revolution, took criticism of Shi'ism a step further by declaring it to be beyond the pale of Islam. Their line of reasoning contributed to an environment in which differences between Shi'ism and Sunnism were no longer issues of doctrinal debate, but fostered sectarian violence. It targeted not only Shi'ism as an ideology, but also Shi'ites as people (Nasir 2000, 139–180). Their thinking sparked a wave of books whose titles suggested that Shi'ites were attacking the core pillars of Islam such as the Qur'an.

The Saudi king Fahd demonstrated his appreciation for the sectarianism of men like Zaheer and Maulana Haq Nawaz Jhangvi, a vice president of the Jamaat-i-Islami, who with the support of General Zia would go on to found Pakistan's most virulently anti-Shi'ite group, Sipah-e-Sahaba, or Guardians/Soldiers of the Prophet's Companions, when he sent his private plane to take Zaheer to Medina after he was seriously wounded in 1987 in a Shi'ite bombing of a mosque in Lahore, the first of many sectarian incidents of that kind. Zaheer died in a Saudi hospital.

Bin Baz, one of his teachers at the IUM, alongside Shaykh Muhammad Nasir al-Din al-Albani, one of the twentieth century's most prominent Salafi thinkers, led Zaheer's funeral prayers (Abou Zahab 2009, 135). Zaheer's "links with the Saudi religious hierarchy and funds made him an important personality within the Jamiat," said journalist Ahmed (Ahmed 2002, n.p.). Zaheer established

Markazi Jamiat Ahl-i Hadith, as a core component of the movement as well as a political party with a jihadi unit, Tehreek al-Mujahideen, that trained fighters in a camp in Afghanistan for engagement in Kashmir (Abou Zahab 2009, 128).

Tehreek al-Mujahideen was funded by the Al-Haramain Islamic Foundation (South Asian Terrorism Portal 1998), a Saudi government-backed charity that in the wake of September 11, 2001, saw many of its overseas branches as well as its head, Aqeel Al-Aqeel, designated as terrorists by the UN Security Council and the US Treasury. Tehreek-al-Mujahideen's patron was Fazlur Rehman Khalil, a specially designated terrorist on the US Treasury's list, who maintains close ties to senior Saudi scholars and counts a Saudi national among his wives. Rehman, a signatory of Usama bin Laden's 1998 *fatwa* declaring the World Islamic Front Against Jews and Crusaders (The World Islamic Front for Jihad Against Jews and Crusaders 1998), operates a madrasa guarded by AK-47-toting guards on the outskirts of Islamabad.

The Floodgates Open

Saudi and Pakistani government support for the anti-Shi'ite militants was evident from day one after the 1979 Iranian Revolution. It highlighted Saudi determination to prevent Iranian revolutionary zeal from inspiring Muslims in Pakistan and across the Muslim world and Iran from emerging as an alternative model of Islamic governance that would challenge the kingdom's autocratic family rule. It also served Pakistani strongman General Zia's Islamist policies and his effort to align his country with Saudi Arabia. The bonds between Saudi Arabia and Pakistan have been maintained by successive Pakistani governments, even if subsequent administrations have backed away from encouraging and supporting Sunni anti-Shi'ite militancy. Most of Zia's successors feared that it would further destabilize Pakistan and undermine its efforts to be seen as an important node in the fight against militancy, rather than as part of the problem.

A 2008 cable from the US consulate in Lahore reported that "financial support estimated at nearly US$100 million annually was making its way to (conservative) Deobandi and Ahl-e-Hadith clerics in the region from 'missionary' and 'Islamic charitable' organizations in Saudi Arabia and the United Arab Emirates ostensibly with the direct support of those governments." US diplomat Bryan Hunt estimated in the cable that up to 200 madrasas in southern Punjab in towns like Multan and Dera Ghazi Khan at the juncture of four Pakistani provinces, and in the central city of Bahawalpur, served as recruitment grounds for militant Islamist groups (Dawn 2011, n.p.).

Pakistani security consultant Muhammad Amir Rana reported that Saudi Arabia in the first decade of the twenty-first century had donated $2.7 million to the education department of the municipality of Jhang for the funding of madrasas (interview, 2018, Islamabad). Jhang was Jhangvi's hometown and a stronghold of Sipah-e-Sahaba as well as its successor, Ahle Sunnat Wal Jama'at (ASWJ), which was established after the former group was banned first in 2002 and again in 2012.

The scale of Saudi government, semi-government, and private funding, particularly with the launch of the insurgency by militant Islamists against the Soviet occupation of Afghanistan, convinced Deobandis, a back-to-basics movement founded in the mid-nineteenth century in opposition to British colonial rule, that they could not afford to miss the opportunity to benefit from generous financing of madrasas, publications, and fighters. Deobandis were far more influential than the Ahl-i Hadith and boasted a far larger footprint in Pakistan as well as in Afghanistan. Deobandism's rejection of core Wahhabi principles and of Ibn 'Abd al-Wahhab as anti-Muslim notwithstanding, Deobandism and Wahhabism agreed on the centrality of the *shari'a* and the threat posed by Iran and Shi'ites. Massive support from multiple Saudi sources for the Deobandis allowed the kingdom to catch three birds with one stone: expand their reach in Afghanistan; counter emboldened Shi'ites whom Saudis viewed as an Iranian fifth column; and, at least initially, ensure that the Deobandis gained the upper hand against Barelvis, their arch-rivals who tend to fuse ultra-conservatism with Sufi practices.

Syed Badiuddin Soharwardy, a sixty-two-year-old Canadian-Pakistani imam, experienced how Saudi-funded ultra-conservatism altered the demography of the Pakistani armed forces. The son of a prayer leader and teacher, Soharwardy recalls accompanying his father to mosques across Pakistan on bases of the Pakistani army air force and navy to celebrate the Prophet's birthday, a ritual frowned upon by ultra-conservatives. "My father would participate in the celebration and the kids would sing rhymes praising the Prophet," Soharwardy said. "I remember, in Karachi, hundreds of military personnel would come on trucks dressed in civilian clothes. They would shout 'Nara e haideri,' 'Shout the name of Ali,' and the crowd would respond 'Ya, 'Ali, Oh 'Ali,'" Sohawardy said. The motivational chants, denounced by ultra-conservatives, praised 'Ali, the son-in-law and companion of the Prophet most revered by Shi'ites. They were banned by General Zia when he seized power in 1978. "It was a sign of Saudization," said Soharwardy, a Sufi scholar and president of the Islamic Supreme Council of Canada (interview, 2018, Singapore).

Soharwardy went on to quantify the religious affiliation of Pakistani mosques on the basis of prayer schedules for holidays that are published in newspapers according to sect. He concluded that, starting with Zia, ultra-conservativism had made significant inroads into the Pakistani military. If 70 percent of mosques were Sufi in the late 1970s, that number had shifted 30 years later to 55 percent adhering to Deobandism, he calculated. The shift in military mosques was even more dramatic, with 85 percent currently following Deobandism as opposed to the 90 percent in the 1970s that aligned themselves with Sufism. Soharwardy attributed the change to Saudi funding and promotion of ultra-conservative literature. "The Wahhabis and Salafis are inside the Pakistani state. They have changed Pakistan from a Sufi-dominated state to a Salafi-dominated state," he said (interview, 2017, Singapore, February 23).

The son a of a military officer, Tareq Parvez, a former head of the Federal Investigation Authority (FIA) and the Counter Terrorism Authority (NCTA), recalled that his "father never spoke of jihad, he spoke of Pakistan. Now every officer talks of jihad in the way of Allah." Speaking in an interview after he stepped down as NCTA's national coordinator, Parvez suggested that the approach of Saudi funders toward Pakistani groups had expanded since the beginning of the twenty-first century to include the Barelvis. Barelvis have since made blasphemy a major issue, leading to mob justice against alleged blasphemers and assassinations of opponents of Pakistan's draconian anti-blasphemy law (interview, 2017, Islambad).

Sectarianism and polarization allowed Saudi-backed Islamists to weave themselves into the fabric of Pakistan's military-civil bureaucracy and intelligence apparatus (Haqqani 2004–2005, 93). As a result, years of religious rhetoric, including legitimization of concepts of jihad in Kashmir and Afghanistan, influenced a generation of military officers as well as officials of the powerful Inter-Services Intelligence (ISI), the country's premier intelligence agency. "This has enabled Islamists to exercise greater influence than would have been possible in an open, democratic political system, given the poor electoral performance of Islamic groups in Pakistan's intermittent elections since gaining independence," said South Asia scholar and former Pakistani ambassador to the United States Husain Haqqani (Haqqani 2004–2005, 91).

The impact of Saudi support for ultra-conservatives and militants sparked concern among some Pakistani officials. Federal minister for Inter-Provincial Coordination (IPC) Riaz Hussain Pirzada accused the Saudi government in early 2015 of creating instability across the Muslim world by distributing money in order to promote religious extremism (Haider 2015).

Similarly, Tariq Khosa, a former director-general of the FIA and senior police officer, recounted in testimony to the Pakistani Senate's defense committee how Zia ordered him to release Jhangvi, the Sipah-e-Sahaba founder, in the 1980s after Khosa had detained him for delivering an inflammatory sectarian speech. Khosa related to the committee how as a police commander he witnessed the abuse of Islamic laws that had been introduced by a Pakistani judge and unidentified Saudi advisers. "They were practiced in such a way that many atrocities were committed," Khosa said. Zia's order to release Jhangvi came after Khosa entered a mosque to stop the preacher from proceeding with an anti-Shi'ite speech at the very moment that Shi'ites were celebrating the holiday of Muharram in the streets of the city. "I was with 25 policemen and the Shias were saying that they will retaliate if he did not stop his offensive speech," Khosa recounted (Testimony of Tariq Khosa 2012, n.p.).

A Cast of Characters

Zia's shielding of Sipah/ASWJ and other militants set a pattern followed by many of his successors, including former prime minister Nawaz Sharif. Sharif recognized the militants' ability to deliver votes in key Punjabi constituencies. In return, the government reigned in the police and the courts. Malik Ishaq, a one-time Sipah leader who founded Lashkar-e-Jhangvi, a more violent Sunni supremacist offshoot of Sipah, was released after fourteen years in prison as a reward for Sipah's support of a candidate of Sharif's Pakistan Muslim League–Nawaz (PMLN) in a key by-election in a Jhang district (Khan, Chaudhry, and Ahmed 2016).

Malik, one of a cast of controversial and notorious militant characters and groups that were part of Saudi Arabia's Pakistani orbit, was the kind of militant the kingdom had publicly long kept at arm's length, but that effectively did its bidding in confronting Shi'ites as an alleged Iranian fifth column and helped in-grain Saudi-backed religious ultra-conservatism and sectarianism in significant segments of Pakistani society (Khan, Chaudhry, and Ahmed 2016).

Within a year of his release, Ishaq was invited by the Saudi embassy in Islamabad to go on an all-expense-paid pilgrimage to Mecca that would coincide with a high-level meeting in the kingdom of the Saudi-dominated Organization of Islamic Cooperation (OIC). Iranian president Mahmoud Ahmadinejad was scheduled to attend the summit, and it was Ishaq's first and only known visit to the kingdom (interview, 2017, Islambad; interview, 2017, Islamabad). "He was received on arrival by 12 Saudi intelligence officers and given a letter saying he was a guest of the state. Ludhianvi, the ASWJ leader, never got that treatment. The Saudis feared that Saudi Shi'ites, who had invited Ahmadinejad to visit Qatif, a predominantly Shi'ite city in the kingdom's oil-rich Eastern Province, would stage anti-government protests. Ishak, surrounded by armed Saudi guards, was in the kingdom to draw Shi'ite attention away from the government. [Saudi prince and then intelligence chief] Turki [al-Faisal] assigned a total of 150 of his men to Ishak," said a Sipah cofounder (interview, 2016, Islamabad).

A senior Pakistani counterterrorism official, who met Ishaq at least once a week after his release, said the militant had spent most of his time in Saudi Arabia with Pakistanis from his hometown of Rahim Yar Khan. The official, who had Ishak followed while he was in the kingdom, described his visit as a low-key fundraising trip that was not widely publicized. The official said the only Saudi officials that met with Ishak were low-level representatives of the ministry of religious affairs. "Malik tried to act big but wasn't big," the official said. He said Ishak, who was killed by police together with his sons in 2015 at a time that the government was cracking down on his group, had raised 9.8 million rupees ($97,000) during his visit (interview, 2018, Islamabad).

ASWJ put Pakistani government and Saudi support on public display when in 2015 it hosted a dinner in Islamabad's prestigious Marriot Hotel for Abdallah Ben Abdel Mohsen Al-Turki, a former Saudi religious affairs minister and general secretary of the MWL. Hundreds of guests, including Pakistani ministers and religious leaders designated as terrorists by the United States, attended the dinner at the expense of the Saudi embassy in the Pakistani capital (interviews, 2016, Jhang and Islamabad).

The Saudi embassy in Islamabad has on occasion sought to fend off persistent reports that it was funding institutions that promoted militancy. "A section of the media has been propagating a false impression that the Kingdom of Saudi Arabia is funding the extremist mindset in Pakistan through its financial support for religious seminaries. Whenever any seminary, mosque or charity organisations request the kingdom for financial assistance, the embassy refers the matter to the Government of Pakistan through the Ministry of Foreign Affairs for examining suitability of the applicant. When the ministry of foreign affairs informs the embassy in writing that the financial assistance is in the interest of public welfare, the assistance is provided to the applicant. . . . The assistance has always been beyond any sectarian considerations," the embassy said in a statement in February 2015 (Haider 2015, n.p.).

Tapping the Fountain

Saudi Arabia allowed Sipah/ASWJ to raise funds among Pakistanis working in Saudi Arabia and elsewhere in the Gulf. "We don't know where they got their money from. It's possible that they were fronting for Saudis," said the Sipah cofounder as he allowed this writer to review his voluminous records of those donations. Donations ranged on average from 2,000 to 10,000 Pakistani rupees, the highest in that initial period being 75,000 at a 1986 exchange rate of US$1 equaling twenty rupees. The donations jumped after Zia-ur-Rehman Farooqi, who took over the group after Jhangvi's successor, Azam Tariq, was killed by Shi'ite militants, decided to open branches in twenty-eight countries, often exploiting local Deobandi networks, and toured all of them to raise funds. Arguing that Sunnis need to resist the rise of Iran, Farooqi's gatherings were often attended by up to 1,000 people, according to the cofounder, who at times traveled with him. The cofounder said one Sipah fundraiser would collect 7.5 million rupees in donations a week. Sipah executives moreover traveled every two months to Saudi Arabia to meet in private homes with their supporters in the kingdom, who numbered in the thousands.

"Before Zia ur Rehman, Sipah and Saudi Arabia had mutual interests, but there was no organized Saudi support. But with Zia ur Rehman, Sipah developed very good relations. The Saudis sent huge amounts often through Pakistani tycoons who had a long-standing presence in Saudi Arabia as well as operations in the U.K. and Canada and maintained close relations with the Al Saud family and the Saudi business community. One of them gave 100 million rupees a year. We had so much money, it didn't matter what things cost," the cofounder said (interview, 2017, Islamabad). The cofounder said the group hired Pakistan's best and most expensive lawyers when its militants ran into legal problems and sent wounded operatives to the country's best private hospitals.

For the most part, Saudi officials, members of the ruling family, and businessmen were careful to keep direct contact out of the limelight. They more often than not preferred to operate through middlemen. Saudi officials never visited Sipah office's but would invite the group to attend functions at the kingdom's diplomatic representations in Pakistan and occasionally meet its representatives in hotel lobbies (interview, 2016, Islamabad). Senior officials of the Saudi religious affairs ministry and prominent Saudi scholars initially restricted their relations to contacts with Shaykh Mohammed Ashfaq, one of Sipah's founders, who had long-standing relationships in the kingdom (interview, 2017, Islamabad, January 3). "The Saudis really support us," the cofounder quoted Farooqi as telling a Sipah leadership meeting. "A senior official kissed my hand and said: 'I am a great supporter of yours. You are doing great work. But don't identify us publicly.'" Farooqi quoted senior scholars and members of the kingdom's religious council as saying they would help Sipah with whatever it needs but could not do so openly (interview, 2017, Islamabad).

Abdul Hafeez Makki, an Islamic scholar from Faisalabad, a city renamed in 1979 in honor of the late Saudi king, who had been resident in Mecca since the 1970s when he obtained Saudi nationality and was well-connected to Saudi Arabia's religious establishment and influential in Deobandi circles, visited Jhangvi in Jhang two years after Sipah's establishment. Makki, a scion of an originally Kashmiri family of influential Deobandi scholars and international head of Aalmi Majlis Tahaffuz Khatm-e-Nubuwwat (AMTKN), a militant Pakistan-based, anti-Ahmadi group with a history of Saudi backing in its various guises since it first was established in 1953, quickly emerged as Sipah's key conduit to members of the kingdom's Council of Senior Scholars, members of the kingdom's ruling family, and Pakistani businessmen (interview, 2016, Islamabad).

"Makki is a patron of Sipah. He tours the world to propagate their brand of Islam. He's their ambassador," said Fazlur Rehman Khalil, who together with Masood Azhar, a Pakistani militant who with backing of the military and the Pakistani intelligence focused on India and Kashmir, founded the since-banned group Harakat ul-Mujahedeen (HuM). Backed by the military and the Pakistani intelligence, the group focused on India and Kashmir. HuM initially recruited its rank and file among Sipah-i-Sabaha militants (Abou Zahab and Roy 2004, 30). Scholars like Mariam Abou Zahab and Olivier Roy and journalists like Mubasher Bukhari, who have long covered Pakistani militancy, argue that Sipah, Jaish-e-Mohammed (JM)—a Pakistani intelligence-sponsored anti-Indian group founded by HuM activists—and Lashkar-e-Jhangvi were wings of one and the same group. Abou Zahab and Roy wrote, "The SSP was a political umbrella while JM and Lashkar-e-Jhangvi (LeJ), named after Sipah founder Haq Nawaz Jhangvi, were the jihadi and domestic military wings respectively" (Abou Zahab and Roy 2004, 30).

The cofounder, as well as a senior Sipah executive, said Makki helped Qari Yacoub, a cleric and Sipah's representative in Saudi Arabia who moved to Mecca in 1994, gain access to the kingdom's Saudi and Pakistani business communities (interviews, 2016, Islamabad). "He got him to meet wealthy Saudis with close ties to the ruling family. Yacoub however never met directly with members of the family. Nevertheless, we'd get whatever we need from Saudi Arabia and our needs were infinite," the cofounder said. The Saudi government courted Makki, the author of a biography of Saudi King Faisal, and "wanted to reward him," added Yunus Qasmi, ASWJ chairman Ludhianvi's personal secretary (interview, 2017, Islamabad). The US Department of State reported that "Makki in 2002 frequently visited the Middle East and viewed it as a main source of funding" (The Guardian 2010, n.p.), while Pakistani bankers and militants described Makki as "financially savvy." One banker said Makki was not only a good fundraiser, but also a knowledgeable fund manager who operated through offshore Pakistani foreign currency accounts. "Makki set up these accounts so that the sources of the funds did not have to be legally revealed," the banker said (interviews, 2017, Islamabad).

The cofounder said that local hires at the Saudi embassy in Islamabad had been assigned to deal with the various militant Islamist and jihadist groups, including Sipah. He said former Saudi intelligence chief Prince Turki, the Saudi point man in the kingdom's support for the Afghan mujahidin, who later served as the kingdom's ambassador to Britain and the United States, had discreetly maintained close ties to the group, particularly after Zia-ur-Rehman's visit to the kingdom in 1995. Ur-Rehman's contact with Prince Turki, widely viewed in Washington as one of the kingdom's most trustworthy officials, in part because of his fervent anti-communism, had been facilitated by his deputy, Shoaib Nadeem, who was a frequent visitor to the kingdom, had close ties to its ruling family, and at times had intervened to get visas for Sipah members who initially were rejected. It was Nadeem who took Tariq on his first visit as Sipah leader to the kingdom (interviews, 2017, Islamabad).

No Top-Down Flick of the Button

Saudi-funded madrasas dominate the educational landscape of the Pakistani province of Balochistan that borders on Iran. "A majority of Baloch school-children go to madrasas. They are in better condition than other schools in Balochistan. Most madrasas are operated by Deobandis and Ahl-i Hadith," said the cofounder of Sipah, whose successors and offshoots have a strong presence in Balochistan (interview, 2017, Islamabad). He said the mosques funneled funds from various sources in Saudi Arabia to the militants.

The cofounder said the leaders of Sipah and Lashkar-e-Jhangvi (LeJ), Maulana Ramzan Mengal and Maulana Wali Farooqi, enjoyed government and military protection because their anti-Shi'ite sentiments made them targets of Iran. He said the two men, who maintained close ties to Saudi Arabia, traveled in Balochistan in convoys of up to ten vehicles that included military guards. Policemen stand guard outside Mengal's madrasa in the Baloch capital of Quetta. "Ramzan gets whatever he needs from the Saudis," the cofounder said. Close relations between Sipah and LeJ, on the one hand, and pro-government tribesmen in Balochistan complicate occasional government efforts to reign in the militants, as does the militants' involvement in drug smuggling that gives them an independent source of funding.

Khosa, the law enforcement official, who also at one point served as Balochistan's police chief, said militancy in the province was fueled by government and military support for proscribed religious extremists in a bid to crush a fourteen-year-old nationalist insurgency (Ahmed 2018). The policy enabled an environment in which militants and law enforcement often operate with impunity. A video showing police officers firing dozens of rounds at point blank into a parked car in broad daylight in the city of Sahiwal went viral after it emerged that the victims were parents and their four children, three of whom survived to tell their story (Agence France Press 2019).

The incident, one of many, was indicative of the degree to which the fabric of Pakistani society and institutions had been impacted by an environment nurtured by decades of Saudi-supported and inspired ultra-conservatism that neither the kingdom nor Pakistani authorities were able or willing to control. To be sure, Saudi Arabia has cut back on funding of religious soft power with the rise of Crown Prince Muhammad bin Salman and has sought to promote its revamped one-time funding vehicles like the MWL as promoters of interfaith dialogue, tolerance, and mutual respect.

Conclusion

The impact, however, of decades of Saudi funding and support, coupled with Pakistani government and military acquiescence and cooperation, cannot be reversed with a top-down flick of the switch. That is no truer than in Balochistan, where continued Saudi funding spotlights the geopolitical drivers of Saudi religious soft-power policy. If anything, Balochistan proves international relations scholar Stephen Tankel's assertion that countries like Pakistan and Saudi Arabia promote militants "to counter external threats, undermine geopolitical competitors, boost domestic legitimacy, and reorient challengers' focus to outside the country's borders" (Tankel 2018, 43). It also proves that they do so at their own peril. The past century is littered with examples of state support of militancy, amounting to letting a genie out of the bottle that ultimately turns on its original backers.

References

Abou Zahab, Mariam. 2009. "Salafism in Pakistan." In *Global Salafism: Islam's New Religious Movement*, edited by Roel Meijer, 126–142. London: Hurst.

Abou Zahab, Mariam, and Olivier Roy. *Islamist Networks: The Afghan-Pakistan Connection*. New York: Columbia University Press.

Agence France-Presse. 2019. "Pakistan Police Culture of Impunity Faces Trial by Social Media." February 4, 2019. https://www.channelnewsasia.com/news/asia/pakistan-police-culture-of-impunity-faces-trial-by-social-media-11202010 (accessed February 4, 2019).

Ahmad, Mumtaz. 1997. "Revivalism, Islamisation, Sectarianism and Violence in Pakistan." In *Pakistan*, edited by Craig Baxter and Charles Kennedy, 101–181. Delhi: Harper Collins.

Ahmed, Khaled. 2002. "The Power of the Ahl-e-Hadith." *The Friday Times*. July 12–18, 2002. http://www.hvk.org/2002/0702/106.html (accessed July 12, 2002).

Ahmed, Maqbool. 2018. "How Death Stalks Policemen in Quetta." *Herald*. April 25. 2018. https://herald.dawn.com/news/1398509/ (accessed April 25, 2018).

Akhtar, Aasim Sajjad. 2018. *The Politics of Common Sense, State, Society and Culture in Pakistan*. Cambridge: Cambridge University Press.

Blood, Peter (ed.). 1994. *Pakistan: A Country Study*. Washington, DC: Government Publishing Office (GPO) for the Library of Congress. http://countrystudies.us/pakistan/19.htm.

Cohen, Stephen Philip. 2004. *The Idea of Pakistan*. Washington, DC: Brookings Institution.

Constitution of the Islamic Republic of Pakistan, Second Amendment. n.d. http://www.pakistani.org/pakistan/constitution/amendments/2amendment.html (accessed January 1, 2017).

Council of Islamic Ideology. 1981. *First Report on Islamization of Laws contained in The Pakistan Code*. Vol. 1: *1836–1871*. Islamabad: Council of Islamic Ideology.

Council on Foreign Relations. 2019. "A Conversation with Prime Minister Imran Khan of Pakistan." September 23, 2019. https://www.cfr.org/event/conversation-prime-minis ter-imran-khan-pakistan-0 (accessed October 13, 2020).

Dawn. 2011. "Extremist Recruitment on the Rise in South Punjab Madrassahs." May 21, 2011. http://www.dawn.com/news/630656/2008-extremist-recruitment-on-the-rise- in-south-punjab-madrassahs (accessed May 21, 2011).

Dorsey, James M. 2018. "The Saudi Export of Ultra-conservatism in the Era of MbS: An Update." The Turbulent World of Middle East Soccer blog. April 18, 2018. https:// mideastsoccer.blogspot.com/2018/04/the-saudi-export-of-ultra-conservatism.html (accessed April 18, 2018).

The Economist. 2016. "Bomb in Lahore: The Hard Choice for Pakistan." April 2, 2016. http://www.economist.com/news/leaders/21695903-country-threatened-not-just- terrorism-widespread-religious-extremism-hard (accessed April 2, 2016).

Farquhar, Michael. 2016. *Circuits of Faith: Migration, Education, and the Wahhabi Mission*. Stanford, CA: Stanford University Press.

Ghattas, Kim. 2020. *Black Wave, Saudi Arabia, Iran and the Rivalry That Unravelled the Middle East*. London: Wildfire.

The Guardian. 2010. "US Embassy Cables: Lashkar-E-Taiba Terrorists Raise Funds in Saudi Arabia." December 5, 2010. https://www.theguardian.com/world/us-embassy- cables-documents/220186 (accessed December 5, 2010).

Haider, Ejaz. 2016. "Terror's Whack-a-Mole Problem." *Newsweek Pakistan*. August 9, 2016. http://newsweekpakistan.com/terrors-whack-a-mole-problem/.

Haider, Irfan. 2015. "Saudi Arabia denies funding 'extremist mindset' in Pakistan." *Dawn*, February 9, 2015. http://www.dawn.com/news/1162507 (accessed August 9, 2016).

Hakim, Khalifa Abdul. 2006. "Islamic Ideology." Lahore: Institute of Islamic Culture. https://www.mediafire.com/file/oh0iur7bpgpf8gm/file+islamic+ideology.pdf (accessed May 1, 2014).

Haqqani, Hussain. 2004. "The Role of Islam in Pakistan's Future." *The Washington Quarterly* 28(1): 83–96. doi: https://doi.org/10.1162/0163660042518161.

Hashim, Asad. 2020. "HRW Slams Exclusion of Ahmadis from Pakistan Minority Commission." *Al Jazeera*. May 8. https://www.aljazeera.com/news/2020/05/hrw- slams-exclusion-ahmadis-pakistan-minority-commission-200508090414467.html (accessed May 8, 2020).

Hussein, Rizwan. 2005. *Pakistan and the Emergence of Islamic Militancy in Afghanistan*. Burlington, VT: Ashgate.

Iqbal Academy Pakistan. n.d. "Biography." http://www.allamaiqbal.com/person/biogra phy/biotxtread.html (accessed October 13, 2020).

Jalal, Ayesha. 2014. *The Struggle for Pakistan, A Muslim Homeland and Global Politics*. Cambridge, MA: The Belknap Press of Harvard University Press.

Khan, Sher Ali, Fareedullah Chaudhry, and Shakeel Ahmed. 2016. "Punjab's 'Encounters' with Sectarianism." *Herald*. October 21, 2016. http://herald.dawn.com/news/1153564/ punjabs-encounters-with-sectarianism (accessed October 21, 2016).

The Lahore Ahmadiyya Movement. n.d. "Maudoodi's Letter Saying Lahore Ahmadiyya Is a Muslim Group." https://www.muslim.org/movement/maudoodi/letter.htm (accessed January 1, 2017).

Mawudūdi, S. Abdul Al'a. n,.d. *The Qadiani Problem*. Lahore: Islamic Publications (PVT). http://www.quranenglish.com/new/Books/04%20The%20Qadiani%20Problem.pdf (accessed January 1, 2017).

Nasir, S. V. R. 2000. "The Rise of Sunni Militancy in Pakistan: The Changing Role of Islamism and the Ulama in Society and Politics." *Modern Asian Studies* 34(1): 139–118. https://www.jstor.org/stable/313114.

Paracha, Nadeem F. 2017. "Smokers' Corner: Curbing the Mullah." *Dawn*. April 28, 2017. https://www.dawn.com/news/1329822/smokers-corner-curbing-the-mullahIbid (accessed April 28, 2017).

Rizvi Hasan Askari. 2017. "Major Dilemmas of Countering Terrorism." *The Express Tribune*, 26 February 26, 2017. https://tribune.com.pk/story/1339960/major-dilem mas-countering-terrorism/ (accessed February 26, 2017).

Rubin, B. R. 1997. "Arab Islamists in Afghanistan." In *Political Islam: Revolution, Radicalism, or Reform?*, edited by John L. Esposito, 179–206. Boulder, CO: Lynne Rienner.

Siddiqa, Ayesha. 2010. "Red Hot Chilli Peppers Islam: Is the Youth in Elite Universities in Pakistan Radical?" *Heinrich Boell Stiftung*. https://pk.boell.org/sites/default/files/downloads/Red_Hot_Chilli_Peppers_Islam_-_Complete_Study_Report.pdf.

Sikand, Yoginder. 2007. "Stoking the Flames: Intra-Muslim Rivalries in India and the Saudi Connection." *Comparative Studies of South Asia, Africa and the Middle East* 27(1): 95–108.

Sikand, Yoginder. 2010. "Wahabi/Ahle Hadith, Deobandi and Saudi Connection." Sunniciter.com. April 14, 2010. https://sunninews.wordpress.com/2010/04/14/wah abiahle-hadith-deobandi-and-saudi-connection/ (accessed April 14, 2010).

South Asian Terrorism Portal. 1998. http://www.satp.org/satporgtp/countries/india/sta tes/jandk/terrorist_outfits/Tehreek_ul_Mujahideen.htm.

Talbot, Ian. 2000. *India and Pakistan*. London: Bloomsbury Academic.

Tankel, Stephen. 2018. *With Us and Against Us: How America's Partners Help and Hinder the War on Terror*. New York: Columbia University Press.

Testimony of Tariq Khosa before the Senate Committee on Defense and Defense Production. September 28, 2012. http://www.senate.gov.pk/uploads/documents/136 5092265_822.pdf (accessed September 28, 2012).

Wasti, Tahir. 2009. *The Application of Islamic Criminal Law in Pakistan: Sharia in Practice*. Leiden: Brill.

The World Islamic Front for Jihad Against Jews and Crusaders. 1998. *Fatwa*. February 23, 1998. https://web.archive.org/web/20060422210853/http:/www.ict.org.il/articles/fat wah.htm (accessed February 25, 2005).

Zaidi, Syed Manzar Abbas. 2013. "Madrassa Education in Pakistan: Controversies, Challenges and Prospects, Centre for International and Strategic Analysis." SISA report no. 3. http://strategiskanalyse.no/publikasjoner%202013/2013-03-04__SISA3_Madr assa_Education_-_Syed_Manzar_Abbas_Zaidi.pdf (accessed December 12, 2013).

10

"Working for a Living in the Land of Allah"

Labor Migration from Bangladesh to Saudi Arabia and Remittances of Wahhabism

Nazli Kibria and Sultan Mohammed Zakaria

Across the Muslim world, the late twentieth and early twenty-first centuries have been a time of religious resurgence with an expansion of Islamic movements that advocate a greater and renewed focus on religion in the lives of Muslims (Hefner 2005). Saudi Arabia, an important force in this resurgence, has promoted Wahhabism, the distinctly Saudi brand of Salafi Islam that emphasizes strict orthodoxy and a return to the earliest practices of Islam. In this chapter, we consider the growth of Wahhabism in Bangladesh, a Muslim-majority country with strong countervailing historical traditions of Sufism and secular nationalism. Our focus is on labor migration from Bangladesh to Saudi Arabia as a channel of transnational remittances of religion, or the movement of resources and ideas about religion across borders.

Foreign workers on temporary labor contracts constitute a prominent segment of the Saudi workforce (Kapiszewski 2001). However, relatively little is known about the role of these workers within the broader Saudi state project of global political and religious influence. In Bangladesh, a Muslim-majority country that is an important source of foreign workers for Saudi Arabia, the Bangladesh to Saudi Arabia labor migration circuit is widely understood to be part of a broader nexus of Saudi influence on the political and religious landscape of Bangladesh (Riaz 2008). Returned labor migrants from the Arab Gulf states are viewed as agents of religious change who bring back Saudi religious practices to their home communities. In what follows we explore these ideas, drawing on the qualitative accounts of less-skilled Bangladeshi labor migrants about their religious experiences in Saudi Arabia and after their return home. Our findings highlight labor migration as both an important and contested channel of Saudi influence. Depending on job histories, gender, and other differences, Saudi migration episodes shape the religious understandings and identities of Bangladeshis in varied ways. These differences are reflected in how migrants position themselves in the religious fields of their home communities in Bangladesh.

Nazli Kibria and Sultan Mohammed Zakaria, *"Working for a Living in the Land of Allah"* In: *Wahhabism and the World*. Edited by: Peter Mandaville, Oxford University Press. © Oxford University Press 2022.
DOI: 10.1093/oso/9780197532560.003.0010

The Politics of Saudi Influence in Bangladesh

Bangladesh, meaning "Bengal nation," is located on the Bay of Bengal between Burma and India. The country has a territory of 56,977 square miles (147,570 sq. km) and, in 2019, had a population of over 160 million people, making it the eighth most populous country in the world as well as one of the most densely populated (World Population Review 2019). Bangladesh is a Muslim-majority country. About 90 percent of the population is Sunni Muslim, with numerous sub-traditions and influences, most notably Sufism. Historians of East Bengal describe how Muslim rulers, later remembered as "Sufis," brought Islam to the region in the fourteenth century (Ahmed 2001). The religious culture that emerged from their conquests was one in which Islam came to intermingle with local indigenous rituals and beliefs, including those of Hindu and Buddhist origin. This "folk" religion, with its harvest festivals, reverence of popular saints, and tolerance of different faiths, has been an increasingly contested feature of the country's cultural and political landscape. The growth of militant Islamist groups, coupled with extremist attacks on religious-minority communities, progressive intellectuals, and foreigners, has been evident since the early 2000s (Fair et al. 2017).

Indeed, the place of religion and more specifically of Islam in national identity and institutions has been a defining point of tension in the contemporary history of Bangladesh. Set against the historical backdrop of the 1947 partition of India, the country emerged in 1971 following a brutal war of separation from the Islamic Republic of Pakistan. The founders articulated a secular nationalist "Bangalee" identity. The Awami League leader and prime minister Sheikh Mujibur Rahman was assassinated in a 1975 military coup. The country's movement at this time away from the founding ethos of secular nationalism coincided with the establishment of formal diplomatic relations between Bangladesh and Saudi Arabia. Prior to 1975, Saudi Arabia had resisted formal recognition of Bangladesh as a nation due to close Saudi ties with Pakistan.

The military regime of General Ziaur Rahman (known as Zia; 1976–1981) saw the introduction of Islam into the official institutions of Bangladesh. Zia rescinded the ban on religion-based political parties, thereby facilitating the rehabilitation and integration of Jamaat-e-Islami, a political group aspiring to create an Islamic state in Bangladesh. Zia's military successor, Hussain Muhammad Ershad (1982–1990), continued these policies. Ershad approved amendments to the constitution of Bangladesh declaring Islam the state religion. Both Zia and Ershad actively cultivated strong political, economic, and cultural ties with Saudi Arabia and encouraged the formation of Islamic charities and schools with support from Middle Eastern donors (Fernando 2011).

The late twentieth and early twenty-first centuries have seen a continuation of these trends of deepening institutional linkages and networks between the Arab Gulf states and Bangladesh. The ascension to power of the Awami League (1996–2001, 2009–present), a political party with a historical legacy of secular nationalism, has given rise to certain tensions in these relationships. In alliance with Pakistan, Saudi Arabia has opposed the prosecution by the Awami League–led government of the leaders of the Islamist religious party Jamaat-e-Islami. However, the Awami League–led government has also worked to establish cooperative political and economic ties with Saudi Arabia. In 2015 Bangladesh joined a Saudi Arabia–based 34-state Islamic military coalition to combat terrorism. There are also ongoing efforts to generate investments and other business ties with Saudi Arabia. In March 2019, Saudi Arabia and Bangladesh signed a series of wide-ranging agreements on Saudi involvement in different development projects in Bangladesh connected with energy, industries, and infrastructure (Dhaka Tribune 2019).

Along with business and commercial interests, the nongovernmental organization (NGO) sector in Bangladesh has been an important institutional channel for Saudi influence. The precise scope and significance of the Saudi NGO channel is difficult to assess given the absence of complete and accurate data on funding streams (Berkley Center for Religion, Peace, and World Affairs 2016). However, available evidence does suggest significant Saudi financial transfers into Bangladesh through the NGO sector. Kumar identifies several charitable NGOs operating in Bangladesh with significant amounts of funding from Saudi Arabia, Kuwait, and the United Arab Emirates, including the Islamic Relief Organization, Al Markajul Islami, Ishra Islamic Foundation, Ishrahul Muslimin, Al Forkan Foundations, and Al Maghrib Eye Hospital (Kumar 2009). These organizations combine humanitarian goals with *da'wa*, or practices of disseminating and encouraging the practices of Islam. Through charitable NGOs, Saudi Arabia has sponsored the construction of mosques, madrasas, and orphanages in Bangladesh. By doing so, Saudi Arabia has created an organizational structure for a wide range of Wahhabi propagation activities. These include scholarships for religious study in Saudi Arabia for promising madrasa postgraduates. Several institutions in Saudi Arabia, such as the Islamic University of Medina and Imam Muhammad Ibn Saud Islamic University, offer scholarships based on selective admission to foreign students from around the world, including from Bangladesh.

The growth of Saudi influence in Bangladesh has taken place within a national social and political context fraught with tensions over the role of Islam in the country's identity and institutions. Echoing global trends, publicly visible and self-conscious Islamic practice and identity have flourished in late twentieth- and early twenty-first-century Bangladesh (Fair et al. 2017; Kibria 2011; Riaz

2008). These developments have occurred alongside changes that have included the growing visibility of women in rural economies, fostered by developmental organizations such as the renowned Grameen Bank, which offers small loans to rural poor women. There has been the growth, since the 1980s, of a large export garments-manufacturing sector that has employed women.

On the political front, the two major political parties, the Awami League and Bangladesh Nationalist Party, have pursued opportunistic alliances with Islamist groups. In addition, the country's major religious party, Jamaat-e-Islami, has developed a significant institutional presence. Following its re-entry into the Bangladeshi political scene in the late 1970s, Jamaat engaged in a wide range of activities to consolidate its position in the country, reportedly with funding from Saudi Arabia and other Arab Gulf sources. These include the development of an elaborate and widespread network of Jamaat-based institutions, including banks, hospitals, schools, universities, and NGOs (Rahman 2018).

The post-2009 Awami League–led government took steps to fulfill its popular 2008 election mandate to prosecute 1971 war criminals, resulting in the conviction and execution of several Jamaat leaders. The Bangladeshi Jamaat-e-Islami was barred from participating in the 2018 national election. At the same time, the Awami League has come under fire from progressive groups for forming strategic alliances with Islamist parties and caving in to pressure from them. In 2011, the government withdrew its support for equal property inheritance rights for women in the National Women Development Policy after protests from Jamaat and other Islamist groups and parties (Gayen 2019). In 2017, the demands of Hefazat-e-Islam, a conservative Islamic organization, eventually led the Awami League government to change textbooks to remove poems and stories deemed "atheistic" and to take down a statue of the Greek goddess Themis on the Supreme Court grounds (Barry and Manik 2017).

Labor Migration from Bangladesh to Saudi Arabia

Since the late 1970s, the movement of contract labor migrants from Bangladesh to Saudi Arabia has been a core aspect of relations between the two countries. Saudi Arabia, the biggest economy in the Arab world, has relied on foreign workers since the oil boom of the 1970s. For Bangladesh, the remittances sent by labor migrants from abroad have been a major source of foreign currency. According to the official figures of Bangladesh's Bureau of Manpower, Employment, and Training (BMET), during the 1976–2018 period over 12 million Bangladeshis went to the Gulf Cooperation Council (GCC) states (Bahrain, Kuwait, Oman, Qatar, Saudi Arabia, and the United Arab Emirates) in search of their livelihoods. Over three million, or 30 percent of them, went to Saudi

Arabia, the top destination. Many have worked in semi-skilled and unskilled jobs and entered Saudi Arabia under the *kafala* sponsorship system. The system assigns responsibility and control of the migrant worker's immigration status to the *kafil* or employer.

Reflecting the financial importance of remittances, successive Bangladeshi governments, regardless of political party, have actively cultivated opportunities for citizens to work in Saudi Arabia. Indeed, the management of labor migration and its associated problems has been a dominant theme in diplomatic relations with Saudi Arabia. By the early 2000s, amidst concerns about high unemployment rates among its own nationals, the Saudi government began moving toward reducing dependence on foreign workers. In 2018, the Saudi government decided to nationalize several jobs, many in the sales and retail sector, barring foreign workers from them. Citing irregularities in the recruitment and placement pipeline for Bangladeshi workers, Saudi Arabia banned workers from Bangladesh (with the exception of domestic workers) from 2009 to 2016.

Along with political pressures to negotiate with Saudi Arabia for a lifting of this ban, the Bangladeshi government faced intense criticism for its failure to protect its labor migrant citizens from the abuses of the system, especially from mistreatment by employers and exploitation by recruiting agents. Historically, much of the labor migration from Bangladesh to Saudi Arabia has involved men. Since the first decade of the twenty-first century, women workers, often in domestic service, have constituted an important element of the flows. Reports of women migrants returning from Saudi Arabia due to employer abuse have fueled calls from human rights activists in Bangladesh to stop sending women to Saudi Arabia to work as maids (Devnath 2019).

Research on labor migration from Bangladesh to Saudi Arabia has focused on financial remittances—their scope, use, and consequences for the economic well-being for migrants and their families (Rahman 2011). Social remittances, or the ideas, practices, skills, identities, and social connections that move through the migration circuit, are relatively unexplored (Levitt 1998). In this chapter, we consider social remittances of Wahhabism with a focus on returned labor migrants as potential agents of religious change in their families and communities. Rather than a fixed and discrete set of impacts, we emphasize the processual and contested character of religious remittances, as well as their embeddedness in the broader political and cultural landscape of Bangladesh. How do Bangladeshi labor migrants experience and understand the religious environment of Saudi Arabia? How, if at all, do they bring the lessons of Wahhabism back with them to shape their local communities upon return to Bangladesh? In considering these questions, we draw on qualitative materials from research on labor migrants from the Dhaka, Chittagong, and Sylhet regions returned from the Arab Gulf states (Kibria 2011). Of the 60 in-depth interviews conducted from 2001 to 2007, 33 involved persons who had lived and worked in Saudi Arabia. Most (30) were men with relatively low levels of education who had worked in semi-skilled or unskilled jobs while abroad.

Agents of Authentic Islam

The following account was gathered from Jashim, a man who worked for 12 years in Saudi Arabia as a truck driver.

> By living in a Muslim country [Saudi Arabia] I have learned a great deal about the correct practice of Islam. As soon as the *ajaan* [call to prayer] is heard, the shops close and all Muslims are required to pray. The punishment is that the person is made to read 50–60 *rakat* [a unit of Islamic prayer'] of extra prayer. Sometimes he may be locked up in a bathroom or a red mark put on his work permit. So even if one does not want to say his prayers, one is forced to do so and it becomes a habit. In our religion, it is said that you should encourage people to do good. It is because their laws are strict that they do not have crime. In our country we have laws that are not followed and nobody fears the police. The way they say their prayers is also a little different. For example, there is no head cap required there for prayer. And here in our country we say "amen" softly after Sura Fatiha [the first surah of the Qu'ran that is recited at the start of each unit of prayer] but there they say it loudly. In our country, the *monajat* [invocation] is given more importance. I have talked to the *maulana* [religious leader] of our mosque in the village and I have told him to start these practices.
>
> Since returning to Bangladesh, I try my best to live in accordance with Islamic rules as I have learned in the land of Allah. My eldest son used to be in an English medium school in the village but the standards there are not good. That is why I have put him in a madrasa. I hope he becomes a *hafiz* [scholar of Islam who has memorized the Qu'ran] as it is of great value if one's son reads the Qu'ran at the grave of his parents. I have also asked my wife to tell the women workers of our house to maintain *purdah* [separation of men and women]. We do not let the women go near the men workers in the farms and the pond. They have separate places to eat and the men are not allowed to come inside the house. I try to do all the transactions with the men and my wife with the women.

After returning to Bangladesh, Jashim took up a well-paying job as an office driver for a multinational company in the capital city. He planned to work for just a few more years as an office driver before retiring to his village where his wife and children were living with his mother. There he had bought a fish pond and land with savings from his time in Saudi Arabia. He hoped to live comfortably from these investments in his old age.

Jashim was confident that he had benefited from his time in Saudi Arabia, not just economically, but also from the religious lessons gained there. Claims of deeper knowledge of Islam are widespread among returned migrants. Formal opportunities for religious study that are open to labor migrants in Saudi Arabia include free classes in public learning centers where attendees are taught the proper ways to pray and conduct oneself in conformity with *shari'a* laws (Ai 2019). In some cases, companies employing migrant workers provide weekly Islamic lessons to them. Well-established Bangladeshi entrepreneurs and community leaders in Saudi Arabia take an active role in the religious education of fellow Bangladeshis by organizing Islamic study meetings in Bangla and distributing free religious books translated into Bangla for them.

Even as they acknowledged opportunities for active religious learning in Saudi Arabia, returned labor migrants emphasized the inability of most Bangladeshi workers to take advantage of them. For many less skilled workers, long working hours and employer-imposed restrictions on mobility resulted in high levels of social isolation. This was especially so for women working as domestics in private households, many of whom had little to no exposure to Saudi society outside the confines of the household. Reflecting these conditions, the acquisition of authentic religious knowledge in Saudi Arabia was attributed not to exposure to formal learning opportunities but to adaptation to the strict religious environment of Saudi Arabia. Anchored in a narrative actively promoted by the Saudi state, of Saudi Arabia as the authentic and pure Islamic society, Bangladeshis offered extensive accounts of the heavily policed nature of religious practice in Saudi society. They had seen and experienced the authority of the Saudi religious police, or *Muttawa* (the Committee for the Promotion of Virtue and the Prevention of Vice), charged with ensuring compliance to religious rules. Those found by the *Muttawa* to violate the rules could face cancellation of their visas, followed by deportation. Those living in this environment developed the religious habits of praying five times a day, ceasing all business activities during prayer time, fasting during Ramadan, and following strict practices of segregation between women and men. Bangladeshi labor migrants identified these habits of practice as part of the religious knowledge gained in Saudi Arabia, which they brought back to Bangladesh.

Studies of South Asian Muslim male labor migrants describe how they use their histories of living and working in the Arab Gulf states to garner religious authority in their local communities (Gardner and Osella 2004). This is especially so for those who go to Saudi Arabia, a country holding special stature for Muslims as the birthplace and center of Islam. Referring to a deepened understanding of Islam as a result of time spent in Saudi Arabia, a returned migrant in Tangail said: "I speak to everyone at our mosque for the sake of removing their misunderstandings about Islam as a person who went to Saudi Arabia and learned about Islam there" (Ai 2019, 14). Self-consciously identifying themselves as agents of religious change, these men express a sense of religious duty and responsibility for instructing family and community members on correct practices as learned in the "land of Allah," whether about how precisely to pray or the importance of enforcing the rules of separation between men and women. This stance meshes easily with the populist project of religious reform advanced by Jamaat-e-Islami and other conservative religious elements in contemporary Bangladesh. Aspiring to an original Islam based on literalist interpretations of the Qur'an, these movements depict the Islam of Bangladesh as impure and corrupt, in need of a thorough purging of local cultural influences. Returned male migrants draw on these ideas in their self-identification as agents of religious reform.

Among the local practices targeted by Islamic reformists in Bangladesh are those of pilgrimage and prayer at *mazaar*s or shrines dedicated to Sufi saints, known as *pirs*. The eradication of these popular and deeply entrenched traditions, viewed as a deep violation of core Islamic principles, is part of the Jamaat platform in Bangladesh and throughout South Asia. Drawing on this discourse, returned male migrants emphasize their commitment to purging their own families and communities of these practices. When we interviewed him, Alamgir was at home in a semi-rural area outside of Dhaka. He was on a three-month holiday and expected to return to his job at a welding workshop in Saudi Arabia where he had been employed for almost five years. Alamgir spoke at length about the need to reform popular religious practices in Bangladesh. Like other returned male migrants (Ai 2019; Riaz 2008), Alamgir regularly gave money to Islamic charities, especially for the upkeep of a mosque and madrasa near his home town. It was a matter of pride for him that he had arranged for an Islamic scholar who had received training in Saudi Arabia to come and instruct local clerics on correct Islamic practice. Alamgir was also at the forefront of an organized effort to close down and prohibit people from going to the Sufi shrines in his area. His participation in this campaign had brought him into contact with networks of reformist groups and organizations. For Alamgir, then, the identity of religious reformer was anchored both in his history of living and working in Saudi Arabia and a local political context in which reformist Islamic movements and institutions are a prominent presence.

Migration Histories of Loss and Disenchantment

The following account was gathered in a rural area in Chittagong from Khalil, about two years after the interviewee, Khalil, had been deported from Saudi Arabia.

> I returned from Saudi Arabia three years ago without a single *taka*. Before that I had gone to Kuwait. I could not stay there because I became sick and the supervisor treated me badly, withholding drink and food. I came home. Two years after that, I decided to go to Saudi Arabia. I still owed money for the time I went to Kuwait and I needed to pay it back. I borrowed more money to go to Saudi Arabia. I was happy because I thought I would have a chance to see Mecca with my own eyes. I planned to perform *hajj* before returning. But my fate was bad. When I arrived there I found out I had been tricked. There was no job waiting for me. The agent told me I had to find a job on my own. I worked for a few months as a gardener and then the authorities took me to jail because I did not have the required papers. They sent me back on a plane.
>
> Now I am a broken man. My brother and son support me. I am in debt, I have sold my land. My family and neighbors give me little respect. Going to Saudi Arabia taught me about what it is like to be discarded like trash. That is the only thing I gained from going there.

Khalil told a horrific story of being duped by unscrupulous agents who had left him to fend for himself in Saudi Arabia without a *kafil* or sponsor. His account, a sharp contrast to that of Jashim, described earlier, provokes questions about homogeneous portrayals of the success of South Asian Muslim men labor migrants and their lives after return to the homeland. Scholars note the importance of economic resources to the entwined dynamics of community status and religious authority among returned male migrants (Gardner 2005; Kurien 2002). Religious practices and involvements offer a site within which to deploy the economic and symbolic capital of migration for the achievement of status and mobility. Gardner and Osella (2004) describe the role of consumption, of the simultaneous displays of religiosity and prosperity that can mark these strategies: "as migrants and their families reinvent themselves as high-status members of their community, how they worship and how they spend their earnings—activities which are often closely linked—tend to take centre stage" (xii).

However, as poignantly shown in Khalil's story, migration to the Arab Gulf states is filled with risks and dangers. Studies of low-wage Bangladeshi international labor migrants note the diversity of economic outcomes amongst them (Rahman 2011). As in the case of Jashim, some are able to use their overseas earnings not only to maintain families, but also to finance such investments as land purchase, home construction, and business ownership that enhance long-term financial security. But for others, the migration episode is less lucrative and even a cause of added loss and debt. Thus, not all those who come back do so with the financial resources to either display a prosperous religiosity or make substantial donations to local religious and community institutions. This was certainly so for Khalil, who had experienced devastating financial losses in addition to the humiliations of arrest and deportation.

Albeit in less extreme ways than it was for Khalil, the migration episode for many others failed to generate tangible and sustained economic gains. As suggested by the case of Masum, these circumstances did not always deter returned migrants from asserting their religious authority. Masum was the head of a large household consisting of his widowed mother and three younger siblings, as well as his wife and two children. He had worked in Saudi Arabia as a building cleaner for about four years in an effort to improve their economic situation. While in Saudi Arabia he had managed to meet basic household expenses but had not made enough to amass any savings or make investments that could result in long-term economic stability. Just one year after returning, he found himself floundering to keep up with expenses and pay back a number of debts. Nonetheless, Masum enjoyed considerable community respect. He was the eldest son and head of a large household who was also presumed to be knowledgeable about the correct practices of Islam from his time in Saudi Arabia. A neighbor remarked to us: "He [Masum] is a respected elder (*morrobbi*). He is our older brother who can teach us about many things. He has lived in the land of Allah and he can tell us about our religion." Patriarchal family and community dynamics play a mediating role in allowing returned men migrants to assert their religious authority despite the absence of prosperity.

The role of gender in shaping the significance of histories of labor migration to Saudi Arabia is further highlighted by the experiences of women migrants. Research on Bangladeshi women labor migrants to the Arab Gulf suggests that they are less likely than their male counterparts to enjoy elevated status upon return to Bangladesh (Bélanger and Rahman 2013). Women migrants typically earn less than men while abroad, thereby giving them less ability to deploy displays of prosperity to enhance their status upon return to Bangladesh (Afsar 2011). It is also the case that histories of labor migration abroad have gendered meanings. Women in Bangladesh who travel and work abroad without the guardianship of male family members face stigmatization for violating the norms and values of *purdah*, or the separation of men and women. They are suspected of engaging in illicit sexual activities while abroad, thereby bringing dishonor to both themselves and their families. These notions of labor migrant women as "fallen women" may be unintentionally reinforced by popular media reports of the exploitation and sexual abuse faced by Bangladeshi

women in domestic service jobs in Saudi Arabia. The significance of these sexu-
alized stigmas is highlighted by the dual meanings of post-migration prosperity
for women. Bélanger and Rahman (2011) observe that while economic success
is associated with higher status in the home community for women migrants,
it is also the case that "having been too successful led to questions and doubts.
Returnees are commonly accused by community members of having had a 'loose
lifestyle'" (Bélanger and Rahman 2011, 369).

Informed by these gendered status dynamics, women migrants are less likely to
be viewed as agents of authentic Islam or to make such claims for themselves upon
return to Bangladesh. Given both their concentration in domestic service as well
as the general restrictions on women's movements in the public sphere in Saudi
Arabia, women migrants do not have the organized opportunities for religious
learning that are identified by some men to be part of their experience in Saudi
Arabia. The absorption of Saudi religious practices from the public environment
that is described by men may also be less relevant for women working in private
homes, where there is less direct monitoring and surveillance of religious behavior.

However, domestic service offered opportunities to Bangladeshi migrant
women for direct and close interactions with Saudi nationals—experiences that
are largely absent for less-skilled migrant men. Speaking of these conditions,
some women spoke of observing and forming regular religious habits, such as
praying five times a day, from their time in Saudi Arabia. For others, however, the
realities of daily household life fostered a critical view of the narrative of Saudi
society as an exemplar of Islamic piety. The account of Meena, who had worked
as a maid in Saudi Arabia for three years, suggests that the environment of private homes was not always conducive to religious practice and learning:

> I cannot say that I was treated very badly by the Madam or very well. They did
> not hit me or mistreat me. But it is true that they did not give me the consid-
> eration I expected for saying my prayers regularly. Saudi Arabia is the place of
> our Prophet (peace be upon him) but in the house it was not like that, they did
> whatever they wanted to do. Once when I was saying my prayers the madam
> of the house came to me and said, why haven't you prepared the tea for us? She
> said, it's more important that you take care of us. You can pray later. It was like
> that. It was not a pious environment.

Conclusions

Bangladesh, a Muslim majority country, has been a focus of the Saudi state
project of global political and religious influence since the 1980s. Along with

the financing of NGOs in Bangladesh that merge the work of humanitarianism and *da'wa*, Saudi Arabia has been an important source of foreign exchange, through migrant remittances, for Bangladesh. In this chapter we have explored the Bangladesh to Saudi Arabia labor migration circuit as one of the channels through which Wahhabism takes meaning and shape in Bangladesh. Our findings both affirm and complicate the narrative of migrants returning to Bangladesh from the "land of Allah" as agents of religious change, working to propagate Saudi practices of Islam. Supported by an extensive network of Islamic reformist institutions, including those of Jamaat-e-Islami, a political group aspiring to create an Islamic state in Bangladesh, some migrants, especially economically successful men, do take on this role. Others, however, lack the economic and social capital to present themselves as religious leaders in their communities. This includes women, who constitute an increasingly prominent segment of the Bangladesh to Saudi Arabia labor migration circuit.

References

Afsar, Rita. 2011. "Contextualizing Gender and Migration in South Asia: Critical Insights." *Gender, Technology and Development* 15(3): 389–410. doi:https://doi.org/10.1177/097185241101500304.

Ahmed, Rafiuddin. 2001. "The Emergence of the Bengali Muslims." In *Understanding the Bengal Muslims: Interpretive Essays*, edited by Rafiuddin Ahmed, 1–25. New Delhi: Oxford University Press.

Ai, Sugie. 2019. "Disembedding Islamic Locale: the Spread and Deepening of Islamic Knowledge in Rural Bangladesh." *Journal of Urban and Regional Studies on Contemporary India* 2: 1–21. https://core.ac.uk/reader/222963404.

Bangladesh Population 2019. *World Population Review*. http://worldpopulationreview.com/countries/bangladesh-population/ (accessed September 9, 2019).

"Bangladesh Signs 2 Deals; 4 MoUs with Saudi Arabia." 2019. *Dhaka Tribune*. March 7, 2019. https://www.dhakatribune.com/bangladesh/foreign-affairs/2019/03/07/dhaka-riyadh-ink-six-instruments.

Barry, Ellen, and Julfikar Ali Manik. 2017. "To Secular Bangladeshis, Textbook Changes are a Harbinger." *New York Times*. January 22, 2017. https://www.nytimes.com/2017/01/22/world/asia/bangladesh-textbooks-radical-islam.html?rref=collection%2Ftimestopic%2FBangladesh&action=click&contentCollection=world&region=stream&module=stream_unit&version=search&contentPlacement=1&pgtype=collection.

Bélanger, Danièle, and Mahmuda Rahman. 2013. "Migrating against All the Odds: International Labour Migration of Bangladeshi Women." *Current Sociology* 61(3): 356–373. doi: https://doi.org/10.1177/0011392113484453

Berkeley Center for Religion, Peace, and World Affairs Report. "Islam and Development in Bangladesh: A Grassroots Perspective." 2016. Georgetown University. October 24, 2016. https://berkleycenter.georgetown.edu/publications/islam-and-development-in-bangladesh-a-grassroots-perspective.

Devnath, Bishakha. 2019. "Hounded out of Saudi Arabia." *Daily Star*. September 13, 2019. https://www.thedailystar.net/frontpage/torture-in-saudi-arabia-to-bangladeshi-fem ale-workers-1799344 (accessed October 6, 2019).

Fair, Christine, Ali Hamza, and Rebecca Heller. 2017. "Who Supports Suicide Terrorism in Bangladesh? What the Data Say." *Politics and Religion* 10: 622–661. doi: https:// doi:10.1017/S1755048317000347.

Fernando, Jude. 2011. *The Political Economy of NGOs: State Formation in Bangladesh and Sri Lanka* . London: Pluto Press.

Gardner, Katy. 2005. *Global Migrants, Local Lives: Migration and Transformation in Rural Bangladesh*. Oxford: Oxford University Press.

Gardner, Katy, and Filippo Osella. 2004. "Migration, Modernity and Social Transformation in South Asia: An Introduction." In *Migration, Modernity and Social Transformation in South Asia*, edited by Filippo Osella and Katy Gardner, xi–xlviii. New Delhi: Sage.

Gayen, Kaberi. 2019. "'Equal Property Right': Much Ado about Nothing." *Daily Star*. March 8, 2019. https://www.thedailystar.net/star-weekend/news/equal-property- right-1711810.

Hefner, Robert. 2005. "Introduction: Modernity and the Remaking of Muslim Politics." In *Remaking Muslim Politics: Pluralism, Contestation and Democratization*, edited by Robert W. Hefner, 1–36. Princeton, NJ: Princeton University Press.

Kibria, Nazli. 2011. *Muslims in Motion: Islam and National Identity in the Bangladeshi Diaspora*. New Brunswick, NJ: Rutgers University Press.

Kumar, Anand. 2009. "Terror Financing in Bangladesh." *Strategic Analysis* 33(6): 903– 917. doi:https://doi.org/10.1080/09700160903255913.

Kurien, Prema. 2002. *Kaleidoscopic Ethnicity: International Migration and the Reconstruction of Community Identities in India*. New Brunswick, NJ: Rutgers University Press.

Levitt, Peggy. 1998. "Social Remittances: Migration Driven Local-Level Forms of Cultural Diffusion." *The International Migration Review* 4: 926–948, www.jstor.org/stable/ 2547666.

Rahman, Mizanur. 2011. "Does Labour Migration Bring about Economic Advantage? A Case of Bangladeshi Migrants in Saudi Arabia." ISAS Working Paper No. 135. October 4, 2011. http://dx.doi.org/10.2139/ssrn.1938168.

Rahman, Md Mizanur. 2018. "The Making of an Islamist Public Sphere in Bangladesh." *Asian Journal of Comparative Politics* 4(4): 1–23. doi: https://doi.org/10.1177/20578 91118811952.

Riaz, Ali. 2008. *Islamic Militancy in Bangladesh: A Complex Web*. London: Routledge.

11

Ethiopia and Saudi Arabia

Between Proximity and Distance

Terje Østebø

Introduction

Geographical proximity has enabled deep connections between peoples on the Arabian Peninsula and in the Horn of Africa. Contacts between the Peninsula and today's Ethiopia go back millennia, initially embodied in migrants crossing the Red Sea who became the ancestors of the Semitic-speaking population of northern Ethiopia. Later, in the sixth century, the Christian kingdom of Axum expanded its territory and occupied parts of Yemen before expanding north and threatening to destroy the Ka'ba in Mecca. The first contact between Islam and Ethiopia was similarly early, in 615 CE, when the Prophet's first followers found protection under the benevolent Christian king of Axum.

While geographical proximity enabled important ethnic, cultural, and, not the least, religious points of contact between Muslims on the Peninsula and in the Horn, Ethiopia's historical relations to the Peninsula have, in contrast, been characterized by distance. The Axumite *hijra* signaled a harmonious relation-ship between Ethiopia and Islam, but this was gradually unseated by more con-flictual relations, particularly after the so-called conquest of Ahmad Gragn in the sixteenth century. The memory of this produced what Haggai Erlich (1994, 31f) has labeled the "Ahmad Gragn Syndrome"—a distinct trauma where Islam is viewed as an external threat to the country's survival. Depicting itself as the "Christian island" in the middle of a hostile Muslim "sea," Ethiopia adopted xenophobic attitudes and protective policies toward the outside world—and par-ticularly toward its Muslim neighbors. The religious fault line also extended to Ethiopia's own Muslim population, which was viewed as potential allies with outside Muslim forces, resulting in a policy of alienation of the Muslims whereby the Christian state made significant efforts to keep them at distance from such "foreign" Muslims.

These proximity-distance dynamics are crucial when trying to understand the contacts between Saudi Arabia and Ethiopia. Paying particular attention to the religious aspect of interactions, wherein Salafism is of importance, this chapter

Terje Østebø, *Ethiopia and Saudi Arabia* In: *Wahhabism and the World*. Edited by: Peter Mandaville, Oxford University Press. © Oxford University Press 2022. DOI: 10.1093/oso/9780197532560.003.0011 will examine Saudi outreach activities, Ethiopia's efforts to thwart these, and how Ethiopian Muslims' attempts to negotiate within this dynamic produced complex relations characterized by a combination of proximity, restrictions, distance, and contact. When trying to understand Saudi influences, we too often, as pointedly argued by Laurent Bonnefoy (2011), focus on the Saudi state as a well-funded machine exporting Salafi teachings, causing us to overlook the role of a range of nongovernmental organizations (NGOs) and private individuals (cf. Al-Rasheed 2008, 8).[1] These actors may have agendas and motivations different from each other, and it is similarly important to recognize that Saudi funding does not necessarily translate into the expansion of Salafism. As noted by Oliver Roy, international Salafi institutions tended to be "networks of finance and diffusion rather than command and organization" (Roy 1992, 144).

It is, moreover, crucial to recognize the role of Ethiopian Muslims as the key actors in ferrying religious ideas across the Red Sea. This chapter reverses the too common perceptions of active Arabs and passive Africans in the spread of Salafism—in turn reproducing a colonial subject–object relationship, in which Africans are located at the subaltern end of a power pendulum. It also thwarts the notion of Salafism as a Saudi or foreign form of Islam forcefully imposed upon "traditional" and tolerant African Muslims, and where the former is perceived as a threat to the latter. Paying attention to local agency also enables us to understand Salafism as something subject to change over time and as constantly produced through the dynamics of local contexts. Building on my book *Localising Salafism* (Østebø 2012), I argue for an approach that recognizes the dialectical dimensions of religious reform as a process where new and alternative messages are introduced in a given locality and which are negotiated in relation to the involved actors' context. Such processes would follow a number of trajectories and produce a number of possible, and sometimes unexpected, results. This means that we need to bypass the oft-used, yet unqualified, global–local dichotomy when talking about Salafism and Saudi Arabian influences. Although Salafism surely is a global phenomenon, it is not something existing on some sort of meta-level detached from local space—as a core, disconnected, and essentialized phenomenon. My suggestion is that Salafism as a global movement can only be properly understood through its appearances in numerous interconnected local realities around the globe, which in sum make what we call global Salafism (cf. Østebø 2015).[2]

Saudi Arabia in Ethiopia

Diplomatic connections between Ethiopia and the Kingdom of Saudi Arabia date back to 1934, yet contacts between the two were at this stage rather sporadic as bilateral relations were not prioritized by either of the two (Erlich 2007, 99, 110f.). Relations between Ethiopia and Saudi Arabia improved from the 1960s, as the two shared the concern over Egypt's—and later the Soviets'—increasing presence in the Horn. While the two viewed each other as stabilizing actors in the region, relations between the two remained tenuous. The Saudis remained, for instance, concerned over the Ethiopian government's treatment of the Muslim population, made evident through its *Voice of Islam* radio broadcasts. The Ethiopian Revolution in 1974 and the arrival of the Derg regime negatively impacted diplomatic relations. Concerned over growing Soviet influence in the region, the Saudis embarked on a policy called "the Arabization of the Red Sea," which included supporting the Eritrean secessionist movement and providing important military support to Somalia during the Ogaden war in 1977–1978.

The arrival of the Ethiopian People's Revolutionary Democratic Front (EPRDF) as the new governing party in 1991 paved the way for diplomatic rapprochement between Ethiopia and Saudi Arabia. It is here interesting to note how the Ethiopian government came to underscore the ancient and deep bonds between Ethiopia and Saudi Arabia, by explicitly referring to Ethiopia's role in giving refuge to the persecuted Muslims during the Axumite Hijra (The Federal Democratic Republic of Ethiopia, n.d.). Saudi focus on Ethiopia and the broader Horn of Africa increased significantly in the 2000s, spurred by Iran's growing presence on the continent in the early 2000s, by the need for partners in the conflict in Yemen from 2015, and as a consequence of the Qatar crisis. Cooperation has mostly been of an economic nature, and Ethiopia looked to Saudi Arabia as a trading partner and as important in contributing to Ethiopia's development. Investment opportunities and regional geopolitics have also in recent years led to the involvement of actors such as the United Arab Emirates (UAE), Turkey, and Qatar—and have paved the way for competition between these (International Crisis Group 2019). The political transition in Ethiopia in 2018, with the arrival of Prime Minister Abiy Ahmed, has intensified this; a peace treaty between Ethiopia and Eritrea was signed in Riyadh in September 2019 which resulted in a US$3 billion aid package from the UAE ("Ethiopia, Eritrea Sign Peace Deal at Saudi Arabia Summit," 2019; "In Peace between Ethiopia and Eritrea, UAE Lends a Helping Hand," 2018). Ethiopia has, on its part, tried to balance the different Gulf actors against each other, accepting assistance from both Saudi Arabia and the UAE, while keeping the door open for Qatar.

Saudi presence and support for *religious* activities in Ethiopia were, however, very limited during the 1960s and 1970s. This was in contrast to an increasingly active Saudi religious foreign policy launched by King Saʿud ibn ʿAbd al-ʿAziz (r. 1953–1964) and later by his successor King Faysal bin ʿAbd al-ʿAziz al-Saʿud (r. 1964–1975) that came to focus on Africa. In addition to blocking Egypt's outreach activities, the objective was to "'save' the African Muslim from the influence of Sufism" (Ahmed 2015, 142). The Saudis connected with local organizations, offered scholarships for studies in Saudi Africa, funded construction of schools and mosques, and distributed Salafi literature (Hunwick 1997; Kane 2003, 66, 123f.; Sirriyeh 1999: 158f.; Thurston 2016, 74f.). Delegations from the newly established Muslim World League (MWL) were sent to Africa in the 1960s, and while these also visited Ethiopia, no efforts were made to support religious infrastructure.

The only exception was Saudi support for the Awaliyya School in Addis Ababa. The school was originally established by wealthy Arab expatriates in 1961, but was taken over by Ethiopian Muslims a few years later. The new owners received financial support from the MWL from 1966 and were provided with Saudi instructors in 1970 (Bauer Oumer 2006, 79; Nega Aba Jebel 1986, 10f.). A MWL delegation led by its secretary-general visited Ethiopia in 1973, visiting Muslim centers and delivering sermons in the main mosques (Erlich 2007, 117). The MWL continued to support the Awaliyya School after the revolution in 1974, providing funds and teachers throughout the 1970s and 1980s (Nega Aba Jebel 1986, 14f.). The MWL, moreover, became active in providing relief during the Ethiopian famine of 1984–1985, which became an important precursor for the opening of the first MWL office in Addis Ababa in 1987. The organization subsequently contributed to the building of schools and clinics in the country, and at the end of the 1980s, the MWL leadership paid another visit to Ethiopia, where they were warmly welcomed by the Ethiopian president, Mengistu Haile-Mariam (Erlich 2007, 167).

The new EPRDF policies opened the doors to the outside world—lifting limits on the *hajj*, suspending the ban on import of religious literature, and enabling foreign religious actors to enter the country. The MWL increased its presence in Ethiopia during the 1990s and its activities were mainly carried out by the organization's development wing, the International Islamic Relief Organization (IIRO). The MWL's own magazine, *al-Alam al-Islami*, claimed that the IIRO was the largest foreign NGO in Ethiopia in the early 1990s. It had its own office in Addis Ababa, and was engaged in a broad array of development schemes, contributing funds for the construction of mosques throughout the country, providing religious literature, organizing seminars for Ethiopian 'ulama, and supporting religious education for children (Erlich 2007, 189; interview, 2020, Addis Ababa, January 24). The Awaliyya School remained the IIRO's main focus, and in 1993, the formal ownership of the school was transferred to the IIRO and it was renamed as the Awaliyya School & Mission Center. The school adopted a secular curriculum required by the state for all schools in Ethiopia, whereas Arabic and Islam became extracurricular education (Bauer Oumer 2006, 79).

In addition to the MWL, the early 1990s saw the arrival of the World Assembly of Muslim Youth (WAMY), the Sultan bin 'Abd al-'Aziz al- Sa'ud Foundation, with its office located at the Awaliyya School, and later the al-Haramain Foundation. The Saudi Prince Turki bin Fahd Foundation provided funding for different local organizations, and there are, in addition, reports that the Islamic Development Bank offered scholarships for students in areas of engineering, medicine, and agriculture ("Allah in Ethiopia: Mostly Quiet on the Islamic Front," 1997). It is also important to note that influences came from different directions—from Sudan, Egypt, and Kuwait.

Religion continued, however, to be a complicating factor in the relationship between Ethiopia and Saudi Arabia, as the Ethiopian government remained fearful that Saudi religious influence could lead to radicalization among its Muslim population. The specter of so-called Islamic extremism came to the fore in 1995, in a series of events—in particular, the failed assassination attempt on the then-Egyptian president Hosni Mubarak in June 1995 as he visited Addis Ababa to attend the African Union (AU) Summit. The incident shaped Ethiopia's policies toward religious developments in the region, enhancing the government's fear of increased radicalization of the Muslim community and of "dangerous" outside influence. Although there were no accusations directed at Saudi Arabia, the government made no attempts to differentiate between different sources of outside influence.[3] The year 1995 constituted in many ways a watershed for Ethiopia's Muslims. The government reacted swiftly by closing organizations and arresting hundreds of leading figures, and it started to keep a closer eye on the Muslim community.

While Saudi organizations continued their presence throughout the 1990s, this changed with the 9/11 Al-Qaeda attacks and the subsequent War on Terror. Shortly after the attacks, the Ethiopian government curbed much of Saudi Arabia's activities in Ethiopia, and in 2004, it closed the Addis Ababa office of the al-Haramain Foundation (Shinn 2005). The government and the broader Christian population remained concerned about radicalization among Ethiopia's Muslims, where increased visibility of Islam in the form of the growth in the number of mosques across the country and the increasing number of Muslims holding governmental and public positions were interpreted as proof of such a development. Such concerns were shared by some foreign observers, arguing that Ethiopian Salafis, in cooperation with the Saudi Arabian Salafi establishment and the Saudi regime, were working relentlessly to disseminate militant Islamism within Ethiopia—and how this threatened "traditional" Muslims, who "have remained loyal to their own apolitical traditions" (Erlich 2007, 179). Such perceptions also informed international policymakers, and the United States, which saw Ethiopia as an important ally in the War on Terror, labeled Salafism as "foreign" and as Saudi-funded "cultural imperialism" attempting to subvert "moderate" Sufi Ethiopian Islam ("Countering Wahabi Influence in Ethiopia through Cultural Programming," 2009).

The IIRO was the last Saudi organization to be ousted from Ethiopia in 2010. Disagreements between the school and the Ministry of Education over the Awaliyya School's Arabic courses emerged, and the ministry moreover required the IIRO to be registered as a religious organization. Unable to reach an agreement, the IIRO lost its license and was forced to end its activities in 2011. The Awaliyya School was subsequently brought under the auspices of the Ethiopian Islamic Affairs Supreme Council (EIASC). The MWL reported in 2018, however, through Twitter, that it had spent over US$25 million on various activities in Ethiopia, claiming to have reached more than three million beneficiaries and spending over US$1 million on dissemination of Qur'ans and nearly US$3 million on education (Muslim World League, n.d.).[4]

Current Saudi support for local religious infrastructure goes through two different channels. The first is aid formalized and structured through the Saudi Arabian Cultural Attaché. While in English it is formally referred to as the *Cultural* Attaché, the office is in Arabic called *Mulhaq al-Dini*, or religious attaché, and falls under the Saudi Arabian Department of Religious Affairs. It provides support for local *iftar* celebrations, sponsors *hajj* for selected Ethiopians, and funds the publication of religious literature. In fact, the Saudi government requires that all requests for the funding of religious projects go through the attaché in Addis Ababa. The extent of such support seems limited, however, and at the time of writing, there are only four projects funded through the attaché. The second channel, which has become more important in recent years, is of an informal nature. It takes the form of Ethiopians approaching wealthy Saudi individuals, who then contact so-called brokers, Saudis who travel to Ethiopia and examine the proposals, who report back to the donors, and who collect a certain percentage if the projects are funded. Most of such support goes toward the construction of mosques (interview, 2020, Addis Ababa, January 14).

Developments in Saudi Arabia are likely to further such informal points of contacts. The ascent of Crown Prince Muhammad bin Salman and his policy of moderation indicate that the kingdom is less focused on exerting religious influence beyond its borders. Eager not to be perceived as a harbinger of so-called Islamic extremism, the new leadership has worked hard to present itself as devoted to tolerance and religious coexistence. The same is true for the MWL, which has been said to have steered away from proselytization and to fight what it calls extremism ("Are Saudi Arabia's Reforms for Real? A Recent Visit Says Yes," 2018). Salafism in Saudi Arabia is, however, represented by a heterogenous set of actors still seeking to export Salafi teaching to countries like Ethiopia.

This situation has opened the door for other religious actors, some of which had a presence in Ethiopia from the early 1990s. One important actor was the Kuwaiti Africa Muslims Agency (AMA), which was much involved in disseminating literature. The organization still operates in Ethiopia under the name Direct

Aid, but is solely focused on development aid. Recent years have, as noted, seen an increase presence of the UAE, mainly in the area of development aid. The UAE government has given some support for local religious infrastructure, funding the construction of a new mosque and the renovation of another in Addis Ababa. The EIASC leadership, moreover, recently traveled to the UAE for a religious workshop organized by the Sufi-leaning Tabah Foundation in Abu Dabi (interview, 2020, Addis Ababa, January 12; "The Return of Sufism to UAE," 2018). Informants argued that the UAE is presenting itself as representing a "moderate" version of Islam, and thus is welcomed by the Ethiopian government (interview, 2020, Addis Ababa, January 12 and 21). However, Prime Minister Abiy Ahmed refused UAE's Crown Prince Muhammad bin Zayed's offer to build an Islamic center in Ethiopia during a visit to Abu Dhabi, claiming to have said to the prince, "We don't need to learn the religion from you. You've lost the religion." (" 'You've Lost Islam': Ethiopian PM Recounts Snub to Abu Dhabi Crown Prince," 2018). This seems not to have made any immediate impact, and in May 2020, the two countries explored further cooperation in the area of "culture" ("UAE, Ethiopia Discuss Cultural Cooperation," 2020).

Ethiopians in Saudi Arabia

Proximity has also enabled Muslims in the Horn to easily cross the Red Sea, and for centuries they have traveled to the peninsula for *hajj* and in search of religious education, where the main centers of education were Mecca, Medina, Jizan, Asir, Mocha, Tarim, and Zabid. While improved means of communication in the twentieth century enabled more Muslims to travel for *hajj*, the number of pilgrims from Ethiopia remained relatively low. This changed, in a somewhat ironic twist, during the Italian occupation (1935–1942). Seeking to generate support from Ethiopia's Muslim population against the Christian-dominated political elite and to legitimize their colonial project in the eyes of the Saudis, the Italians actively facilitated the pilgrimage from Ethiopia (Erlich 2007, 39f.; Temam Haji 2002, 48).[5] Exposed to Salafi teaching, actively promoted by the newly established Kingdom of Saudi Arabia, returning Ethiopians soon made efforts to disseminate such ideas in their respective localities. The initial appearance of Salafism was found in the southeastern town of Harar (Erlich 2007, 26, 81f.), before gradually spreading to the surrounding Oromo areas. Centers for Salafi teaching were established in the southeastern region of Hararge, and from there the new teaching spread to the neighboring areas of Arsi and Bale in the late 1950s.

The 1960s became a crucial period for Ethiopian Muslims' connections to Saudi Arabia and the spread of Salafi teachings. This was obviously connected to the establishment of the Islamic University of Medina in 1961, which was key to the kingdom's strategy of disseminating Salafism beyond its borders; to educate students "from the entire Muslim world and to train *ulama* able to undertake *da'wa* after finishing their studies" (cited in Ahmed 2015, 137). The university's regulations called for 75 percent of its students to be recruited from overseas, who were offered scholarships from the Saudi state (Commins 2006, 112; Layish 1984, 36f.). News about the possibilities for higher religious education in Saudi Arabia soon spread across southeastern Ethiopia, and during the 1960s and 1970s an increasing number of Muslims crossed the Red Sea in search of knowledge. The area that was most significantly affected was the Bale region, and the relatively high number of people from Bale educated in Saudi Arabia made it an early Salafi stronghold in Ethiopia (Østebø 2012). After graduation and returning home, these returnees became active in disseminating what they had learned: "They [the Saudis] gave us an assignment to teach, to open *madaris* when we got home. They sent us books we were supposed to teach . . . some also got salaries when they returned" (interview, 2006, Robe, June 10). Salafism was thus gradually and subtly dispersed through teaching institutions that emerged across the southeast, slowly influencing future generations and laying the ground for more significant changes to come.

Opportunities for travels across the Red Sea were significantly reduced during the Derg period. This was particularly done through limiting the *hajj*, and the regime formally granted a maximum of 2,000 exit visas annually; the cumbersome and costly process for obtaining such permissions made it likely that they issued fewer. Hussein Ahmed (1994, 791) claimed that the number of pilgrims was usually never above 1,000 per year throughout the Derg period.[6] The possibility for higher religious education in Saudi Arabia also diminished during the 1980, as the priorities of the Islamic University of Medina—in the course of the Soviet intervention in Afghanistan—shifted toward Central and South Asia (Ahmed 2015, 142). It was no longer possible to travel for 'umra or hajj and then subsequently enroll in the university (interview, 2020, Addis Ababa, January 12).

Restrictions on travels to Saudi Arabia were eased from the early 1990s, and led to an increase of migrant workers, seeking jobs in the different sectors of the Saudi Arabian economy. A high number of these migrant workers were illegal, and had consequently to live rather sheltered from the gaze of the authorities. Most were not particularly interested in pursuing religious education, and those who were interested could not openly attend institutions of learning. The Saudi government's crackdown on illegal migration and limitations on *hajj* in the 2000s, however, have thwarted possibilities to travel to Saudi. It is generally limited to those with established contacts in the kingdom, and who, as noted earlier, are able to locate funds from wealthy donors.

Saudi Arabia and Ethiopian Salafism

The limited Saudi presence in Ethiopia and the Ethiopian government's efforts to distance the Muslims from Saudi influence have contributed much to make Ethiopian Salafism rather informal and decentered. The EPRDF's initial liberal policy toward religion meant an end to former restrictions on religious practice, paving the way for the construction of mosques, the surfacing of Islamic newspapers and magazines, and the establishment of Islamic organizations (Haustein and Østebø 2011; Hussein Ahmed 1994, 791; Østebø 2008). The first main Salafi organization was the Islamic Daʿwa and Knowledge Association, directed by a graduate from the Islamic University of Medina with good connections with wealthy Saudi donors. This organization played a decisive role in translating and publishing religious literature, constructing mosques, and supporting various forms of daʿwa (interview, 2006, Addis Ababa, September 26). Similarly important was the Ethiopian Muslim Youth Association, which offered courses on Islam, organized training and camps for the youth, and had representatives actively recruiting followers through frequent visits to the capital's mosques (interview, 2006, Addis Ababa, June 17). While it had not had much of a Salafi leaning from the beginning, something changed as it started to receive funding from the World Association of Muslim Youth (WAMY).

The previously discussed incidents and the government's crackdown in 1994–1995 severely reduced opportunities for Muslim organizations, consequently solidifying the earlier decentered and informal character of the Salafis and other reform movements. This was accelerated post–9/11 and after the IIRO was kicked out in 2010. From the early 2000s, a group of Oromo ʿulama led by Dr. Jeylan Kadir, the most prominent Salafi scholar in Ethiopia, emerged. These individuals had returned from Saudi Arabia in the early 1990s and had settled in Aiyr Tena, one of the suburbs of Addis Ababa (Bauer Oumer 2006, 75f.; interview, 2006, Addis Ababa, January 22). Aiyr Tena was also the site for Markaz al-Ansar al-Shariʿa, which also included a school offering higher Islamic education to shaykhs from across the country (interview, 2020, Addis Ababa, January 22).

The lack of organizational structures paved the way for a more internally fragmented Ethiopian Salafism. One important sub-stream of Salafism emerging in Addis Ababa in the 2000s was represented by the Madkhaliyya group, which, as the name indicates, was inspired by the Saudi ʿalim Shaykh Rabiʿ al-Madkhali. The group initially revolved around a few individuals—some of whom had spent some time in Saudi Arabia—but has gradually grown in strength. Its activities are concentrated around the Ibnu al-Masoud Islamic Center and it runs, in addition, the Mewedda School (interview, 2006, Addis Ababa, May 20; interview, 2006, Addis Ababa, October 10). In addition to Saudi Arabia, the group was also ideologically linked to the Yemeni Salafi scholar Muqbil al-Wadiʿi (d.

2001), and unconfirmed reports claim that a number of Ethiopian Salafis spent time in Yemen, studying at his Dar al-Hadith institute in Dammaj (Bonnefoy 2011: 54f.).[7] Advocating a "stricter" version of Salafism, and often secluding themselves from both non-Salafis and other Salafis, they were often labeled the "Super Salafis," while internal fragmentation birthed a faction referred to as the "Super-Super Salafis." This latter faction is a rather small group represented by the Jamiyya al-Sunna organization (interview, 2020, Addis Ababa, January 12). Another, and more exclusivist, Salafi faction was the Takfir wal Hijrah group, arriving through Sudan and emerging in 1994–1995.[8] The Takfir wal Hijra was soon able to attract quite a number of followers among the capital's young residents, and for a period the issue of *takfir* was on everybody's lips. Distancing themselves from Christians, they also severed their connections with other Muslims, including Salafis, refusing to pray with them (Østebø 2012, 253f.). The group's popularity waned in the middle of the first decade of the 2000s, but reports indicate that they played an important role in escalating inter-religious tensions later in that decade (Zelalem Temesgen 2010, 81; interview, 2010, Addis Ababa, February 20).

Contrary to the authorities' claim that Ethiopian Salafis were promoting so-called Islamic extremism, they were, as I have argued elsewhere, little interested in political activism (Østebø 2014). This dates back to the time of the early returnees, and one of my informants, who spent over ten years studying in Saudi Arabia in the 1960s, claimed: "we were advised by our [Saudi] teachers not to get into conflict with the regime, to teach deeply about *tawhid*, and to advice against *shirk*. We followed all their advices" (interview, 2005, Robe, November 19). The Ethiopian returnees were by and large influenced by a "mainstream" Saudi state-endorsed form of Salafism, and there is no indication that they were exposed to more politically oriented currents arriving at Saudi Arabian institutions of higher education at that time (Lacroix 2011, 89, 212). The Madkhaliyya and the Takfir wal Hijrah group have in particular been erroneously accused of having political goals. The former has, however, followed the teaching of al-Madkhali and the *hadith* scholar Muhammad Nasir al-Din al-Albani (d. 1999) who have staunchly opposed any form of Islamist political engagement, arguing that the purging of all innovations has to precede the creation of an Islamic political order (Lacroix 2009, 69; Østebø 2012, 258; interview, 2013, Addis Ababa, November 5). While the Takfir wal Hijrah held a radical position toward the Ethiopian state, seen by its refusal to hold ID cards and to pay taxes, the group has been similarly uninterested in the establishment of an Islamic state and more occupied with carving out symbolic space for the realization of their ideological program.

While the decentered character of Ethiopian Salafism contributed to a complex ideological picture, Ethiopian Salafis' main focus was on purification within the religious sphere. They never adhered strictly to a blueprint of Saudi teachings, and the new ideas that gradually spread in Ethiopia were tailored to local realities. The main targets of the early Salafi returnees were Sufi and local cultural practices viewed as irreconcilable with Islam, but in contrast to many parts of West Africa where Salafis battled with strong Sufi brotherhoods, Ethiopian Salafis' focus was the widespread veneration of so-called Muslim saints (*awliya*) and pilgrimages to their tombs. During the 1990s, the attention shifted from issues related to local culture to questions related to piety. A generation of young Salafis was now increasingly attacking fellow Muslims for religious laxness and indifference to the requirements of Islam, rebuking things like smoking, chewing *khat*, listening to pop music, and "improper" sexual interactions. Seeking to produce a new pious subject, they advocated for a strict observance of the duties of Islam, particularly the regular observance of the daily prayers (*salat*) and were zealously committed to the issue of the Sunna—the practice of following the example of the Prophet in all aspects of life. This meant much attention was paid to certain outward issues, such as growing one's beard, shortening one's trousers (to fall above the ankles), and, for women, the usage of a black veil, the *niqab*.

This generation of Salafis was far from a coherent group, and included autodidactics with little formal religious education and individuals who had spent time as migrant workers in Saudi Arabia. The latter were exposed to Salafi ideas in a rather idiosyncratic manner, and many were seeking out and selecting ideas that appealed to them, and came to develop a certain degree of ideological independence. The arrival of new interpretations of Salafism exacerbated the ideological fragmentation, producing what Søren Gilsaa (2015) calls "Salafi eclecticism," and illustrating how an evolving globalization enabled new and disparate groups to transcend local boundaries, to be exposed to alternative ideas, and pointing, moreover, to the unpredictable nature of religious reform.

What is interesting is that these young Salafis held very critical views of Saudi Arabia, compared with the more senior Salafis. The returning migrant workers, who had suffered under tough living conditions in Saudi Arabia, with long hours and abusive employers, were largely negative toward the Saudi kingdom, where the royal family's excessive lifestyle and overindulgence were lamented, and where the Saudi 'ulama were accused of being in league with the corrupt Saudi regime. Such critique was extended to the local senior Salafis, who were accused of being religiously lax, corrupt, and compromising, and who, moreover, were chastised for their connections with wealthy Saudi donors and for keeping Saudi donations for themselves rather than distributing them to the Muslim community. One activist in Bale lamented that the old *shaykh*s "were too fat and that this was due to their lack of thinking about the last day [of judgment]" (interview, 2005, Robe, August 14).

The informal and decentered nature of Saudi funding makes it difficult to determine the amount of money reaching Ethiopia and how it is spent. It seems clear from my findings that most religious infrastructure was financed by local means. In Bale, my main area of research, funding was of a random nature, and Saudi Arabia seemed not to be the main source of funding of local religious infrastructure. Two new mosques constructed in early 1990s were partly funded by foreign contributions, but were mainly financed by the local community. The local Salafiyya Madrasa received some sporadic aid from the Kuwaiti African Muslims Agency and the IIRO, but that ended in the late 1990s. It managed to get some support from a local organization in Addis Ababa, but most of its funds came from local contributions.

Post-Salafism

The growing complexity of Salafism has made it increasingly difficult to conceptualize it. Earlier attempts to categorize different sub-streams seem inadequate (International Crisis Group 2004; Wiktorowicz 2006), thus making it critical to refine our analytical apparatus. Alex Thurston's notion of "post-Salafism" might be a step in the right direction, where he argues that there are indications that leading Salafi figures no longer appear completely committed to Salafi exclusivism (Thurston 2018). This seems to be applicable to the Ethiopian case, though there are, at the same time, many uncertainties as to where future developments may lead.

While the 1990s were characterized by rigid ideological positions and polarizing debates, the situation changed gradually in the 2000s as people were getting tired of doctrinal disagreements—particularly between Salafi- and Sufi-oriented factions in Ethiopia. While this dovetails with how Salafism in other African contexts was becoming more accommodating toward Sufism (Kobo 2015; Loimeier 1997, 308), the unique feature in Ethiopia was the creation of concrete forums aimed at alleviating the tense relations. The Addis Ababa Ulama Unity Forum (AAUUF), established in 2007, spent nearly two years mediating between leading scholars from both sides, discussing a range of controversial religious issues. The two sides were gradually finding some common ground, but this came to an abrupt halt in 2009 when the forum was shut down by the government (Feyissa and Lawrence 2014).

Ideological rapprochement continued, however, in the course of widespread Muslim protests from early 2012. These protests were directed toward the arrival of the Lebanese Association of Islamic Charitable Projects (AICP), or the al-Ahbash, as it commonly was called. The al-Ahbash is devoted to combating any form of "extremist" Islam, viewing itself as the leading force for moderation (al-itidal),[9] and from the fall of 2011, enforced al-Ahbash trainings were conducted throughout the country, where Lebanese instructors and government officials sought to warn Muslims about the alleged rise of Islamic extremism in Ethiopia, instructing them to adhere to a more moderate version of Islam. The reactions from the Muslim community were immediate and negative, accusing the government of illegal interference in religious affairs and violating the constitutional separation of state and religion. Weekly protests emerged in the mosques, which soon spread to the streets of Addis Ababa during the spring of 2012. This continued until August 2013, when the authorities violently ended the protests. What is important here is how the protests managed to unite the Muslims across ideological divisions. They were led and coordinated by the so-called arbitration committee consisting of seventeen members, which was composed of members from the Intellectualist and Salafi movements, as well as more "traditional" religious scholars. Such unity was, moreover, made explicit when Dr. Jeylan Khadir appeared at one of the protests holding hands with Mufti Hajj Umar Idris, the main Sufi-oriented figure in Ethiopia. The arrest—and later sentencing—of the committee, for instigating terrorism, further enhanced feelings of unity, and the committee members were praised as heroes in the Muslims' struggle.

This is not to say that all differences were erased, but attempts of ideological reconciliation have continued in recent years. One such instance was the reconfiguration of the EIASC in 2018. The arrival of Abiy Ahmed as the new prime minister and new political realities ended the authorities' co-option of the council and gave the Muslim community the freedom to choose the members of the council. A committee of people with different ideological positions was selected, and after some months of negotiations, a new council with both Salafis and Sufis was formed. Mufti Hajj Umar Idris became the president, while Dr. Jeylan Khadir was elected as vice president.

The dwindling of Saudi funding, some said, provided opportunities for Ethiopian Muslims to further develop their own Islam. Dr. Jeylan Khadir himself lamented how outside funding had created internal competition among the Muslims, saying "everyone was running after the Saudi money. Now we are more independent, there is more trust among us" (interview 2020, Addis Ababa, January 21). Others, in turn, claim that the lack of outside support has severely weakened Salafism in Ethiopia (interview, 2020, Robe, January 18).

Signs of such shifts have appeared in Ethiopia, noticeable, for example, during a recent public meeting organized by the Saudi embassy, the Saudi Cultural Attaché, and a representative from the Saudi Waqf Ministry. At the meeting, some Salafis announced that they were preparing a book outlining the Salafi creed, but were immediately interrupted by the representative from the Waqf Ministry, who said that rather than writing on such topics, they should rather focus on the main tenets of Islam (interview, 2020, Addis Ababa, January 24). A key point to be made here is that these developments highlight the continued agency among Ethiopian Muslims—that they are defining their own ideological positions and deciding on their strategies for action. Similarly important is that, while drawing upon currents from the broader Muslim world, ideological distinctions have become less pronounced and are being selected and appropriated to fit the local realities. Saudi—and other—influences remain relevant, yet in a less explicit and direct manner, being juxtaposed with other currents.

Notes

1. It is, at the same time, important is recognize how non-state actors such as Saudi NGOs remain intimately connected with the Saudi state, consequently blurring the boundaries between state and non-state interventions.
2. Similar arguments have been made by Scott Reese (2014).
3. The Egyptian organization Jama'at al-Islamiyya took responsibility for the attack, with alleged support from Sudan (Haustein and Østebø 2011).
4. The tweet had no mention of what period the aid was distributed.
5. In contrast to before the occupation, when only eleven Ethiopians left for pilgrimage (1933), the number rose to somewhere between 1,600 and 1,900 in 1936 (Erlich 2007: 73f.).
6. The Derg allowed for the departure of 3,000 pilgrims to the Hijaz in 1974–1975, in an attempt to establish good relations with the neighboring Saudi kingdom (Erlich 2007, 137).
7. Shaykh Mukbil al-Wadi'i was leading Salafi scholar in Yemen, much inspired by al-Albani and close to Shaykh Rabi al-Madkhali.
8. Takfir wal Hijra first emerged in Egypt in 1977, where its leader, Shukri Mustafa, advocated a radical interpretation of Islam, rejecting any Muslim except his own followers as *kuffar*. In Sudan there are reports that the group was behind several attacks on mosques in the 1990s and that they tried to assassinate Osama bin Laden in 1994. See Carney (2005, 122).
9. The name al-Ahbash (Arabic) refers to the people of Ethiopia, and the explicit Ethiopian connection was embodied by Shaykh Abdullah ibn Muhammad ibn Yusuf al-Harari (1910–2006), a religious scholar from Harar, who after fleeing Ethiopia became the long-time spiritual leader of al-Ahbash in the 1950s.

References

Ahmed, Chanfi. 2015. *West African 'Ulama' and Salafism in Mecca and Medina: Jawab Al-Ifriqi: The Response of the African*. Leiden: Brill.
"Allah in Ethiopia: Mostly Quiet on the Islamic Front." 1997. (Cable from US Embassy in Addis Ababa, Ethiopia), *Wikileaks*. April 1, 1997.
https://wikileaks.org/plusd/cables/97ADDISABABA2584_a.html (accessed November 26, 2019).

"Are Saudi Arabia's Reforms for Real? A Recent Visit Says Yes." 2018. *Washington Post*. March 1, 2018. https://www.washingtonpost.com/opinions/global-opinions/are-saudi-arabias-reforms-for-real-a-recent-visit-says-yes/2018/03/01/a11a4ca8-1d9d-11e8-9de1-147dd2df3829_story.html (accessed May 4, 2020).

Bauer Oumer. 2006. *The Development of Islamic Propagation (Da'wa) in Addis Ababa and Its Surroundings*. MA thesis in History, Addis Ababa University.

Bonnefoy, Laurent. 2011. *Salafism in Yemen: Transnationalism and Religious Identity*. New York: Columbia University Press.

Carney, Timothy. 2005. "The Sudan: Political Islam and Terrorism." In *Battling Terrorism in the Horn of Africa*, edited by Robert I. Rotberg, 119–140. Washington DC: Brooking Institution Press.

Commins, David. 2006. *The Wahhabi Mission and Saudi Arabia*. London: I. B. Tauris.

"Countering Wahabi Influence in Ethiopia through Cultural Programming." 2009. (Cable from US Embassy in Addis Ababa, Ethiopia), *Wikileaks*. http://wikileaks.org/cable/2009/07/09ADDISABABA1675.html (accessed November 9, 2011).

Erlich, Haggai. *Ethiopia and the Middle East*. 1994. Boulder, CO; London: Lynne Rienner.

Erlich, Haggai. 2007. *Saudi Arabia and Ethiopia: Islam, Christianity, and Politics Entwined*. Boulder, CO; London: Lynne Rienner.

"Ethiopia, Eritrea Sign Peace Deal at Saudi Arabia Summit." 2019. *Al Jazeera*. September 17, 2019. https://www.aljazeera.com/news/2018/09/ethiopia-eritrea-sign-peace-deal-saudi-arabia-summit-180917055913813.html (accessed May 14, 2020).

Federal Democratic Republic of Ethiopia. n.d. "Ethiopia–Saudi Arabia." Edited by the Ministry of Foreign Affairs. Addis Ababa. http://www.mfa.gov.et/BilateralMore.php?pg=50 (accessed May 14, 2014).

Feyissa, Dereje, and Bruce Lawrence. 2014. "Muslims Renegotiating Marginality in Contemporary Ethiopia." *The Muslim World* 104(3): 281–305. doi: https://doi.org/10.1111/muwo.12056

Gilsaa, Søren. 2015. "Salafism(s) in Tanzania: Theological Roots and *Political Subtexts of the* Ansar Sunna." *Islamic Africa* 6(1–2): 30–59. doi: https://doi.org/10.1163/21540993-00602002

Haustein, Jürg, and Terje Østebø. 2011. "EPRDF's Revolutionary Democracy and Religious Plurality: Islam and Christianity in Post-*Derg* Ethiopia." *Journal of Eastern African Studies* 5(4): 755–772. doi: https://doi.org/10.1080/17531055.2011.642539

Hunwick, John. 1997. "Sub-Saharan Africa and the Wider World of Islam: Historical and Contemporary Perspectives." In *African Islam and Islam in Africa: Encounters between Sufis and Islamists*, edited by David Westerlund and Eva Evers Rosander, 28–54. London: Hurst.

Hussein, Ahmed. 1994. "Islam and Islamic Discourse in Ethiopia (1973–1993)." In *New Trends in Ethiopian Studies: Papers of the 12th International Conference of Ethiopian Studies*, edited by Harold G. Marcus and Grover Hudson, 775–801. Lawrenceville, NJ: The Red Sea Press.

"In Peace between Ethiopia and Eritrea, UAE Lends a Helping Hand." 2018. *Reuters*. August 8, 2018. https://www.reuters.com/article/us-ethiopia-eritrea-emirates-insight/in-peace-between-ethiopia-and-eritrea-uae-lends-a-helping-hand-idUSKBN1KT1QX (accessed May 13, 2020).

International Crisis Group. 2004. "Saudi Arabia Backgrounder: Who are the Islamists." Middle East Report no. 31.

International Crisis Group. 2019. "Intra-Gulf Competition in Africa's Horn: Lessening the Impact." Middle East & North Africa Report no. 206. https://www.crisisgroup.org/middle-east-north-africa/gulf-and-arabian-peninsula/206-intra-gulf-competition-africas-horn-lessening-impact.

Kane, Ousmane. 2003. *Muslim Modernity in Postcolonial Nigeria: A Study of the Society for the Removal of Innovation and Reinstatement of Tradition*. Leiden: Brill.

Kobo, Ousman Murzik. 2015. "Shifting Trajectory of Salafi/Ahl-Sunna Reformism in Ghana." *Islamic Africa* 6(1–2): 60–81. doi: https://doi.org/10.1163/21540993-00602003

Lacroix, Stéphane. 2009. "Between Revolution and Apoliticism: Nasir Al-Din Al-Albani and His Impact on the Shaping of Contemporary Salafism." In *Global Salafism: Islam's New Religious Movement*, edited by Roel Meijer, 58–80. London: Hurst, 2009.

Lacroix, Stéphane. 2011. *Awakening Islam: The Politics of Religious Dissent in Contemporary Saudi Arabia*. Cambrdge, MA: Harvard University Press.

Layish, Aharon. 1984. "'Ulama' and Politics in Saudi Arabia." In *Islam and Politics in the Modern Middle East*, edited by Metin Heper and Raphael Israeli, 29–63. New York: St. Martin Press.

Loimeier, Roman. 1997. *Islamic Reform and Political Change in Northern Nigeria*. Evanston, IL: Northwestern University Press.

Muslim World League. n.d. Twitter. https://twitter.com/MWLOrg_en/status/10094583 09995343872 (accessed November 26, 2019).

Nega Aba Jebel. 1986. "The History of the Awaliyya School 1961–1986." BA thesis, Addis Ababa University.

Østebø, Terje. 2008. "The Question of Becoming: Islamic Reform Movements in Contemporary Ethiopia." *Journal of Religion in Africa* 38(4): 416–46.

Østebø, Terje. 2012. *Localising Salafism: Religious Change among Oromo Muslims in Bale, Ethiopia*. Leiden: Brill.

Østebø, Terje. 2014. "Salafism, State Politics, and the Question of 'Extremism' in Ethiopia." *Comparative Islamic Studies* 8(1): 165–184.

Østebø, Terje. 2015. "African Salafism: Religious Purity and the Politicization of Purity." *Islamic Africa* 6(1–2): 1–29.

Al-Rasheed, Madawi. 2008. "Introduction: An Assessment of Saudi Political, Religious and Media Expansion." In *Kingdom without Borders: Saudi Political, Religious and Media Frontiers*, edited by Madawi Al-Rasheed, 1–38. New York: Columbia University Press.

Reese, Scott S. 2014. "Islam in Africa/Africans and Islam." *Journal of African History* 55(1): 17–26.

"The Return of Sufism to UAE." 2018. *Al Mesbar Studies and Research Center*. April 16, 2018. https://mesbar.org/the-return-of-sufism-to-the-uae/ (accessed May 11, 2020).

Roy, Oliver. 1992. *L'échec Du L'islam Du Politique*. Paris: Seuil.

Shinn, David. 2005. "Ethiopia: Governance and Terrorism." In *Battling Terrorism in the Horn of Africa*, edited by Robert I. Rotberg, 93–118. Washington, DC: Brookings Institution Press.

Sirriyeh, Elizabeth. 1999. *Sufis and Anti Sufis: The Defence, Rethinking and Rejection of Sufism in the Modern World*. Richmond, UK: Curzon.

Temam Haji. 2002. "Islam in Arsi, Southeast Ethiopia (ca. 1840–1974)." MA thesis, Addis Ababa University.

Thurston, Alexander. 2016. *Salafism in Nigeria: Islam, Preaching, and Politics*. London: Cambridge University Press.

Thurston, Alexander. 2018. "An Emerging Post-Salafi Current in West Africa and Beyond." *The Maydan*. October 15, 2018. https://themaydan.com/2018/10/emerging-post-salafi-current-west-africa-beyond/ (accessed September 14, 2021).

"UAE, Ethiopia Discuss Cultural Cooperation." 2020. Emirates News Agency. May 9, 2020. https://wam.ae/en/details/1395302841687 (accessed May 13, 2020).

Wiktorowicz, Quintan. 2006. "Anatomy of the Salafi Movement." *Studies in Conflict & Terrorism* 29(3): 207–239.

"'You've Lost Islam': Ethiopian PM Recounts Snub to Abu Dhabi Crown Prince." 2018. *Middle East Monitor*. July 31, 2018. https://www.middleeasteye.net/fr/news/ethiopian-pm-says-gulf-countries-not-fit-teach-islam-1372998477 (accessed May 11, 2020).

Zelalem Temesgen. 2010. *The 2006 Religious Conflict in Didessa and Gomma Waradas of Western Oromia*. MA thesis, Addis Ababa University.

12

Wahhabi Compromises and "Soft Salafization" in the Sahel

Alexander Thurston

Crossing the King Fahd Bridge on the way to the King Faysal Mosque in Bamako, Mali's capital, one could be forgiven for thinking that Saudi Arabian influence permeates the city's physical and religious landscape. But one could also be forgiven for asking whether such influence peaked, at least in its most concentrated form, years or even decades ago. Faysal, after all, was king of Saudi Arabia from 1964 to 1975, and Fahd from 1982 to 2005. And even if the press still periodically carries readers on a "voyage to the heart of Wahhabi Bamako" (Ahmed 2011), other dynamics have also shaped the 2010s, including compromises that Mali's Salafis have made with some of their ostensible arch-rivals.

This chapter argues that the contours and content of Salafism[1] have become ambiguous in Mali. Leading figures in the movement no longer appear completely committed to Salafi exclusivism—some of their postures even gesture toward what might be called "post-Salafism" (Thurston 2018). Meanwhile, ordinary sympathizers' degree of affiliation to the movement has become fluid and unclear. The idea that "a Salafi is immediately recognizable to others through distinctive dress, social and religious habits and prayer postures, and the content and form of his speech" (Haykel 2009, 33) applies less now in the Sahel than it did previously. Operating as a contested label and multilayered identity throughout the twentieth century, "Wahhabism" was most clearly demarcated and most aggressive against Sufis and others in the 1980s and 1990s. By the 2010s, Salafi-Wahhabi identities had become less stark and distinct than they were a generation ago. At the same time, more diffuse forms of what I call "soft Salafization" are visible: in some Malian contexts, Salafism has become more a set of practices and styles from which lay Muslims choose selectively, rather than an identity that requires total commitment, high visibility, and criticism of other Muslims.

At the level of the leadership and the laity, these ambiguities over Salafi identity are driven by multiple causes, among them: decisions by leading Salafi clerics to pursue alliances or accommodations with non-Salafis; exhaustion among clerics and followers with doctrinal controversies and religious exclusivism; and

Alexander Thurston, *Wahhabi Compromises and "Soft Salafization" in the Sahel* In: *Wahhabism and the World*. Edited by: Peter Mandaville, Oxford University Press. © Oxford University Press 2022.
DOI: 10.1093/oso/9780197532560.003.0012

the growing sense that there are viable and meaningful positions inbetween exclusivist Salafism and the traditionalist package of Ash'arism,[2] Malikism,[3] and Sufism. Moreover, the spread of Salafi-jihadi movements across peripheral regions of the Sahel since the early 2000s has led some prominent Salafi clerics in Sahelian capitals and beyond to take pains to distinguish themselves from the jihadis—even as Salafis' critics accuse jihadis and mainstream Salafis of being in league. The result is a spectrum of Salafi religio-political identities that are partly shaped by creed and political worldview, but also heavily shaped by individual, communal, and political contexts.

There have even been ambiguities concerning the role and meaning of Salafism in northern Mali, where jihadis have had a presence since at least the early 2000s and a substantial presence since the early 2010s (Thurston 2020). On the one hand, jihadis' entrance into the rebellion of 2012 brought dramatic and often tragic enactments of Salafi-jihadi theology on bodies and landscapes as Al-Qaeda-aligned officials ordered the severing of hands and the destruction of Sufi sites. On the other hand, top Malian jihadis have sometimes shown a hint of a very limited theological toleration of other Islamic perspectives, as well as moments of political calculation that have the potential to conflict with Salafi-jihadi doctrine. Meanwhile, the roles of Saudi Arabia, Qatar, and Wahhabism itself remain hotly debated in Mali, even as the available evidence for assessing foreign influence in the conflict zones remains very meager.

Sahelian Wahhabism: A Contested Label and a Complex History

In Sahelian countries such as Mali, Senegal, Mauritania, Burkina Faso, Niger, and Chad, as well as in nearby northern Nigeria, the appearance of so-called reformist movements dates to at least the 1930s. In that decade and especially in the 1940s and 1950s, a loose network of would-be reformers emerged. Some were returning home from North Africa, while others became homegrown counterweights to colonial models of education or to Sufi-dominated local hierarchies. Interestingly, other would-be reformers emerged out of the very same colonial schools that sought to fashion "modernized" Muslims; one example is Nigeria's Abubakar Gumi (1924–1992), whose own colonial education was formative (Gumi with Tsiga 1992).

Sahelian and northern Nigerian reformers, especially in the period before independence, often pursued a relatively generic critique of Sufism and traditionalism, rather than attempting to impose a specifically Wahhabi-Hanbali version of creed and jurisprudence. In the Sahel, as elsewhere in the world, "Wahhabism" largely functioned as an exonym applied by critics of the movement, rather than by its members. The label was favored by French colonial authorities and by leaders of a "counter-reform" movement (Kaba 1974; Brenner 2001; Loimeier 2016).

It is likely that reformers such as Mahmoud Ba (1905–1978) from present-day Mauritania and Cheikh Touré (1925–2005) from present-day Senegal did not consider themselves "Wahhabis" or even Salafis in the same sense as figures whose careers flourished beginning in the late twentieth century, such as Mali's Mahmoud Dicko. The late colonial reformists were more influenced by Islamic modernist currents in North Africa than they were by Saudi Arabian Wahhabism or by later iterations of global Salafism. As Louis Brenner writes, "There is no clear record of Mahmoud Ba having embraced Wahhabism as such, in spite of his continued connections with Saudi Arabia and the Middle East. On the other hand, he had certainly returned from the Middle East with perceptions of Islam and of Islamic religious education which were not easily accepted in the West African milieu" (Brenner 2001, 72).

Colonial authorities considered the reformers threatening partly because of the reformers' actual stances on doctrinal issues, but more so for two other reasons: first, the reformers challenged the social and political dominance of Sufi orders; and second, the schools that reformers created had the potential to outcompete the educational offerings the colonial administration provided. In this atmosphere, the label "Wahhabi" came to function as an epithet for individuals the colonial authorities perceived as troublemakers, rather than as a precise theological descriptor. A sense that the word is a crude and foreign-imposed label has persisted up to the present: in my January 2018 interview in Bamako with Dicko, which turned sour as I attempted to pin down his stances on various theological and jurisprudential matters, he said in exasperation, "Just write that I am a Wahhabi. That is what you are going to call me anyway."

Turning back to the mid-twentieth century, more recognizably Salafi and Saudi-influenced religious leaders emerged in this period, whether from the ranks of returning pilgrims and scholars, early graduates of the Islamic University of Medina, or Sahelians who had settled in the Hijaz but then turned their attention back to their homelands. One figure in the third category was the Mauritanian cleric Muhammad al-Amin al-Shinqiti (d. 1973), who rose to the heights of the Saudi Arabian religious establishment and also became a leading figure on several outreach tours conducted by Saudi Arabia–based institutions such as the Islamic University of Medina and the Muslim World League in the 1960s. Two key Malian figures were 'Abd al-Rahman al-Ifriqi (d. 1957) and Hammad al-Ansari (d. 1997), who took key posts in Saudi Arabian educational institutions (Ahmed 2015). As the influence of Saudi-based Western African clerics, returning Medina graduates, and locally trained Salafis grew, there was rivalry between the "arabisants" (Arabophones) and the Francophone,

Western-educated elite that dominated the civil service, the universities, and other key sectors. Yet across the Sahel and West Africa, Salafi clerics also found allies among certain merchants and Western-educated elites, some of whom had begun to turn a critical eye on Sufi *shaykh*s in the region. These relationships between clerics, merchants, and professionals allowed for the spread of Salafism, including in Sahelian cities such as Bamako and Ouagadougou, and in the northern Nigerian cities of Kano, Kaduna, and Jos (Loimeier 1997; Kane 2003; Ben Amara 2011; Kobo 2012; Thurston 2016).

The twentieth century, and especially the 1970s and 1980s, brought fierce polemics, with Sahelian and West African Salafis turning their full ire on Sufis, especially the Tijaniyya Sufi order. Part of the context for these polemics included not just the expansion of Salafism, but also the expansion of Sufism. Starting in the first half of the twentieth century, charismatic Tijani *shaykh*s such as Ahmad Hamaullah (d. 1943) and Ibrahim Niasse (1900–1975) revitalized the order, bringing it into new areas and often transforming Sufism from an elite scholarly affiliation into a mass movement (Soares 2005; Seesemann 2011).

The Salafis were thus not on the offensive against a passive and stagnant Sufism, but rather competing in a highly dynamic religious field. The most outspoken Salafis sought to undercut the core of Sufi charismatic authority and mass appeal by depicting Sufism, and especially the Tijaniyya, as unorthodox—a borderline, if not outright, heretical mishmash of saint-worship, un-Islamic magic, and con artistry (Gumi 1972). Such struggles were, moreover, not simply doctrinal but also related to a wider question of paradigms of authority: Sufi *shaykh*s, as noted earlier, were typically not just Sufi in orientation but also Ash'ari in creed and Maliki in jurisprudence. As bitter conflicts broke out over issues such as celebrating the Prophet Muhammad's birthday (*mawlid*) or where to position one's hands during the standing portion of prayer, at stake were not just these particular issues but also the Salafi paradigm versus the Sufi-Ash'ari-Maliki paradigm of authority that had dominated parts of northwest Africa for nearly a millennium.

Saudi Arabian support played a crucial role in shaping these struggles, especially between the 1960s and the 1990s. The 1960s brought the creation of crucial new Saudi Arabian or Saudi-backed institutions, particularly the Islamic University of Medina and the Muslim World League. On the Sahelian side, in the 1960s and 1970s a lack of resources, exacerbated by droughts, led Sahelian leaders (including Christian heads of state, such as Chad's François Tombalbaye) to open their arms to Saudi outreach. Various factors made Africa an attractive zone of outreach for Saudi Arabia: African states' independence and attendant influence as a bloc in the United Nations General Assembly; the Arab states' 1967 loss to Israel, which elevated Saudi Arabia's influence over Egypt's but also led Saudi authorities to seek out new means of countering Israeli influence; and a growing awareness among Arab Muslims that Islam had a substantial presence in much of Saharan and sub-Saharan Africa (Haseeb 1985). King Faysal paid personal attention to the Sahel, visiting Mali in 1966 and then stopping in Chad, Niger, Mauritania, and Senegal on a five-nation African tour (the other stop was Uganda) in 1972.

Famine, poverty, and state weakness are part of the wider context for enhanced Saudi Arabian outreach to Mali and the Sahel in the 1970s and 1980s. As Gregory Mann has written, during the Sahelian drought of 1973–1974, "the practice of relief was changing the meaning of government by prying open a new political space of imported initiatives, controlled distribution, and constrained sovereignty" (Mann 2015, 11). Mann's comments largely refer to Western NGOs, but Sahelian and Malian poverty were one factor in making the country a destination for Saudi Arabian and other Gulf aid. Gulf-funded NGOs were, and often still are, highly active in the humanitarian, health, and education sectors, as well as in the construction of mosques (Kaag 2016). The dynamics and effects of Gulf aid in the Sahel are still largely under-researched, although some research has been done on Gulf NGOs in northern Mali, particularly their impact in the 1990s. These NGOs appear to have had some impact in fostering greater competition within the Islamic sphere: in that decade, the global missionary/piety movement Jama'at al-Tabligh (known locally as da'wa) and Salafism both appear to have gained in popularity, partly at the expense of traditionalist clerics and hierarchies, although Tabligh's popularity may have begun to decline even by the early 2000s (Benthall 2006; Gutelius 2007; Lecocq and Schrijver 2007). Conflict in the north, meanwhile, has made it difficult to conduct sustained ethnographic research about the growth of Salafism there and the role of Gulf influence in that growth.

Experimentation and Compromise since the 1990s

Politically, the 1990s were a pivotal decade in the Sahel. Pressures for liberalization and democratization spread in tandem with the end of the Cold War and a surge in popular mobilization. Long-ruling military regimes collapsed in Mali and Niger, giving way to a twenty-year run of civilian-led electoral democracy in the former and to a period of alternating civilian and military control in the latter (Villalón 2010). Elsewhere in the region, relatively new military dictators in Burkina Faso, Chad, and Mauritania retained power but made performative gestures toward the liberal-democratic model. For Muslim clerics and activists, this period brought opportunities to create new media platforms and civic associations, but it also brought the challenge of navigating roles within electoral politics; certain Muslim umbrella bodies also had internal quasi-democratic structures whose mastery posed challenges to clerics.

In contrast to the later, post–Arab Spring period in North Africa, the opening of civil society and electoral politics in the Sahel in the 1990s did not massively empower Islamist political parties. Would-be Islamist parties in the Sahel had weak roots and no infrastructures comparable to the decades of institution-building and recruitment that the Muslim Brotherhood had undertaken in Egypt. Would-be Sahelian Islamists were, in all countries except the Islamic Republic of Mauritania, further constrained by the hegemony of *laïcité*, a French-derived political principle that seeks to protect the state and public life from explicit religiosity and religious influence. The new Sahelian constitutions of the early 1990s, like their antecedents, re-enshrined the *laïc* nature of the state and banned explicitly religious parties (Thurston forthcoming). Even in Mauritania, the only Sahelian country with a legally recognized Islamist party, such parties were banned until 2007. For the most part, activists with Islamist ambitions had to adapt themselves to contexts where the Islamist project had to be pursued indirectly, for example by running Islamist candidates as independents in elections, or by mobilizing Islamist constituencies as pressure blocs rather than as political parties.

As elsewhere in the world (Lacroix 2011), the relationship between Islamism and Salafism has been extremely complex and variable in the Sahel. And as elsewhere, Sahelian Salafis are not merely a subset of Islamists—rather, Salafis adopt a range of theologically informed political stances that range from quietism to jihadism. Yet in Mali, some of the most prominent Salafi or Salafi-leaning figures gravitated toward Islamist organizations or Islamist rhetoric. The Salafi luminary Mahmoud Dicko pursued an Islamist-esque agenda with increasing visibility during the 2000s and 2010s, harnessing the power of a state-backed Islamic council. Yet Dicko made substantial compromises as his political and clerical profile rose. His case instantiates the seeming dilution of Wahhabi exclusivism amid political change and emerging Wahhabi-Sufi détentes and alliances.

Born in 1954 in the Timbuktu Region of northern Mali, Dicko came from a scholarly family. As a young man, he studied in Mauritania and then in Medina. In the Hijaz, he became part of an intellectual lineage of West African Salafis that included one of Dicko's primary teachers, the Mali-born Hammad al-Ansari. In the early 1980s, Dicko became the imam of a mosque in the Badalabougou neighborhood of Mali's capital Bamako. Throughout the 1980s and 1990s, he seems to have been theologically combative, at a time when Salafi-Sufi conflicts broke out in much of West Africa. His career has overlapped with a period of intensifying competition not just between traditionalists and reformists, but between different types of reformists, including Salafis but also Sufi-influenced populist movements (Holder 2012).

Dicko's role began to change when he was elected president of the High Islamic Council of Mali (HCIM) in 2008. Dicko's tenure at the HCIM allowed him to expand his political influence, but also involved many accommodations with non-Salafis. In terms of influence, Dicko and other leading *shaykh*s were instrumental in successfully opposing revisions to Mali's family code between 2009 and 2011, eventually forcing the National Assembly and President Amadou Toumani Touré (in office 2002–2012) to revise the revisions in a much more conservative direction than politicians had initially intended. In the family code debate and at other times, Dicko displayed a capacity to fill "March 26 Stadium" in Bamako with thousands of sympathizers.

In 2012, a multifaceted security and political crisis gripped Mali: a separatist rebellion in the north; a jihadi project that quickly overshadowed the separatists and seized control of key northern cities; a junior officers' coup in the capital; and a humanitarian emergency. The crisis thrust Dicko into the spotlight in new ways—on the one hand, further elevating him as he put himself forward as a potential mediator with jihadis; on the other hand, exposing him to questions about what really distinguished him, ideologically, from those same jihadis. Among the many fraught discourses in the Malian public sphere at that moment, one line of analysis that some commentators pursued was to blame Gulf religious influence for Mali's predicament.

During the campaign for the 2013 presidential elections, Dicko intervened in electoral politics. Indeed, preparations for the elections had begun earlier; the vote was initially scheduled for 2012, but was derailed by the coup that year. Allying himself with the candidate and eventual winner, former prime minister Ibrahim Boubacar Keïta ("IBK"), Dicko helped to create an association called Sabati 2012, which was resuscitated for the 2013 elections. The relationship between Dicko and IBK dated back years, and Dicko had supported Keïta's 2002 presidential bid. The group was headed by a young activist with degrees in law and civil engineering, Moussa Boubacar Bah (b. 1974) (*L'Essor* 2019).

Sabati 2012 was cast in the Francophone media as the electoral vehicle for Wahhabism in Mali. Yet, as some of that very same media coverage noted, Sabati 2012 also benefited from the spiritual and financial patronage of Mali's most prominent Sufi leader, Mohamed Ould Cheicknè, popularly known as the Chérif of Nioro du Sahel (*Le Monde* 2013). Already by the 2013 elections, Dicko was capable of and interesting in forging Salafi-Sufi coalitions in the service of political interests. Moreover, Sabati 2012's memorandum, which it asked candidates to endorse, did not contain any specifically "Wahhabi" provisions—in fact, much of the memorandum did not focus on strictly religious questions at all, but rather on policy recommendations for areas such as public health, conflict resolution, and the justice sector. The few recommendations explicitly relating to religion were the following:

- Create training centers for imams and preachers;
- Fully involve religious leaders in the organization of *hajj*;
- Extend public financing of political parties to core religious structures (*structures faitières religieuses*, which might even be translated as "load-bearing religious structures");
- Make the first day of the *hijri* year a public holiday (*Sabati 2012*, 2013).

The memorandum also included a section on "our ethical and moral values," where "our" was presumably intended to mean the Malian nation, rather than just Sabati 2012. These recommendations were:

- Adapt the content of audiovisual media programs to our sociocultural values;
- Rigorously apply the regulation relating to bars and brothels;
- Forbid all advertising for tobacco and alcohol throughout the entire expanse of Mali's national territory;
- Criminalize all behavior tending to promote homosexuality in Mali (*Sabati 2012*, 2013).

A conservative agenda, no doubt, but not necessarily an exclusively Salafi one. Here it is crucial to note that although Sufism and "moderate Islam" have become synonyms in many Western policymakers' and journalists' minds, many Sufis are deeply socially conservative—Malian Sufis are unlikely, for example, to call for the legalization of homosexuality or the toleration of prostitution in Mali. The memorandum, moreover, did not advance explicitly Salafi positions on any of the major religious controversies—whether to celebrate the Prophet Muhammad's birthday, whether it is permissible to visit the tombs of deceased *shaykh*s, etc.—that have divided Salafis and Sufis in West Africa and beyond. Finally, Sabati 2012 may have had more to do with installing Keïta in office, rather than with Islamization per se. Later, one Sabati 2012 official would state simply, "We created Sabati 2012 with the one goal of supporting the candidate IBK. . . . We did not accord any importance to the other candidates who were promising us that they would make Mali an Islamic state" (Mali Actu 2016).

It is difficult to determine how much weight Sabati 2012 had in Keïta's election victory. Keïta scored nearly 40 percent of the vote in the first round and nearly 80 percent in the second, defeating another former minister from the 1990s, Soumaïla Cissé, and a host of other politicians. Keïta's victory likely owed much to his own long tenure in politics and his image—at the time—as someone with the experience to help Mali turn the page on its crises. Sabati 2012's Bah himself pointed to these factors in determining the organization's choice of endorsement: "Among the criteria that led to the choice of IBK [were] his political weight, his audience among the populations, the fact that he embodies the authority of the State, [and] the acceptance of our memorandum" (Diallo 2013). Whether Sabati 2012's endorsement of Keïta represented a bandwagon effect or an actual factor in his victory, the temporary alignment of prominent clerics' lobbying vehicle and the winning candidate seemed to represent a new level of clerical influence on Malian politics.

Keïta's government did not promote Wahhabism. Within weeks of taking office in September 2013, IBK hosted King Mohamed VI of Morocco in Bamako. They signed two accords—one for the installation of a temporary field hospital in the capital, and another for the Moroccan state to train 500 Malian imams. The latter agreement was explicitly predicated on a valorization of traditionalist Islam, particularly its northwest African variant. Morocco's ambassador to Mali explained, "We share the Maliki rite with Mali. So there is a perfect cohesion when it comes to religious practice of moderate Sunni Islam (*l'islam sunnite modéré*). It's for us to train these imams according to the principles of tolerance relating to Islam" (RFI 2013). Arguably, participation in the imam training program represented the Malian government's tacit acceptance the idea that "Wahhabism" was a core problem in the country. Since the early 2000s, Morocco's own state policies vis-à-vis Islam have focused on the promotion of a traditionalist framework that emphasizes the Maliki jurisprudential school, the Ashʿari theological school, and Sufism—currents that Salafis reject, particularly when it comes to Ashʿarism and Sufism. Moroccan foreign policy has begun to promote this model for other African countries as well (Wainscott 2017, chapter 8).

During Keïta's first term, Dicko experimented with a variety of roles and postures. In April 2014, he was re-elected president of the HCIM, reportedly with the financial and political support of both IBK and the Chérif of Nioro (Keita 2014). Yet relations between the president and both Dicko and the Chérif began to degrade, hitting a new low with the arrival of an influential prime minister, Soumeylou Boubèye Maïga, in late 2017—for example, Dicko, who had been temporarily tasked with opening a dialogue with jihadis in central Mali, was pushed out of that role.

Yet the *shaykhs*' ability to influence politics did not extend to shaping presidential elections—in the 2018 vote, they openly opposed IBK. The president, failing to obtain an outright majority in July, was forced into a second round in August, but he won it handily, once again defeating Soumaïla Cissé. Dicko was not, it turned out, a kingmaker.

The 2019 elections for the HCIM leadership were another instance that showed that there were limits to Dicko's influence. Dicko had reached his two-term limit and—according to his detractors, at least—had overplayed his hand, politicizing and personalizing the HCIM to an extent that neither the Keïta administration nor Dicko's rivals within the HCIM could tolerate. Dicko stepped aside without even designating a clear potential successor. According to one insider (and anti-Dicko) account, the election process then became a kind of bargaining between Sufis and Salafis; the Sufi-leaning Ousmane Madani Haïdara was selected as president, but the Salafis claimed the first vice president slot, the Tijaniyya claimed the second vice president slot, and so forth. If Dicko was unable to hand the HCIM presidency to a person of his choosing, Salafis nevertheless retained influence—albeit on the condition that they consented to divvy up the HCIM cake with Sufis and others.

In Keïta's second term, Dicko continued to make his political influence felt, but now once again in a more oppositional role. In late 2018, he and other clerics forced the government to modify plans for a new school curriculum that included sexual education content deemed inappropriate by clerics. And in February 2019, Dicko and the Chérif held a mass rally to demand Maïga's resignation. The prime minister eventually stepped down in April 2019, following an ethnic massacre in central Mali. Dicko and the Chérif claimed credit. Most dramatically, in the summer of 2020, Dicko led a coalition of clerics, civil society actors, and opposition politicians who held a series of protests demanding Keïta's resignation. The protests became part of the impetus for a military coup against Keïta in August 2020. Dicko's role, however, remained ambivalent throughout the process (including a military-to-civilian transition whose parameters and timetable remained contested as of late 2021, when this volume went to press). After the coup, Dicko stated, "I am going back to the mosque" (*Le Figaro* 2020)— a promise that few believed, but that underlined the fluid nature of his role as someone with profound influence over Malian politics, but also with reluctance to become fully transformed into a politician. Wahhabism, per se, was also a relatively muted theme during the protests of summer 2020; and social media clips showed some of Dicko's supporters dancing, singing, or taking other actions contrary to what Wahhabism is so often assumed to entail.

Salafi-Jihadism in Northern and Central Mali: The Power and Limits of Salafism?

The various jihadi movements that have moved into and emerged out of northern Mali, and then later central Mali, all brand themselves as not merely jihadi but specifically as Salafi-jihadi. Such groups include Al-Qaeda in the Islamic Maghreb (AQIM, founded in the late 1990s and initially known as the Salafi Group for Preaching and Combat), the Movement for Unity and Jihad in West Africa (MUJWA, founded in 2011), Ansar al-Din (Defenders of the Faith, founded in late 2011), Ansar al-Din's Katibat Macina (Macina Battalion, founded circa 2015), the Islamic State in the Greater Sahara (ISGS, founded in

2015), and Jama'at Nusrat al-Islam wa-l-Muslimin (the Group for Supporting Islam and Muslims, JNIM, an AQIM-backed coalition created in 2017). If these organizations sometimes refer opportunistically to precolonial Islamic movements in northwest Africa, from the eleventh–twelfth century Murabitun/ Almoravid empire to the *diina* of Seku Amadu (d. 1845), the contemporary ji-hadi movements nevertheless completely reject Sufism and other hallmarks of those past movements (Kane 2008). Jihadis are even suspected of destroying part of the mausoleum of Seku Amadu himself, in a May 2015 explosion in the central Malian region of Mopti.

Yet certain Malian jihadis have also shown themselves to be politically flex-ible, and therefore also flexible on what are typically assumed to be core Salafi-jihadi doctrines. During the 2012 rebellion, Ansar al-Din initially cooperated with the Tuareg-led separatist organization called the National Movement for the Liberation of Azawad (French acronym MNLA). Ansar al-Din also wel-comed into its own ranks various top northern Malian politicians in 2012, in-cluding sitting parliamentary deputies, and then tolerated—with launching assassinations—those politicians' departure from Ansar al-Din after the French-led intervention called Operation Serval began in January 2013. More recently, in March 2020, JNIM issued a statement at least theoretically accepting an offer from the Malian government to hold a dialogue with the group, with the pre-condition that French troops exit the country (Jama'at Nusrat al-Islam wa-l-Muslimin 2020).

One could attribute such decisions and statements to what some analysts argue is an overall strategy of cunning and sophistication on the part of Al-Qaeda and its affiliates around the world. That is, one could argue that Al-Qaeda and its fellow travelers are stronger than ever, and that part of that strength flows from their (presumed) ability to woo civilians in conflict zones, trick and befuddle governments, and adapt to changing circumstances. On the other hand, however, one could treat these instances of compromise and flexibility as manifestations of a kind of "dilution" of the jihadi project (Bunzel 2017). Put differently, one could argue that in some circumstances, including in northern Mali, Salafi-jihadis are sometimes tacitly acknowledging the untenability of an absolute insistence on principles that are constitutive of Salafi-jihadism itself. These are principles such as *hakimiyya* (for Salafi-jihadis, the absolute sover-eignty of God over earthly legislation) or *al-wala' wa-l-bara'* (loyalty only to those acknowledged as fellow Muslims and disavowal of any perceived un-Islamic actors and systems) (Maher 2016). The Islamic State's fierce criticisms of JNIM's willingness to negotiate with the Malian government (Islamic State 2020, 11) underline the fact that arguably, Al-Qaeda's affiliates are not neces-sarily just becoming savvier but are in some instances moving beyond the horizons of the Salafi-jihadi project.

For further context, the top leader of JNIM is Iyad ag Ghali, a Tuareg politician (in the broadest sense) with a complex history as a nationalist rebel, a government-aligned mediator, a Tabligh activist, a diplomat, and a jihadi. Ag Ghali has, in contrast to the usual Salafi skepticism regarding Tabligh, spoken fondly of his time in that movement (*Al-Masra* 2017). And alongside widespread perceptions that ag Ghali became religiously radicalized throughout the 1990s and 2000s, some of his maneuvers through Ansar al-Din and JNIM arguably represent the same political instincts he showed in earlier guises. It appears unlikely that Salafi-jihadism is merely a cloak that figures such as ag Ghali wear or doff at will—but it also appears unlikely that figures such as ag Ghali are completely trapped by Salafi-jihadism in their thinking and their choices.

What influence has Saudi Arabia, or the Arab Gulf more broadly, had over the course of the jihadi insurgency in the north and the center of Mali? First of all, even before assessing foreign influence, it appears that there was no linear trajectory leading from the growth of the Salafism to the rise of Salafi-jihadism. Mathieu Pellerin, making a distinction between Salafism and Wahhabism, writes, "In northern Mali, the sole region where the followers of Wahhabi Islam were numerous before the 2012 crisis was the region of Gao." Pellerin goes on to note that although some Wahhabis from the later infamous village of Kadji gravitated toward MUJWA when it took control of Gao in 2012, their adherence was essentially "naïve," reflecting a limited knowledge of MUJWA and its goals; meanwhile, prominent Wahhabis in Gao publicly rejected the jihadist project (2017, 14–15). As Michael Kenney has written regarding the very different context of the United Kingdom, the notion of a single "conveyor belt" leading from hardline religiosity to violent action is simplistic and inaccurate (2018, 28–29).

Second, there have been more rumors of Qatari influence than Saudi Arabian influence in the north. If Saudi Arabia is sometimes blamed in a generic (but I think much too sweeping) way, accused of planting a Wahhabi seed that blossomed into a jihadi tree (again, a very problematic argument), then Qatar is accused much more specifically of directly promoting the jihadi movements in the north. In 2012 and 2013, several French newspapers and politicians, including Marine Le Pen, accused Qatar of supporting multiple armed movements, including jihadis (France24 2013). These accusations were discussed by Anglophone outlets and think tanks as well. Yet the accusations are extremely difficult to substantiate. Meanwhile, the Qatari government has periodically condemned terrorist attacks in Mali (Qatar Ministry of Foreign Affairs 2018).

Third, Malian jihadis have sometimes explicitly condemned Saudi Arabia and other Gulf countries. In 2017, a heated exchange broke out between the central Malian jihadi leader Amadou Kouffa and the former speaker of the National Assembly, Ali Nouhoum Diallo. The two men belong to the same ethnic group, the Peul, but Diallo's efforts to open a dialogue with Kouffa quickly led to a war of words. After hearing that Diallo had called him a "slave of the Arabs," Kouffa responded with a long audio message in which he said, in one portion:

> Which Arabs are our masters? Saudi, Emirati, Qatari, Iraqi, Iranian [sic]? Are we their allies? Go ask these countries the number of Islamist militants imprisoned in their jails. Islamist militants are imprisoned in all the Arab countries from Morocco to [Saudi] Arabia.... We are hunted down in Bamako, in [Saudi] Arabia, in the Emirates, in Qatar, and everywhere in the world: the prison or the tomb. The different donations in kind and in cash on the part of the monarchies of the Gulf (Saudi Arabia, United Arab Emirates, Kuwait, Qatar) that the government of Mali receives—has one ever provided for the portion of the Malian jihadists? Ask your scholars who are, incidentally, the distributors of these gifts—have they ever once thought of the Malian jihadists in this division? Never! (Kouffa/Sow 2017, n.p.)

A public relations maneuver, perhaps—but more likely, I think, a reminder that some jihadists consider the Gulf countries to be just as corrupted as other regimes in the Muslim-majority world.

In the same statement, moreover, Kouffa went from denouncing Diallo and other interlocutors to hinting that some kind of dialogue might be possible—especially if Salafi clerics such as Mahmoud Dicko were willing to act as mediators. There is a reminder here of certain Malian jihadists' tentative curiosity about exploring political paths that might lead beyond Salafi-jihadi exclusivism. And there is an indication that the compromises Dicko has himself made in the more mainstream political arena have not destroyed his theological credibility with jihadis.

Conclusion: A Soft Salafization?

In this conclusion I would like to return briefly to topics more connected with nonviolent Salafism than with Salafi-jihadism. If leading lights of the Salafi da'wa in the Sahel have become less recognizably Salafi than they were twenty or thirty years ago, and if such figures have become more rather than less prone to compromise and collaborate with Sufis, this does not mean that Salafi influence has waned in the region. Rather, Salafi influence may have widened but simultaneously weakened: that is, more people are influenced by Salafism previously, but to a lesser degree than the Salafi adherents of yesteryear.

In other words, a "soft Salafization" may be taking place. Such a trend would be hard to measure quantitatively, but in ethnographic terms I have observed that at least in Nouakchott and Bamako, it is a minority of mosque congregants who pray with their arms hanging in *sadl*, the traditionalist Maliki posture; many more pray with hands folded across their chests in *qabd*, and it is common to see congregants lifting their hands not just at the start of prayer, as all Muslims do, but also before and after bowing; such lifting of the hands is, again, not part of the traditionalist Maliki prayer style. It is often the older congregants, if any, who continue to pray in *sadl*. Some of this shift, in my view, represents Salafization—but a soft Salafization, because the young men praying in *qabd* and lifting their hands often lack the long beards and short trousers so often associated with Salafism. Such young men (and women)—and a number of not-so-young men and women—may not necessarily think of themselves as Salafis, but their religious practice is marked by the headway that Salafis have made against Maliki traditionalism, Sufism, and other opponents.

Another sign of soft Salafization is what people read. Here, again, it is hard to assemble compelling quantitative data. Yet in perusing the bookshops of Nouakchott and Bamako, I have been struck by how easy it is to find books of *hadith*, which are not at all the exclusive property of Salafism but which are its textual currency. Simultaneously, it seems to be getting a bit harder to find advanced Maliki materials. Even in Sufi-saturated Dakar, the capital of Senegal, this trend appears to some extent. In June 2019, I stepped into a well-stocked Islamic bookstore that was empty of other customers. The clerk, who may also have been the manager or owner, appeared to be well into middle age. He looked at me in wonderment when I requested *Al-Fawakih al-Dawani*, a commentary by the Maliki scholar Ahmad al-Nafrawi (d. 1810/1811). He pulled a dusty copy with yellowed pages from a high shelf and told me, "No one reads these books anymore." The massive availability of printed *hadith* texts, especially the accessible compilations by figures such as Yahya bin Sharaf al-Nawawi (1233–1277) and Ahmad bin Hajar al-'Asqalani (1372–1449), seems to have had a dual impact: more laypeople study Islamic texts than ever before, and these lay audiences prefer *hadith* to classical *fiqh* (jurisprudence). Yet if this is Salafization it is, once again, a soft Salafization. The audiences who consume *hadith* texts are not necessarily interested in pronouncing *takfir* against Sufis or even in abandoning Sufism, Malikism, and other schools altogether.

A final interesting question is whether the *shaykhs* described in this chapter are shaping or following trends in Muslim publics at large. Are figures such as Dicko softening their stances vis-à-vis other Muslims and then bringing followers along with them, or are these *shaykhs* responding to their audiences' fatigue or even boredom with the debates that raged in the 1980s and 1990s in the region? The answer to this question will loom large for the future of Salafism in the Sahel and beyond.

Notes

1. My own usage defines "Salafism" as the contemporary, global movement of ultra-Sunni literalism, while restricting the term "Wahhabism" to the Saudi Arabian religious establishment, especially during the period between the life of Muhammad ibn ʿAbd al-Wahhab (1703–1792) and the Grand Mufti Muhammad bin Ibrahim Al al-Shaykh (1893–1969).
2. Ashʿarism is a major Sunni theological school. Salafis denounce Ashʿaris' metaphorical readings of certain Qurʾanic descriptions of God's attributes, as well as various other Ashʿari positions.
3. Malikism is one of the four main Sunni legal schools. Some Salafis regard the legal schools as overly rigid and as disconnected from the study of the original source texts, namely Qurʾan and *hadith*.

References

Ahmed, Baba. 2011. 'Mali: Voyage au coeur du Bamako wahhabite'. *Jeune Afrique*. October 11, 2011. https://www.jeuneafrique.com/179054/societe/mali-voyage-au-coeur-du-bamako-wahhabite/.

Ahmed, Chanfi. 2015. *West African ʿUlamāʾ and Salafism in Mecca and Medina: Jawâb al-Ifrîqî, the Response of the African*. Leiden: Brill.

Ben Amara, Ramzi. 2011. *The Izala Movement in Nigeria: Its Split, Relationship to Sufis and Perception of Sharīʿa Re-Implementation*. PhD dissertation, Bayreuth University.

Benthall, Jonathan. 2006. "Islamic Aid in a North Malian Enclave." *Anthropology Today* 22(4) (August): 19–21.

Brenner, Louis. 2001. *Controlling Knowledge: Religion, Power, and Schooling in a West African Muslim Society*. Bloomington: Indiana University Press.

Bunzel, Cole. 2017. "Diluting Jihad: Tahrir al-Sham and the Concerns of Abu Muhammad al-Maqdisi." *Jihadica*. March 29, 2017. http://www.jihadica.com/diluting-jihad/.

Diallo, Youssouf. 2013. "Présidentielle 2013: Le Mouvement Sabati 2012 tranche pour IBK." *Mali Actu*, July 22, 2013. https://maliactu.net/presidentielle-2013-le-mouvement-sabati-2012-tranche-pour-ibk-2/.

L'Essor. 2019. "Mali: Moussa Boubacar Bah." May 7, 2019. https://maliactu.net/mali-moussa-boubacar-bah-secretaire-detat-aupres-du-ministre-de-leducation-nationale-charge-de-la-promotion-et-de-lintegration-de-lenseignement-bilingue/.

Le Figaro. 2020. "Mali: 'Je retourne à la mosquée,' affirme l'imam Dicko, figure de l'opposition, après la chute du président Keïta." August 21, 2020. https://www.lefigaro.fr/flash-actu/mali-je-retourne-a-la-mosquee-affirme-l-imam-dicko-figure-de-l-opposition-apres-la-chute-du-president-keita-20200821.

France24. 2013. "Is Qatar Fuelling the Crisis in North Mali?" January 21, 2013. https://www.france24.com/en/20130121-qatar-mali-france-ansar-dine-mnla-al-qaeda-sunni-islam-doha.

Gumi, Abubakar. 1972. *Al-ʿAqida al-Sahiha bi-Muwafaqat al-Shariʿa*. Beirut: no publisher.

Gumi, Abubakar, with Ismaila Tsiga. 1992. *Where I Stand*. Ibadan: Spectrum Books.

Gutelius, David. 2007. "Islam in Northern Mali and the War on Terror." *Journal of Contemporary African Studies* 25(1) (January): 59–76.

Haseeb, Khair El-Din, ed. 1985. *The Arabs and Africa*. London; Sydney; Dover, NH: Centre for Arab Unity Studies.

Haykel, Bernard. 2009. "On the Nature of Salafi Thought and Action." In *Global Salafism: Islam's New Religious Movement*, edited by Roel Meijer, 33–58. New York: Columbia University Press.

Holder, Gilles. 2012. "Chérif Ousmane Madani Haïdara et l'association islamique Ançar Dine: Un réformisme malien populaire en quête d'autonomie." *Cahiers d'Études Africaines* 206–207: 389–425.

Islamic State. 2020. "'Qa'idat Mali' Musta'idda 'Li-l-Hiwar' ma'a al-Hukuma wa-Tulammih anna 'al-Niza'' baynahuma 'Faradatha Faransa!.'" *Al-Naba'* 225(March 12): 11. https://jihadology.net/wp-content/uploads/_pda/2020/03/The-Islamic-State-al-Nabā'-Newsletter-225.pdf.

Jama'at Nusrat al-Islam wa-l-Muslimin. 2020. "Bayan bi-Sha'n Da'awat al-Tafawud." March 8, 2020. https://twitter.com/MENASTREAM/status/1236702975374036992/photo/2.

Kaag, Mayke. 2016. "Islamic Charities from the Arab World in Africa: Intercultural Encounters of Humanitarianism and Morality." In *Humanitarianism and Challenges of Cooperation*, edited by Volker Heins, Kai Koddenbrock, and Christine Unrau, 155–167. New York: Routledge.

Kaba, Lansiné. 1974. *The Wahhabiyya: Islamic Reform and Politics in French West Africa*. Evanston, IL: Northwestern University Press.

Kane, Ousmane. 2003. *Muslim Modernity in Postcolonial Nigeria: A Study of the Society for the Removal and Reinstatement of Tradition*. Leiden: Brill.

Kane, Ousmane. 2008. "Islamism: What Is New, What Is Not? Lessons from West Africa." *African Journal of International Affairs* 11(2): 157–187.

Keita, Sinaly. 2014. "Haut conseil islamique du Mali: IBK intronise Mahamoud Dicko avec 25 millions Fcfa." *Le Reporter*. April 22, 2014. https://maliactu.net/haut-conseil-islamique-du-mali-ibk-intronise-mahamoud-dicko-avec-25-millions-fcfa/.

Kenney, Michael. 2018. *The Islamic State in Britain: Radicalization and Resilience in an Activist Network*. Cambridge: Cambridge University Press.

Kobo, Ousman. 2012. *Unveiling Modernity in Twentieth-Century West African Islamic Reforms*. Leiden: Brill.

Kouffa, Amadou. 2017. Untitled audio recording. Unpublished translation from Fulfulde to French by Oumar Sow.

Lacroix, Stéphane. 2011. *Awakening Islam: The Politics of Religious Dissent in Contemporary Saudi Arabia*. Translated by George Holoch. Cambridge, MA: Harvard University Press.

Lecocq, Baz, and Paul Schrijver. 2007. "The War on Terror in a Haze of Dust: Potholes and Pitfalls on the Saharan Front." *Journal of Contemporary African Studies* 25(1) (January): 141–166.

Loimeier, Roman. 1997. *Islamic Reform and Political Change in Northern Nigeria*. Evanston, IL: Northwestern University Press.

Loimeier, Roman. 2016. *Islamic Reform in Twentieth-Century Africa*. Edinburgh: Edinburgh University Press.

Maher, Shiraz. 2016. *Salafi-Jihadism: The History of an Idea*. Oxford: Oxford University Press.

Mali Actu. 2016. "'Nous avons crée Sabati 2012 uniquement pour soutenir le candidat IBK à la demande de Mahmoud Dicko' (Chouala Haidara, vice président de Sabati 2012)." January 10, 2016. https://maliactu.net/nous-avons-cree-sabati-2012-uniquem

ent-pour-soutenir-le-candidat-ibk-a-la-demande-de-mahmoud-dicko-chouala-haid ara-vice-president-de-sabati-2012/.

Mann, Gregory. 2015. *From Empires to NGOs in the West Africa Sahel: The Road to Nongovernmentality*. Cambridge: Cambridge University Press.

Al-Masra. 2017. "'Al-Masra' Tuhawir al-Shaykh Aba al-Fadl Iyad Ghali." *Al-Masra* 45(April 3): 4. https://azelin.files.wordpress.com/2017/04/al-masracc84-newspaper-45.pdf.

Le Monde. 2013. "Au Mali, les wahhabites de Sabati veulent peser sur la présidentielle." July 27, 2013. https://www.lemonde.fr/afrique/article/2013/07/27/au-mali-les-wah habites-de-sabati-veulent-peser-sur-la-presidentielle_3454516_3212.html.

Pellerin, Mathieu. 2017. "Les trajectoires de radicalisation religieuse au Sahel." IFRI, February. https://www.ifri.org/sites/default/files/atoms/files/pellerin_radicalisation_ religieuse_sahel_2017.pdf.

Qatar Ministry of Foreign Affairs. 2018. "Qatar Condemns Explosion in Northern Mali." November 13, 2018. https://www.mofa.gov.qa/en/statements/qatar-condemns-explos ion-in-northern-mali.

RFI. 2013. "Mali: Mohammed VI et IBK lancent deux projets de cooperation." September 21, 2013. http://www.rfi.fr/afrique/20130921-mali-mohamed-vi-ibk-lancent-deux-projets-cooperation-maroc-imams.

Sabati 2012. 2013. "Mémorandum du Mouvement Sabati 2012 aux candidats." July. https://www.maliweb.net/societe/memorandum-du-mouvement-sabati-2012-aux-candidats-158754.html.

Seesemann, Rüdiger. 2011. *The Divine Flood: Ibrahim Niasse and the Roots of a Twentieth-century Sufi Revival*. Oxford: Oxford University Press.

Soares, Benjamin. 2005. *Islam and the Prayer Economy: History and Authority in a Malian Town*. Ann Arbor,: University of Michigan Press.

Thurston, Alexander. 2016. *Salafism in Nigeria: Islam, Preaching and Politics*. Cambridge: Cambridge University Press.

Thurston, Alexander. 2018. "An Emerging Post-Salafi Current in West Africa and Beyond." *The Maydan*, October 15, 2018. https://www.themaydan.com/2018/10/ emerging-post-salafi-current-west-africa-beyond/.

Thurston, Alexander. 2020. *Jihadists of North Africa and the Sahel: Local Politics and Rebel Groups*. Cambridge: Cambridge University Press.

Thurston, Alexander. Forthcoming. "Negotiating Secularism in the Sahel." In *The Oxford Handbook of the African Sahel*, edited by Léonardo Villalón. Oxford: Oxford University Press.

Villalón, Leonardo. "From Argument to Negotiation: Constructing Democracy in African Muslim Contexts." *Comparative Politics* 42(4) (July): 375–393.

Wainscott, Ann. 2017. *Bureaucratizing Islam: Morocco and the War on Terror*. Cambridge: Cambridge University Press.

13

Unpacking the Saudi-Salafi Connection in Egypt

Stéphane Lacroix

A common trope in Middle Eastern politics is to portray Salafis across the region as being remote-controlled by the Saudi state. This reading was commonly applied to Egypt after 2011, in order to explain the quick rise and apparently bizarre political choices made by the largest Salafi political party, the Nour Party.[1] In the run-up to the country's first free and fair presidential election, the party did all it could to undermine Muslim Brotherhood candidate Muhammad Morsi, and, despite its rigid religious conservatism, it decided for that purpose to back a liberal Islamist candidate, ʿAbd al-Munʿim Abu al-Futuh. Later, on July 3, 2013, a year into the Morsi presidency, the Nour Party openly supported the military coup against the elected president, and it has since then been the only Islamist party allowed to sit in Egypt's parliament. For some, this was the ultimate proof of the Salafis' alignment with Riyadh: the Saudis, who were a key external force behind the coup, hated the Brothers and wanted them out of office, and so Egypt's Salafis had merely done what their "masters" had told them to. The main problem with this reading is that it ignores the internal complexity of Egypt's Salafi movement and, more importantly, the ambiguities of its ties to Saudi Arabia.

The purpose of this chapter is thus twofold. First, it aims at historicizing the Salafi movement in Egypt in order to present a more nuanced account of its diversity and to properly introduce the diverse nuances of its relationship to the Saudi kingdom. Second, it aims to show that the most organized and grassroots part of Egypt's Salafi movement, the Salafi Call (*al-daʿwa al-salafiyya*), which is also the Nour Party's mother organization, has since its creation in the late 1970s not enjoyed particularly close ties to the Saudi kingdom. Its political behavior thus needs to be accounted for as the reflection of domestic political calculations, without resorting to the alleged influence of external actors.

Stéphane Lacroix, *Unpacking the Saudi-Salafi Connection in Egypt* In: *Wahhabism and the World.* Edited by: Peter Mandaville, Oxford University Press. © Oxford University Press 2022. DOI: 10.1093/oso/9780197532560.003.0013

Early Connections: Muhammad Rashid Rida
and Ansar al-Sunna

There is no doubt that the Salafi ideology that spread across the Middle East throughout the twentieth century owes a lot to Saudi Arabia. Its main modern inspiration is Muhammad bin 'Abd al-Wahhab (1703–1792), who cofounded the Saudi state in 1744 together with Muhammad bin Sa'ud, and whose "Book of Tawhid" (*kitab al-tawhid*) remains core reading for all Salafis. Ibn 'Abd al-Wahhab's message relies on his interpretation of the works of medieval scholars, including, most importantly, Ahmad Taqi al-Din bin Taymiyya (1263–1328).[2] Those scholars were first introduced to the broader Egyptian public in the 1920s as part of a concerted effort carried out by a group of reformist scholars and intellectuals, the most prominent of whom was Muhammad Rashid Rida (1865–1935). Though Rida had first shown modernist tendencies inherited from his erstwhile teacher Muhammad 'Abduh (1849–1905),[3] he had grown more conservative in the wake of World War I. This conservative turn coincided with Rida's growing interest in the development of the Saudi state under Sultan (who adopted the title of king in 1932) 'Abd al-'Aziz bin Sa'ud (1902–1953) (Lauzière 2015, 64). At a time when most of the Islamic world was under the yoke of colonial powers, Saudi Arabia remained one of the very few Muslim countries free from foreign interference, with a political system derived from Islam instead of European political institutions. 'Abd al-'Aziz's conquest of the holy two cities of Mecca and Medina in 1924 would only make him more legitimate in the eyes of Rida.

The two men, Rashid Rida and 'Abd al-'Aziz bin Sa'ud, established a direct relationship of mutual admiration and friendship, and Rida started receiving money grants from 'Abd al-'Aziz (Al-Samhan 2011, 141–148). Saudi Arabia was a poor country then—oil would only be exploited there from the 1930s onward, and the income derived from it would only become significant in the 1950s—so the sums were relatively small, but they allowed Rida to keep his publishing house afloat. For 'Abd al-'Aziz, Rida was a precious ally: in the 1920s, Saudi Arabia was widely considered with suspicion across the Muslim world, and its brand of Islam was often considered "extremist" or "heretic," as it was described by the pro-Ottoman scholars who had written against it since its early days (Commins 2006, 30, 41). Yet, in the wake of his conquest of the holy cities, 'Abd al-'Aziz was seeking normalization with his neighbors and recognition from the region's foreign powers, and for that purpose the support of a shrewd and respected intellectual like Rida was crucial (Commins 2006, 138–139). Throughout the 1920s, Rida's journal—the widely read *al-Manar*—would reflect its editor's growing interest in the Saudi political experiment, which he defended vigorously (Rida 1925, 6–7). In parallel, Rida grew interested in the religious message propagated by the scholars of the Saudi state, to the point of adopting part of their language and some of their main ideas (Rida 1925, 7–8). Rida would use the printing press of *al-Manar* to publish for the Egyptian public books by Ibn Taymiyya and his disciples such Ibn al-Qayyim al-Jawziyya, as well as by Saudi scholars—many of which had not been circulated in Egypt before.

Muhammad Rashid Rida was not the only intellectual or scholar in Egypt to follow that path. Muhibb al-Din al-Khatib, another Syrian who ran the so-called Salafiyya bookstore and publishing house, also played a similar role. Yet, the member of Rida's circle who pushed the logic of embracing the Saudi political and religious discourse the furthest was Muhammad Hamid al-Fiqi, a former student of Rida. In 1926, he founded an organization called Ansar al-Sunna al-Muhammadiyya ("The Supporters of the Prophetic Tradition," here Ansar al-Sunna) whose stated goal was to promote the Salafi message in Egypt (Al-Tahir 2004). The organization was apparently established with the financial support of Saudi Arabia's ambassador to Egypt (Shahada 2013), and al-Fiqi himself would, not long after the creation of Ansar al-Sunna, spend a few years working in Saudi Arabia, where 'Abd al-'Aziz put him in charge, first of a magazine, and later of the newly founded directorate of edition and publication. For the decades to come, Ansar al-Sunna remained closely tied to the Saudi kingdom to the extent that, during a visit to Cairo in 1954, Prince Nayef bin 'Abd al-'Aziz famously referred to the organization as "our ambassadors" (*sufara'una*) (Al-Sayyid 2009, 153–154). In its publications, notably its journals *al-Hadi al-Nabawi* (until 1967) and *al-Tawhid* (from 1973), Ansar al-Sunna constantly praised the Saudi political-religious model, advising Egyptian rulers to take inspiration from it. Individual Ansar al-Sunna scholars also glorified Saudi Arabia and its figures in their books, as in Muhammad al-Fiqi's hagiographic biography of 'Abd al-'Aziz bin Sa'ud entitled "Flower in the Gardens: The Biography of the Just Imam 'Abd al-'Aziz al-Faysal Al Sa'ud," or Muhammad Khalil al-Harras's "The Wahhabi Movement: A Response to Muhammad al-Bahi's Article Criticizing Wahhabism" (Al-Fiqi 2008; Harras 1985).

Ansar al-Sunna, whose membership grew from less than a thousand before World War II to about ten thousand members (and a thousand mosques under its control) in the 2000s (Munib 2010, 55), has continued throughout the decades to act as an Egyptian satellite of both the Saudi political and religious establishments. It was common for members of the association to spend extended periods of time working in Saudi Arabia, and some of its figures even had stellar careers in the Saudi religious establishment. Such was the case with 'Abd al-Razzaq 'Afifi, who was briefly president of Ansar al-Sunna from 1959 to 1960 and ended his career as a member of the kingdom's highest religious body, the Committee of Senior Scholars (*hay'at kibar al-'ulama*), where he was appointed in 1971. This makes Ansar al-Sunna an exception from the perspective of Saudi religious scholars. Though starting in the 1950s the Saudi religious establishment partnered with a large number of Islamic movements across the Muslim world, their members were usually kept on the margins of the Saudi religious sphere. Only Ansar al-Sunna's members were considered as peers and could be integrated to the kingdom's highest religious bodies and its religious universities' departments of creed ('aqida), which represented the strongholds of the Wahhabi religious establishment (Lacroix 2011, 47).

In addition, there is evidence that Ansar al-Sunna continued to receive funding from Saudi Arabia—either the Saudi state or Saudi individuals—during the many decades of its existence. King 'Abd al-'Aziz paid part of the costs of the building hosting the association (Al-Tahir 2004, 91). And in 1954, for instance, Prince Nayef, during his aforementioned visit, pledged to give a yearly grant of 200 pounds from his personal wealth to the association (Al-Sayyid 2009, 153). Saudi Arabia was, however, not the only foreign country funding Ansar al-Sunna. An investigation run by a special commission established in 2011 in the wake of the Egyptian revolution proved that Ansar al-Sunna had received hundreds of millions of pounds from the Qatari Eid Charity Foundation and the Kuwaiti Association for the Revival of Islamic Heritage (both are Salafi organizations with close ties to the Saudi religious establishment) (Al-nas al-kamil 2012).

One might think that those links and the organization's openly pro-Saudi stance were to eventually harm Ansar al-Sunna's standing in Egypt, especially since Egypt and Saudi Arabia were on opposite sides of the "Arab cold war" that raged through the region in the 1950s and 1960s. Yet, in Egypt, Ansar al-Sunna's stance—in line with Wahhabi teachings that call for obedience to the rulers (ta'at wali al-amr)—was to adopt an unambiguously loyalist position toward the successive regimes. Ansar al-Sunna publications glorified Egyptian kings until 1952, for instance asking God to bless "the always wise" King Farouk in the wake of his coronation in 1936 (Al-Sayyid 2009, 65–67). And they did the same with the free officers behind the 1952 Egyptian revolution, whom they described as "heroes sent by God to save the country from despotic tyrants and purify it from corruption" (Al-Sayyid 2009, 119).

This meant that the successive regimes had little reason to crack down on the organization, and Gamal 'Abd al-Nasser might even have thought them as useful at a time when the Saudi propaganda machine was attacking his religious credentials and calling him an "atheist" (Schulze 1990, 162). Under Nasser, they were even one of the very few religious organizations to remain intact after the 1954 repression against the Muslim Brotherhood. Thus, apart from a small period from 1967 to 1972 when Ansar al-Sunna was forced to merge with another religious organization called al-Jam'iyya al-Shar'iyya (which, as a result, would also end up adopting more obvious Salafi undertones, especially in matters of creed) (Al-Tahir 2004, 148), Ansar al-Sunna has been active in Egypt continuously for almost a hundred years.

Apart from running mosques, Ansar al-Sunna's most visible activity was publishing important works of Salafi literature—thereby continuing what Rida and al-Khatib had started—as well as its own magazines. Its unrelenting publishing efforts would eventually contribute to the transformation of the mainstream religious corpus used in Egypt. Books by Ibn Taymiyya, Ibn Qayyim al-Jawziyya, and even Muhammad bin 'Abd al-Wahhab would, throughout the decades, come to exert increasing influence over Egypt's religious sphere, thereby redefining what is seen as religiously orthodox. Ideas promoted by Ansar al-Sunna, such as the un-Islamic nature of Sufism and Shi'ism, as well as certain ultra-conservative social practices favored by the organization (together with its counterpart al-Jam'iyya al-Shar'iyya), also gained enormous ground among the Egyptian public. The neutering and eventual co-optation of al-Azhar by the Nasserist state, the general decline of Sufism, together with the relentless attempts at destroying the Muslim Brotherhood and banning their books in the 1950s and 1960s, weakened all possible counter-discourses. Thus, well before the 1970s onslaught of Saudi religious influence across the Islamic world, conservative circles in Egypt were already increasingly influenced by elements of a Salafi worldview.

The Complexification of Egyptian Salafism

Egypt's "Islamic Awakening" in the 1970s has been the subject of many studies and books.[4] They tend to focus on this Awakening's two main manifestations during that decade: the rise of Islamist student activists, organized in what became known as *jama'at islamiyya* ("Islamic groups"); and the development of a clandestine milieu of radical activists pledging to overthrow the regime and establish an Islamic state. It is the convergence of both that eventually led to the assassination of President Anwar al-Sadat in 1981. Most of the existing academic literature insists on the influence exerted by the ideas of radical Muslim Brotherhood ideologue Sayyid Qutb on that generation of activists. Yet, the impact of Salafi ideas on that generation has not been sufficiently noted. In a forthcoming book, I am making the argument that the initial religious socialization of many of those activists was deeply Salafi. One key reason for this was that the only non-state Islam available under Nasser was Salafi Islam, since Ansar al-Sunna and al-Jam'iyya al-Shar'iyya (whose Salafi undertones had only grown more obvious as a result of its state-led rapprochement with the former) were among the only Islamic associations able to maintain a social presence during those years, and their mosques were where independent-minded Muslims would seek religious training. The Salafi outlook was most obvious among *jama'at islamiyya* members, whose initial activism on Egyptian campuses was all about fighting gender-mixing, denouncing the ills of Sufism, and promoting the adoption of what they called *al-hadi al-zahir* (roughly translated as "ostentatious piety," meaning "Salafi" dress and attitudes). Only at a later stage would those groups become politicized, through—but not exclusively—their intellectual encounter with the ideas of Sayyid Qutb.[5]

This is an important argument because it undermines the widespread idea that Salafism in Egypt merely grew out of the religious influence exerted by Saudi Arabia in the 1970s, either indirectly through the migration of Egyptians moving for work in Saudi Arabia, or directly through the kingdom's well-funded pros-elytization bodies, the Muslim World League, the World Assembly of Muslim Youth, and the Islamic University of Medina. My point is not to say that these bodies did not matter on the ground. They certainly had an impact, although a number of caveats must be added. An important one is that these bodies, which had been formed at the height of King Faysal's campaign for "Islamic solidarity" (*al-tadamun al-islami*) in the early 1960s, were, throughout the 1970s and 1980s, far from being purely Salafi bodies. For instance, many of the World Assembly of Muslim Youth and the Muslim World League's leadership came from the Muslim Brotherhood, either foreign Brothers or Saudi Brothers (Lacroix 2011, 68; Schulze 1990). And in Egypt, the two organizations' ties to the Muslim Brotherhood were at least as strong as they were to Salafis. Though these organizations were active in supporting Egypt's broader "Islamic Awakening," they thus cannot be singled out as an explanation for the particular growth of Egypt's Salafi movement. What I have been willing to show in the previous paragraphs is that, first, Salafism had been present in Egypt since the 1920s, and its influence had si-lently been growing during the subsequent decades, including the Nasser period. And second, 1970s Egyptian Islamist activists were partly the product of that si-lent influence, which means that most of them became Salafi before traveling to Saudi Arabia or partnering with Saudi religious associations. To be sure, many of them would later spend time in Saudi Arabia, but they would go as Salafis (and sometimes being Salafi is what opened doors for them in the kingdom), not the other way around.

The release of the imprisoned leaders of the Muslim Brotherhood in 1974 made the situation more complex. Faced with a new generation of activists that had developed independently from them, the Brothers were keen on trying to assimilate them to rebuild their organization.[6] Thus, the Brothers established dialogues with the leaders of the campus groups, and slowly convinced them to join, despite those leaders' initial reluctance because the Brothers were seen as too "liberal." Around 1978–1979, a clarification happened among the *jama'at islamiyya*: most of their leaders, and the members under their authority, announced that they were joining the Muslim Brotherhood (some actually did so with the explicit aim of correcting the Muslim Brotherhood's path in a Salafi way) (interview with Khalid Da'ud, 2013, Alexandria, January). Certain chapters of the *jama'at islamiyya* refused the decision however, arguing that the Brothers were not Salafi enough. In Upper Egypt, most of the *jama'at islamiyya*'s members went their own way, forming the group that would later be called al-Jama'a al-Islamiyya (in the singular form). They blended a Salafi outlook and Salafi conceptions of creed with Sayyid Qutb's revolutionary political ideas. The group was heavily involved in the assassination of al-Sadat in 1981, and many of its members were arrested—though the group came back with added strength in the 1980s. In Alexandria, another group pledged to follow the "Salafi method" (*al-manhaj al-salafi*), cleansed of any Muslim Brotherhood ideological influence, and created "the Salafi school" (*al-madrasa al-salafiyya*), which would be renamed "the Salafi Call" (*al-da'wa al-salafiyya*) in 1984 (Shalata 2015).

In the 1980s, al-Jama'a al-Islamiyya and the Salafi Call were thus, among the new generation of the activists, the two main organized flag bearers of Salafism in Egypt. Both had the aim of becoming mass movements, and adopted modes of socialization, mobilization, and organization inherited from their experience as student activists and from their encounters with the Muslim Brotherhood.[7] They established bodies of governance, sections devoted to different activities, and chapters across Egypt. They were extremely proactive in their recruitment efforts. This is what made them radically different from Ansar al-Sunna, which remained a traditional organization with little outreach. Gradually the two became the loudest Salafi voices in Egypt, with very different understandings of Salafism and its patterns of action: the Salafi Call shunned all political activism, and concentrated instead on preaching and teaching through the network of mosques that the organization controlled; whereas al-Jama'a al-Islamiyya, though also preaching and teaching to expand its religious base, advocated the necessity of "correcting vice by force" (*taghyir al-munkar bi-l-yad*), thereby acting as moral vigilantes (*Mithaq al-'amal al-islami* 1984). This would put al-Jama'a al-Islamiyya on a collision course with the Egyptian state, and after a few years of relative peace, a bloody confrontation between the two started that would last until the late 1990s, when the group announced a series of revisions to its ideology, renouncing the use of violence and adopting an approach to Salafism quite similar to the one followed by the Salafi Call.

After the 1980s, other smaller Salafi groups emerged across the country, generally organized around the authority of a particular *shaykh*. Instead of going into the details of those different groups, the following paragraphs will concentrate on the relationship that the two main Salafi mass movements—the Salafi Call and al-Jama'a al-Islamiyya—had with Saudi Arabia.

The Evolving Relationship with Saudi Arabia

We should start here with a few useful reminders on the kingdom's religious sphere and how it relates to the Saudi ruling family. First, the historical relationship between the princes and the 'ulama in the country has been based on a distribution of tasks, according to which the 'ulama define religious and social norms, and the princes govern. This has engendered a two-headed system, where each "head" backs the other, while enjoying a large measure of autonomy within its own perimeter (Lacroix 2011, 8–10). Second, the Saudi religious sphere has witnessed an enormous amount of diversification throughout the twentieth century: starting in the 1920s, Islamic activists from the entire Muslim world started converging to Saudi Arabia, exerting influence over its religious brand. This was particularly true for the members of the Muslim Brotherhood and other related movements who immigrated to Saudi Arabia in droves in order to escape the persecution of Arab nationalist and leftist regimes across the Middle East starting in the 1950s. The influence they exerted, particularly through the Saudi education system, where many of them ended up playing an important role, led to the politicization of Salafi Islam, especially among the young generation of Saudis (Lacroix 2011, 37–73). The politicized Salafism that resulted from this input is locally known as the Sahwa (from al-Sahwa al-Islamiyya, the Islamic Awakening). In the 1980s, the Sahwa had a huge presence in the Saudi religious sphere, where it shared space with more traditional forms of Salafism, themselves quite diversified. The measure of autonomy religious actors enjoyed at this point meant that the regime barely interfered with that diversity (Lacroix 2011, 77–78).

Al-Jama'a al-Islamiyya developed early connections to members of the Sahwa, who shared its ideological mix of Salafism and Qutbism. This would allow al-Jama'a al-Islamiyya activists to travel to Saudi Arabia relatively freely, escaping persecution in Egypt.[8] The Salafi Call's relationship with the Sahwa was more distant, because of the ideological differences between the two, though individual contacts did take place (interviews, 2011–2012, Egypt). In the 1990s, a religious controversy over whether someone who abandons one of the key pillars of Islam is still a Muslim (thus involving the delicate question of takfir, excommunication) even opposed one of the leading figures of the Salafi Call, Yasir Burhami, and Sahwa firebrand Safar al-Hawali.[9] As for the traditional Salafis who still controlled the highest echelons of the Saudi religious establishment, they didn't show much interest in either of the two groups. The connections they had to Egyptian Salafism were mainly through their historical partner Ansar al-Sunna, and the fact that Ansar al-Sunna did not have a strong relationship with either of the two groups—which Ansar al-Sunna shaykhs saw as competitors, and with whom they sometimes openly clashed (especially al-Jama'a al-Islamiyya)—meant that traditional Saudi Salafis wouldn't either. This is particularly visible in the memoirs written by the founders of the Salafi Call. Though they mention meetings with the famed Saudi Salafi *shaykhs* of their time, 'Abd al-'Aziz bin Baz and Muhammad bin 'Uthaymin, it is obvious from the account they give that those meetings happened as part of a larger group, and didn't denote any close relationship.[10]

As opposed to Ansar al-Sunna, the Salafi Call would even proudly emphasize its Egyptianness. In his conferences on the history of the Call, Shaykh Mahmud Abd al-Hamid insists on Ibn Taymiyya's travels to Egypt and his imprisonment in the citadel of Alexandria. He does of course talk about Muhammad bin 'Abd al-Wahhab, but only as one of the stages in the long history of Salafism. He delves into the story of Rashid Rida, Muhibb al-Din al-Khatib, and Ansar al-Sunna, before recounting how Ansar al-Sunna members 'Abd al-Razzaq 'Afifi and Muhammad Khalil Harras trained many of the Saudi *ulama*. He concludes: "And this is how Egypt became the center of the Salafi message" (Abd al-Hamid 2013). When I asked Shaykh Sa'id Abd al-'Azim, one of the Call's founders, about Saudi Arabia, he responded the same thing in his unmistakably Alexandrian accent: "It is we who influenced them, not the other way around!" (interview, 2013, Alexandria, January). Since the Call was meant to become a mass movement in Egypt, such a narrative was no doubt tailored for a public that remained deeply suspicious of Saudi Arabia. During the first two decades of the Salafi Call, Saudi Salafi authorities, especially *shaykhs* Ibn Baz and Ibn 'Uthaymin, whose authority went unquestioned by Salafis across the world, were initially extensively quoted by the Egyptian *shaykhs*. After their deaths in 1999 and 2001, the Call would more systematically refer to its own *shaykhs* and no longer to Saudi religious authorities.

The Salafi Call was also never shy about its disagreements, however minor, with the way Salafism is sometimes practiced in Saudi Arabia. Shaykh Yasir Burhami explains that he wrote his famous "The Benefits of the Rich and Worthy of Praise to Explain the Book of *Tawhid*" in 1980 to avoid "certain misunderstanding regarding excommunication (*takfir*)" in Muhammad bin 'Abd-Wahhab's Book of *Tawhid* (Burhami 2019). The key question here is that of the extent to which ignorance can excuse impious behavior (*al-'adhr bi-l-jahl*). Saudi Salafis tend to adopt a relatively intransigent view, especially when impiety concerns the creed. Sufis, for instance, are regularly denounced by Saudi *shaykhs* as apostates. In a mixed society like Egypt's, where Sufism remains strong, such a position was untenable, as it would risk setting the Call against its environment. Thus, the *shaykhs* of the Salafi Call opted for a slightly more lenient view. On the face veil (*niqab*) for women, they also went for the more lenient view that, though recommended, it is not an obligation, following the opinion of Syrian Salafi *shaykh* Nasir al-Din al-Albani instead of that of most in the Saudi religious establishment (that disagreement was actually one of the reasons why al-Albani was expelled from his teaching position at the Islamic University of Medina in 1963). As Bassam al-Zarqa, a prominent member of the Salafi Call, put it: "We had to clean the *fiqh* from the social pressures that have become sacralized in the Arabian Peninsula" (interview, 2012, Alexandria, September).

All of this should not be taken to mean that the Salafi Call and even, to some extent, al-Jama'a al-Islamiyya were not able to benefit from Saudi cashflows in those years: the autonomy of Saudi religious actors, facilitated through a range of Islamic NGOs; the enormous amounts of money they had at their disposal for proselytism; and the fluidity of the Salafi scene in Egypt (where, for instance, the Salafi Call and al-Jama'a al-Islamiyya were sometimes able to take over entire sections of Ansar al-Sunna in certain provinces), allowed them to receive their share. But they were not seen as privileged partners. Still, suspicion of Saudi funding was one of the reasons for the crackdown that targeted the Salafi Call in 1994—although the organization was able to resume its activities (interviews, 2011, Alexandria).

The 1990s were a turning point in the relationship of Saudi Arabia with what, for lack of a better term, can be called "political Islam." By the late 1980s, the Sahwa had become emboldened by the enormous influence it now had on Saudi society, and it started applying its political criticism to the quietism of the religious establishment's traditional scholars, as well as to the ruling family. In this already tense context, Iraq's invasion of Kuwait in 1990, and the subsequent royal decision to call on US troops to protect the kingdom, triggered what Saudi historiographers call the "Sahwa's intifada" (*intifadat al-Sahwa*): a period of open dissent led by Sahwa figures who demanded far-ranging reforms. Many of the region's Islamist groups—including al-Jama'a al-Islamiyya and the Salafi Call, but also the Muslim Brotherhood—joined the Sahwa in condemning the call for US troops. That period only ended in 1994 with a full state-led crackdown on the Sahwa's figures, as well as on thousands of their followers. This episode prompted a profound reconfiguration of the Saudi state's relationship with religious actors, that would unravel during the next couple of decades (Lacroix 2014). First, the Saudi ruling family would work to establish much firmer control over the country's religious sphere, thereby gradually ending its autonomy. And all forms of organized Islamic activism were now seen with growing suspicion in Riyadh. This applied first and foremost to the Muslim Brotherhood—whom Prince Nayef, then Saudi minister of interior, would famously call "the root of all evil" in Saudi Arabia in a 2002 interview (Al-Bayan 2002)—but also to all organized Salafi groups. As a result, Saudi Arabia stepped up its security cooperation with Egypt, arresting members of al-Jama'a al-Islamiyya on Cairo's behalf.[11]

As for the Salafi Call, whose relations with Saudi Arabia had not been particularly strong, it was now seen with open suspicion. The problem was not its discourse—as opposed to the Sahwa, the Call shunned politics—but the fact that it was an organized grassroots force, that could easily be assimilated to the Islamist groups that the Saudi regime now distrusted. A member of the Call who lived in Saudi Arabia between 2001 and 2010 and acted as its local representative recalls: "The Salafi Call was not welcome in Saudi Arabia, it could only operate there in a discrete manner" (online interview, 2015, January).

Hizb al-Nur's Saudi Connections?

The years preceding Egypt's 2011 revolution witnessed the growth of what has been dubbed "popular Salafism" among Egyptian crowds (Al-Anani and Maszlee 2013). This happened mainly because of the creation of numerous Salafi channels on NileSat, starting with Qanat al-Nas in 2006. Those channels, duly licensed by the Mubarak authorities who thought of them as a way to counter the politicized discourse of the Muslim Brotherhood, hosted tens of *shaykhs* who preached ultra-conservative social norms. Despite the fact that most of those preachers were independent figures not affiliated with any of the previously discussed organizations, the huge audience garnered by their shows clearly contributed to the growing hegemony of Salafi discourse in Egypt's religious sphere, thereby indirectly reinforcing the existing Salafi groups.

In the wake of Egypt's 2011 revolution, many of the country's Salafi groups decided to form political parties. This was a major surprise at the time, given that most of those groups had previously shunned party politics (if not politics altogether). The most successful of those new political parties was the Nour Party (Hizb al-Nur), which was established in June 2011 by members of the Salafi Call—by far the largest Salafi grassroots organization in the country. In the parliamentary elections that took place during the autumn of 2011, the Nour Party received more than a quarter of the votes, emerging as the country's second political force after the Muslim Brotherhood's Freedom and Justice Party. The stellar rise of the Nour Party prompted suspicions of links to Saudi Arabia, especially as the party had been able to quickly mobilize an impressive amount of financial resources for its campaign. The subsequent political behavior of the Nour Party puzzled observers even more: it supported 'Abd al-Mun'im Abu al-Futuh, a liberal Islamist candidate, for the presidential election; it actively opposed Muslim Brotherhood president Muhammad Morsi after his election; and it openly backed the July 3, 2013, military coup against the Brotherhood. Again, the dominant view among Egyptian and foreign commentators was that this behavior could only be explained by the Nour Party's alleged alignment with (and dependence on) Saudi Arabia, a country that, for the reasons mentioned earlier, abhorred the Brotherhood and whose influence was instrumental in the

Egyptian military's takeover.[12] The following paragraphs are meant to undo that theory, by offering a radically different account of why the Nour Party did what it did.

First of all, it has been shown that the Salafi Call's relationship to Saudi Arabia was at most shallow before 2011. It is entirely possible—yet impossible to prove, except via anecdotal evidence—that the Nour Party received financial support from individuals (including Egyptian expatriates) in Saudi Arabia, but a more systematic and/or state-level funding scheme seems highly unlikely. Besides, what those who saw a Saudi hand in the initial success of the Nour Party tend to forget is that the Call, which was behind the party, represented by then (though many were not yet aware of this) the second largest religious organization across Egypt after the Muslim Brotherhood, with membership cutting across social classes. It was thus relatively easy for the Call to raise substantial amounts of campaign funding among its followers, especially wealthy ones.[13]

One central misunderstanding about the Nour Party was that it was an Islamist party akin to the Muslim Brotherhood but with a Salafi outlook, i.e., a party whose aim was to conquer power to establish an Islamic state. Yet, the shaykhs of the Call—who took over the party after an initial moment of tension with its nominal founders (Lacroix 2016, 7–10)—had a very peculiar conception of politics. As Salafis, they never stopped believing that reform will only come through what Salafi shaykh Nasir al-Din al-Albani famously called "purification and education" (al-tasfiya wa-l-tarbiya) (Burhami 1412). By this, he meant purifying the Muslim creed from blameworthy innovations, and teaching people the purified creed through preaching. For those shaykhs, then, change could only come from below, by expanding people's adherence to Salafism. There is thus no incentive to take over the state before society has been transformed. This was already the main reason why the Salafi Call didn't support the January–February 2011 protests against Mubarak.

In Egypt's post-revolutionary context, though, the shaykhs of the Call understood that their religious organization needed a political arm, not as a vehicle to seize power, but as an instrument meant to defend the interests of the organization in the political sphere. In other words, the Nour Party was to be first and foremost a political lobby on behalf of a religious organization (Lacroix 2016, 7–8). As prominent Salafi Call and Nour Party member Ashraf Thabit put it: "The parliament is not, has never been, and will not be the solution for us. We believe change will only come from below, not by simply changing the laws. The parliament is only a means to help us practice what is the basis for us, da'wa. This is our manhaj [methodology]. What matters most is purifying the ummah's creed" (interview, 2012, Alexandria, January). Concretely speaking, the Call hoped its MPs would be able to advance an agenda favorable to the expansion of the religious organization, and to block any decision that could harm it. Naturally, there was never talk of presenting a candidate for the presidency.

The group that the Call feared the most was the Muslim Brotherhood. Seen from the Call's perspective, the Brothers were not just preaching an Islam that didn't match Salafi standards. They were also formidable competitors who, just as they did, vied for the control of the country's mosques, but who could use their political hegemony—should they achieve it—in order to gain religious hegemony, thereby threatening the Salafi project, and the Salafi Call itself. This explains why, after the Brotherhood announced in April 2012 that it was presenting a candidate for the presidential election, the Nour Party did all it could to prevent his victory. After an internal consultation, the *shaykhs* decided to back liberal Islamist Abd al-Mun'im 'Abd al-Futuh, despite their strong disagreement with his religious views, because he was a fierce enemy of the Brotherhood (which he had left in 2011) and the only religious candidate with a chance of winning. The plan failed and Brotherhood candidate Muhammad Morsi was elected in June 2012.

Six months into the Morsi presidency, the Nour Party started denouncing what they saw as a "Brotherhoodization of the state" (*akhwanat al-dawla*) (Al-Arabiyya 2013). Though the accusation was also leveled by liberals, for the Nour Party it mainly referred to the appointment of Brotherhood members at the ministry of religious endowments, as well as a number of decisions which they saw as aimed at reducing the Salafis' religious influence and increasing the Brotherhood's. This led to an uneasy rapprochement between the Nour Party and the liberals, and the Salafis' eventual decision to back the June 30, 2013, demonstrations against Morsi (without explicitly calling for their followers to join, which is not surprising given the traditional Salafi stance on demonstrations) (Al-Masry al-Yawm 2013). On July 3, 2013, when General 'Abd al-Fattah al-Sisi announced that Morsi was no longer president and that a new political phase was about to begin, a senior representative of the Nour Party was among the people sitting behind him.

The Salafi Call was apparently hoping to make itself indispensable to the new regime. After all, they were the only Islamist force to back the coup, and would therefore be needed to regain control of the religious sphere. And by doing that, they would be able to expand their presence. The Salafi Call certainly underestimated the army's unwillingness to rely on a non-state group for social and religious control, and therefore saw many of its initial hopes shattered. Despite that, the Salafi Call has managed to at least keep its presence, and the Nour Party is the only Islamist party represented in Egypt's parliament (Lacroix and Shalata 2018).

What the previous demonstration shows is thus that the behavior of the Nour Party can perfectly be accounted for by understanding what their domestic priorities were, and how they conceived of politics. There is no need to bring into the explanation an alleged relationship to Saudi Arabia, especially since the kingdom saw them with distrust—and the establishment of the Nour Party only added to that distrust, since the Saudi regime feared it could give ideas to its own Salafi opposition.

Conclusion

There has been in the media and some of the academic literature a tendency to see Saudi Arabia as the *Komintern* of a global Salafi movement guided by Riyadh. This is problematic in that it underestimates the diversity of Saudi Arabia's Salafi scene, and the relatively high level of autonomy religious actors once enjoyed in the kingdom—meaning that the relationships they established cannot always be interpreted as responding to clear political contingencies. That said, it is true that until the 1990s, most Salafi movements across the globe had some degree of contact with Saudi religious actors, and were able to benefit from generous Saudi cashflows. Yet, not all groups had the same level of proximity to the kingdom, depending on their histories. The case of Egypt illustrates that quite well. While Ansar al-Sunna was and remained the Saudi religious establishment's leading religious partner across the Red Sea, groups like the Salafi Call—which developed much later and independently from Saudi Arabia—didn't enjoy the same level of influence in Riyadh. After the 1990s, Saudi Arabia became much more selective in its support for foreign Salafi groups, gradually distancing itself from anything it considered to be "political Islam."

This means that, by 2011, many of the region's Salafis could no longer be seen as proxies of Riyadh (if they had ever been proxies in the first place, which is already a far-fetched assumption). Yet, this misconception continued after the Arab revolutions, with commentators interpreting the rise of Salafi political influence across the region as the effect of deliberate Saudi policies. The case of the Salafi Call and the Nour Party shows that this reading is inaccurate, and that the political behavior of Salafi groups—however different from that of better-known groups such as the Muslim Brotherhood—can perfectly be understood on their own terms.

Notes

1. For two examples among many: Patrycja Sasnal, "Saudi Arabia: On the Inside Track in Egypt," July 31, 2015, https:// www.thegl obal ist.com/ saudi- ara bia- mid dle- east- extrem ism- egypt/ (accessed July 31, 2020); "Al- Sa'udiyya wa- l- salafiyya

al-sakandariyya: ayya ʿilaqa?," June 12, 2018, https://politicalstreet.org/2018/06/12/
السعودية-والسلفية-السكندرية/ (accessed July 31, 2020).

2. On Muhammad ʿAbd al-Wahhab and his message, see, for instance, David Commins, *The Wahhabi Mission and Saudi Arabia* (London: I. B. Tauris, 2006); Michael Crawford, *Ibn Abd al-Wahhab* (London: Oneworld Publications, 2014).

3. Some of the academic literature distinguishes a conservative Salafi movement (the one this article refers to, which traces its roots back to Muhammad bin ʿAbd al-Wahhab) and a modernist Salafi movement, inspired by Muhammad ʿAbduh. In his book *The Making of Salafism*, Henri Lauzière has shown that the boundaries between those in the first half of the twentieth century in Egypt were quite blurry, and that the term *Salafi* was initially used in a relatively loose way. He also argues that the secondary literature added to the confusion, since ʿAbduh himself never referred to his project as *salafiyya*. After the 1950s, the term *Salafi* was almost exclusively used to designate the conservative, Saudi-inspired, strain. This chapter uses the term *Salafi* exclusively in this sense.

4. See, for instance, Gilles Kepel, *Muslim Extremism in Egypt: The Prophet and the Pharaoh* (Berkeley: University of California Press, 1992).

5. The memoirs of former *jamaʿat islamiyya* leader Abd al-Munʿim Abu al-Futuh are one of many sources illustrating that point. See Husam Tammam, *Abd al-Munʿim Abu al-Futuh: Shahid ʿala taʾrikh al-haraka al-islamiyya fi masr 1970–1984* (Cairo: Dar al-Shuruq, 2010).

6. On this period, see Abdullah al-Arian, *Answering the Call: Popular Islamic Activism in Sadat's Egypt* (Oxford: Oxford University Press, 2014).

7. On al-Jamaʿa al-Islamiyya, one of the best sources is Salwa Muhammad al-ʿAwwa, *Al-jamaʿa al-islamiyya al-musallaha fi masr 1974–2004* (Cairo: Maktabat al-shuruq al-duwaliyya, 2006); on al-Jamaʿa al-Islamiyya as a Salafi social movement, see Roel Meijer, "Commanding Right and Forbidding Wrong as a Principle of Social Action," in Roel Meijer (ed.), *Global Salafism: Islam's New Religious Movement* (Oxford: Oxford University Press, 2009), 189–220.

8. There are numerous examples of al-Jamaʿa al-Islamiyya members who spent time in Saudi Arabia in the 1980s, sometimes before leaving for Pakistan and Afghanistan. This was the case, for instance, for Rifaʿi Taha.

9. The book at the root of controversy was Safar al-Hawali's *The Phenomenon of irjaʾ in Islamic Thought* (*zahirat al-irjaʾ fi-l-fikr al-islami*). Yasir Burhami of the Salafi Call tried to put an end to the dispute with his book *A Critical Reading of Some of What Was Written in the Book on the Phenomenon of irjaʾ* (*qiraʾa naqdiyya li baʿd ma warada fi kitab zahirat al-irjaʾ*). The notion of *irjaʾ* here refers to a group of Muslim scholars from the first centuries of Islam who were known to dissociate faith from works, thereby refusing the excommunication of sinners.

10. See, for instance, the memoirs of Ahmad Farid, *Hadith al-Dhikrayat* (Alexandria: Dar Ibn al-Jawzi, 2012).

11. This is what I heard from several interviewees when I was conducting interviews in Saudi Arabia in the early 2000s. In 1998, both Egypt and Saudi Arabia would be

signatories to the "Arab agreement on combating terrorism" (see https://www.aljaze era.net/2004/10/03/الاتفاقية-العربية-لمكافحة-الإرهاب; accessed July 31, 2020).

12. For a (critical) view of those explanations, see Mu'taz Zahir, *Min al-masjid ila-l-barlaman: Dirasa hawla al-da'wa al-salafiyya wa hizb al-nur* (London: Takween Center, 2015), 132.

13. This is confirmed by months of fieldwork in Egypt during the run-up to the parliamentary elections.

References

Al-Arabiyya. 2013. "Hizb al-Nur al-salafi: Muhawalat akhwanat al-dawla al-masriyya ghayr maqbula." January 29, 2013. http://www.alarabiya.net/articles/2013/01/29/263 205.html (accessed July 31, 2020).

Al-nas al-kamil li-taqrir lajnat taqassi al-haqa'iq hawla al-tamwil al-ajnabi li-l-jam'iyyat al-ahliyya bi- masr. 2012. https://aljaras.wordpress.com/2012/01/04/النص-الكامل-لتق-ارير-لجنة-تقصى-الحقائق-ح/ (accessed July 31, 2020).

Abd al-Hamid, Mahmud. 2013. *Ta'rikh al-da'wa al-salafiyya*. https://www.youtube.com/watch?v=bEW4xx0j66Q (accessed July 31, 2020).

Al-Anani, Khalil, and Maszlee, Malik. 2013. "Pious Way to Politics: The Rise of Political Salafism in Post-Mubarak Egypt." *Digest of Middle East Studies* 22(1): 57–73.

Al-Bayan. 2002. "Nayif: Al-ikhwan al-muslimun asl al-bala'." November 26, 2002. https://www.albayan.ae/one-world/2002-11-26-1.1366263 (accessed September 22, 2021).

Burhami, Yasir. 1412 [corresponding to 1991–1992]. *Al-salafiyya wa manahij al-taghyir*. Sawt al-Da'wa, 3.

Burhami, Yasir. 2019. Interview with the website of al-Jama'a al-Islamiyya, 2nd part, August 13, 2019. https://www.anasalafy.com/play.php?catsmktba=82634.

Commins, David. 2006. *The Wahhabi Mission and Saudi Arabia*. London: I. B. Tauris.

Al-Fiqi, Muhammad Hamid. 2008. *Azhar min Riyadh: Sirat al-imam al-'adil 'Abd al-'Aziz bin 'Abd al-Rahman Al-Faysal Al Sa'ud*. Cairo: Dar 'ilm al-salaf.

Harras, Muhammad Khalil. 1985. *Al-haraka al-wahhabiyya: Radd 'ala maqal Muhammad al-Bahi fi naqd al-wahhabiyya*. Beirut: Dar al-kitab al-'arabi.

Lacroix, Stéphane. 2011. *Awakening Islam: The Politics of Religious Dissent in Contemporary Saudi Arabia*. Cambridge, MA: Harvard University Press.

Lacroix, Stéphane. 2014. "Saudi Arabia's Muslim Brotherhood Predicament." *Project on Middle East Political Science (POMEPS)*. March 9, 2014. https://pomeps.org/saudi-arab ias-muslim-brotherhood-predicament (accessed July 31, 2020).

Lacroix, Stéphane. 2016. *Egypt's Pragmatic Salafis: The Politics of Hizb al-Nour*. Washington, DC: Carnegie Endowment for International Peace.

Lacroix, Stéphane, and Ahmed Zaghloul Shalata. 2018. "Les strategies religieuses du régime et leurs complications dans l'Egypte de al-Sissi." *Critique Internationale* 78(1): 21–39.

Lauzière, Henri. 2015. *The Making of Salafism: Islamic Reform in the Twentieth Century*. New York: Columbia University Press.

Al-Masry al-Youm. 2013. "Yasir Burhami: Idha kjaraja al-malayin fi 30 yunyu sa-atlub Mursi bi-l-istaqala." 5 June 5. 2013. http://www.almasryalyoum.com/news/details/215 693 (accessed July 31, 2020).

Mithaq al-'amal al-islami. 1984. http://www.ilmway.com/site/maqdis/MS_36681.html (accessed July 31, 2020).

Munib, Abd al-Mun'im. 2010. *Dalil al-harakat al-islamiyya*. Cairo: Maktabat Madbuli.

Rida, Muhammad Rashid. 1925. *Al-wahhabiyyun wa-l-hijaz*. Cairo: Matba'at al-Manar.

Al-Samhan, Faysal bin Abd al-Aziz. 2011. *Al-Imam al-sayyid Rashid Rida fi mayadin al-muwajaha*. Kuwait: Maktabat ahl al-athar.

Al-Sayyid, 'Adil. 2009. *Al-hakimiyya wa-l-siyasa al-shar'iyya 'inda shuyukh jama'at Ansar al-Sunna al-muhammadiyya*. Cairo: Dar al-Ibana.

Schulze, Reinhardt. 1990. *Islamicher Internationalismus im 20? Jahrhundert: Untersuchungen zur Geschichte der Islamischen Weltliga*. Leiden: Brill.

Shahada, Usama. 2013. *Silsilat rumuz al-islah 19—al-'allama Muhammad Hamid al-Fiqi*. http://www.alrased.net/main/articles.aspx?selected_article_no=6412 (accessed July 31, 2020).

Shalata, Ahmad Zaghlul. 2015. *Al-da'wa al-salafiyya al-sakandariyya: Masarat al-tanzim wa malat al-siyasa*. Beirut: Markaz dirasat al-wahda al-'arabiyya.

Al-Tahir, Ahmad Muhammad. 2004. *Jama'at Ansar al-Sunna al-muhammadiyya: Nash'atuha, ahdafuha, manhajuha, juhuduha*. Riyadh: Dar al-fadila/Dar al-hadi al-nabawi.

14

Arab Brothers, Arms, and Food Rations

How Salafism Made Its Way to Bosnia and Herzegovina

Harun Karčić

Introduction

The visibility of Islam in Bosnia and Herzegovina, particularly in its capital city Sarajevo, continues to intrigue the average foreign observer. A European city with its Austro-Hungarian architecture, topped with Ottoman-era minarets and a majority population of white, Slavic-speaking Muslims, is certainly not the everyday picture so many are accustomed to. In such an environment, men donning long beards and ankle-length trousers and women covered in *niqab*s—though a minority—unambiguously stand out from the rest of the crowd.

A closer look as to why some Bosnian Muslims dress differently from the majority population will point to one connection—Saudi Salafism.

How exactly Salafism made its way from the Saudi peninsula to Bosnia and Herzegovina and how strong an influence it wields today are questions that have been subject to much debate over the past three decades. A plethora of answers has been suggested—one side claimed that they came uninvited (Ćidić 2018), another claimed they were brought in by Western intelligence agencies (Subašić 2019), while a third claimed they were invited by the Bosnian Muslim leadership to help beleaguered Bosnian Muslims (Lučić 2017). Whatever the facts may be, Salafism today is a reality in Bosnia and Herzegovina, and it is no longer an imported ideology. It now has homegrown followers.

The aim of this chapter is to examine how exactly Saudi Salafism made its way to Bosnia and Herzegovina, why it found fertile ground in the war-ravaged country, which Saudi governmental and nongovernmental channels were employed to disseminate Salafi ideas, and how it was all received by the Bosnian Muslim population. However, simply analyzing the situation today without delving into the recent past will not yield many results. In order to understand the new visibility of Islam in Bosnia and Herzegovina, and particularly the foreign factors influencing Bosnia's interpretation of Islam, it is necessary to place events into the context of the country's recent history.

Harun Karčić, *Arab Brothers, Arms, and Food Rations* In: *Wahhabism and the World.* Edited by: Peter Mandaville, Oxford University Press. © Oxford University Press 2022. DOI: 10.1093/oso/9780197532560.003.0014

Islam in the Turbulent Balkans

Bosnians have been living in the Western Balkans since the Middle Ages. Following the Ottoman conquest of the region and the annexation of Bosnia and Herzegovina in the fourteenth century, gradual conversions to Islam began which lasted almost until the late seventeenth century (Malcolm 2011). Though Ottoman rule in the Balkans is still referred to as *Pax Ottomanica*, the decades that followed were particularly turbulent and arduous for Bosnian Muslims (also known as Bosniaks). Namely, the Ottomans lost Bosnia and Herzegovina at the Congress of Berlin in 1878 and ceded their province to the Austro-Hungarians. Following the Young Turk Revolution in Istanbul in 1908 and the ensuing political turmoil in the foundering empire, the Austro-Hungarians used the opportunity to annex Bosnia. After World War I, the Austro-Hungarian Empire collapsed, and Bosnia and Herzegovina became part of the Kingdom of Yugoslavia (initially called the Kingdom of Serbs, Croats, and Slovenes). Then, following the end of World War II, precisely from 1946 until 1991, the country was part of communist Yugoslavia. Hence, in a period slightly longer than 100 years, its citizens changed personal documents four times—or, to make use of Xavier Bougarel's 2018 book title, Bosnian Muslims *survived* empires (Bougarel 2018).

State-sponsored atheism in communist Yugoslavia heavily influenced Bosnian Muslims and their practice of Islam, perhaps more than any other previous state. Islamic activists and religious officials, just like priests and clergy, were persecuted by the secret police, particularly in the early years of the regime (Trhulj 1992). Some of the most visible Islamic institutions were targeted in an attempt to weaken the religion's societal influence. For instance, *shari'a* courts were abolished in 1946, and Islamic law as a legal system ceased to have a binding legal force for Yugoslav Muslims (F. Karčić 2011). Then, in 1950, the full-face veil commonly known as *niqab* (in Bosnia also known as the *zar* or *faraja*) was banned. Though the headscarf was never explicitly banned, its removal was heavily encouraged by the government and various communist female associations (H. Karčić 2018). In 1952, the government ordered all Islamic religious educational schools (madrasas) closed. Of the 100 in Yugoslavia, only two were left functioning—one in Sarajevo and the other in Skopje (F. Karčić 2011). Finally, the economic independence of the Islamic community was greatly reduced after the state nationalized land, buildings, hotels, and spas registered as Islamic pious endowments (*waqf*).

On the political level, Bosnian Muslims and Yugoslav Muslims in general experienced a great deal of national and cultural suppression. Unlike Serbs, Croats, and Slovenes, Bosnian Muslims (*Bošnjaci*) were not recognized as a separate nation, but only as a religious group. Hence, they could only identify themselves as *Muslimani* (Muslims) (Lučić 2018).

Even though practicing religion was theoretically allowed under the country's laws, public manifestations of such were severely curtailed (H. Fazlić 2015). In the private sphere, Muslims in Yugoslavia were among the most religious Yugoslavs. According to a 1964 survey, the percentage of self-declared believers was highest among Kosovar Albanian Muslims (91 percent), followed by Bosnian Muslims (83.8 percent) (H. Fazlić 2012). However, believers praying at mosques or fasting during the month of Ramadan were watched, followed, and often questioned by the secret police. This instilled a sense of fear among Yugoslav Muslims, who gradually abandoned prayers and Ramadan fasting in an attempt to blend in with the larger non-Muslim population and communist mindset. Two decades later, in a 1985 survey of 6,500 people, 62.3 percent of Catholic families said they were religious, as compared to 43.8 percent of Muslim families and 26.2 percent of Orthodox Christian families (Mirescu 2003). Finally, surveys from 1990–1991 indicate that Bosnia-Herzegovina had the highest percentage (29 percent) of any republic not declaring any confessional orientation, and that Bosnian Muslims (88 percent) valued their affinity with Yugoslavia more than either Bosnia's Serbs (85 percent) or Bosnia's Croats (63 percent) (H. Fazlić 2012). In other words, Bosnian Muslims and Yugoslav Muslims in general became greatly detached from Islam during the five decades of communism.

The Collapse of Communism and the Breakout of War

The year 1990 was a time of great political upheaval in Europe. The Cold War was officially over, and Western liberal democracy had triumphed over communism. In Yugoslavia, Muslims in Bosnia-Herzegovina had felt not only confident and free to openly declare themselves as "Bosniaks" but to publicly practice Islam as well. Sometimes this freedom paved the way for individuals to overemphasize and even exaggerate their religious affiliation by the use of Muslim greetings, Islamic symbols, flags, songs, etc. This was a time of mixed feelings—genuine euphoria because of communism's demise and the first multiparty elections, but also a palpable sense of fear due to the uncertain future.

Yugoslavia was collapsing. A war broke out in Slovenia after it declared independence, then another one broke out in Croatia after *its* independence. In both cases, the newly independent states were attacked by Serb-dominated rump Yugoslavia. After a national referendum in 1992, Bosnia-Herzegovina declared independence. Bosnian Serb nationalists, not wanting to share a state with a Muslim majority, declared their own rebellious "autonomous regions" along with parallel political and military institutions in the eastern and northern parts of the country where they constituted significant numbers. In the spring of 1992, two years after the first democratic elections, war erupted as Serb rebels refused to recognize the newly independent government led by a Bosniak Muslim, Alija Izetbegović.

The war had a drastic impact on reawakening the Bosniak Muslim masses. Innocent Muslim civilians found themselves targets of a genocidal campaign while the country's territory became the aim of irredentist and hostile neighbors (Serbia and Croatia) intent on achieving their expansionist aspirations (Gow 2003). Although this war was primarily a war over territory, the intentional killing of Bosniak Muslims in the process of "cleansing" Serb-held territory, as well as the destruction of mosques and acts such as forced baptizing, made many Muslims realize they were targets simply because of their religious affiliation (Cushman and Meštrović 1996). This is an important factor to bear in mind when analyzing increased religiosity among Bosniak Muslims during the war. The misery and suffering of war and the uncertainness of life and death resulted in many individuals turning to God for help.

While the democratically elected and multinational government led by Bosnia's Muslim president Alija Izetbegović shuttled between Western capitals in an attempt to find a diplomatic solution to the rapidly deteriorating political and humanitarian situation, the Islamic Community in Bosnia and Herzegovina, the official institution representing all Muslims in the country, toured Middle Eastern capitals in an attempt to draw attention to the plight of the country's Muslims.

Their lobbying, but more importantly extensive Western media coverage of the plight of Bosnian Muslims, yielded significant results. Over the following years, the arrival of humanitarian aid from Muslim countries, including weapons, money, and medicine, established a lifeline for the country. This humanitarian aid coming from Muslim countries, in the absence of any significant Western support, was instrumental in the defense of Bosnian Muslims.

However, aid came with strings attached. Islamic humanitarian organizations, charities, missionaries, and fighters not only helped defend the country's Muslims against Serbian and Croat aggression, but also used the opportunity to disseminate their own visions of Islam, mostly Salafism. There were a number of channels for the dissemination of such teachings, and they will be discussed in the following sections.

How Salafism Made Its Way to Bosnia and Herzegovina

Prior to the 1992–1995 war, *Salafism* was a term known to and used by a very limited number of individuals, who were mostly scholars and students of Islam and the Middle East. It was used in literature as a descriptor of early Islam and not an identifier of fellow Muslims in Yugoslavia. This is because Islam practiced in Yugoslavia generally, and Bosnia specifically, is liberal in worldview, rich in Sufi tradition and popular folk practices, and unquestioningly subservient to the secular state and its laws. This "Bosnian Islam," as it is more commonly known today, is practiced by an overwhelming majority of Bosniak Muslims throughout the country. The war, however, changed the notion and understanding of Salafism, which became an identity marker.

Although a number of Muslim states promoted their interpretations of Islam during and after the war, the aim of this chapter is to solely focus on Saudi influence in Bosnia-Herzegovina. Namely, there were four channels through which Salafi ideas were disseminated in Bosnia and Herzegovina: Saudi institutions, Saudi-funded nongovernmental and humanitarian organizations, Arab volunteer fighters, and graduates of Middle Eastern universities.

State-Level Channeling of Salafism

Financial donations and humanitarian aid started pouring in from Saudi Arabia in mid-1992, mostly through individuals and pious foundations. The situation changed in 1993 when Saudi Arabia appointed then Prince Salman bin 'Abd al-'Aziz, later king of Saudi Arabia, to direct the Saudi High Commission for Relief of Bosnia and Herzegovina (SHC) (Weinberg 2015). He had previous experience in organizing and funding the Afghan resistance against Soviet occupation in the 1980s, and it seems that he applied similar tactics to Bosnia-Herzegovina as well (Riedel 2017). Through the Saudi High Commission, millions of dollars were funneled into the country—from 1992 until 2011 the Saudi High Commission officially collected some US$600 million (Weinberg 2015). The actual amount, according to many insiders, is much higher, as a lot of Saudi money was passed through back channels. At its peak, the Commission funded hundreds of orphans and thousands of families of fallen Muslim soldiers. It also fully operated eighteen refugee camps, provided school equipment for children, food, medicine, fuel for heating, water, and milk. It organized lectures on Islam, summer schools and Qur'an courses, and published large numbers of Islamic books and distributed them for free (Ardat 1995). Such activities during and immediately after the war became crucibles for spreading Salafi teachings and attracting new followers.

The Saudi High Commission would mostly donate money to the central Bosnian government in Sarajevo, which was then distributed to the lower levels. But in case of heavy fighting, money and aid were also distributed to other towns under the control of the central government, such as Zenica, Travnik, and Tuzla. The Commission also maintained close ties with the Islamic Community in Bosnia-Herzegovina and used their networks of imams or religious leaders to distribute aid throughout the country and help repair damaged mosques. Arabic-speaking imams were also employed to help translate books from Arabic to Bosnian.

NGO-Level Channeling of Salafism

Saudi-funded organizations—such as the Muslim World League, Al Haramain Foundation, the International Islamic Relief Organization, World Assembly of Muslim Youth (WAMY), Saudi Arabian Red Crescent Society, the Islamic Waqf Organization, Society for the Revival of Islamic Heritage, Centre for the Affirmation of Islamic Sciences, Muwafaq Foundation, Third World Relief Agency, Al Furqan, and the Makkah Humanitarian Organization—were active in Bosnia-Herzegovina throughout the war. Their work sometimes overlapped with the Saudi High Commission when it came to social programs for orphans, families of fallen soldiers, and the reconstruction of homes, mosques, and Islamic institutions. They also provided school equipment and stipends for Muslim children in the country and scholarships for university-level study in Saudi Arabia and other Arab countries (such as Jordan). Many of these organizations often used humanitarian aid as an incentive to encourage Bosniak Muslims to fulfill their religious duties, such as praying, wearing the hijab, attending lectures on Islam, etc. Even during the war, these organizations organized lectures on Islam, summer schools, and Arabic-language courses in areas controlled by the Bosnian Army. Some Islamic humanitarian organizations such as Third World Relief Agency and Muwafaq Foundation allegedly helped channel money and weapons for the Bosnian army (Pomfret 1996).

Sometimes financial aid and scholarships were conditioned by the fulfillment of Islamic religious duties, growing beards for men or wearing the hijab for women. My wife, Senada Maličević, is a case in point. As an eight-year-old, she lost her father to the war. Left alone with a younger brother and a mother, they struggled to make ends meet in the besieged town of Goražde. They were soon approached by a Kuwaiti Salafi organization which offered to provide them with monthly stipends, an offer they could not refuse in the dire circumstances of war. Over the following months and years, this financial aid and similar food donations from Saudi humanitarian organizations proved to be instrumental for their livelihood. My wife, however, had to regularly attend various Islamic lectures, and every month she had to put on a headscarf and wear a black *abaya* (along with other child-recipients of financial aid) for a photo session. These pictures, so they were told, were sent back to Kuwaiti and Saudi donors as proof of their humanitarian activities in Bosnia-Herzegovina. (It is perhaps worth mentioning that after the photo session, my wife and the other girls would take off their headscarves.) Her brother, Senad, was required to wear a plain-white Islamic skull cap for the photo session and was also required to attend regular Islamic lectures organized by the Kuwaiti organization.

The Distribution of Salafi Literature

There was an influx of foreign Islamic literature during the war in Bosnia-Herzegovina. Both state and non-state actors and even individuals played an active role in the translation, publication, and distribution of such literature. Today most of these books and booklets are difficult to come across, save for some rare copies in the archives of libraries such as the King Fahd Center in Sarajevo. Most of them were published by the Islamic Center "Balkan," the Saudi High Commission, and the World Assembly of Muslim Youth. Some of the titles published include *Useful Ways of Leading a Happy Life*, written by Abdul Rahman b. Nasir Es-Seadi; *The Collection of Hadith from the Riyadus-Salihin*, edited by Muhammed Mustafa El-ʿAzami; *The Truth about Jesus*, written by Maneh Hammad Al-Johani; *Take Your Belief from the Qurʾan and Sunnah*, written by Muhammad Bin Jamil Zino; *The Triumph of Truth* (Izhar ul-Haqq) by Shaykh Rahmetullah Bin Khalil al Hindi; Muhammad ibn ʿAbd al-Wahhab's *Three Foundational Principles*; and Shaykh Bin Baz's *The Prophet's Prayer*; a collection of Bin Baz's *fatawa* were also translated into Bosnian and published by the Saudi Ministry for Islamic Affairs, Endowments, and Guidance.

Moreover, the Saudi High Commission translated and published older books, such as Emir Shakib Arslan's *Our Decline: Its Causes and Remedies* and several works by Bosniak Muslim scholars who had earlier graduated from Saudi universities, such as *Ramadan Fast*, written by Muharem Štulanović. All these books and booklets were published in astonishing numbers and multiple editions. For instance, Muhammed Bin Jamil Zino's *Take Your Belief from the Qurʾan and Sunnah* was printed in 100,000 copies, while *Ramadan Fast* had 80,000 copies and multiple editions (sometimes up to ten editions). Some of these books were printed in Zagreb (in neighboring Croatia), while others were printed in Bosnian towns such as Zenica and Sarajevo.

To what extent these books were read by Bosniak Muslims is questionable. An anecdote from the war—several Bosniak Muslim friends of mine told me how they would use books donated by "Arabs" to light up their improvised stoves to heat themselves or cook food during the war. Not many admit to reading these books, let alone absorbing their Salafi message.

The Saudis used their visits to Bosnia-Herzegovina during the war to promote the kingdom and its role in the Muslim world. For example, in February 1995, the secretary-general of the Muslim World League, Ahmed Muhammad Ali, on a visit to Sarajevo, said:

> ... Saudi Arabia is a country based on Islamic principles and tenets. Therefore, the interest that it shows towards developments in the Islamic world is one of the most important factors in determining its foreign policy, regardless of bilateral or multilateral relations. Then, the position that Saudi Arabia enjoys in the world as the country with the two Holy Mosques, which are visited by millions of Muslims from all over the world during the pilgrimage, should not be forgotten. On the other hand, the Saudi people are one of the most emotional people in the world and they sympathize with their brothers in pain. Hence, from there comes Saudi Arabia's duty to be above the rest in providing aid. (Ali 1995)

Along similar lines, the secretary-general of the WAMY, who also visited Sarajevo during the war, said: "I would also convey a message to our brothers in Bosnia ... that the majority of their brothers who come from Islamic countries of the Arabian Peninsula know Islam better than the rest. I do not wish to underestimate other Arabs. To the contrary, Arabs generally know Islam better than the rest ... because the Qur'an and the Hadith (Prophet's sayings) are in Arabic, and these sources can be used in their original language" (El-Džuheni 1995).

In both interviews, the emphasis was on the Saudis having more political and religious legitimacy because of their knowledge of Islam and the Arabic language.

Salafi-Oriented Foreign Fighters

The first foreign fighters arrived in Bosnia-Herzegovina in the summer of 1992. Initially, fighters came individually, but then in 1993, when the Pakistani government ordered Afghan war-era training camps closed and threatened those remaining fighters with deportation, they came to Bosnia-Herzegovina in much larger groups (Donnely, Sanderson, and Feldman 2020). Babar Ahmad, who came from England, admitted to having been strongly moved by images of slaughtered Muslim civilians, so much so that he decided to personally take part in military action (Verkaik 2016).

The Bosnian government was reluctant to accept them, as manpower was not an issue, rather the main issue was the lack of weapons and ammunition. Furthermore, the Bosnian government was worried that Arab fighters would tarnish its image in the West—a fear that years later proved well founded.

The number of foreign fighters in the Bosnian army's El-Mujaheed unit at its peak was around 700—including Bosniak Muslims—a majority of whom had accepted Salafism (Karup 1998). Arab fighters considered some Bosniak Muslims as having deviated from the true path of Islam. A case in point is the Egyptian Imad El Misri, who authored a booklet titled "Practices That Need to be Changed," where he claimed that deviant Bosniak Muslim practices can only be corrected by returning to the *Salaf* (Al Misri 1993). Another example is Abu Hamza, a Syrian from the same military unit, who become one of the most vocal Salafi leaders after the war. He accused Bosniak Muslims of practicing "communist Islam" (Dnevnik 2016).

Many of these Arab fighters married local Bosniak Muslim women and disseminated their interpretations of Salafi Islam to family and friends. This was also the case with Bosniak Muslim fighters from the El-Mujaheed unit who openly admitted to having been heavily influenced by the Islamic practices of fellow Arab fighters (Karup 1998). It is worth noting that villages where mujahidin fighters settled after the war became, years later, epicenters of illegal Salafi mosques and congregations, recognized neither by the state nor by the Islamic Community in Bosnia-Herzegovina (Turčalo and Veljan 2018).

Toward the end of the war, foreign fighters took the implementation of Islamic religious norms into their own hands. Senad Omerašević, a journalist from the Bosnian town of Zavidovići, told me how in 1995 and 1996 mujahidin fighters would even fire rounds into the air to scare off young Bosnian teenage boys and girls who were swimming in the Krivaja River. The mujahidin considered such mixing of sexes as un-Islamic and saw themselves as the implementers of Islamic norms. However, their behavior drew the ire of local Bosnian Muslims, who were happy to see them leave after the war.

Postwar Saudi Influence in Bosnia and Herzegovina

The postwar period was associated with increased religiosity. According to a research carried out in 2000, 89.5 percent of Croats and 78.3 percent of Bosniak Muslims declared themselves as "religious persons." Other research from the same year in the town of Doboj showed that 88 percent of Croats, 84.8 percent of Bosniak Muslims, and 81.6 percent of Serbs declared themselves as "very religious" or "medium religious" (Fazlić 2012). Compared to the earlier cited levels of religiosity during the communist republic of Yugoslavia, the postwar change in religiosity is evident.

After every war, reconstruction begins. Bosniak Muslims started seeking donations to reconstruct the country as early as 1996. Apart from the tens of thousands of destroyed homes and buildings, Bosnian Serb and Croat forces had also destroyed a total of 614 of the 1,144 mosques active in the country, as well as 405 out of the 1,425 Islamic religious endowments (Racimora 2013). It was a systematic campaign of cleansing their territory of any traces of Islamic heritage. Though European countries helped reconstruct schools, hospitals, and cultural institutions, they were reluctant to rebuild destroyed mosques. Bosnian Muslims turned to Muslim-majority countries for help, and it was the latter that willingly answered their call.

It was mostly the same countries that had aided Bosnia and Herzegovina during the war that continued their support after the war. The postwar period was marked by the continued activities of Saudi state institutions and nongovernmental organizations, the departure and eventual deportation of foreign Salafi fighters, and the increased number of Bosniak Muslim students pursuing their higher education in the Middle East.

Saudi State-Funded Activities in Postwar Bosnia

After the war, the Saudi High Commission financed the construction of hundreds of new houses for Bosniak Muslims forcefully displaced by Bosnian Serb forces during the war or whose homes were destroyed as a result of fighting (Hadžić 2000). The Saudis also donated money for the reconstruction of public schools, hospitals, and drinking water networks in the country.[1] It should be stressed that many of these projects benefited all Bosnian citizens, regardless of religious affiliation. In the field of Islamic da'wa, the Saudi High Commission continued translating and publishing Islamic books as it had done during the war. So-called family libraries consisting of a dozen Islamic books were distributed free of charge to many Bosnian Muslims families. The authors or translators of such books were in most cases Bosnian graduates of Middle Eastern universities. According to a Saudi official, from 1992 until 1998 the Saudi High Commission had published and distributed half a million copies of the Qur'an in the Bosnian language, 1.5 million other Islamic books, and 200,000 audio cassettes with recitations of the Qur'an. The Committee had also organized ninety courses for the memorization of the Qur'an, and 118 one-month shari'a courses, and had given out 200,000 headscarves to Bosnian Muslim women (Ibn Abdur-Rahman 1998). The Saudis also funded the construction of the two Islamic pedagogical academies in the towns of Zenica and Bihać and the renovation of numerous waqf properties.

Although countries such as Malaysia, Qatar, Turkey, Kuwait, and Indonesia paid for the construction of new mosques in Bosnia and Herzegovina, the Saudis topped the list. According to a 2011 report presented at the closing ceremony of the Saudi High Commission, the Saudis had by then built twenty brand new mosques, reconstructed 165 damaged mosques, and additionally helped refurbish another 400 (Blijesak 2011). The most *éclatant* and visible example of Saudi influence is the King Fahd Mosque in Sarajevo, opened in 2000. Although nominally under the control of the Islamic Community, it remains a major meeting place of Salafis in the country. In fact, several researchers believe that financial support for Salafi preaching in the country was and perhaps still is being channeled through the King Fahd Cultural Center, which is located within the same compound as the mosque (Bećirević 2016).

Since 2011 until 2020, only a handful of mosques have been reconstructed or renovated by the Saudis. In fact, the overwhelming majority of new mosques constructed over the past decade (2010–2020) have been financed by Bosnian Muslims themselves (Zorlak 2018).

Saudi-Funded Nongovernmental Organizations in Bosnia

Perhaps the most talked about Islamic youth organization in postwar Bosnia and Herzegovina was the now-defunct Active Islamic Youth (AIY). The AIY, initially funded by the Saudi High Commission, was established in the years following the end of the war by former Bosnian members of the El-Mujaheed unit with the aim of continuing their *da'wa* (Islamic proselytism) after the war (Karup 1998). The years 1999 and 2000 were the apex of their activism—they organized weekly lectures, round table discussions, monthly *shari'a* courses, summer schools, and youth camps (Karup 1998). This helped attract many young, self-searching Muslims, particularly those from the margins of society. However, the AIY was shut down in 2003 due to both a lack of funding and also because of US pressure following the 9/11 Al-Qaeda attacks (Bećirević 2018). Its mouthpiece, the *SAFF Magazine*, made a transition from being an exclusively Salafi magazine to becoming a purely Bosniak nationalist media outlet, focusing extensively on local politics, and was largely supportive of the Party of Democratic Action (SDA).

Organizations funded by Saudi Arabia—such as the Muslim World League, Al Haramain Foundation, World Assembly of Muslim Youth, Saudi Arabian Red Crescent Society, Islamic Waqf Organization, Society for the Revival of Islamic Heritage, Muwafaq Foundation, Third World Relief Agency, and the Makkah Humanitarian Organization—all continued their activities in Bosnia and Herzegovina after the war. They built homes for the internally displaced, organized lectures and courses on Islam, and financially helped orphans and families of fallen Bosnian Muslim soldiers. Most of these organizations continued publishing and disseminating Islamic literature until they were forcibly shut down following the 9/11 attacks.

Saudi Scholarships for Bosnian Muslim Students

Before the war, small groups of Bosniak Muslim students had traveled to Arab countries for undergraduate degrees in Islamic studies and Arabic language, mostly to Cairo and Baghdad. Toward the end of the 1980s, Saudi Arabia also became a destination. However, during those years, studying in the Arab world was strictly controlled by the communist regime, and students received scholarships through official lines of communication between then-Yugoslavia and various Arab countries. However, during and immediately after the war, the chaotic atmosphere in the country resulted in little transparency and state oversight as to who was going where.

I was told by Muhamed Jusić, the spokesperson of the Islamic Community, that they do not have precise statistics on the number of Bosnian Muslim students who have graduated from Middle Eastern universities (personal interview, November 25, 2019). Bosnian state institutions have no details either, while the embassies of Arab countries in Sarajevo are not very forthcoming in sharing such information. Rough estimates are that a few hundred Bosnian Muslim students have graduated from Middle Eastern universities since the end of the war, mostly in Egypt, Saudi Arabia, Jordan, and Kuwait. The question of whether these students adopted different interpretations of Islam has become the subject of much debate in recent years. However, research has shown that the Saudis targeted two specific groups among Bosnian Muslim students. The first were youth who had accepted Salafism and showed intertest in Salafi preaching, while the second group were Bosnian Muslim students who showed interest in religion but had not yet adopted Salafism (Turčalo and Veljan 2018).

Bosnian Muslim Reactions to Saudi Salafism

From the 1992–1995 war until the present day, there have been verbal arguments in the public sphere between proponents of "traditional Bosnian Muslims" and Salafis. The most common disagreements have revolved around alleged innovations (bid'a) in Islam (including celebrating the Prophet's birthday, the position of the hands and feet during prayer, use of prayer beads, and raising hands in supplication—du'a). The Islamic Community realized the gravity of the problem at an early stage. As a reaction to Salafi influence, as early as in 1993, the grand mufti of the Islamic Community issued a fatwa making it compulsory for all Muslim religious leaders in the country to adhere to the official Hanafi school of law (Cerić 1993).

A second wave of criticism of Salafism came in mid-1995 in the form of articles published in the official newspaper of the Islamic Community Preporod from Islamic religious leaders ('*ulama*) such as Mustafa Effendi Spahić and Ferid Effendi Dautović. Both openly blamed Islamic humanitarian organizations and Islamic missionaries for the spread of Salafism. Bearing in mind that these reactions came in 1995, it is clear that the Islamic Community was aware from the onset of the challenge posed by Saudi Salafism. Reactions against Salafi interpretations of Islam continued and reached their peak in 2006 and 2007, when the Islamic Community issued two resolutions against "alternative" interpretations of Islam and promoted the *Islamic Tradition of Bosniaks* (Karčić 2006).

Today, a vetting system has been introduced to limit foreign influence. The Islamic Community requires all foreign degrees in Islamic studies to be recognized by the Faculty of Islamic Studies in Sarajevo. They have the discretionary power to decide whether they recognize a certain degree or not. Additionally, to become an imam, the Islamic Community requires candidates to have completed education at a Bosnian madrasa (equivalent to a secondary school). Unlike similar schools in Pakistan and Afghanistan, Bosnian madrasas are generally seen as the incubators of a moderate "Bosnian Islam."

In private conversations, a number of high-ranking former and serving Islamic Community officials have told me that during and immediately after the war, Saudi Arabia was a major donor in the reconstruction of Bosnia's destroyed Islamic heritage and hence they were cautious when criticizing Saudi Salafism so as not to offend their donors. Saudi Salafis clearly took advantage of the wartime and postwar structural cleavages and financial weaknesses to establish their own base of followers. At one time, so emboldened were they that some Salafi preachers called for Bosniak Muslims to avoid praying behind Bosnian Muslim imams, whom they accused of practicing *bid'a* or innovations to Islam (Turčalo and Veljan 2018).

In 2017, in an attempt to rein in informal Salafi congregations and under-the-radar mosques (usually in private homes of Salafi leaders), the Islamic Community gave an ultimatum to all Salafi groups to recognize the authority of the Islamic Community and integrate. Most obliged, and the few that refused to integrate were raided by Bosnian security agencies.

Making Sense of Salafism among Bosniak Muslims

Bosnia's postwar transition has been marred by widespread socioeconomic deprivation, mistrust, and mass corruption. Among Bosniak Muslims, who were victims of genocide, feelings of injustice and utter defeatism prevail. Though a majority in the country, they remain cornered on some 51 percent of the country's territory.

Looking back at the 1992–1995 war from today's perspective, many researchers might wonder why Bosnia accepted financial and military aid from Muslim-majority countries. It should be taken into consideration that the United Nations had an arms embargo placed on Bosnia, ostensibly to limit fighting capabilities of *all* three sides. However, Bosnian Serb and Bosnian Croat forces had the upper hand, as they were armed and financed by neighboring Serbia and Croatia, respectively, while the embargo left Bosniak Muslims defenseless. Wartime prime minister Haris Silajdžić explained it succinctly in the following words: "The atmosphere is such that everyone is saying: Enough is enough. We will accept arms from anyone who offers. It is our right. To keep an embargo on a country being devastated by a war machine is simply not right. The world should either stop the aggression or let us stop it. The alternative for us is to lie down and die" (Murphy 1992).

Similarly, in an interview with British journalist Robert Fisk in December 1992, a Bosniak Muslim commander said, "Of course we need guns. We need help—and yes, why not from the Arabs? We need money, food, clothes. We need to train our officers because the Serbs had most of the officer posts in the Yugoslav army. The Arabs are our brothers and they want to help us. The UN does not help us. How can you blame us for accepting Arab assistance?" (Fisk 1992).

However, what Bosnian Muslims in those years had not expected was that along with arms, food rations, medicine, and money, Muslim-majority countries—in this case, Saudi Arabia in particular—would use the chaotic situation and their leverage as a major donor country to promote their interpretation of Islam. The seeds of Saudi Salafism were planted during the war, nurtured in postwar years, and are bearing fruit today in the form of homegrown Salafis.

Though Saudi activities dwindled following the 9/11 attacks and greater scrutiny of Middle Eastern money flowing to Bosnia, this by no means stopped their activities. As recently as 2019, the Saudis donated 150,000 euros to renovate a dilapidated student dormitory in Sarajevo which will also feature an Islamic center (M.N. 2019). But as a sign of changing times, Saudis donated money for non-religious activities as well—in 2018 Saudi Arabia donated one million euros for upgrading ammunition storage facilities of Bosnia's Armed Forces.

Certain "push" factors ought to be considered when analyzing the lure of Salafism among young Muslims. For a start, although all ethnic groups suffered losses during the war, Bosniak Muslims faced genocide. Given the fact that a majority of pre-war Bosniak Muslims were not religious, the notion that "their lack of true belief was to blame for ethnic cleansing and genocide" was often used by Salafis to strengthen their recruitment narrative (Ruge 2017).

In addition, large segments of society today lack any sensible vision of the future and remain disillusioned with and skeptical of their religious and political leaders. Such an atmosphere of uncertainty enables foreign elements to push forward their agenda. Here Salafism provides certainty and clear-cut answers to many life issues.

Perhaps an additionally important push factor is the continued war-mongering by Bosnian Serbs and Croat nationalist politicians and their constant threats of secession and a redrawing of state borders. For a nation that has survived genocide and continues to live as a minority in a non-Muslim region, Salafism perhaps provides a safe haven and a sense of belonging to the wider Muslim ummah. Some Salafis have in fact gained numerous followers by pointing to continuing dangers of Serb aggression that will not disappear until Bosnian Muslims embrace "true Islam."

Then, there were the "pull" factors, such as conditioned scholarships, financial aid, and direct proselytizing by Saudi and Saudi-inspired Bosniak Muslim preachers during and after the war.

What do Bosniak Muslims think of Saudi Arabia today? According to a 2017 IRI study, when asked what their opinion was of Saudi Arabia, 56 percent of Bosniak Muslims said they had a "mostly or somewhat positive opinion" of the kingdom. For comparison's sake, 55 percent of Bosniak Muslims had a "mostly or somewhat positive opinion" of the United States, while 76 percent of Bosniak Muslims had a "mostly or somewhat positive opinion" of Turkey (IRI 2017).

Yet, when asked which country they considered to be Bosnia's biggest ally, 51 percent of Bosniak Muslims polled said Turkey, 17 percent considered Germany to be their major ally, and 11 percent considered the United States their major ally.

While considering Turkey an ally and having a rather positive view of Saudi Arabia, a significant percentage of Bosniak Muslims strongly support Bosnia's accession to NATO. Precisely, 58 percent of Bosniak Muslims support the country entering the Western military alliance, compared to just 5 percent of Bosnian Serbs and 44 percent of Bosnian Croats. Similarly, a high percentage of Bosniak Muslims support the country joining the European Union. Precisely, 68 percent of Bosniak Muslims strongly support Bosnia joining the European Union, compared to just 21 percent of Bosnian Serbs and 53 percent of Bosnian Croats (IRI 2017).

Hence, Bosnian Muslims seem to be a reflection of their geographical position—religiously turned toward the East, but politically toward the West.

Note

1. For more on the activities of the King Fahd Cultural Center, see "Aktivnosti" https://www.kf-cc.ba/aktivnosti/5.

References

"Abu Hamza se ispričao muslimanima u BiH." 2016. *Dnevnik.* https://dnevnik.hr/vijesti/svijet/abu-hamza-se-ispricao-muslimanima-u-bih.html (accessed April 25, 2020).

Ali, Ahmed Muhammad. 1995. "Saudijski narod je jedan od najosjećajnijih naroda koji znaju da suosjećaju sa svojom braćom u nevolji." *Preporod* 3(574) (March): 16–17.

Ardat, Muhamed. 1995. "Allah dž.š. neće zaboraviti narod koji ga poštuje." *Preporod* 4(575) (April): 24.

Bećirević, Edina. 2016. *Salafism vs. Moderate Islam: A Rhetorical Fight for the Hearts and Minds of Bosnian Muslims.* Sarajevo: Atlantska inicijativa.

Bećirević, Edina. 2018. "Extremism Research Forum: Bosnia and Herzegovina Report." *British Council.* https://wb-iisg.com/wp-content/uploads/bp-attachments/5595/erf_bih_report_British-Council.pdf (accessed April 25, 2020), p. 17.

Bljesak. 2011. "Saudijski komitet u BiH zaključio svoj rad sa preko 560 milijuna dolara pomoći." *Bljesak.* December 22, 2011. https://www.bljesak.info/vijesti/flash/saudijski-komitet-u-bih-zakljucio-svoj-rad-sa-preko-560-milijuna-dolara-pomoci/52127 (accessed September 20, 2021).

"Bosnia and Herzegovina: Attitudes on Violent Extremism and Foreign Influence." 2017. International Republican Institute. https://www.iri.org/sites/default/files/iri_bosnia_poll_february_2016_v9_0.pdf (accessed April 25, 2020).

Bougarel, Xavier. 2018. *Islam and Nationhood in Bosnia-Herzegovina: Surviving Empires.* London: Bloomsbury Academic.

Cerić, Mustafa. 1993. "Fetva o obavezi pridržavanja hanefijskog mezheba." *Islamic Community in Bosnia and Herzegovina.* Available at the official website of the Islamic Community. https://static.islamskazajednica.ba/fetve-i-rezolucije/193-fetva-o-obavezi-pridrfavanja-henefijskog-mezheba.

Ćidić, Ismail. 2018. "Profesor Darryl Li: Alija Izetbegović nije doveo mudžahedine." *Al Jazeera Balkans.* http://balkans.aljazeera.net/vijesti/profesor-darryl-li-alija-izetbegovic-nije-doveo-mudzahedine (accessed April 25, 2020).

Cohen, J. Lenard. 1998. "Bosnia's 'Tribal Gods': The Role of Religion in Nationalist Politics." In *Religion and the War in Bosnia,* edited by Paul Mojzes, 43–73. Atlanta, GA: Scholars Press.

Cushman, Thomas, and Stjepan G. Meštrović, eds. 1996. *This Time We Knew: Western Responses to Genocide in Bosnia.* New York: New York University Press.

Donnely, Maria Galperin, Thomas M. Sanderson, and Zack Fellman. 2020. *Case Studies in History: Afghanistan, Bosnia, Chechnya.* http://foreignfighters.csis.org/history/case-studies.html (accessed April 20, 2020).

El-Džuheni, Mani'. 1995. "Ne potencirati razlike među mezhebima." *Preporod* 4(575) (April): 4.

Fazlić, Hazim. 2015. "The Elements That Contributed to the Survival of Islam in Tito's Yugoslavia." *Journal of Islamic Studies* 26(3): 289–304.

Fazlić, Hazim. 2012. *Islam in the Successor States of Former Yugoslavia: Religious Changes in the Post-Communist Balkans from 1989–2009.* PhD dissertation, University of Birmingham. https://etheses.bham.ac.uk/id/eprint/3997/ (accessed April 25, 2020).

Fisk, Robert. 1992. "'Arab Brothers' Come to Aid of Bosnian Forces: Muslim Fighters Are Getting Help from the East." *The Independent.* https://www.independent.co.uk/news/world/europe/arab-brothers-come-to-aid-of-bosnian-forces-muslim-fighters-are-getting-help-from-the-east-robert-1561377.html (accessed April 25, 2020).

Gow, James. 2003. *The Serbian Project and Its Adversaries*. Montreal: McGill-Queen's University Press.

Hadžić, Hasan. 2000. "Arizona Deal." *BH Dani*. https://www.bhdani.ba/portal/arhiva-67-281/167/t16708.htm (accessed April 25, 2020).

Halilović, Safvet. 2012. "Saudijska Arabija je dokazani prijatelj Bosne i Hercegovine i svih njenih naroda." *Bošnjaci*. https://www.bosnjaci.net/prilog.php?pid=47042 (accessed April 25, 2020).

Ibn Abdur-Rahman es-Seid, Sheikh Nasir. 1998. "Bratska pomoć bez ikakvog uslovljavanja." *Preporod* 7(633) (1 Apri):l 16–17.

Karčić, Fikret. 2006. "Šta je to 'Islamska tradicija Bošnjaka?" *Preporod*, No.23/841, 1 December 2006, 14–15.

Karčić, Fikret. 2011. *Studije o šerijatskom pravu i institucijama*. Drugo dopunjeno izdanje. Sarajevo: IC El-Kalem i Centar za Napredne Studije.

Karčić, Fikret. 2014. *Muslimanki Balkana: "Istočno pitanje" u XX. Vijeku*. Drugo Izdanje. Sarajevo: Centar za napredne studije.

Karčić, Harun. 2018. *Šerijat i pravni pluralizam u Evropi: Primjeri koegzistencije religijskog i sekularnog prava na Starom kontinentu*. Sarajevo: Centar za Napredne Studije.

Karup, Dženana. 1998. "Kur'an je naš ustav." *BH Dani* 72 (30 Mart): 14–19.

Lučić, Iva. 2018. "Kako je Bošnjacima priznat nacionalni identitet 'Muslimani'?" Intervju sa Ivom Lučić. *Preporod*. https://www.preporod.com/index.php/intervju/item/9210-kako-je-bosnjacima-priznat-nacionalni-identitet-muslimani (accessed April 25, 2020).

Lučić, Ivo. 2017. "Nevjerojatno! Bakir kao i Alija Izetbegović tvrdi da su mudžahedine doveli Hrvati!" *Jutarnji List*. https://www.jutarnji.hr/globus/Globus-politika/nevjeroja tno-bakir-kao-i-alija-izetbegovic-tvrdi-da-su-mudzahedine-doveli-hrvati/6555240/ (accessed April 25, 2020).

Malcolm, Noel. 2011. *Bosna: Kratka povijest*. Sarajevo: Buybook.

Mirescu, Alexander. 2003. "Religion and Ethnic Identity Formation in the Former Yugoslavia." *Occasional Papers on Religion in Eastern Europe* 23(1): 1–18.

Misri, Imad. 1993. Shvatanja koja trebamo ispraviti. *Švedska davetska organizacija*. https://www.scribd.com/doc/179027450/Shvatanja-Koja-Trebamo-Ispraviti (accessed April 20, 2020).

M.N. 2019. "Studentski dom u Sarajevu dobija još jedan moderni paviljon, finansiraju ga Arapi." *Klix*. https://www.klix.ba/vijesti/bih/studentski-dom-u-sarajevu-dobija-jos-jedan-moderni-paviljon-finansiraju-ga-arapi/191119113 (accessed April 25, 2020).

Murphy, Kim. 1992. "Islamic Nations to Press for Military Aid to Bosnia." *Los Angeles Times*. December 1, 1992. https://www.latimes.com/archives/la-xpm-1992-12-01-mn-1538-story.html (accessed April 25, 2020).

Powers, Gerard F. 1996 "Religion, Conflict and Prospects for Peace in Bosnia, Croatia and Yugoslavia." *Occasional Papers on Religion in Eastern Europe* 16(5): 221–252.

Pomfret, John. 1996. "Bosnia's Muslims Dodged Embargo." *Washington Post*. September 22, 1996. https://www.washingtonpost.com/wp-srv/inatl/longterm/bosvote/front.htm (accessed April 25, 2020).

Racimora, W. 2013. "Salafist/Wahhabite Financial Support to Educational, Social and Religious Institutions." Belgium: Policy Department of Directorate-General for External Policies of the European Union. https://www.europarl.europa.eu/RegData/etudes/etudes/join/2013/457136/EXPO-AFET_ET(2013)457136_EN.pdf.

Riedel, Bruce. 2017. "The Next King of the Saudis: Salman, the Family Sheriff." *The Daily Beast*. April 14, 2017. https://www.thedailybeast.com/the-next-king-of-the-saudis-sal man-the-family-sheriff (accessed April 25, 2020).

Ruge, Majda. "Radicalization among Muslim Communities in the Balkans: Trends and Issues." June 14, 2017. Hearing on: Southeast Europe: Strengthening Democracy and Countering Malign Foreign Influence. https://www.foreign.senate.gov/imo/media/doc/061417_Ruge_Testimony_REVISED.pdf (accessed April 25, 2020).

"Saudijski komitet u BiH zaključio svoj rad sa preko 560 milijuna dolara pomoći" 2011. *Bljesak info*. https://www.bljesak.info/vijesti/flash/saudijski-komitet-u-bih-zakljucio-svoj-rad-sa-preko-560-milijuna-dolara-pomoci/52127 (accessed April 25, 2020).

Spahić, Mustafa. 1995. "Rušenje posljednjeg utočišta." *Preporod* 6(577) (July): 24.

Subašić, Edin. 2019. "'Džihad' u BIH: Mudžahedini su podvala Zapada." *Al Jazeera Balkans*. http://balkans.aljazeera.net/vijesti/dzihad-u-bih-1-mudzahedini-su-podv ala-zapada (accessed April 25, 2020).

Trhulj, Sead. 1992. *Mladi muslimani*. Sarajevo: Globus.

Turčalo, Sead, and Nejra Veljan. 2018. "Community Perspectives on the Prevention of Violent Extremism in Bosnia and Herzegovina." Country Case, Study 2. *Berghof Foundation*. https://www.berghof-foundation.org/fileadmin/redaktion/Publications/Other_Resources/WB_PVE/CTR_CaseStudy2BiH_e.pdf (accessed April 25, 2020).

Verkaik, Robert. 2016. "The Trials of Babar Ahmad: From Jihad in Bosnia to a US Prison via Met Brutality." *The Guardian*. https://www.theguardian.com/uk-news/2016/mar/12/babar-ahmad-jihad-bosnia-us-police-interview (accessed April 25, 2020).

Weinberg, David Andrew. 2015. "King Salman's Shady History." *Foreign Policy*. January 27, 2015. https://foreignpolicy.com/2015/01/27/king-salmans-shady-history-saudi-arabia-jihadi-ties/ (accessed April 25, 2020).

Zorlak, Kemal. 2018. "Dan džamija: Od rata do sada u BiH obnovljeno 1.175 džamija i mesdžida." *Anadolu Ajansi*. https://www.aa.com.tr/ba/balkan/dan-d%C5%BEamija-od-rata-do-sada-u-bih-obnovljeno-1175-d%C5%BEamija-i-mesd%C5%BEida/1137409 (accessed September 7, 2020).

15

The Shifting Contours of Saudi Influence in Britain

Hira Amin

It is undeniable that Saudi Arabia has played a significant role in shaping the British Muslim landscape. Yet, far from being static, its influence has shifted over time. This chapter suggests that since the late 1960s to the present day there have been four broad stages of Saudi Arabia's impact on the development and evolution of Islam in Britain.

The first stage is marked by institution building, religious diplomacy, pan-Islamic networks, and a spectacular show of wealth, as Saudi Arabia attempted to pave the way to become a dominant force in the Muslim world. This period laid the foundations of Saudi influence in Britain and paved the way for the second stage, from the mid-1980s to the mid-1990s, when Saudi-style Salafism[1] captivated the hearts and minds of many young British Muslims. Salafi scholars and graduates of the Islamic University of Medina projected an "authentic," "universal," and "deculturized" Islam that appealed to the new British-born generation, eager to connect to the wider ummah. They trumped other sectarian rivals, who were either still deeply embedded within South Asian cultural mores, or were largely political, without a strong connection to the Qur'an and *hadith*. However, from the mid-1990s, things began to unravel—this was the third stage. Spurred by Salafism's success, other sectarian rivals adapted to the British context, becoming attractive alternatives; the burgeoning Salafi movement internally fractured, and segments of British Salafis, as well as British Muslims overall, began to turn their focus toward establishing an Islam that was more conducive to the West. The post–9/11 and 7/7 context exacerbated things further and marked the beginning of the fourth stage. The rise of new social, political, and intellectual challenges, coupled with the disillusionment of oppositional politics and sectarian polemics, led to an alteration of priorities and paradigms. In this new climate, Saudi Salafi institutions and their scholars are no longer the prime model.

Hira Amin, *The Shifting Contours of Saudi Influence in Britain* In: *Wahhabism and the World*. Edited by: Peter Mandaville, Oxford University Press. © Oxford University Press 2022. DOI: 10.1093/oso/9780197532560.003.0015

The Foundations, 1960–1985: Saudi Arabia's Pan-Islamic Outreach and the Ahl-e-Hadith

Between the 1880s and 1920s, the collective experience of imperialism sparked a wave of pan-Islamic solidarity throughout the Muslim world. But this was short-lived. The aftermath of World War II gave birth to a myriad of nation-states, politically dividing Muslim societies more than before, eclipsing Muslim unity with secular Third World internationalism. Particularly in the Arab world, the Egyptian Revolution of 1952 brought Gamal 'Abd al-Nasser to power, where he promoted a secular, pan-Arab vision, opposing the other Arab monarchies in the region, precipitating what some have called the "Arab Cold War" (Kerr 1971). Against this backdrop, Prince Faisal, who became the Saudi king in 1964, started laying the foundations for pan-Islamic unity with Saudi Arabia at its center. As well as actively fostering bilateral ties with other Muslim nations, he helped to establish international Muslim organizations, such as the Islamic University of Medina (IUM) in 1961, the Muslim World League in 1962, the Organization of Islamic Cooperation in 1969,[2] and the Islamic Development Bank in 1975. Initially, under the fervor of Nasser's secular nationalism, King Faisal's outreach was not met with great enthusiasm. However, the tide soon turned. The violence of decolonization, Cold War politics that disrupted national interests,[3] and re-ligious resurgence precipitated by demographic shifts and rapid urbanization (Arjomand 2010, 173–178) together reignited pan-Islamic unity that bolstered King Faisal's efforts and placed Saudi Arabia in a prime position (Aydin 2017, chapter 6).

It is in this context that Saudi Arabia's gaze turned toward Britain. One of the main projects was the 1976 World of Islam Festival, which was "the largest ever presentation of Islamic material culture in a Western country" (Grinell 2018, 74). Precise figures are unavailable, yet it is uncontested that the bulk of funds for the festival came from countries on the Arabian Peninsula, including Saudi Arabia. Although the plans were initially drawn up before the oil boom of the 1970s, the increased wealth expanded the size and scope of the festival. Held primarily in London, with events scattered around the country, the ceremony was opened by Queen Elizabeth II with other prominent figures present, such as the archbishop of Canterbury, Donald Coggan, and the grand imam of Al-Azhar, Abd al-Halim Mahmud. Despite the sizable number of Muslims in Britain at that time, the event was not about, nor did it include, Islam or Muslims in Britain. The festival's main aim was to showcase a timeless and unified Islamic civilization distinct from modern Britain. In fact, newspapers reported that some British Muslims were apprehensive due to the syncretic and heterodox nature of the art. This was clearly not an issue for Saudi officials, who were more focused on religious and political diplomacy (Grinell 2018).

Seen in this light, it is perhaps not surprising that Saudi Arabia also partly or wholly funded many infrastructural projects in Britain for both Salafi and non-Salafi organizations. Perhaps the most famous is the Islamic Cultural Centre in London, most commonly referred to as Regent's Park Mosque. Initially funded by Prime Minister Winston Churchill and the Egyptian government in the 1940s, Saudi Arabia rebuilt it in the 1970s, paying large sums and also covering the maintenance and administration costs (Al-Rasheed 2005, 157). Other notable mosques and institutions that have received some funding include: East London Mosque in Tower Hamlets; Goodge Street Mosque in London, which is the European headquarters for the Muslim World League; Masjid Tawhid in Leyton; Edinburgh Central Mosque; Al Muntada al-Islami Trust, which is an Islamic center and registered charity in South West London; and the Islamic Foundation in Leicester, which specializes in research, education, and publication (Al-Rasheed 2005; Birt 2007; Eade 1996, 219). As Al-Rasheed points out, "donations for less prestigious organizations tend to be covert, as they pass through personal networks and connections, which people are reluctant to disclose" (Al-Rasheed 2005, 154).

The Afghan-Soviet War in 1979 proved to be another opportunity for Saudi Arabia to take the lead for pan-Islamic unity. Large sums of money were funneled to Afghanistan to train and support the fighters—the mujahidin (Jalali 2017, chapter 9). Common political interests led British officials to allow Saudi emissaries to more or less openly preach and recruit British Muslims for the Afghan "jihad" in the 1980s and 1990s (Al-Rasheed 2005, 156).

Another significant line of Saudi connection in this period was the South Asian Ahl-e-Hadith. As has been heavily documented, the bulk of Muslim migration in the 1960s came largely from South Asia following the Second World War and the passing of the British Nationality Act of 1948 in which former subjects of the British Empire could be granted British citizenship (Abbas 2007; Peach 2006).[4] The initial group of migrants were men, joined by their wives and children. As numbers increased, and communities, mosques, and institutions grew in tandem, they divided along ethnic and sectarian lines, replicating the five main South Asian Sunni schisms: Deobandis, Barelwis, Fultolis, Jamaat-e-Islami, and the Ahl-e-Hadith (Ahmed and Ali 2019; Ansari 2004; Gilliat-Ray 2010).

The Ahl-e-Hadith were a relatively small elite reformist movement born in mid-nineteenth-century British India. As Suroosh Irfani (2004, 148) shows, the Ahl-e-Hadith were among the first to set in motion what he terms as the "Arabist shift," moving away from the Indo-Persian culture prevalent in the region since the eleventh century.[5] Overlapping intellectual genealogies led them to develop bilateral ties with the Wahhabi movement in Arabia, influencing many prominent Salafi scholars and co-establishing institutions, such as the Dar al-Hadith in Medina (Lacroix 2009). From the nineteenth century (and continuing to this day) there has been a constant stream of scholars and students traveling between Saudi Arabia and South Asia. One pertinent example for this chapter is Abdul Ghaffar Hassan—a prominent Ahl-e-Hadith scholar originally from Umarpur who was selected in 1964 by a delegation from Saudi Arabia to teach *hadith* at the IUM (Abou Zahab 2009, 130). Later, as will be discussed later in the chapter, his son, Suhaib Hasan, also graduated from this university and became one of the leaders of the Ahl-e-Hadith in Britain.

These transnational ties helped to lay the foundations of Salafism in Britain. The first British Ahl-e-Hadith mosque in Birmingham, which later became known as Green Lane Masjid, was established in the late 1970s, funded by a Kuwaiti businessman. It was established by Maulana Fazal Karim Asim, a graduate from an Ahl-e Hadith school in Amritsar and Punjab University. Asim, together with other like-minded individuals, created a network of centers and mosques throughout the country, known as the Markaz Jamiat Ahl-e-Hadith (MJAH) (Abou Zahab 2009, 132; Azami 1995, 18–19). Around this time, Asim performed *hajj* and met 'Abd al-'Aziz bin Baz—at that time the chairman of the Saudi Dar al-Ifta—to discuss ways of collaboration. Bin Baz then sent two Pakistani IUM graduates, Mahmud Ahmad Mirpuri and Sharif Ahmad Hafiz, to help MJAH in 1975. Suhaib Hasan also migrated to Britain in 1976 to pursue his doctorate.[6] All three became active leaders of MJAH.

The Ahl-e-Hadith provided a platform for the Arab Salafis. They avidly translated and distributed Salafi books, and translated lectures of Middle Eastern Salafi scholars (MJAH UK 2008). Yet, despite this support, the Ahl-e-Hadith, relative to other South Asian factions, remained a minority in Britain and were largely shunned by the other groups as "Wahhabis," sometimes even considered to be outside the fold of Sunni Islam. Their staunch anti-Sufi and anti-*madhhab* message simply failed to resonate with the predominately Hanafi and Sufi-orientated flavor of South Asian Islam. They also maintained their South Asian flavor of Salafism in terms of dress codes, language, and intellectual lineage (Amin and Majothi 2021). Although in their publications they described themselves as being part of the wider global Salafi movement (Ahmed Mirpuri et al. 1987, 25), to this day they prefer the label "Ahl-e-Hadith."

In this period, the splendor of Saudi wealth manifested primarily in its large, mainly infrastructural projects that did not translate into religious influence with immediate effect. The Ahl-e-Hadith remained a minority in the fledgling British Muslim landscape and anchored themselves in their South Asian tradition. But Saudi Arabia's pan-Islamic outreach included British Muslims in its remit, and this period proved crucial in terms of laying the foundations, institutions, and networks for the next stage.

The Rise: British Salafism and the Aura of Authenticity

The period between the mid-1980s to the mid-1990s was the time when the influence of Saudi Salafism in Britain reached its apex. Arab Salafi scholars, their prominent students, or the few Western-born graduates of Saudi institutes circulated throughout the Western world. With their indefatigable ability to cite Qur'anic verses and *hadith* as primary source evidence, in contrast to "back home" scholars who merely dictated Islamic rulings, young British Muslims were awestruck.[7] Desperately searching for "authentic" Islam and a way of life distinct from Western and South Asian cultural mores, Salafism provided this panacea. Moreover, they were largely unchallenged; the other dominant youth movements in this period were political, allowing the Salafis to position themselves as providing a robust scholarly response.

The first Salafi organization catering to the second generation was Jamiat Ihya Minhaj As Sunnah (JIMAS), founded in 1984 by Muhammad Manwar Ali, who went by the moniker Abu Muntasir (Hamid 2016, 50–67). Originally from a Deobandi and Bangladeshi background, in his teenage years, Abu Muntasir searched for an Islam devoid of cultural baggage. Unwelcomed in many mosques, he found the Ahl-e-Hadith network, including Masjid Tawhid in Leyton—the Ahl-e-Hadith mosque where Suhaib Hasan was based. Thereafter, Abu Muntasir delivered talks in this mosque every Sunday morning for ten years (Usama Hasan, interview with author, May 27, 2015). By traveling to other Ahl-e-Hadith mosques and university Islamic societies, hosting annual conferences in Leicester, and producing short publications, JIMAS and the charismatic and eloquent Abu Muntasir quickly rose to prominence. Initially, approximately 300 people attended their conferences, which were held every two years, but by the 1990s they became an annual event that attracted, on average, 3,000 Muslims.

A sprawling network rapidly developed of predominantly Middle Eastern scholars, particularly students of al-Albani,[8] and a few Western-born scholars, the latter of whom were mainly self-taught or were among the few who had graduated from the IUM.[9] They regularly traveled between the growing network of Salafi organizations in the West, one example being the Al-Quran wa Sunnah Society of North America (QSS); it was common for the same set of speakers to attend both conferences.

Contrary to popular opinion, the success of JIMAS was not due to Saudi Arabia's petrodollars. Abu Muntasir, known for being candid, has always denied any foreign governmental and nongovernmental funding (Inge 2017, 28). Rather, JIMAS had begun to create a new subculture distinct from both South Asian and Western cultural mores. This dual rejection and the shift from an ethnic to a religious identity are one of the dominant tropes in the study of Muslims in Britain (Hinnells 2007; Vertovec and Rogers 1998; McLoughlin and Zavos 2013). Almost all studies on British Muslim youth describe the concerted drive by the British-born, second-generation Muslims to simultaneously reject both the "Western" culture and the "South Asian" culture of their parents; they perceived themselves as part of a global, universal ummah and wanted a "pure" Islam without cultural accretions that they could confidently understand and engage with. This was not simply the result of being a second-generation minority in Britain. Young British Muslims were also swept up in the second wave of pan-Islamic unity and Islamic revival mentioned earlier. Responding to this sentiment, the main international Islamic charities and NGOs were established in this period with their headquarters in Britain but with a global mission: Islamic Relief Worldwide in 1984, Muslim Aid in 1985, Human Appeal in 1991, and Muslim Hands in 1993.

JIMAS also tapped into this vision. It was at the forefront of projecting itself as the main organization of authentic Islam in terms of everyday culture, language, and Islamic knowledge, giving Muslims a sense of global Muslim citizenship, though "global" usually translated into Saudi culture in terms of male and female dress codes, gender segregation, and the preference for Arabic-language pronunciations and phrases (Ramadan 2004, 215).

Seen in this context, it is not surprising that the other two successful youth movements during this time were also advocating a global, universalized Islam: Hizb-ut-Tahrir and Young Muslims UK. Both of these groups were politically oriented, offering very little depth of Islamic knowledge relative to the scholars associated with JIMAS. Other movements, such as the Deobandis, Tablighi Jamaat, and the Barelwis and other Sufis, had yet to adapt themselves to the new British context to attract the new generation. Therefore, in this period between the mid-1980s and mid-1990s, JIMAS had comfortably positioned themselves as the only true followers of an "authentic" Islam, purged of cultural accretions.

Apart from JIMAS, common political and diplomatic interests between the United Kingdom and Saudi Arabia continued. As mentioned earlier, there was the ongoing Saudi support for British jihadis as part of the Afghan-Soviet War effort. Another key event during this time was the Rushdie Affair in the late 1980s, which sparked the formation of nationwide umbrella bodies to coordinate and represent Muslim grievances. One of the dominant organizations was the UK Action Committee on Islamic Affairs (UKACIA), founded in 1989. Its headquarters was based at the Saudi-funded London Central Mosque in Regent's Park, with the director of the mosque, Ali Al-Ghamidi, serving as its chairman. Although by the mid-1990s, the UKACIA had obtained "considerable standing and recognition . . . and a central position as interlocuter" with the British government by utilizing its diplomatic ties, Elshayyal (2018, chapter 4) argues that they had little support among Muslims outside of London, partly due to their connections with the Saudi state.

The Slow Decline: Factions, Fissures, and New Rivals

From the mid-1990s, the peak of Saudi influence began to slowly unravel due to three separate developments: first, the burgeoning British Salafi network internally fractured and entered into a bitter and protracted debate, which still continues to this day; second, partly in reaction to Salafism's success, other sectarian groups entered the scene, breaking the Salafi monopoly of representing "authentic" Islam; third, there was a shift from a global, universal outlook to a focus on new, local challenges and on establishing an Islam more suited to the Western environment.

The Salafi Divide

Salafi movements throughout the Muslim world were constantly evolving, splintering, and mutating as they were buffeted with local, regional, and global struggles—for example, the partition of the Indian subcontinent and the Kashmir crisis, the ongoing struggle for Palestine, the Soviet-Afghan War, and the siege of Mecca in 1979. This led to a wide spectrum of Salafi groups, some of which were in stark contrast to one another. Many of these strands, particularly those in the Arab Gulf states, were replicated in the United Kingdom.

The main disagreement between the Salafis in the Arabian Peninsula was over political engagement. A new splinter movement emerged that blended Salafi theology and social conservatism with the Muslim Brotherhood's approach to politics (Lacroix 2009, 67; International Crisis Group 2004, 2). The key figures of this new offshoot were Abd al-Rahman Abd al-Khaliq, Muhammad Surur Zayn al-Abidin, and the Saudi Sahwa cohort (Lacroix 2011). Despite their reverence for the older scholars linked to the Saudi establishment, such as Bin Baz, the Sahwa scholars were frustrated with their uncritical support for the Saudi regime, lack of political understanding, and myopic concern with Islamic doctrines. The senior scholars claimed, in return, that only privately advising the ruling elite is permissible and that oppositional political engagement, even if nonviolent, was a Western innovation; they prioritized correct religious thought and practice.

The trigger was the 1990 Gulf War *fatwa* when Iraq invaded Kuwait and Saudi Arabia allowed the United Stats to establish an army base on their territory. The Sahwa brazenly criticized the state, gaining immense popularity. By the mid-1990s, Sahwa members were either imprisoned or had fled the country (International Crisis Group 2004, 5). Thereafter, the void left by the repression of political groups and the return of the Afghan-Soviet War veterans also led to the development of jihadi ideologies in the region (Hegghammer 2010).

This fractured the Salafi movement into a spectrum ranging from those who remained fiercely loyal to the Saudi regime to those who criticized them, including those who believed in militant strategies.

This fracture created a ripple effect in the Salafi movement in the West.[10] Either through migration, exile, or travel, Britain became a hub, hosting many of these tendencies. Their ties to Salafism meant that JIMAS and Salafi mosques were their natural home. Up until this point, JIMAS was still unified, but by the mid-1990s each tendency had reached a critical mass which came to a head.

Muhammad al-Masari and Saad al-Faqih were among the Saudi dissents who fled to Britain in 1994. Welcomed by many politically active British Muslims—for example, those linked to Islamist groups and Hizb-ut-Tahrir—they founded the Committee for the Defense of Legitimate Rights in Saudi Arabia. They organized demonstrations outside of the Saudi embassy and press conferences with the mainstream British media (Al-Rasheed 2005, 161). Another dissident who arrived much earlier was Muhammad Surur Zayn al-Abidin—mentioned earlier. He was exiled from Saudi Arabia and, after a short stint in Kuwait, finally settled in Britain in 1984. In Birmingham, Surur helped establish an organization called Markaz Dirasat al-Sunna al-Nabawiya and, in London, the Al-Muntada Trust. He produced a magazine called *As-Sunnah*, and later another entitled *Al-Jumuah* (Bowen 2014, 63). The arrival of these dissidents further fueled internal Salafi debates and undermined Saudi Arabia's credibility among British Muslims overall.

On the other side of the spectrum, more people were returning after their studies in Saudi Arabia. Two key figures were Dawud Burbank, a British Muslim convert, and Abu Hakeem Bilal Davis, an Afro-Caribbean convert. Although neither completed their studies and graduated from the IUM, they were both heavily influenced by al-Albani and Rabi al-Madkhali, a staunch loyalist to the Saudi regime. Upon their return, they avidly translated and disseminated the writings of their mentors, particularly their criticisms of Islamism. They joined the British Muslim preachers Abu Khadeejah and Abu Iyad Amjad, who was also a prolific translator, and together they established the famous website and publishing house Salafi Publications—known primarily for their refutations of other Muslim groups.

Another significant group of dissidents were the *takfiri*-jihadis.[11] Among this group were: Abdullah el Faisal, a graduate of Islamic Studies from Imam Muhammad ibn Saud University, who preached briefly at Brixton Masjid in the 1990s and was later dismissed following his increasingly extreme beliefs; Abu Qatada, former student of al-Albani who interacted mainly with Arab Islamist exiles; and Abu Hamza Muhammad al-Masri, the main student of Abu Qatadah, most famously known for his hand hook and preaching at Finsbury Park Mosque (Baker 2011). Ironically, as Baker (2011, 6–7) illustrates, other Salafi groups

could effectively counter their narrative by providing a contextualized understanding of the Islamic texts they used as justification.

With these conflicting strands, British Salafism had internally imploded.
Much time was spent infighting; each group claimed to be the "true" Salafis.
Eventually, JIMAS whittled down as key players left, either to form new Salafi
splinter groups or to join other movements. To make matters worse, it was at this
precise moment that the other sectarian factions were gaining strength.

Sectarian Rivals

One significant competitor that arose in the 1990s was known as the Traditional
Islam network. Spearheaded mainly by converts, this Sufi-oriented movement
offered an alternative, more spiritually infused understanding of Islam.[12] They
managed to weaken the Salafi claim to textual authority and orthodoxy, arguing
that it was in fact they, not the Salafis, who were keeping in accordance with the
historical "Islamic tradition" by following one of the four legal schools of thought
and practicing *tassawuf* (Sufism). Fluent in English and born and raised in the
West, they became a strong, viable alternative in the British Muslim scene.

The traditional *tariqa*-based Sufism arguably had borne the brunt of the Salafi
onslaught. As Geaves points out, the majority of Muslims in Britain originate
from countries where this form of Sufism is embedded in their social and historical fabric (Geaves 2006, 142). This explains why Britain has the second strongest
Sufi presence in Europe, the first being France (Abo-Alabbas 2015, 9). Yet despite
this numerical majority they were divided, as each group was centered on a charismatic *pir*, their descendants, customs, and shrines—all of which were indelibly
marked by their different geographic areas of origin. As a result, they struggled
to attract the new generation, who were consciously moving away from ethnic
markers and labels. In a bid to pass on their traditions and resist losing the youth
to Salafism, during this time some *tariqas* actively attempted to move beyond
ethnic boundaries and were successful. One example was Faiz-ul-Aqtab of the
Naqshabandi *tariqa*, who became the first British-born *pir* in 1994 (Geaves 2006,
148–149).[13] The Barelwis also began to define themselves as the "Ahlus Sunnah
Wal Jamaa" to underscore that they are the "legitimate" version of Sunni Islam
(Geaves 2006, 148).

The mid-1990s also proved to be a watershed moment for the Tablighi Jamaat.
Timol (2015, 2019) marks this period as the beginning of the second phase of the
Tablighi Jamaat in Britain, where thousands of British-born youth took part in
the *khuruj* (outing), many of whom, he notes, still remain active to this day.[14] In
some regions, they also reacted to Salafi groups. While the northern towns and
cities and the Midlands remained Tablighi Jamaat and Deobandi strongholds, in

other cities, namely London and Birmingham, where Salafis and Hizb-ut-Tahrir were more popular, followers forged their identities in relation to these rivals. In these areas, they relied on Deobandi scholars to produce scholarly responses to Salafism's critiques, and some Tablighi Jamaat followers learned Arabic so that they could also engage directly with the Islamic texts (Timol 2020).[15]

The UK-based Deobandi seminaries were also producing a new generation of British-born Muslims, some of whom opened up new seminaries in the United Kingdom.[16] Razavian and Spannnaus (2018, 180) consider these new initiatives as part of "second-wave" institutions also found in North America, which are "attempting to adjust Deobandi *fiqh* to the needs of Western Muslims . . . and expanding the scope of their activities beyond the South Asian Deobandi community." Even older, established seminaries are undergoing an internal transformation, albeit at a much slower pace, by adopting new pedagogical techniques aimed at making their learning experience more relevant to their context (Sidat 2018).

While Salafis mainly focused on criticizing Sunni revival groups and later other Salafi schisms (Inge 2017, 122), which was one factor causing each of them to react and internally develop, to date there have been a relatively small number of booklets published against Shi'ism (Majothi 2020). As Monaghan (2018, 96–97) has pointed out in her study on Salafi-Shi'ite relations in Britain, each group has very little physical interaction with the other, and they live in their own bubbles.[17] It is interesting to note, however, that British South Asian Twelver Shi'ite Muslims have internally divided; a small group, pejoratively known as "Wahhabi Shi'a," advocate a piety-led life outside the month of Muharram, such as daily prayers and reciting the Qur'an, as well as standardized forms of commemorating Muharram in line with official Iranian guidelines, which crucially do not allow for self-flagellation (Dogra 2019). This emphasis on piety, rituals, and the demystification of the *ahl al-bayt* have led the opposing Shi'ite majority in Britain to accuse them of being an "apologetic response" to the "growing influence of Salafis and the Tablighi Jamaat in Sunni Muslim public spheres" (Dogra 2019, 307).

Establishing Islam in the West

Another key development which began in the mid-1990s was the increased interest in making Islam more suitable to the Western context and focusing on domestic issues rather than matters relating to Muslim-majority countries. To this end, Salafi speakers began to demarcate the "Islamic world" from the "Western world" in order to conceptualize an Islam in the West. One example is JIMAS's 1997 annual conference, which was entitled "Establishing Islam in the West," where speakers discussed how the earlier generations used Islamic principles to find solutions to novel issues that had not occurred during the time of the Prophet (At-Tamimi 1997). In lectures, scholars started using the term "we" to mean specifically "Muslims in the West," as opposed to the wider ummah (Philips 1997a, 1997b).

These early sentiments on rooting Islam in the West, found in Salafi circles, were not isolated incidents but reflected the overall mood during the 1990s in Britain and, indeed, in Western Europe and North America. In the aftermath of local events such as the Rushdie and Honeyford Affairs and international events such as the Bosnian War, the First Gulf War, and the ongoing Palestinian crisis, there was a broad consensus that Muslims needed to better represent themselves and their interests and focus more on domestic issues. In 1997, the same year of the aforementioned JIMAS conference, the Muslim Council of Britain was established. This was a cross-sectarian civic society organization designed to work for British Muslim interests, particularly representing them to the government (Elshayyal 2018). It was also in this year that the European Council for Fatwa and Research (ECFR) was established to develop specialized rulings to help Muslims easily integrate and navigate some of the challenges of living in the West.

This shift in the 1990s was also intellectually bolstered by the concept of *fiqh al-aqalliyat* (jurisprudence of minorities) developed by two prominent and highly influential jurists in the 1990s: Taha Jabir al-Alwani (d. 2016) and Yusuf al-Qaradawi (b. 1926). Grounding their arguments in established legal maxims and the Qur'an and Sunna, they legitimized "the production of context-specific and needs-based rulings for Muslim minorities living in the West" (Whyte 2017, 55). Al-Qaradawi has served as the chairman of the ECFR since its establishment and, in 2004, the *fiqh* of minorities became their official policy (Whyte 2017, 56). The Fiqh Council of North America, established in 1989, also began with similar goals, with Taha al-Alwani acting as its chairman (Whyte 2017).

The September 11, 2001, attacks, the London bombings in 2005, and the subsequent War on Terror ushered in a new era of securitization, rising Islamophobia, and intrusive government agendas aimed at rooting out extremism. Muslims were under intense scrutiny as politicians and the media questioned their loyalty to the nation-state. Undercover reporters secretly recorded video and audio in mosques, capturing snippets of sermons to "frame" their attendees as supporters of radicalism and Islam as an inherently violent religion (Morey and Yaqin 2011); Suhaib Hasan at Green Lane Masjid was among those whom they filmed (Dispatches 2007). These pressing issues accelerated the focus even more to matters pertaining to Muslims in the West. Imams and preachers were now facing unprecedented challenges for which their Salafi training did not prepare them, and for which senior Salafi scholars had little relevant experience.

These three separate developments—internal Salafi divisions and polemics, the rise of other sectarian factions who became viable alternatives, and a reorientation toward developing an Islam of the West—inadvertently worked together to decenter Salafi movements within the British Muslim landscape and weaken the specter of Saudi influence.

Diversification: Post-Sectarianism, New Paradigms and Priorities

In the past decade, the British Muslim landscape has undergone a new turn. This can be described as "post-sectarianism," a term I am using to describe two different yet related phenomena. First is the slow and steady establishment of many issue-based organizations which are not rooted in one of the major global trends in Islam but, instead, are defined by their particular cause, such as the environment, combating Islamophobia, women's empowerment, or mental health. Second is the decline of internal sectarian schisms in favor of broad partnerships to better tackle issues pertaining to Western Muslims, such as rising levels of atheism among Muslims or engaging with local authorities. This is not to say that sectarian factions are no longer suffering from internal polemics or that sectarian organizations are no longer being established, but rather that there is a growing, tangible apathy for labels and disputes, and the focus is being redirected to social or political issues and concerns, rather than the sectarian or doctrinal differences that were characteristic features of the 1990s.[18]

Post-sectarian, issue-based organizations can also be seen as part of the wider disillusionment and even failure of both local and global Muslim political activism. Scholars have described this as "post-Islamism," where oppositional and revolutionary politics is being replaced with new forms of political engagement and expression, largely due to activist fatigue and disenchantment with the ideal Islamic utopia promised by the Islamist project (Bayat 2013). As Boubekeur (2012) has shown, Islamist groups in Europe also experienced a post-Islamist turn, favoring a secular, human rights framework.[19] The rise of organizations distinct from the religious groups rooted in the late twentieth century indicates that this disillusionment and the need for new forms of engagement was not limited to Islamist-inspired movements.

A sizable portion of these new organizations are third-generation—or young, second-generation—Muslims who are not overshadowed by the oppositional politics and the culture wars (South Asian or Western vs. "Islamic" culture) that defined the 1980s and early 1990s. They are confidently experimenting with hybrid identities, combining their faith with different modern cultural trends in a way that pushes all boundaries (Herding 2013). Without the weighty rhetoric of idealized utopian forms of Islam, they are not overburdened with the struggle of re-creating a "pure" Islamic culture; rather, they are creating one that resonates with their everyday life and surroundings. Millennial Muslims, or "Generation M," as Shelina Janmohamed (2016) puts it, are young Muslims who are unapologetically proud of their faith, dynamic, creative, and modern. This can also be linked to the broader intellectual shift taking place from the *fiqh* of minorities to the *fiqh* of citizenship—where a weak, minority mindset is being replaced with a confident mantra of equal citizenship for all (Mestiri 2016, 33–37; Ramadan 2004, 53; Whyte 2017, 58–59).

Disillusionment and fatigue have also spilled over into intra- and inter-sectarian schisms. Established religious groups are also undergoing, or at least are attempting to undergo, a post-sectarian turn.[20] There seems to be a concerted effort in trying to bridge gaps between sectarian factions under the general banner that "unity does not mean uniformity," primarily arguing that there are simply more pressing issues for Muslims in the West to focus their energies on, particularly navigating the increased scrutiny of Western governments and the media. This can be seen by public pledges of scholars (including prominent Salafi scholars) that openly call for unity between different Muslim groups and dropping labels which are seen as divisive (Qadhi 2007; Dawood 2020).[21] Scholars are also establishing non-sectarian, nationwide organizations such as the Mosques and Imams National Advisory Board (MINAB) established in 2006 and, more recently, the British Board of Scholars and Imams (BBSI) in 2013, which describes itself as a "network dedicated to . . . the principle of unity of purpose, as opposed to the uniformity of opinion" (BBSI n.d.).

Salafis in Britain are both adapting and contributing to this changing landscape. Many Salafi mosques and imams are actively engaging with their local communities in dealing with social, political, and ideological challenges. For example, Green Lane Masjid recently won the prestigious title of "Mosque of the Year" at the British Muslim Awards in January 2020 for their community engagement, such as campaigns on knife crime, homelessness, and plastic waste, as well as youth clubs, religious classes, and services (Bentley 2020). A prominent scholar who regularly lectures at this mosque is Abu Usamah adh-Dhahabi—an African American convert and IUM graduate. While discussing his relationship to Saudi Arabia, he underscores his deep gratitude and appreciation for allowing him to learn Arabic and study Islam after years of exploring his faith and not being satisfied with the groups he encountered after conversion. With this he makes an important caveat:

> But . . . this is my host country where I am living in, the UK, I do not believe, that I have to get on that minbar [pulpit] and get before you and praise Saudi Arabia and say "that society is beautiful and we have to"—I don't believe that.

Nor should I use this microphone or that minbar to say, "they are bad and look what they are doing and this"—no. Because we have our own issues right here. We have our own issues right here. Issues right under your nose [presses his nose firmly] like your child, how to stay married, LGBTQ—all of this stuff. We have real issues. What do I look like as a teacher, a dae'ee [preacher] preoccupying people with Saudi Arabia like that. . . . . It [the leaders of Saudi Arabia] doesn't have anything to do with our community . . . it has nothing to do with our reality. . . . I am not going to come and politicise the *dawa* [call to Islam] and make that the issue. No way, that is not going to happen. (Adh-Dhahabi 2019a)

Another example is Shakeel Begg, the senior imam of Lewisham Masjid since 1998. Raised in South London and part of the first batch to graduate and return from the IUM, Begg describes his vision of a *masjid* to be similar to the Prophet's *Masjid*, where it should be at the forefront of social and political issues benefiting the society. Lewisham Masjid, known for its high number of converts particularly from Black African and Black Caribbean backgrounds, also acts as a support hub for many struggling new converts outside the area. When discussing religious teachings, he gives an example of parents who came to him after their children became atheists (Begg 2019). Despite attending Islamic schools, after learning about evolution they lost their faith in God. Remarking on this incident, Begg stresses the need to teach theology that is not theoretical, but practical and relevant to the average British Muslim today. This sentiment of facing new ideological challenges is shared by other prominent Salafi preachers, such as Haitham Al-Haddad—born and raised in Saudi Arabia but from Palestinian origins, he is on the board of many prominent UK and European *fiqh* councils and also has links to Al-Muntada Trust. Al-Haddad argues that ideological challenges facing Muslims in the West must be countered by indigenous Muslims publishing literature written in English directly—as opposed to translations from Arabic writings that overlook the culture and audience of the UK context (Al-Haddad 2013).

Al-Haddad is particularly outspoken about political participation. While the majority of Salafis believe voting is permissible, Al-Haddad argues that it is "almost obligatory" for Muslims to use their vote to bring about positive change for the community and society as a whole (Al-Haddad 2018). In line with the shift toward the *fiqh* of citizenship, he states:

we want to change our mentality . . . you are a Western citizen, so you have rights, as all other Western people have. You are not part of a minority, a subjugated minority, an inferior minority. . . . No, you are a citizen here. You are equal to the prime minister. This is your country, you should change it. (Al-Haddad 2013)

These different social, political, and intellectual challenges have led many to argue for more unity and to move away from "peripheral" areas of disagreement, to focus on promoting the basic fundamentals of Islam that everyone agrees upon. Adh-Dhahabi explains:

> We are living in a time right now where as he [the Prophet] says *salallahu alayi wasalam* [peace be upon him] the people have come together against this community like the people who converge on one plate. The Democrats, Republicans, Labour, Nazis, Far Right, the Left . . . everybody came and the common denominator of hate is Islam and the Muslims. And with that being the case it doesn't make any sense for us to be enemies of one another unnecessarily when we are on the same thing. . . . As for the Muslims who are not on what we are on [Salafiyyah], let's have some *rahma* [mercy] on them. (Adh-Dhahabi 2019b)

This, to a certain extent, includes Shi'ites. As well as regularly giving lectures at Green Lane Masjid, Adh-Dhahabi is also the imam for the Central Mosque of Liverpool that is home to a myriad of ethnicities and sectarian groups in Islam. He describes how he behaves in accordance to the Prophetic advice of giving *da'wa* to people gently and based on their level of understanding and needs, otherwise they would be deterred. This includes performing religious services for Shi'ites such as the funeral prayer (Adh-Dhahabi 2019b). Similarly, Waleed Basyouni—an Egyptian-American Salafi scholar who was one of the first batch of graduates from the IUM and who continues to be a regular speaker in the Western Salafi scene after migrating to the United States in the 1980s—asserts that Muslims should unite on big issues and focus on the fundamentals and basics of the religion, such as the importance of prayer, as opposed to the question of "where do you put your hands when you pray?" (Basyouni 2020a).

Therefore, there is a broad shift toward unity in spite of non-uniformity, tackling specific challenges facing Western Muslims, confident citizenship, and seeking to impact the wider society—all of which has developed in the post–9/11 context and is a definite feature of modern British Salafism.

However, this is not to say that Saudi influence has entirely diminished, or that these new developments have occurred primarily as a result of distancing from Arab Salafi scholars. Many Salafi mosques, including Green Lane Masjid, regularly invite Arab scholars for their conferences and support young British Muslims in applying to study at the IUM. The awe of Arab scholars is still present among some circles, and the relative ease of inviting them means that they are still a part of the British Salafi circuit.

Furthermore, when Salafi scholars in the West discuss the changes outlined earlier, they bring evidence from the Qur'an, *hadith*, or examples from the

Prophet's biography (*sirah*), as opposed to justifying it through being a minority or a new paradigm detached from their studies at the IUM. For example, Basyouni, known for his pragmatic opinions, credits his flexibility to his studies and particularly to Bin Baz (Basyouni 2020b). He narrates how he travels back at least twice a year to visit his teachers. This close relationship does not preclude him from debating and holding different, and even controversial, opinions relative to his teachers (Basyouni 2020b).

In another talk, Adh-Dhahabi stresses that religious authority is not the sole prerogative of Saudi Arabia:

> But . . . respecting them [Saudi Arabia] is one thing but superimposing Saudi Arabia and culture upon the communities that we come from is not Islamic and it doesn't make sense. And the scholars of Saudi Arabia they represent *some* [emphasis in tone] of the scholars of the Muslim world. There are scholars in Libya, in Morocco, in Pakistan, in Egypt, in Syria, in Jordan and all over the world. (Adh-Dhahabi 2019b)

But, there still remains the sub-group formed in the 1990s, described earlier, who meticulously follow Rabi al-Madkhali and scholars he approves of, known in the United Kingdom as the Salafi Publications network. They see these scholars, who are staunch loyalists to the Saudi regime, as "the" primary source of religious authority. They criticize other Salafi groups mainly for political activism and joining with other non-Salafis, as they advocate strict theological purity. While this group is small, they have a disproportionately large online presence and regularly post videos and blog articles refuting other groups. Furthermore, there has been a recent rise of a few young, Salafi social-media personalities, some of whom are critical of this new post-sectarian trend yet do not ascribe themselves to the Salafi Publications network. This is not a coherent group, and their loyalties and positions change frequently, making it difficult to assess their impact.[22]

Salafi Mosques and Funding

One oft-cited statistic that is important to mention here is that the fastest-growing number of mosques in Britain are those with a Salafi-leaning (with a 28 percent increase from 2014 to 2015 alone). This figure is deceptive. First, they still make up only 155 mosques, accounting for 9 percent of the total, the dominant groups being the Deobandis (43 percent) and Barelwis (25 percent) (Naqshabandi 2015). Second, and more importantly, studies show that the influence of imams and mosques has been exaggerated, perhaps due to the perception that imams are the Muslim equivalents of Christian priests and ministers (Van Bruinessen 2010, 6). A mosque's influence in the community depends on many factors, such as the local demographic, the mosque committee members, internal mosque politics, the type of community activities they hold, and the characteristics and qualifications of the imam (Van Bruinessen 2010, 6–9). Third, even if local Muslims do actively attend the mosque, the extent to which they accept and implement the imam's religious advice rests again on many factors, such as their respect for the scholar and his credentials, textual evidence, and contextual realities (Amin 2019). Also, the internet and other spaces for religious activity, such as religious cafes and short courses and events, have decentered the mosque as the sole space for religious authority. Fourth, the extent to which those who attend have a good grasp of sectarian differences is questionable.[23] There is a scale ranging from the leaders and devoted core group of organizers to the average informed follower to the sporadic attendees; only the first group has a good understanding of sectarian differences and histories. Lastly, as I have discussed earlier, not all Salafi preachers, even those educated in Saudi Arabia, advocate Saudi-style Salafism (Farquhar 2017). Therefore, mosque statistics are only one small facet of a much more intricate picture of Salafism in Britain.

What about Saudi-funded mosques? While there are no definitive statistics, it is apparent that the Saudi state does spend a significant amount on propagating their version of Salafism. An important example is the case of Ajmal Masroor, who was fired in 2018 from Saudi-funded Goodge Street Mosque for criticizing Crown Prince Muhammad bin Salman for Saudi Arabia's role in the war in Yemen and the planned assassination of Jamal Khashoggi (Ullah 2018; TRT World 2018). A popular and articulate polymath, Masroor is a Bangladeshi-born British imam, broadcaster, fundraiser, relationship counselor, and politician who regularly participates in televised debates and discussions on mainstream channels. He volunteered at the mosque for twenty-two years as an imam and was reprimanded on multiple occasions for his outspoken political Friday sermons. Yet, Masroor unabashedly continued his criticisms in the mosque and online. His strident condemnation of Muhammad bin Salman and religious scholars whom he deemed complicit through their silence was the final stroke, and he was swiftly removed from his position. Contrary to the crown prince's aims, this incident caught media attention, and articles and videos were avidly shared (Ullah 2018; TRT World 2018).

This incident highlights the complex relationship between the Saudi state's funding of mosques and establishments and its religious influence in Britain. First, Masroor is not Saudi-trained or educated, yet he was allowed to regularly deliver the Friday sermon and use the mosque for his other activities, including a marriage counseling institute. Also, he had been an outspoken critic of Saudi Arabia for a long time, yet only recently was he forced to leave under the new crown prince, which suggests that the Saudi state did not exercise tight control on all mosque activities and preachers. Second, despite removing him from his position, far from silencing him and his message, this event proved to be even more problematic for Saudi Arabia's reputation. Masroor stated that the vast majority of those who attend the *masjid* are non-Arabs and were in "dismay and disbelief" when they heard the news (TRT World 2018). Ironically, his message reached a much wider audience than a typical Friday sermon would through his usage of social media and news coverage of the event by a range of media outlets. Therefore, mere funding does not always lead to favorable outcomes for Saudi Arabia's influence and reputation, and similar to IUM graduates, can even have an inverse effect.

Conclusion

Rather than petrodollars, the primary source of Saudi influence has been the graduates of the IUM. Yet, these graduates are not mere mouthpieces for Saudi Arabia. Many Salafi preachers have become increasingly vocal on the necessity of focusing on issues relevant to Western Muslims, in three different domains: socially, such as crime, drugs, the environment, and mental health; politically, such as Islamophobia and counterproductive government-led initiatives; and intellectually, such as atheism and evolution. In this shifting landscape, Saudi-style Salafism, with its heavy focus on theological purity rooted in a different political context, does not resonate with these new priorities and paradigms that have emerged in Britain. While the glib mantra of "the Qur'an and Sunna are the solution" jibed with the overarching sentiments of the 1980s and early 1990s, it does not speak to the complex and hostile post–9/11 British context where sectarian polemics are taking the back seat as young Muslims are more socially and politically astute.

Although Arab Salafi scholars are still invited by certain segments among British Salafis and there remains a respectful relationship between British Salafi preachers and their teachers, this does not preclude the vast majority of Salafi preachers in the West from mediating their message and adapting it accordingly. Ideas that were foundational to twentieth-century Muslim movements are now being questioned, refashioned, or even abandoned, paving the way for new concepts and social movements in which mainstream Saudi scholars and institutions are no longer leading the way.

Notes

1. I am using this term to mean mainstream Salafism as represented by the Saudi religious establishment. Broadly speaking, this entails a heavy focus on theological purity and eschewing political activism. It also includes conservative social mores, such as gender segregation and Saudi-style dress codes, for example white *thawbs* for men, which rest above the ankle, and typically black *abayas* and hijabs for women. However, this is not to say that this is a coherent, unified static group; there are internal schisms and differences, but these are not pertinent to this chapter. Also, not all that espouse "Saudi-style" Salafism are Saudi nationals, such as Syrian-Albanian scholar Nasir al-Din al-Albani. Hence, the term "Arab Salafi" or "Middle Eastern Salafi" will also be used to reflect this.

2. Formerly known as the Organization of the Islamic Conference.

3. For example, the Suez War in 1956, the Algerian War of Independence in 1954–1963, and the failure to liberate Palestine with the humiliating military defeat in 1967.

4. The bulk of migrants arrived from South Asia and a few from Northern Cyprus. In the 1970s, small pockets of Arab migrants also began to settle in London, joined by political dissidents who found a safe haven in Britain. In the 1990s the picture diversified even further with the arrival of Eastern European, African, and Middle Eastern refugees and asylum seekers. For problems regarding the census data, see Ansari (2004, 169–172).

5. They also wrote and translated many books in both Urdu and Arabic, contributing to the vibrant print culture and the Muslim transnational public sphere. See Robinson (2012).

6. Hasan was originally sent to Kenya where he preached for approximately ten years. Yet due to the difficulties in the *da'wa*, he asked to be relocated to Britain as he wanted to pursue a doctorate. Bin Baz readily granted his request.

7. During my fieldwork, many Salafis described this juxtaposition.

8. This gave the students instant international authority and recognition. Some even argued that they were more popular in the West than the Middle East. An exemplar of this group is Ali al-Halabi. Born in Jordan, he studied with al-Albani for over twenty years, and he traveled widely and participated in conferences in North America, Britain, France, Holland, Hungary, Canada, Indonesia, and Kenya. Another crucial figure is Salim al-Hilali, who was born in Palestine and studied under al-Albani for twenty-five years. He also studied under prominent scholars in India and Pakistan, including Abd al-Ghaffar Hasan—the father of Suhaib Hasan.

9. For example, Jamal Zarabozo was an American convert who taught himself Arabic and *hadith* sciences; Bilal Philips, a Jamaican-Canadian convert who became the first Western-born IUM graduate and then went on further to complete a PhD in Islamic Theology at the University of Wales; and Dr. Ali Al-Tamimi, an American-Iraqi speaker who also graduated from the IUM in the early 1990s and, alongside his Islamic studies, completed a doctorate in computational biology.

10. For Salafism in America and the fracture there, see Elmasry (2010).

11. On the relationship between this group and Salafism and the dangers of seeing Salafism as a precursor to violent jihadism, see Abdul Haqq Baker (2011, 6–12).

12. One of the key figures of this movement was a charismatic American convert, Hamza Yusuf. Even today, Yusuf is one of the most popular speakers circulating the Western Muslim scene as well as the Middle East. Other prominent figures include the British convert Tim Winter (also known as Abdal Hakim Murad), who lectures in Islamic Studies at the University of Cambridge; the American convert Nuh Keller, who moved to Jordan to study Islam, where he currently resides; and, later, the American convert Zaid Shakir who, in 2001, became the first American male to graduate from Syria's Abu Nour University in Islamic Sciences. See Hamid (2016, 68–87).

13. The Hijaz Naqshabandis, led by Pir Wahhab Siddiqi, were acutely aware of the situation and he thus trained his sons to be effective heirs of the *tariqa*, encouraging them to be educated in both the secular and Islamic sciences. When he died in 1994, his son, Faiz-ul-Aqtab Siddiqi, who was also a trained barrister, became the first British-born *pir* of the *tariqa*. Likewise, other *tariqa*s have successfully risen above ethnic lines, attracting the new generation.

14. The catalyst was the 1994 World Ijtima, which was a large gathering of international Tablighi Jamaat activists at their UK headquarters in Dewsbury. This sparked the enrollment of the budding British-born generation, including converts and non–South Asian Muslims, and proved to be a pivotal moment in intergenerational transmission.

15. While the Tablighi Jamaat has a basic policy of avoiding confrontation and debate, some of their scholars, such as Mumtaz ul-Haq, directly respond to Salafi critiques.

16. An important example is British-born Bangladeshi Shams ad-Duha Muhammad, who studied in Deobandi seminaries in Dewsbury, Nottingham, and Bangladesh and thereafter completed an MA in Islamic Studies at Birkbeck College, London. In 2003, Ad-Duha established a modern Deobandi seminary, Ebrahim College, in East London. See Philip and Hamid (2018, chapter 2). In 2009, Abdal Hakim Murad established Cambridge Muslim College with similar aims.

17. Despite some calls for unity and cooperation discussed in the previous section of this chapter, there has also been a recent surge in some Salafis producing anti-Shiʿite YouTube videos and Salafi-Shiʿite debates (usually posted as "Sunnis vs. Shiʿites," but the overwhelming majority of the producers are Salafi men), particularly in Speakers Corner in Hyde Park—a space for open discussion in Central London. These informal debates are usually recorded and uploaded on YouTube, garnering thousands of views and also sparking reactionary videos from Shiʿites. See, for example, Al Ghadeer (2018) and SCDawah Channel (2016).

18. There seems to be some geographical variance to this post-sectarian turn. In regions where there was intense sectarian strife in the 1990s, a sense of fatigue has settled in, pushing this shift toward unity. However, in regions which are strongholds of a particular faction, for example in some Northern towns and cities, the post-sectarian turn is relatively weaker.

19. They shifted from defining their Islamic identity in opposition to the West to one of negotiation. One of their primary methods was by partnering with non-religious

actors, which, as Boubekeur (2012) argues, secularized their Islamic identity as their frame of reference altered from religion to ethics. For example, the ongoing crisis in Palestine—a persistent issue in Muslim politics—becomes an issue of minority rights fought alongside other human rights activist groups. Also, after 9/11, the Muslim Association of Britain partnered with the left-wing Socialist Worker's Party to create the Stop the War Coalition (Elshayyal 2018, 121).

20. It would be inaccurate to say this is an entirely new phenomenon. There have always been pockets of cooperation, during political incidents such as the Rushdie Affair or even more mundane activities such as deciding which day Eid is. However, now there is an active drive to overcome the issue of sectarian politics.

21. There are also other reasons why groups are dropping labels. As Dawood (2020) has shown, the splinter group known as Salafi Publications, known for their stringent refutations, have monopolized the term "Salafi," leading many other Salafi groups and scholars to stop using the term to avoid any form of affiliation. Hamid (2016, 128) also discusses how some Salafi groups did not use the label after 9/11 to avoid negative connotations, as Salafism is associated with Saudi Arabia, where the majority of the hijackers originated from.

22. One example of this trend is Imran Ibn Mansur, more popularly known as "Dawah Man" (Naseeha Sessions 2015).

23. In my own research on Salafism, one of the most surprising findings is how little "religious" Muslims knew about sectarian differences; one of the most common questions I was asked during my fieldwork was to outline the differences between the various groups. Other researchers have also noted this.

References

Abbas, Tahir. 2007. "Muslim Minorities in Britain: Integration, Multiculturalism and Radicalism in the Post-7/7 Period." *Journal of Intercultural Studies* 28(3): 287–300. https://doi.org/10.1080/07256860701429717.

Abo-Alabbas, Belal. 2015. "Sufism in Britain: How Sufi Orders Have Adapted to a Western Context." In *Muslims in the UK and Europe I*, edited by Yasir Suleiman, 9–18. Cambridge: Centre of Islamic Studies, University of Cambridge.

Abou Zahab, Mariam. 2009. "Salafism in Pakistan: The Ahl-e Hadith Movement." In *Global Salafism: Islam's New Religious Movement*, edited by Roel Meijer, 126–143. London: Hurst.

Adh-Dhahabi, Abu Usamah. 2019a. "The 'Moderate' View Concerning Saudi Arabia: Shaykh Abu Usamah At-Thahabi." https://www.youtube.com/watch?v=M6MONrhTeFU&t=9s (accessed June 15, 2020).

Adh-Dhahabi, Abu Usamah. 2019b. "Hijab, SPUBS, Mufti Muneer" Meet Sheikh Abu Usama | Young Smirks Podcast Ep9| Young Smirks Podcast Ep9." https://www.youtube.com/watch?v=PDgvR5ecJRA&t=1090s (accessed June 15, 2020).

Ahmed, Abdul-Azim, and Mansur Ali. 2019. "In Search of Sylhet—The Fultoli Tradition in Britain." *Religions* 10(10): 572.

Amin, Hira. 2019. "British Muslims Navigating between Individualism and Traditional Authority." *Religions* 10(6): 354.

Amin, Hira, and Majothi Azhar. 2021. "Ahl-e-Hadith: from British India to Britain." *Modern Asian Studies*. doi: https://doi.org/10.1017/S0026749X21000093.

Ansari, Humayun. 2004. *The Infidel Within: Muslims in Britain since 1800*. London: Hurst.

Arjomand, Said Amir. 2010. "Islamic Resurgence and Its Aftermath." In *The New Cambridge History of Islam*. Volume 6: *Muslims and Modernity: Culture and Society since 1800*, edited by Robert W. Hefner, 173–197. Cambridge: Cambridge University Press.

At-Tamimi, Ali. 1997. "The Need for Fiqh Suitable for Our Time and Place." http://islamiclectures.us/AT.html (accessed April 15, 2016).

Aydin, Cemil. 2017. *The Idea of the Muslim World: A Global Intellectual History*. Cambridge, MA: Harvard University Press.

Azami, Rashad Ahmad. 1995. *Ahl-e Hadith in Britain: History, Establishment, Organisation, Activities and Objectives*. London: Ta-Ha.

Baker, Abdul Haqq. 2011. *Extremists in Our Midst: Confronting Terror*. London: Palgrave Macmillan.

Basyouni, Waleed. 2020a. "Fiqh of Unity: Waleed Basyouni." https://www.youtube.com/watch?v=C4ranVzScOg&t=499s (accessed June 15, 2020).

Basyouni, Waleed. 2020b. "Unscripted #45: Stories That Touched My Heart: Shaykh Waleed Basyouni." https://www.youtube.com/watch?v=BhZ9STynHgI (accessed June 15, 2020).

Bayat, Asef, ed. 2013. *Post-Islamism: The Changing Faces of Political Islam*. New York: Oxford University Press.

Begg, Shakeel. 2019. "Unscripted #18: Veteran Imam Shakeel Begg Opens Up." https://www.youtube.com/watch?v=6gGVBENffg0 (accessed June 15, 2020).

Bentley, D. 2020. "Birmingham's Green Lane Masjid Celebrates as It Wins Mosque of the Year Award." https://www.birminghammail.co.uk/news/midlands-news/birminghams-green-lane-masjid-celebrates-17683188 (accessed June 15, 2020).

Birt, Yahya. 2007. "Wahhabi Wrangles." https://yahyabirt1.wordpress.com/2007/11/02/wahhabi-wrangles/ (accessed November 29, 2019).

Boubekeur, Amel. 2012. "Reinventing Political Islam: The Disengagement of European Islamists." In *Whatever Happened to the Islamists?: Salafis, Heavy Metal Muslims and the Lure of Consumerist Islam*, edited by O. Roy and A. Boubekeur, 107–128. London: Hurst.

Bowen, Innes. 2014. *Medina in Birmingham, Najaf in Brent: Inside British Islam*. London: Hurst.

British Board of Scholars and Imams (BBSI). n.d. "About us." http://www.bbsi.org.uk/about-us/ (accessed June 15, 2020).

Dawood, Iman. 2020. "Who Is a 'Salafi'? Salafism and the Politics of Labelling in the UK." *Journal of Muslims in Europe* 9(2): 240–261.

Dispatches. 2007. "Undercover Mosque." Originally broadcast January 15, 2007. Channel 4.

Dogra, Sufyan Abid. 2019. "Living a Piety-Led Life beyond Muharram: Becoming or Being a South Asian Shia Muslim in the UK." *Contemporary Islam* 13: 307–324.

Eade, John. 1996. "Nationalism, Community, and the Islamization of the Space in London." In *Making Muslim Space in North America and Europe*, edited by Barbara .D. Metcalf, 217–233. Berkeley: University of California Press.

Elmasry, Shadee. 2010. "The Salafis in America: The Rise, Decline and Prospects for a Sunni Muslim Movement among African-Americans." *Journal of Muslim Minority Affairs* 30(2): 217–236.

Elshayyal, Khadijah. 2018. *Muslim Identity Politics: Islam, Activism and Equality in Britain*. London: I. B. Tauris.

Farquhar, Michael. 2017. *Circuits of Faith: Migration, Education, and the Wahhabi Mission*. Stanford, CA: Stanford University Press.

Geaves, Ron. 2006. "Learning the Lessons from the Neo-Revivalist and Wahhabi Movements: The Counterattack of the New Sufi Movements in the UK." In *Sufism in the West*, edited by Jamal Malik and John Hinells, 152–169. London: Routledge.

Al Ghadeer, Bayat. 2018. "The Divine Reality: God, Islam and the Mirage of Salafis Part 1." https://www.youtube.com/watch?v=u7lwUraSZp0 (accessed September 20, 2020).

Gilliat-Ray, Sophie. 2010. *Muslims in Britain: An Introduction*. Cambridge: Cambridge University Press.

Grinell, Klas. 2018. "Framing Islam at the World of Islam Festival, London, 1976." *Journal of Muslims in Europe* 7(1): 73–93.

Al-Haddad. Haitham. 2013. "Muslims' Role in the West. Part 2.1: Living Islam in the West: Dr. Haitham al-Haddad." https://www.youtube.com/watch?v=dQ4hfO57U54 (accessed June 15, 2020).

Al-Haddad. Haitham. 2018. "Is Voting Really Haram? Sh Haitham al-Haddad Face to Face." https://www.youtube.com/watch?v=x3E_GwLZpww (accessed June 15, 2020).

Hamid, Sadek. 2016. *Sufis, Salafis and Islamists: The Contested Ground of British Islamic Activism*. London: I. B. Tauris.

Hegghammer, Thomas. 2010. *Jihad in Saudi Arabia: Violence and Pan-Islamism since 1979*. Cambridge: Cambridge University Press.

Herding, Maruta. 2013. *Inventing the Muslim Cool: Islamic Youth Culture in Western Europe*. Verlag: Transcript.

Hinnells, John R. 2007. *Religious Reconstruction in the South Asian Diasporas: From One Generation to Another*. Basingstoke: Palgrave Macmillan.

Inge, Anabel. 2017. *The Making of a Salafi Muslim Woman: Paths to Conversion*. New York: Oxford University Press.

International Crisis Group. 2004. "Saudi Arabia Backgrounder: Who Are the Islamists?" Middle East Report No. 31. https://www.crisisgroup.org/middle-east-north-africa/gulf-and-arabian-peninsula/saudi-arabia/saudi-arabia-backgrounder-who-are-islamists

Irfani, Suroosh. 2004. "Pakistan's Sectarian Violence: Between the Arabist Shift and Indo-Persian Culture." In *Religious Radicalism and Security in South Asia*, edited by Satu P. Limaye, Robert G. Wirsing, and Mohan Malik, 147–170. Honolulu: Asia-Pacific Center for Security Studies.

Jalali, Ali Ahmad. 2017. *A Military History of Afghanistan: From the Great Game to the Global War on Terror*. University Press of Kansas.

Janmohamed, Shelina. 2016. *Generation M: Young Muslims Changing the World*. London: I. B. Tauris.

Kerr, Malcom H. 1971. *The Arab Cold War: Gamal 'Abd al-Nasir and His Rivals 1958–1970*. London: Oxford University Press.

Lacroix, Stéphane. 2009. "Between Revolution and Apoliticism: Nasir al-Din al-Albani and His Impact on the Shaping of Contemporary Salafism." In *Global Salafism: Islam's New Religious Movement*, edited by Roel Meijer, pp. 58–80. London: Hurst.

Lacroix, Stéphane. 2011. *Awakening Islam: The Politics of Religious Dissent in Contemporary Saudi Arabia*. Cambridge, MA: Harvard University Press.

Lewis, Philip, and Sadek Hamid. 2018. *British Muslims: New Directions in Islamic Thought, Creativity and Activism*. Edinburgh: Edinburgh University Press.

Majothi, Azhar. Personal correspondence. September 23, 2020.

McLoughlin, Séan, and John Zavos. 2013. *Writing Religion in British Asian Diasporas: Diasporas, Migration and Identities Programme*. University of Leeds. http://eprints.whiterose.ac.uk/76475/.

Mestiri, Mohamed. 2016. "From the Fiqh of Minorities to the Fiqh of Citizenship: Challenges of Conceptualization and Implementation." In *Rethinking Islamic Law for Minorities: Towards a Western-Muslim Identity*, edited by Jasser Auda, 33–43. London: Association for Muslim Social Scientists. https://www.jasserauda.net/new/pdf/kamil_fiqh_alaqalliyaat.pdf.

Markaz Jamiat Ahl-e-Hadith UK (MJAH UK), Scholars of. 2008. *In Defence of MJAH: A Response to the Unjust, Deceptive and Slanderous Allegations Made against Markazi Jamiat Ahle Hadith UK*. Birmingham: MJAH.

Mirpuri, Mahmood Ahmed, et al. 1987. *The Straight Path* 8(6). Birmingham: MJAH.

Monaghan, Misha. 2018. *How Can We Understand Salafi-Shia Relations in Britain?* Unpublished master's thesis, Royal Holloway.

Morey, Peter, and Amina Yaqin. 2011. *Framing Muslims: Stereotyping and Representation after 9/11*. Cambridge, MA: Harvard University Press.

Naseeha Sessions. 2015. "Naseeha Sessions YouTube Channel." https://www.youtube.com/c/NaseehaSessions/ (accessed September 20, 2020).

Naqshbandi, Mehmood. 2015. "UK Mosque Statistics." http://www.muslimsinbritain.org/resources/masjid_report.pdf (accessed January 15, 2017).

Peach, Ceri. 2006. "Muslims in the 2001 Census of England and Wales: Gender and Economic Disadvantage." *Ethnic and Racial Studies* 29(4): 629–655.

Philips, Bilal. 1997a. "Is Establishing a Muslim Society about Establishing Muslim Ghetto?" https://blog.islamiconlineuniversity.com/question/establishing-muslim-community-is-different-from-muslim-ghetto/ (accessed April 15, 2016).

Philips, Bilal. 1997b. "Islamic Education & Establishing Islam in the West." http://islamiclectures.us/BP.html (accessed April 15, 2016).

Qadhi, Yasir. 2007. "Update! Pledge of Mutual Respect and Cooperation." https://muslimmatters.org/2007/09/22/pledge-of-mutual-respect-and-cooperation/ (accessed June 15, 2020).

Ramadan, Tariq. 2004. *Western Muslims and the Future of Islam*. Oxford: Oxford University Press.

Al-Rasheed, Madawi. 2005. "Saudi Religious Transnationalism in London." In *Transnational Connections and the Arab Gulf*, edited by Madawi Al-Rasheed, 149–167. London: Routledge.

Razavian, Christopher, and Nathan Spannaus. 2018. "New Deobandi Institutions in the West." In *Modern Islamic Authority and Social Change: Evolving Debates in the West*, edited by Masooda Bano, 180–210. Edinburgh: Edinburgh University Press.

Robinson, Francis. 2012. "The Islamic Word: World System to 'Religious International.'" In *Religious Internationals in the Modern World: Globalization and Faith Communities since 1750*, edited by Abigail Green and Vincent Viaene, 111–136. Basingstoke: Palgrave Macmillan.

SCDawah Channel. 2016. "SCDawah YouTube Channel." https://www.youtube.com/c/scdawahchannel/ (accessed September 20, 2020).

Sidat, Haroon. 2018. "Between Tradition and Transition: An Islamic Seminary, or Dar Al-Uloom in Modern Britain." *Religions* 9(10): 314.

Timol, Riyaz. 2015. "Religious Travel and Tablighi Jama'at: Modalities of Expansion in Britain and Beyond." In *Muslims in the UK and Europe I*, edited by Yasir Suleiman, 194–206. Centre of Islamic Studies: University of Cambridge.

Timol, Riyaz. 2019. "Structures of Organisation and Loci of Authority in a Glocal Islamic Movement: The Tablighi Jama'at in Britain." *Religions* 10(10): 573.

Timol, Riyaz. 2020. Personal correspondence with the author.

TRT World. 2019. "British Imam Sacked after Criticising Crown Prince Mohammed bin Salman." https://www.youtube.com/watch?v=vPVogXgYnME (accessed June 15, 2020).

Ullah, Areeb. 2018. "UK Imam Fired from Saudi-Funded Mosque for Criticising Saudi Royal Family." *Middle East Eye*. https://www.middleeasteye.net/news/uk-imam-fired-saudi-funded-mosque-criticising-saudi-royal-family (accessed June 15, 2020).

van Bruinessen, Martin. 2010. "Producing Islamic Knowledge in Western Europe: Discipline, Authority, and Personal Quest." In *Producing Islamic Knowledge: Transmission and Dissemination in Western Europe*, edited by Martin van Bruinessen and Stefano Allievi, 1–27. Oxon: Routledge.

Vertovec, Steven, and Alistar Rogers. 1998. *Muslim European Youth: Reproducing Ethnicity, Religion, Culture*. Aldershot: Ashgate.

Whyte, S. 2017. "Whither Minority Jurisprudence? The Case of Fiqh l-Aqalliyat in Australia." *Australian Journal of Islamic Studies* 2(3): 55–75.

Index

Aa Gym (Abdullah Gymnastiar), 151
Aalmi Majlis Tahaffuz Khat\m-e-Nubuwwat (AMTKN), 202
al-'Abbad, 'Abd al-Muhsin, 59, 142, 152–53, 162
al-'Abbudi , Muhammad Nasir, 95
'Abd al Hamid, Mahmud, 263
'Abd al-Khaliq ,'Abd al-Rahman, 87, 296
Abd al-Razzaq 'Afifi, 56, 257, 263
Abd al-Zahir Abu al-Samih, 57
'Abduh, Muhammad, 76–80, 256
'Abdul-Aziz (king of Saudi Arabia), 12, 17, 37, 44, 79
Abdykalykov, Shamsuddin, 164–66, 168
Abu Ghudda, Abd al-Fattah, 83–84
Abu Hamza, 280
Abu Muntasir (Muhammad Manwar Ali), 294
Abu Nida, 135–36, 140–41, 144, 147–48
Abu Qatada, 297
Abu Sayyaf, 107
Abu Turab, Maulana Ali Muhammad, 193
Abu Zayd, Bakr, 84
Active Islamic Youth (AIY), 282
Addis Ababa Ulama Unity Forum (AAUUF), 232
Adh-Dhahabi, Abu Usamah, 302–5
Afghani, Jamal al-Din, 76, 78–80
Afghanistan
    Pakistan and, 190, 192, 199
    Saudi Arabia and, 39, 85, 167, 198, 228, 292
    Soviet war (1980s) in, 13, 85, 188, 192, 196, 198, 228, 292, 295–96
    United States and, 13–14, 85
Africa Muslims Agency (AMA), 226–27, 232
ag Ghali, Iyad, 249
al-Ahbash (Association of Islamic Charitable Projects), 232–33
Ahle Sunnat Wal Jama'at, 198, 200–201
Ahl-i Hadith movement
    Islamic University of Medina and, 56–58
    Pakistan and, 11, 192, 194–97, 204
    Shi'ism opposed in, 195–96
    Sufism opposed in, 195
    United Kingdom and, 292–94
Ahlus- Sunnah Wal-Jama'ah, 65
Ahmadinejad, Mahmoud, 200
Ahmadiyya, 22, 189–91
Ahmed, Abiy, 223, 227, 233

al-'Aishiy, Tariq Samiy Sultan, 141
Akaev, Askar, 164, 166
Akhtar, Aasim Sajjad, 192
Akmal, Abu Munzir Zul, 141, 143
Al al-Shaykh , Abd al-Rahman bin Hasan, 149
Al al-Shaykh, Muhammad ibn Ibrahim, 94
Al al-Shaykh, Salih bin 'Abd al-'Aziz, 104
al-Albani, Muhammad Nasiruddin
    Bin Baz and, 83
    hadith authentication and, 45
    Indonesian followers of, 142
    Islamic University of Medina and, 83
    in Jordan, 66
    jurisprudence of minorities and, 300
    al-Kawthari and, 83–84
    niqab and, 44, 263–64
    "purification and education" emphasis of, 266
    Salafist framework developed by, 77–78, 82–84
    Wahhabism and, 10, 83
Algeria, 106
Ali, Ahmed Muhammad, 279
Ali, Shahnaz Wazir, 187
Allama, Rahmatullah, 162
al-Alusi, Mahmoud Shukri, 56
Alwaleed Philanthropies, 118, 121
al-Alwani, Taha Jabir, 300
al-'Alwani, Muhammad, 94
Amadu, Seku, 248
al- Amir, Ibrahim, 153
Ansar al-Din, 247–49
Ansar al-Sunna al-Muhammadiyya, 56, 66, 78, 257–59, 261–62
al-Ansari, Hammad, 57, 240, 243
al-Ansari, 'Abdullah Ibrahim, 86, 94
Ansarullah, 169
al-'Aqil, 'Aqil 'Abd al-'Aziz, 118, 197
al-'Aqqad , 'Abbas, 79
Arab Gulf Program for Development (AGFUND), 121
Arab-Israel War (1967), 137, 188, 241
Arab League, 13, 123
al-'Arifi, Muhammad, 18, 121
al-Ash'ari, Abu Hasan, 148
Ash'arites, 148–49, 241, 246
Ashfaq, Mohammed, 202

Asim, Maulana Fazal Karim, 293
al-'Asqalani, Ahmad bin Hajar, 251
Association for the Revival of Islamic
    Heritage, 258
al-Astal, Yasin, 66–67
Atambaev, Almazbek, 167–68
al-Athari, Muhammad Bahjat, 56
Al-Athari Islamic Education Foundation, 147
Awaliyya School (Ethiopia), 224–26
Awami League, 210–11
al-Awdah, Salman, 18, 121
al-Azhar, 85, 100, 259
'Azzam, 'Abdullah, 109, 142

Ba, Mahmoud, 240
Ba'asyir, Abu Bakar, 142
Babakhanov, Ziauddin, 162
Badakhan, Ishan, 162
al-Badr militia, 193
al-Baghdadi, al-Khatib, 81
Bah, Moussa Boubacar, 244–45
Bahrain, 211
Bakiev, Kurmanbek, 166
Bakir Uulu, Tursunbai, 159
Bangladesh
    gender relations in, 211, 215, 217–18
    independence of, 191–92, 209
    Islam and national identity in, 209
    Jamaat-e-Islami and, 210–11, 215
    knowledge of Islam among return migrants
        from Saudi Arabia in, 208, 212–15, 217
    migration to Saudi Arabia from, 18, 208,
        211–18
    Sufi shrines in, 215
Bangladesh Nationalist Party, 211
al-Banna, Hasan, 80, 109, 189
Barelvis, 198–99, 298, 305
al-Barrak, Abd al-Rahman, 106
Basyouni, Waleed, 304–5
Batyrov, Kadyrzhan, 177
al-Bayhani, Muhammad Salim, 56
al-Baytar, Muhammad Bahjat, 79
Bayumi, Sayyed, 170
Bayzakov, Arlen, 168
Begg, Shakeel, 303
Belgium, 28
Bhutto, Zulfikar Ali, 189–91
bid'a (corrupting innovations), 10, 40, 43, 46,
    54, 146, 148
Bin Baz, Abd al-'Aziz
    Ahl-i Hadith and, 195
    al-Albani and, 83
    Council of Senior 'Ulama and, 137

Gulf War and, 141
Islamic University of Medina and, 55–56, 66
Muslim World League and, 94, 106
niqab and, 44
social media accounts of, 18
al-Wadi'i and, 47
Bin Baz Islamic Center, 135, 144
Bin Laden, Usama, 47, 107
Bin Sadiq, Sadiq bin Salim, 84
al-Bitar, Muhammad Bahjat, 56
Bosnia and Herzegovina
    Austro-Hungarian Empire and, 273
    civil war in, 274–75, 285, 300
    European Union and, 286
    foreign fighters in, 279–80
    humanitarian aid and, 275–77, 280, 282–84
    niqab and, 272–73
    Ottoman Empire and, 273
    postwar reconstruction in, 39, 280–82
    Al-Qaeda, 99
    Salafi literature in, 278–79
    Saudi Arabia and, 39, 276–78, 281, 285–86
    Turkey and, 286
    Yugoslavia and, 273–74
Boulaouali, Tijani, 107
Britain. See United Kingdom
British Board of Scholars and Imams (BBSI), 302
Bukhari, 77, 88, 150
Burbank, Dawud, 297
Burhami, Yasir, 262–63
Burkina Faso, 239, 242

Chad, 239, 241
Chechnya, 163, 166
Cheema, Afzal, 193–94
Chérif of Nioro du Sahel (Mohamed Ould
    Cheicknè), 244, 246–47
China, 29, 177
Chubak ajy Zhalilov, 164
Churchill, Winston, 292
Cissé, Soumaïla, 245–46
Cold War, 13, 42, 96–97, 258, 291
Commins, David, 102
Commission for the Promotion of Virtue and
    the Prevention of Vice (CPVPV), 38, 48,
    85, 121, 214
Committee for the Defense of Legitimate Rights
    in Saudi Arabia, 297

al-Dakhir, Fauz, 171
Dar al-Arqam, 86
Dar al-Hadith, 57, 62, 293
al-Darimi, 'Uthman bin Said, 82

Darussalam publishing house, 88
Dautović, Ferid Effendi, 284
Davis, Abu Hakeem Bilal, 297
da'wa (religious propagation)
  humanitarian aid and, 16, 116
  Salafism and, 43
  satellite television and, 152
  Saudi agencies devoted to, 3–4, 14–16, 24–25, 39
  Saudi media organizations and, 16–17
  Wahhabism and, 41–42
Deobandism
  origins of, 11
  Pakistan and, 198–99, 204
  Saudi funding of, 198
  United Kingdom and, 295, 298–99, 305
  Wahhabism and, 198
Diallo, Ali Nouhoum, 249–50
Dicko, Mahmoud
  biographical background of, 243
  election (2013) and, 244
  High Islamic Council of Mali and, 244, 246–47
  Keïta and, 244, 247
al-Dihlawi, Ahmad ibn Muhammad, 57, 68n1
Dualibi, Marouf, 193
Dzul Akmal, 143
Dzulqarnain Muhammad Sunusi, 135, 143–44, 147–48, 152–53

Egypt
  coup (2013) in, 255, 265, 267
  migration to Saudi Arabia from, 19
  revolution (1952) in, 258, 291
  revolution (2011) in, 265
  Salafism in, 11, 45, 65–66, 78–81, 255–56, 259–68
  Saudi Arabia and, 257–58, 260, 262–68
  Sufism in, 259
Eid Charity Foundation, 258
El Misri, Imad, 280
Erdoğan, Recep Tayyip, 182
Ershad, Hussain Muhammad, 209
Ethiopia
  ancient history of, 221
  Christian-Muslim relations in, 225
  Eritrea's peace treaty (2019) with, 223
  famine (1984-5) in, 224
  hajj and, 224, 226–28
  International Islamic Relief Organization and, 224, 226, 229, 232
  Italian occupation (1935-42) of, 227
  migration to Saudi Arabia from, 231

  Muslim World League and, 224
  revolution (1974) in, 223
  Soviet Union and, 223
  United Arab Emirates and, 227
  United States and, 225
  World Assembly of Muslim Youth and, 224, 229
Ethiopian Islamic Affairs Supreme Council (EIASC), 226–27, 233
Ethiopian Muslim Youth Association, 229
Ethiopian People's Revolutionary Democratic Front (EPRDF), 223–24, 229
European Council for Fatwa and Research (ECFR), 300
Evangelical Christianity, 3, 258

Fahd (king of Saudi Arabia), 24, 83, 85, 106, 196
el Faisal, Abdullah, 297
Faiz-ul-Aqtab, 298
Fallata, 'Umar, 57
al-Faqih, Saad, 297
Farooqi, Maulana Wali, 204
Farooqi, Zia-ur-Rehman, 201–4
Farouk (king of Egypt), 258
al-Fawzan, 'Abd al-Aziz, 18
al-Fawzan, Salih ibn Fawzan, 43, 106, 143–44, 153
Faysal (king of Saudi Arabia)
  Ahmadiyya and, 190–91
  assassination of, 13
  Muslim Brotherhood and, 96
  Muslim World League and, 12, 95–96, 100
  Organization of Islamic Cooperation and, 97
  Sahelian countries and, 242
  Saud and, 12, 93
  Saudi religious transnationalism and, 12–13, 96, 117, 260, 291
Fiqh Council of North America, 300
al-Fiqi, Muhammad Hamid, 78–79, 81, 257
Firanda Andirja, 152–54
France, 27, 248, 298
Freedom and Justice Party, 265
al-Futuh, 'Abd al-Mun'im Abu, 255, 265, 267

Gaziev, Moldogazy, 164–65
Germany, 27, 286
al-Ghamidi, Ali, 295
Ghana, 64–65
Ghazali, 77
al-Ghaznawi, Muhammad Dawud, 56
Ghondalavi, Hafiz Mohammad, 195
al-Ghumari, Ahmad, 84
Goodge Street Mosque (London), 292, 307
Grameen Bank, 211

Green Lane Masjid (Birmingham, UK), 293, 302, 304
Gülen, Fethullah, 9, 158, 180
Gulf Cooperation Council (GCC), 6, 211
Gulf War (1990-1)
  US troops in Saudi Arabia during, 47, 106, 141, 264, 296
  Wahhabist opposition to Saudi regime regarding, 106, 117, 141, 264, 296, 300
Gumi, Abubakar, 64, 239
Gumi, Ahmad, 64
Guraba publishing house, 86

al-Haddad, Haitham, 303
Hafiz, Sharif Ahmad, 293
Haïdara, Ousmane Madani, 247
Haile-Mariam, Mengistu, 224
hajj (pilgrimage)
  Ahmadiyya and, 191
  Ethiopia and, 224, 226–28
  growth during twentieth century of, 93–94
  Kyrgyzstan and, 171–72
  Qur'an distribution during, 19
  Saudi government's stewardship of, 12, 19
  Wahhabist literature distributed during, 87
Hamas, 16
Hamaullah, Ahmad, 241
Hanafism
  Bosnia and Herzegovina and, 283
  Deobandism and, 11
  hadith and, 82
  Kyrgyzstan and, 160–62, 168–69, 172, 181
  ultimate judgment and, 81
Hanbalism
  Ibn Taymiyya and, 65, 77–78
  ultimate judgment and, 81
  Wahhabism and, 40–41, 54, 83, 85, 195
Harakat ul-Mujahedeen (HuM), 203
al-Haramain Foundation
  Bosnia and Herzegovina and, 277, 282
  establishment (1989) of, 118
  Ethiopia and, 225
  Indonesia and, 140
  Tehreek al-Mujahideen and, 197
  terrorism and, 39, 122
  Wahhabism and, 16, 118
al-Harkan, Muhammad 'Ali, 95, 100
Harras, Muhammad Khalil, 263
Hasan, Suhaib, 293–94, 300
Hassan, Abdul Ghaffar, 293
al-Hawali, Safar, 141, 262
Haykal, Muhammad Husayn, 79
Hefazat-e-Islam, 211

Hijaz region (Saudi Arabia)
  merchant families of, 95, 97–98
  Muslim holy cities in, 187
  Muslim World League and, 97–98, 101, 104
  Ottoman era and, 54
  Saudi expansion during 1920s in, 79
al-Hilali, Muhammad Taqi ud-Din, 17
al-Hindi, Abdul Ghaffar Hasan, 195
Hizb al-Nur. See Nour Party
Hizb ut-Tahrir, 179, 295, 297, 299
Holy Qur'an Memorization Association, 119–20
humanitarian aid. See also specific organizations
  Bosnia and Herzegovina, 275–77, 280, 282–84
  da'wa and, 16, 116
  Saudi Arabia's annual levels of, 115
  Saudi state and, 114–15, 121–27
  terrorism and, 5, 16, 39, 98–99, 105–7, 122, 127
  Wahhabi proselytization and, 114, 116–18, 125
  zakat and, 116, 119, 125
Husayn, Taha, 79
al-Husayn, Salih 'Abd al-Rahman, 94
al-Husayni, Amin, 95
Hussein, Ameena, 21
al-Huzaymi, Nasir, 84

Ibn Abdul Wahhab, Muhammad. See also Wahhabism
  bid'a criticized by, 10, 54
  hadith authentication and, 45
  Ibn Sa'ud and, 53
  Ibn Taymiyya and, 10
  revivalism and, 41, 117
  Sufism criticized by, 10
  tawhid and, 54, 145
Ibn al-Qayyim al-Jawziyya, 87, 140, 257, 259
Ibn Hazm, 87
Ibn Humayd, 'Abdullah, 94–95, 189
Ibn Kathir, 87
Ibn Qudama, 87
Ibn Sa'ud, Muhammad, 53–54, 67
Ibn Taymiyya
  Hanbalism and, 65, 77–78
  al-Kawthari and, 80–82
  Salafism and, 76–78, 81, 84, 137
  state authority and, 137
  Sufism and, 81
  tawhid and, 149
  Wahhabism and, 10, 77, 137
Ibnu al-Masoud Islamic Center, 229
Ibrahim, Umar, 64–65

Idris, Hajj Umar, 233
al-Ifriqi, ʿAbd al-Rahman, 57, 64, 68n1, 240
ijtihad (direct access to earliest sources), 40, 78
Ikhwan, 37–38, 43–44
Ilham, Muhammad Arifin, 151–52
Ilmiyanov, Ikrom, 172–73
al-ʿIlmiyya, 78
Imam al-Shafiʿi College for Islamic Studies, 150
Imam Muhammad bin Saud University, 15,
    173, 210
India
    India-Pakistan War (1971) and, 191
    Kashmir and, 13, 188, 197, 199, 203, 296
    migration to Saudi Arabia from, 19
    Mumbai terrorist attacks (2008) in, 193
    partition (1947) of, 186, 188
Indonesia
    Ashʿarites in, 148–49
    cultural resistance against Salafism in, 146
    Darul Islam rebellion in, 142
    hadith education in, 149–50
    al-Haramain Foundation and, 140
    International Islamic Relief Organization
        and, 106, 138
    Jamʿiyyat Ihya al-Turath al-Islami and, 140–41
    Muslim-Christian skirmishes (1998) in, 142
    Pancasila ideology in, 142
    Salafi madrassas in, 145–47
    Salafi publishing in, 150–53
    Salafi social media in, 136, 147, 150–51
    Salafi television programming in, 147–48,
        150, 152–54
    Saudi universities and, 139–40, 153
Indonesian Council for Islamic Proselytizing
    (DDII), 138–40
Institute for the Study of Islam and Arabic
    (LIPIA), 139
International Commission of Jurists, 108
International Islamic Relief Organization (IIRO)
    Bosnia and Herzegovina and, 277
    decline of, 127
    disaster relief and, 99
    establishment (1978) of, 98, 118
    Ethiopia and, 224, 226, 229, 232
    Indonesia and, 106, 138
    Muslim World League and, 98, 118
    The Philippines and, 106
    terrorism and, 39, 98–99, 105–7, 122, 229
    Wahhabism and, 118
International Organization for Relief, Welfare
    and Development, 16, 108. See also
    International Islamic Relief Organization
    (IIRO)

International Supreme Council of Mosques, 98
Inter-Services Intelligence (ISI, Pakistan), 199
Iqbal, Allama, 186
Iran
    Horn of Africa and, 223
    Pakistan and, 192, 204
    revolution (1979) in, 3, 13, 85, 117, 137, 188,
        191, 195–97
    Saudi Arabia and, 3–4, 13–14, 19, 25, 29, 42,
        48, 195–97
    Shiʿa Islam and, 25, 29, 48, 191
Iraq, 14, 106, 163, 168, 173, 264, 296
al-Irsyad, 139
Ishaq, Malik, 200–201
Islamic Community in Bosnia and Herzegovina
    (organization), 275–76, 280, 283–84
Islamic Daʿwa and Knowledge Association, 229
Islamic Development Bank, 13, 121, 225, 291
Islamic Movement of Uzbekistan (IMU), 163
Islamic Research and Reformation Centre
    (IRRC, Ghana), 65
Islamic Spiritual Administration, 161
Islamic State (ISIS)
    civil wars in Iraq and Syria and, 168
    exclusionary religious identity and, 23
    Muslim World League and, 107
    Salafi quietism criticized by, 58
    Saudi religious transnationalism and, 18, 28
    Wahhabism and, 47
Islamic State in the Greater Sahara (ISGS),
    247–48
Islamic University of Medina
    African graduates of, 63–65
    Ahl-i Hadith movement and, 56–58
    al-Albani and, 83
    Bin Baz and, 55–56, 66
    curriculum at, 54, 59–60
    Egyptian graduates of, 66
    establishment (1961) of, 15, 54, 291
    faculty at, 56–59
    Indonesian graduates of, 139
    Jordanian graduates of, 66
    Muslim Brotherhood and, 56–58
    Palestinian graduates of, 66–67
    pedagogy at, 58–59
    Sahelian students and, 241
    Saudi Arabia's international influence and,
        55, 67–68, 228, 307
    scholarships for international students at, 15,
        54–55, 210, 228
    Wahhabism and, 60–61, 68, 100
    women students at, 48
    Yemeni graduates of, 62–63

Israel, 137, 188, 241
al-ʿIssa, Muhammad, 28, 108, 126
Itar-Zharkyn Zhashtar Foundation, 170–71
Izetbegović, Alija, 275

Jabhat al-Nusra, 168
Jaish-e-Mohammed (JM), 203
Jamaat Ahl al-Hadith, 162
Jamaat-e-Islami
    Afghanistan and, 190
    Bangladesh and, 210–11, 215
    Mawdudi and, 189
    Muslim World League and, 15
    sharia courts and, 192
    World Assembly of Muslim Youth and, 102
Jamaat-ud-Dawa, 193, 196
al-Jamaʿa al-Islamiyya, 87, 99, 261–64
al-Jamaʿa al-Salafiyya al-Muhtasiba, 83, 142
Jamaʿat al-Muslimin, 87
Jamaʿat Nusrat al-Islam wa-l-Muslimin (JNIM),
    248–49
al-Jami, Muhammad Aman, 58, 87
Jamiat Ihya Minhaj As Sunnah (JIMAS), 294–95,
    297–300
Jamilurrahman teaching center, 135
Jamiyya al-Sunna, 230
al-Jamʿiyya al-Sharʿiyya, 258–59
Jamʿiyyat Ihya al-Turath al-Islami, 140–41
Jauhari, 143
Jawwas, Yazid Abdul Qadir, 135, 140–41, 150
Jeenbekov, Sooronbai, 168
Jemaah Islamiyah (JI), 142
al-Jetaily, Samer, 114, 125–26
Jhangvi, Maulana Haq Nawaz, 196, 199–200
Jordan, 19, 66
Jund al-Khalifat, 169
Justice and Development Party (AKP,
    Turkey), 86

Kamalov brothers, 168, 177
Karimov, Islam, 163
Kashmir, 13, 188, 197, 199, 203, 296
al-Kawthari (Zahid Kevseri), 80–84
Kazakhstan, 159, 164, 174, 179
Keïta, Ibrahim Boubacar ("IBK"), 244–47
Kenya, 99, 106
Khadir, Jeylan, 229, 233
Khalid, Kamali, 64
Khalifa, Muhammad Jalal, 107
Khamis, Bakr ʿAbbas, 139
Khan, Imran, 187
Khashoggi, Jamal, 306
al-Khatib, Muhibb al-Din, 78, 257, 259, 263

Khizmet movement, 9, 158, 166, 180–81
Khomeini, Ruhollah, 13, 109, 191
Khosa, Tariq, 199–200, 204
King Fahd Complex for the Printing of the Holy
    Qurʾan, 16–17, 19, 39, 85, 120, 127
King Fahd Mosque (Sarajevo), 282
King Khalid Foundation, 118, 122
King Salman Humanitarian Aid and Relief
    Center (KSRelief)
    as clearinghouse for Saudi overseas aid
        donations, 114, 121–22, 124, 127
    Code of Ethics at, 124–25
    establishment (2015) of, 114
    international partnerships of, 123
    Saudi state control of, 114, 122–24
King Saud University, 173
Kitab al-Tawhid (al-Wahhab), 41, 88, 145,
    149, 256
Kouffa, Amadou, 249–50
Kulov, Umar, 165, 167–68, 172
al- Kurdi, Allah, 78
Kuwait
    Africa Muslims Agency (AMA)
        and, 226–27, 232
    Association for the Revival of Islamic
        Heritage and, 258
    Bangladesh and, 210–11
    Bosnia and Herzegovina and, 277–78, 281
    global Islamic organizations supported by, 6
    Gulf War (1990-91) and, 264, 296
    Jamʿiyyat Ihya al-Turath al-Islami and,
        140–41
    Kyrgyzstan and, 160, 171
    Mali and, 250
Kyrgyzstan
    criminal organizations in, 178
    ethnic minority populations in, 177
    Evangelical Christians in, 158
    Ferghana Valley in, 162–63, 177
    hajj and, 171–72
    Hanafism and, 160–62, 168–69, 172, 181
    Khizmet movement in, 158, 166, 180–81
    Kuwait and, 160, 171
    Law on the Freedom of Religion (2005)
        in, 158
    madrassas in, 164–65, 176
    media in, 175
    mosque construction in, 169–70
    Muftiyat (Spiritual Board of Muslims) in,
        165, 167–68, 171–73, 177, 181
    Muslim Brotherhood in, 167, 179–80
    Qatar and, 160, 171
    revolution (2010) in, 166

Russian-speaking population in, 176–77
Security Council in, 167–68
social media in, 159, 175
Soviet era in, 161–63, 176
Sufism in, 162
Tablighi Jamaat and, 158, 166, 179–80, 182
traditional imams in, 180–81
Turkey and, 182
Wahhabism in, 161, 166
women in, 178
Kyrgyz State University of Construction,
    Transport, and Architecture, 171

Lajnat Birr al-Islami, 138
Lashkar-e-Jhangvi, 203–4
Lashkar-e-Taiba, 16, 193
Laskar Jihad, 143
La Tahzan (Don't Be Sad), 151–52
Lembaga Pengajaran Bahasa Arab (LPBA), 139
Le Pen, Marine, 249
London terrorist bombings (2005), 300
al-Luhaydan, Salih bin Muhammad, 95
Lukman Baabduh, 135, 143–44, 147–48, 152

al-Madkhali, Rabee', 10, 58, 106, 143, 305
Madkhaliyya group, 109, 229–30
Madrasa Minhaj al-Sunnah, 146
Ma'had al-Sunnah, 143
Mahri, Usamah Faisal, 141
Maïga, Soumeylou Boubèye, 246–47
al-Majdhub, Muhammad, 56
Majelis Ulama Indonesia, 138
Majlis Ihya al-Turats al-Islami, 141
Makhluf, Hasanayn Muhammad, 56
Makki, Abdul Hafeez, 202–3
Maksutov, Ilyas, 164–65, 168
al-Maktab al-Islami publishing house, 85–87
Mali
    elections (2018) and, 246
    elections (2013) in, 244–46
    French intervention (2013) in, 248
    northern separatist movement in, 244
    Qatar and, 239, 249–50
    Salafism in, 64, 238–50
    Saudi Arabia and, 238, 240–42, 249
    Sufism in, 64, 239, 241, 243, 245
    Tablighi Jamaat in, 242, 249
Maličević, Senada, 277–78
al-Manar, 78, 256–57
al-Manea, 'Abdullah bin Sulayman, 118
al-Maqdisi, Abu Muhammad, 47–48, 66, 87,
    106, 142
al-Maraghi, Mustafa, 79

Markaz al-Ansar al-Shari'a, 229
Markaz Dirasat al-Sunna al-Nabawiya, 297
al-Masari, Muhammad, 297
al-Masri, Abu Hamza Muhammad, 297
Masroor, Ajmal, 306–7
Matba'at al-Taraqqi, 86
al-Maturidi, Abu Mansyur, 148, 166
Mauritania, 239, 242–43
Mawdudi, Abul A'la
    Ahmadiyya and, 189
    Islamic University of Medina and, 58–59, 189
    Jamaat-e-Islami and, 189
    Muslim World League and, 95, 110, 189–90
    Pakistani government's conflict with, 189–90
al-Ma'sumi, Muhammad Sultan, 86
al-Ma'sumi, Muhammad Sultan, 86
Mecca Grand Mosque attack (1979)
    global Muslim community's response to, 296
    Juhayman al-'Utaybi as perpetrators of, 48,
        105, 117, 138
    Sahwa movement and, 138
    Saudi government's response to, 13, 85
Mengal, Maulana Ramzan, 204
Ministry of Islamic Affairs, Da'wa, and
        Guidance (Saudi Arabia)
    curricula developed by, 27
    da'wa and, 3
    al-Haramain Foundation and, 140
    humanitarian aid and, 119–21
    Islamic endowments *(awaqf)* and, 120–21
    religious attachés stationed in foreign
        countries by, 24–25
    religious propagation activities by, 3, 14
al-Minyawi, Muhammad Hilmi, 80
Mirpuri, Mahmud Ahmad, 293
Mirzoev, Abduvoli-Qori, 162
Mohamed VI (king of Morocco), 246
Morghilani, Hakimjon-Qori, 162
Morghilani, Mullah Hakimjon-Qori, 162
Morocco, 24, 26, 44, 246, 250
Morsi, Muhammad, 66, 189, 255, 265, 267
Mosques and Imams National Advisory Board
        (MINAB), 302
Movement for Unity and Jihad in West Africa
        (MUJWA), 247, 249
Mubarak, Hosni, 66, 225, 265–66
al-Mubarak, Muhammad, 56
Muhaimin, 149
Muhammad, Ghulam, 189
Muhammad bin Salman (prince of Saudi Arabia)
    Commission for the Promotion of Virtue and
        the Prevention of Vice and, 121
    al-'Issa and, 126

Muhammad bin Salman (prince of
   Saudi Arabia) (*cont.*)
  Khashoggi killing and, 306
  Saudi religious transnationalism and, 28–30,
   204–5, 226
  Vision 2030 strategy and, 27, 29, 115
Muhammad bin Zayed (Emirati prince), 227
Muhammadiyah, 139, 149
Muhsin Khan, Muhammad, 17
El-Mujaheed unit, 279–80, 282
al-Muntada Trust, 297, 303
Muntasir, Abu Hasan, 164, 168
Muslim Brotherhood
  dissidents in Saudi Arabia from, 9–10, 262
  Egyptian electoral politics and, 255, 265, 267
  grassroots organization in Egypt by, 260–61
  Gulf War (1991) and, 264
  Islamic University of Medina and, 56–58
  Kyrgyzstan and, 167, 179–80
  Madkhaliyya and, 109
  Muslim World League and, 15, 97, 108–10
  publishing industry of, 80
  Sahwa movement and, 10, 106, 121, 138
  Salafi Call and, 267
  Saudi religious transnationalism and, 14, 24–25
  Shi'a Muslims and, 109
  Somalia and, 27
  Syria and, 9–10, 56
  World Assembly of Muslim Youth and, 15,
   102, 109
Muslim Council of Britain, 300
Muslim World League (MWL)
  Ahmadiyya and, 191
  anti-Semitism and, 28–29
  Bosnia and Herzegovina and, 277, 282
  Constituent Council of, 94–95, 98, 100, 108
  educational institutions supported by, 99
  Egypt and, 260
  establishment (1962) of, 15, 94, 291
  Ethiopia and, 224, 226
  Faysal and, 12, 95–96, 100
  Hijaz origins of, 97–98, 101, 104
  Indonesia and, 138
  International Islamic Relief Organization
   and, 98, 118
  International Supreme Council of Mosques
   and, 98
  Islamic jurisprudence and, 99–100, 108
  Islamic State and, 107
  al-Issa and, 28
  Jamaat-e-Islami and, 15
  Mawdudi and, 95, 110, 189–90
  Muslim Brotherhood and, 15, 97, 108–10

  organizational challenges at, 105
  public interest in, 103
  rabita (bond) and, 96–97
  Sahelian countries and, 241
  Saudi Arabia's international influence and,
   55, 96, 137
  Supreme Council of, 108
  terrorism and, 105–7
  Wahhabism and, 97–101, 105–6
  World Assembly of Muslim Youth and, 101, 104
al-Mu'allimi, 'Abd al-Rahman, 83

Nadeem, Shoaib, 203–4
al-Nadwi, Abul Hasan 'Ali, 56, 58, 95
al-Nafrawi, Ahmad, 251
Nahdlatul 'Ulama, 139
Naik, Zakir, 18
Najd region (Saudi Arabia), 38, 42, 53–54, 119
Namangani, Juma, 163
Nasif, Abdullah bin 'Umar, 100, 104
Nasif, Muhammad, 79, 81, 83
al-Nasser, Gamal 'Abd, 3, 12, 55, 117, 258, 291
National Medical Ambulance Society, 119
National Movement for the Liberation of
  Azawad (MNLA), 248
Natsir, Muhammad, 138
Nayef bin 'Abd al-'Aziz (prince of Saudi
  Arabia), 257–58, 264
Nazili, Sayyid, 56
Negara-Islam Indonesia (NII) movement, 142
Niasse, Ibrahim, 241
Nida al-Islam radio station, 17
Niger, 239, 242
Nigeria, 63–64, 239
niqab (veil)
  Bosnia and Herzegovina and, 272–73
  Ethiopia and, 231
  Salafi Call and, 263
  Salafism and, 44, 136, 138, 169
  Saudi religious funding and global spread
   of, 20–21
  Wahhabism and, 44
al-Nishapuri, 81
Nour Party, 255, 265–68

Oman, 211
Organization of Islamic Cooperation (OIC), 13,
  39, 97, 100, 200
Ottoman Empire, 41, 54, 78, 273

Padri movement, 137
Pakistan
  Afghanistan and, 190, 192, 199

Ahl-i Hadith movement and, 11, 192, 194–97, 204
Ahmadiyya in, 22, 189–91
Council of Islamic Ideology in, 193–94
Deobandism in, 198–99, 204
establishment (1947) of, 186, 188
India-Pakistan War (1971) and, 191
intelligence services in, 199
Iran and, 192, 204
Kashmir and, 13, 188, 197, 199, 203, 296
madrasas in, 188, 195–97, 204
militias in, 193
Saudi Arabia and, 18, 20, 22, 186–88, 190–91, 195–205
Shi'a population in, 22, 190–91, 193, 197–200
Sufism in, 198–99
Zia's Islamization campaign in, 13, 189, 191, 193, 197
Palestine, 19, 66–67, 119, 296, 300
Penny for Palestine Society, 119
Pentecostal Christianity, 3, 13
Persis, 139
The Philippines, 14, 19, 107
pilgrimage. *See hajj* (pilgrimage)
Pirzada, Riaz Hussain, 199
Prince Turki bin Fahd Foundation, 225

Al-Qaeda
  Abu Turab and, 193
  Bosnia and Herzegovina and, 99
  Islamic charity organizations and, 99, 106–7, 122
  quietist Salafism criticized by, 58
  Sahel region of Africa and, 239, 249
  Saudi royal family and, 28
  September 11 terrorist attacks (2001) and, 67, 85
  US-led global counterterrorism campaign against, 282
  Wahhabism and, 47, 85
Al-Qaeda in the Arabian Peninsula (AQAP), 38
Al-Qaeda in the Islamic Maghreb (AQIM), 247–48
al-Qahtani, Muhammad, 105
al-Qaradawi, Yusuf, 108–9, 189, 300
al-Qari, 'Abd al-Fattah, 56–57
al-Qari, 'Abd al-'Aziz, 57–58
al-Qarni, 'A'id, 87–88, 141, 151
Qatar
  Ansar al-Sunna and, 258
  Bangladesh and, 211
  Bosnia and Herzegovina and, 281
  diplomatic crisis (2017) in, 223

global Islamic organizations supported by, 6
Kyrgyzstan and, 160, 171
Mali and, 239, 249–50
Wahhabism and, 6, 36, 85–86
Qazzaz, Muhammad Salih, 95
Qur'an
  English translations of, 17
  King Fahd Complex for the Printing of the Holy Qur'an and, 16–17, 19, 39, 85, 120, 127
  Sura al-Nisa passage in, 120
  zakat and, 116
Al-Quran wa Sunnah Society of North America (QSS), 294
Qutb, Sayyid
  Egypt's Islamic Awakening and, 259–61
  Muslim Brotherhood publishing and, 80
  Sahwa movement and, 105
  Saudi publishing industry and, 85
  Wahhabi critics of, 102

Rahman, Mujibur, 209
al-Rajhi, Ahmad bin Sulayman, 120
Ramadan, Sa'id, 109
al-Rasheed, Madawi, 6
Rasul Sayyaf, 142
al-Raziq, Ali 'Abd, 79
Regent's Park Mosque (London), 292, 295
Rehman Khalil, Fazlur, 197, 203
Rida, Muhammad Rashid, 77–79, 256–57, 259, 263
Rushdie, Salman, 295
Russia, 159

Sabati 2012 organization, 244–46
as-Sabban, Muhammad Surur, 95, 97
Sabirov, Ravshan, 177
Sabri, Mustafa, 80
al-Sadat, Anwar, 259, 261
Saeed, Hafiz, 193
As-Safa Foundation, 170–71
Sahwa movement
  arrests of members of, 121
  Gulf War (1991) and, 264, 296
  al-Jama'a al-Islamiyya and, 262
  Mecca Grand Mosque attack (1979) and, 138
  Muslim Brotherhood and, 10, 106, 121, 138
  opposition to Saudi regime and, 101, 264, 296
  Qutb and, 105
  Salafi Call and, 262
Salafi Bookstore of Birmingham, 88
Salafi Call (Egypt)
  coup (2013) and, 267
  establishment (1984) of, 261

Salafi Call (Egypt) (*cont.*)
  Muslim Brotherhood and, 267
  Nour Party and, 255, 265–68
  Sahwa movement and, 262
  Saudi Arabia and, 255, 263–66, 268
Salafism
  bid'a and, 43, 46, 146, 148
  da'wa and, 43
  global growth of, 10–11
  hadith and, 45
  Ibn Taymiyya and, 76–78, 81, 84, 137
  ijtihad and, 78
  modernity and, 43–45
  niqab and, 44, 136, 138, 169
  performativity and, 46
  publishing industry and, 78–89
  quietism and, 42–43
  satellite television and, 18
  Shi'a Muslims and, 48, 77, 299
  state authority and, 46
  Sufism and, 64, 77, 241, 243, 245, 260
  tawhid and, 43, 45, 145
  terrorism and, 35
  vigilantism and, 43
  Wahhabism and, 4, 10, 35–36, 40–49
  women and, 48–49
As-Salam Foundation, 170–71
Salman (king of Saudi Arabia), 120–21, 125, 276
satellite television, 17–18, 150, 152–54
Saud bin 'Abdul-Aziz (king of Saudi Arabia)
  Ahl-i Hadith movement and, 195
  Ansar al-Sunna and, 258
  Faysal and, 12, 93
  Mawdudi and, 190
  Mecca and Medina conquered by, 195
  Saudi foreign policy and, 12, 223
  zakat and, 119
Saudi Arabia
  Afghanistan and, 39, 85, 167, 196, 198, 228, 292
  Bangladesh and, 208–19
  Bosnia and Herzegovina and, 39, 276–78, 281, 285–86
  Council of Senior 'Ulama in, 12, 36, 137
  Egypt and, 257–58, 260, 262–68
  Ethiopia and, 221–34
  Gulf War (1990–1) and, 47, 106, 117, 141, 264, 296, 300
  High Commission for Oversight of Charities in, 122
  Iran and, 3–4, 13–14, 19, 25, 29, 42, 48, 195–97
  Kyrgyzstan and, 159–82
  labor migration to, 18–19
  Mali and, 238, 240–42, 249

Pakistan and, 18, 20, 22, 186–88, 190–91, 195–205
petrodollars and, 39
publishing industry in, 84–88
religious transnationalism and, 6–9, 12–13–14, 20–30, 137
Shi'a Muslims and, 13, 36–38, 200
terrorist attacks in, 106, 122
United Kingdom and, 290, 295–96, 306–7
United States and, 4, 13, 47, 106, 141, 264, 296
Vision 2030 strategy in, 27, 29, 42, 115
Saudi Fund for Development (SDF), 121, 126
Saudi High Commission for Relief of Bosnia and Herzegovina (SHC), 276–78, 281
Saudi Islamic Relief Organization, 64
Saudi Red Crescent Society, 39, 119, 126–27, 277, 282
al-Sawwaf, Muhammad Mahmoud, 56
Sa'd ibn 'Atiq, 57
Seidu, Afa, 65
Senegal, 26, 239
September 11 terrorist attacks (United States, 2001)
  Al-Haramain Islamic Foundation and, 197
  International Islamic Relief Organization and, 122, 229
  Muslim World League and, 105–6
  Al-Qaeda and, 67, 85
  regulation of Islamic charities following, 16, 127, 282
  Saudi citizens among the perpetrators of, 4, 122
  Wahhabism and, 35, 67, 85
Al-Shabab, 27
Shaltut, Mahmud, 79
Shambetov, Kylych, 164
al-Shams militia, 193
Shaqra, Muhammad Ibrahim, 66
Sharab, Salim, 66–67
Sharif, Nawaz, 200
al-Shawish, Zuhayr, 85
al-Shaybi, Amin Muhammad, 95
al-Shaykh, Abd al-Aziz, 18
Shi'a Muslims
  Iran and, 25, 29, 48, 191
  Muslim Brotherhood and, 109
  Pakistan and, 22, 190–91, 193, 197–200
  Salafism and, 48, 77, 299
  Saudi Arabia and, 13, 36–38, 200
  United Kingdom and, 299, 304
  Wahhabism and, 20, 22, 25, 42, 48, 67
al-Shinqiti, Muhammad al-Amin al-Jakani, 57–58, 240
al-Siba'i, 'Abd al-'Aziz Ahmad, 95

Sipah-e-Sahaba, 196, 198, 200, 202–4. *See also*
    Ahle Sunnat Wal Jama'at
al-Sisi, Abd al-Fattah, 267
social media
    in Kyrgyzstan, 159, 175
    Salafism in Indonesia and, 136, 147, 150–51
    Saudi Arabia's broad adoption of, 38
    Wahhabism and, 5, 18
Society of Majid bin 'Abd al-'Aziz for
    Development and Social Services, 118
Soharwardy, Syed Badiuddin, 198–99
Somalia, 27, 223
Soviet Union
    Afghanistan War (1980s) and, 13, 85, 188,
        192, 196, 198, 228, 292, 295–96
    Ethiopia and, 223
    fall (1991) of, 14
    Kyrgyzstan and, 161–63, 176
Spahić, Mustafa Effendi, 284
Spiritual Board of Muslims of Central Asia
    (SADUM), 162–63, 177
Sri Lanka, 19–21, 26
Stalin, Joseph, 162
al-Sudais, 'Abd al-Rahman, 18
Sufism
    in Bangladesh, 215
    in Egypt, 259
    Ibn Taymiyya and, 81
    in Kyrgyzstan, 162
    in Mali, 64, 239, 241, 243, 245
    in Pakistan, 198–99
    Salafism and, 64, 77, 241, 243, 245, 260
    Saudi religious transnationalism and, 26
    Tijaniyya order and, 64, 241
    Wahhabism and, 20–21, 42
Suharto, 135, 139, 142, 144
Sultan bin 'Abd al-'Aziz al-Sa'ud Foundation,
    224–25
Sungkar, Abdullah, 142
Sunna (Prophet Muhammad's example), 40–41,
    43, 145, 148
Supreme Council for Islamic Call and Research
    (SCICR), 65
Surur Zayn al-Abidin, Muhammad, 9, 95, 97,
    105, 141
Syria, 86, 127, 163, 168, 173

al-Tabbani, Muhammad al-'Arabi ibn, 84
Tablighi Jamaat
    Kyrgyzstan and, 158, 166, 179–80, 182
    in Mali, 242, 249
    United Kingdom and, 295, 298–99
al-Tahawi, Abu Ja'far, 83

Tajikistan, 163–64
takfir (apostasy), 10, 37, 40–42
Takfir wal Hijrah group, 230
The Taliban, 192
Tanzania, 106
At-Taqfir wal-Hijra, 169
Tarbiyya movement, 147
Tariq, Azam, 201
tawhid (monotheism), 10, 37, 41, 43, 45, 54,
    145, 149
tawhid 3 curriculum, 149, 154
Tehreek al-Mujahideen, 197
Tengirchiler, 181
terrorism
    humanitarian aid and, 5, 16, 39, 98–99, 105–
        7, 122, 127
    London terrorist bombings (2005) and, 300
    Mumbai terrorist attacks (2008) and, 193
    in Saudi Arabia, 106, 122
    September 11 attacks (2001) and, 4, 16, 35,
        67, 85, 105–6, 122, 127, 197, 229, 282
    US Embassy in Africa attacks (1998) and, 106
    Wahhabism and, 8, 22–23, 35, 39, 67, 85, 105
Thalib, Ja'far Umar, 135, 141–44
Al Thani , 'Ali ibn 'Abdullah, 85
Tijaniyya Sufis, 64, 241
Timur (Tamerlane), 161
Tombalbaye, François, 241
Touré, Amadou Toumani, 244
Touré, Cheikh, 240
Turkey, 23, 86, 182, 223, 281, 286
al-Turki, 'Abdullah bin 'Abd al-Muhsin, 101,
    105–7, 139, 201
Turki al-Faisal (prince of Saudi Arabia), 200, 203

al-'Ubayd, 'Abdullah bin Salih, 101, 105, 139
UK Action Committee on Islamic Affairs
    (UKACIA), 295
Umm Al-Qura University, 15, 173
United Arab Emirates
    Bangladesh and, 210–11, 213
    Ethiopia and, 223, 227
    global Islamic organizations supported by, 6
    Mali and, 250
    Pakistan and, 197
United Kingdom
    Ahl-i Hadith movement and, 292–94
    Barelwis and, 305
    Deobandism in, 295, 298–99, 305
    foreign donations for mosque construction
        in, 292
    London terrorist bombings (2005) in, 300
    millennial Muslims in, 302

United Kingdom (*cont.*)
  Muslim middle class in, 27
  Salafi mosques in, 305–7
  Saudi Arabia and, 290, 295–96, 306–7
  Saudi dissidents in, 297
  Shi'a Muslims in, 299, 304
  Sufism in, 298
  Tablighi Jamaat and, 295, 298–99
  World of Islam Festival (1976) in, 291–92
United States
  Afghanistan and, 13–14, 85
  Ethiopia and, 225
  Gulf War (1990-1) and, 47, 106, 141, 264, 296
  Saudi Arabia and, 4, 13, 47, 106, 141, 264, 296
  Saudi students in, 101–2
  September 11 terrorist attacks (2001) and, 4,
    16, 35, 67, 85, 105–6, 122, 127, 197, 229, 282
al-'Utaybi, Juhayman, 13, 48, 62, 66, 84, 105,
    117, 138
al-Uthaymeen, Muhammad ibn, 10, 18, 84–85,
    106, 263
al-'Uyayri, Yusuf, 47
Uyghurs, 177, 182
Uzbekistan, 163–64
Uzbek population in Kyrgyzstan, 177, 182

Vision 2030 strategy (Saudi Arabia), 27, 29, 42, 115

al-Wadi'i, Muqbil bin Hadi, 47, 62, 87, 141, 143,
    229–30
Wahhabism
  da'wa and, 41–42
  defined, 9–10
  hadith and, 45
  Hanbalism and, 40–41, 54, 83, 85, 195
  humanitarian aid and, 114, 116–18, 125
  Ibn Taymiyya and, 10, 77, 137
  jihad and, 5
  loyalty and disavowal doctrine in, 37
  modernity and, 38, 43–44
  Muslim World League and, 97–101, 105–6
  niqab and, 20–21, 44
  Qatar and, 6, 36, 85–86
  revivalism and, 40–41, 117
  Salafism and, 4, 10, 35–36, 40–49
  Saudi agencies devoted to promoting, 3–8,
    24–25, 55
  Saudi publishing industry and, 85–87
  Shi'a Muslims and, 20, 22, 25, 42, 48, 67
  social media and, 5, 18
  state authority and, 46, 54, 117
  Sufism and, 20–21, 42
  takfir and, 10, 37, 40–42
  tawhid and, 10, 37, 41
  terrorism and, 8, 22–23, 35, 39, 67, 85, 105
  women and, 48–49
Wajdi, Muhammad Farid, 80
al-Waqf al-Islami, 3, 16, 117–18, 122, 126,
    164, 170
World Assembly of Muslim Youth (WAMY)
  Bosnia and Herzegovina and, 282
  Egypt and, 260
  establishment (1972) of, 15, 101
  Ethiopia and, 224, 229
  Indonesia and, 138
  Jamaat-e-Islami and, 102
  Kyrgyzstan and, 170
  Muslim Brotherhood and, 15, 102, 109
  Muslim World League and, 101, 104
  proselytization emphasis at, 25
  public interest in, 103
  Saudi Arabia's international influence and, 55
  Saudi students in foreign countries
    and, 101–2
  Supervisory Board of, 102
  Wahhabism and, 101–2
World Council of Mosques, 138
World of Islam Festival (United Kingdom,
    1976), 291–92
al-Wuhaybi, Salih ibn Sulayman, 104

Yacoub, Qari, 203
Yamani, Muhammad 'Abduh, 95
Yemen, 62–63, 127, 223, 306
Yolcu, Abdullah ('Abdullah ibn 'Abd al
    Hamid), 86
Young Muslims UK organization, 295
Yufid Group, 147
Yuldashev, Tohir, 163

Zaheer, Ehsan Elahi, 195–97
zakat (charitable tax), 116, 119, 125, 193
Zaydi population (Yemen), 62–63
Zia (Ziaur Rahman), 209
Zia ul-Haq
  anti-Shia laws under, 193, 196, 198
  Islamiziation campaign of, 13, 189, 191,
    193, 197
  Saudi Arabia and, 197
Zulpukarov, Torobai, 159, 172, 180